THE BOOK OF DANIEL

VOLUME 1

THE BOOK OF DANIEL

Composition and Reception

EDITED BY

JOHN J. COLLINS

AND

PETER W. FLINT

With the Assistance of Cameron VanEpps

VOLUME ONE

BRILL ACADEMIC PUBLISHERS, INC.
BOSTON • LEIDEN
2002

Library of Congress Cataloging-in-Publication Data

The book of Daniel : composition and reception / edited by John J. Collins and
Peter W. Flint ; with the assistance of Cameron VanEpps.
　　p. cm.
　Originally published: Leiden ; Boston : Brill, 2001.
　Includes bibliographical references and indexes.
　　ISBN 0–391–04137–1 (set)—ISBN 0–391–04127–4 (v. 1)—
　ISBN 0–391–04128–2 (vol. 2)
　　　　1. Bible. O.T. Daniel—Criticism, interpretation, etc. I. Collins, John
Joseph, 1946– II. Flint, Peter W. III. VanEpps, Cameron.

　BS1555.2 .B65 2002
　224'.506—dc21

2002066273

ISBN 0–391–04127–4

CONTENTS

PART FOUR

SOCIAL SETTING

VOLUME TWO

PART FIVE

LITERARY CONTEXT, INCLUDING QUMRAN

PART SIX

RECEPTION IN JUDAISM AND CHRISTIANITY

PREFACE

The Book of Daniel: Composition and Reception contains thirty-two essays on a wide range of topics in eight sections: (a) General Topics; (b) Daniel in Its Near Eastern Milieu; (c) Issues in Interpretation of Specific Passages; (d) Social Setting; (e) Literary Context, including Qumran; (f) Reception in Judaism and Christianity; (g) Textual History; and (h) The Theology of Daniel. The contributors were invited with a view to representing the spectrum of opinion in the current interpretation of the Book of Daniel, over a wide range of subjects. Only one of the essays has been published before: Johan Lust's "Cult and Sacrifice in Daniel. The Tamid and the Abomination of Desolation," which appeared in J. Quaegebeur (ed.), *Ritual and Sacrifice in the Ancient Near East* (Orientalia Lovaniensia Analecta 55; Leuven: Peeters, 1993) 283–99.

Because of the length and size of the book, the first fourteen essays are presented in the present volume, with the remaining eighteen (plus indices) to appear shortly in a second volume.

This is the second book in the series "The Formation and Interpretation of Old Testament Literature" (FIOTL), the purpose which is to examine and explore the prehistory, contents and themes of the books of the Old Testament, as well as their reception and interpretation in later Jewish and Christian literature. First to appear in the series was *Writing and Reading the Scroll of Isaiah: Studies in an Interpretive Tradition*, eds. Craig C. Broyles and Craig A. Evans (FIOTL 1.1-2 and VTSup 70.1-2, 1997).

The editors extend thanks to four distinct groups of people. First, to all the contributors for meeting various deadlines and working hard and harmoniously to render the editing process smooth and effective. Second, to several graduate assistants at Trinity Western University whose dedication, research, and computer skills have proved indispensable. Special thanks are due to Cameron Van Epps, for managing this project well and being closely involved with all aspects of the book from its inception. We are also grateful to Jennifer Shepherd for preparing the abbreviation list in this volume, and to Christopher Davis and Ian Spaa for preparing the indices, which will appear in the second volume. Thanks are also due to Professor André Lemaire and the VTSup Board for their support of the FIOTL volumes as part of the VTSup series. Finally, we are grateful to the team at Brill Academic Publishers, especially Desk Editor Mattie Kuiper and Senior Religion Editor Hans van der Meij, for their guidance and encouragement in the production of this book.

John J. Collins   29 October, 2000
Yale University

Peter W. Flint
Langley, British Columbia

TERMS, SIGLA, AND ABBREVIATIONS

For most terms, sigla, and abbreviations of journals and other secondary sources, see P. H. Alexander et al. (eds.), *The SBL Handbook of Style for Ancient Near Eastern, Biblical, and Early Christian Studies* (Peabody, MA: Hendrickson, 1999). For Qumran sigla, see also J. A. Fitzmyer, *The Dead Sea Scrolls: Major Publications and Tools for Study* (rev. ed., SBLRBS 20; Atlanta: Scholars Press, 1990) 1–8.

TERMS AND SIGLA

(?)	Some doubt exists as to the identification of a verse or reading.
X	Denotes a verse/section that is absent from MT (e.g. Ps 118:1, 15, 16, 8, 9, X, 29)
[ ]	The bracketed portions are not extant, but were originally written.
[ ]	Space between fragments or where the leather surface is missing
\	Division between lines in a manuscript
//	Two or more parallel texts (e.g. Ps 18//2 Sam 22)
∘	Ink traces of an unidentified letter remain.
+	Word(s) or a verse have been added.
>	Word(s) or a verse have been omitted.
*	What the scribe originally wrote (e.g. 4QDan^{a*})
⁕	The asterisk here indicates that not all of the verses are indicated (e.g. Dan 1:1–7:27*).
_	Denotes Hebrew pagination (e.g. 42*–45*)
2:4-5	Dead Sea Scrolls: the second extant column of the manuscript, lines 4-5
2.5	Dead Sea Scrolls: fragment 2, line 5
10 ii.4-5	Dead Sea Scrolls: fragment 10, column 2, lines 4-5
§, §§	Section(s), especially in Josephus and Philo
א א א	A certain letter, a probable letter, a possible letter, respectively
AB	Astronomical Book of Enoch
Ag. Ap.	Josephus, *Against Apion*
Ant.	Josephus, *Antiquities*
ar	Aramaic
b.	The Babylonian Talmud (Bavli)
Beih.	Beihefte
BH	Biblical Hebrew
bis	Two times
col(s.)	Column(s)

Comm. in Dan.	*Commentary on Daniel*
Comm. in Matt.	*Commentary on Matthew*
corr.	*correctus, -a, um,* the corrected reading
Dem. Ev.	Eusebius, *Demonstration evangelica* (*Demonstration of the Gospel*)
ed(s).	Edition, editor(s), or edited
Ee	*Enuma Elish*
ET	English translation
fin.	*finis,* end (e.g. 144:13^{fin})
frg(s).	Fragment(s)
𝕲 or LXX	The Old Greek (as in the Göttingen editions)
𝕲*	The (reconstructed) original reading of the Old Greek
HUBP	Hebrew University Bible Project
IAA	Dead Sea Scrolls: Israel Antiquities Authority (photograph accession numbers)
J. W.	Josephus, *The Jewish War*
La	The Vetus Latina or Old Latin translation of the LXX
LXX	The Septuagint
𝔐 or MT	The Masoretic Text
𝔐^{ed}	An edition of the Masoretic Text (usually *BHS*)
𝔐^{L} or B ^{19A}	The Leningrad (St. Petersburg) Codex
𝔐$^{ms(s)}$	Masoretic manuscript(s)
𝔐^{q}	*qere* for the Masoretic Text
m.	Mishnah
MS(S)	Individual manuscript(s)
n.	*nota,* note
n.p.	No publisher (cited)
n.s.	New series
OG	The Old Greek (original Septuagint)
PAM	Dead Sea Scrolls: Palestine Archaeological Museum (photograph accession numbers)
pl(s).	Plates(s)
Praep. Ev.	Eusebius, *Praeparatio Evangelica* (*Preparation for the Gospel*)
Qat.	*Moʿed Qaṭan*
Ra	Rahlfs' edition of the Septuagint
recto	The front, inscribed side of a manuscript: the hair side of a leather scroll, or the side of a papyrus having horizontal ridges
repr.	Reprint(ed)
rev.	Revised
s.v.	*sub verbo* ("under the word," dictonary entry)
Sanh.	*Sanhedrin*
SP	Samaritan Pentateuch
t.	Tosefta

T.	Testament, as in *T.Levi*, etc.
Tg.	Targum
v(v).	Verse(s)
vacat	Indicates that the leather or papyrus was intentionally left blank
verso	The reverse side of a manuscript: the flesh side of a leather scroll, or the side of a papyrus having vertical ridges
vid.	*ut videtur, -entur*, as it seems, as they seem from the available evidence
Vorlage	Hebrew text used by the translator of the Greek or other Version
y.	The Palestinian Talmud (Yerushalmi)

JOURNALS, BOOKS AND SERIES

AASOR	*Annual of the American Schools of Oriental Research*
AB	Anchor Bible
ABD	*The Anchor Bible Dictionary* (6 vols., New York: Doubleday, 1992), ed. D. N. Freedman
AfO	*Archiv für Orientforschung*
AfO Beih.	*Archiv für Orientforschung*, Beihefte
AGJU	Arbeiten zur Geschichte des antiken Judentums und des Urchristentums
AHw	*Akkadisches Handworterbuch* (3 vols., Wiesbaden, 1965-1981), by W. von Soden
AJP	*American Journal of Philology*
AnBib	Analecta biblica
ANEP	*The Ancient Near East in Pictures Relating to the OT* (Princeton: Princeton University Press, 1954), ed. J. B. Pritchard
ANET	*Ancient Near Eastern Texts Relating to the Old Testament* (3rd ed., Princeton: Princeton University Press, 1969), ed. J. B. Pritchard
ANRW	*Aufstieg und Niedergang der römischen Welt* (Berlin: de Gruyter, 1979-), ed. W. Haase and E. Temporini
ANTJ	Arbeiten zum Neuen Testament und Judentum
AOAT	Alter Orient und Altes Testament
ARM X	*Archives royales de Mari: La correspondance féminine*, ed. G. Dossin
ASNU	Acta seminarii neotestamentici upsaliensis
ASOR	American Schools of Oriental Research
AT	Altes Testament
ATAT	Arbeiten zu Text und Sprache im Alten Testament
ATANT	Abhandlungen zur Theologie des Alten und Neuen Testaments
ATD	Das Alte Testament Deutsch
BA	*Biblical Archaeologist*

BAR	*Biblical Archaeologist Reader*
BARev	*Biblical Archaeology Review*
BASOR	*Bulletin of the American Schools of Oriental Research*
BASORSup	*Bulletin of the American Schools of Oriental Research,* Supplements
BBR	*Bulletin for Biblical Research*
BETL	Bibliotheca ephemeridum theologicarum lovaniensium
BGBE	Beitrage zur Geschichte der biblischen Exegese
BHK	*Biblia Hebraica* (R. Kittel)
BHS	*Biblia Hebraica Stuttgartensia*
Bib	*Biblica*
BibOr	Biblica et orientalia
BIOSCS	*Bulletin of the International Organization for Septuagint and Cognate Studies*
BIS	Biblical Interpretation Series
BJS	Brown Judaic Studies
BK	Biblischer Kommentar
BKAT	Biblischer Kommentar: Altes Testament, eds. M. Noth and H. W. Wolff
BN	*Biblische Notizen*
BO	*Bibliotheca orientalis*
BZAW	Beihefte zur *ZAW*
BZNW	Beihefte zur *ZNW*
Cahiers RB	Cahiers de la *Revue Biblique*
CANE	*Civilizations of the Ancient Near East* (4 vols., New York: Charles Scribner's Sons, 1995), ed. J. Sasson
CAD	*The Assyrian Dictionary* of the Oriental Onstitute, University of Chicago
CAT	Commentaire de l'Ancien Testament
CBQ	*Catholic Biblical Quarterly*
CBQMS	Catholical Biblical Quarterly Monograph Series
CCSL	Corpus Christianorum: Series graeca
CCSL	Corpus Christianorum: Series latina
CCL	Classics of Christian Litererature
CJA	Christianity and Judaism in Antiquity
CNT	Commentaire du Nouveau Testament
ConB	Coniectanea biblica
ConBNT	Coniectanea biblica, New Testament
ConBOT	Coniectanea biblica, Old Testament
CRINT	Compendia rerum iudaicarum ad novum testamentum
CS	*The Context of Scripture*, eds. W. W. Hallo and K. Lawson Younger
CT	*Cuneiform Texts from Babylonian Tablets in the British Museum*

CT	*Christianity Today*
CTA	*Corpus des tablelettes en cunéiformes alphabétiques découvertes à Ras Shamra-Ugarit de 1929 à 1939* (Mission de Ras Shamra 10; Paris, 1963), ed. A. Herdner
DB	*Dictionnaire de la Bible* (5 vols., 1895-1912)
DBSup	*Dictionnaire de la Bible, Supplément*
DDD	*Dictionary of Deities and Demons in the Bible* (Leiden: Brill, 1995), ed. K. van der Toorn, B. Becking and P. W. van der Horst
DISO	*Dictionnaire des inscriptions semitiques de líouest* (Leiden: Brill, 1965), ed. Ch. F. Jean and J. Hoftijzer
DJD	Discoveries in the Judaean Desert
DJDJ	Discoveries in the Judaean Desert of Jordan
DSD	*Dead Sea Discoveries*
EB	Echter Bibel
Ebib	Études bibliques
EdF	Erträge der Forschung
ErIsr	*Eretz Israel*
ETL	*Ephemerides theologicae lovanienses*
EvT	*Evangelische Theologie*
FAT	Forschungen zum Alten Testament
FIOTL	The Formation and Interpretation of Old Testament Literature
FO	*Folia Orientalia*
FRLANT	Forschungen zur Religion und Literatur des Alten und Neuen Testaments
GCS	Griechischen christlichen Schriftsteller
GKC	*Gesenius' Hebrew Grammar* (ed. E. Kautzsch, tr. A. E. Cowley, 1910)
HAR	Hebrew Annual Review
HBC	*Harper's Bible Commentary*
HBD	*Harper's Bible Dictionary*
HDR	Harvard Dissertations in Religion
HKAT	Handkommentar zum Alten Testament
HNT	Handbuch zum Neuen Testament
HS	*Hebrew Studies*
HSM	Harvard Semitic Monographs
HSS	Harvard Semitic Studies
HTR	*Harvard Theological Review*
HTS	Harvard Theological Studies
HUCA	*Hebrew Union College Annual*
HUCMon	Hebrew Union College Monographs
ICC	International Critical Commentary
IDBSupp	*Interpreter's Dictionary of the Bible, Supplement*, ed. F. Crim et al.

IEJ	*Israel Exploration Journal*
IES	Israel Exploration Society
Int	*Interpretation*
IOS	Israel Oriental Society
Iraq	*Iraq*
JANESCU	*Journal of the Ancient Near Eastern Society of Columbia University*
JAOS	*Journal of the American Oriental Society*
JBL	*Journal of Biblical Literature*
JCS	*Journal of Cuneiform Studies*
JDS	Judaean Desert Studies
JECS	*Journal of Early Christian Studies*
JJS	*Journal of Jewish Studies*
JNES	*Journal of Near Eastern Studies*
JNSL	*Journal of Northwest Semitic Languages*
JNSLSup	*Journal of Northwest Semitic Languages*, Supplement Series
JQR	*Jewish Quarterly Review*
JQRMS	Jewish Quarterly Review Monograph Series
JSJ	*Journal for the Study of Judaism in the Persian, Hellenistic and Roman Period*
JSJSup	*Journal for the Study of Judaism in the Persian, Hellenistic and Roman Period*, Supplement Series
JSNT	*Journal for the Study of the New Testament*
JSNTSup	*Journal for the Study of the New Testament*, Supplement Series
JSOT	*Journal for the Study of the Old Testament*
JSOTSup	*Journal for the Study of the Old Testament*, Supplement Series
JSP	*Journal for the Study of the Pseudepigrapha*
JSPSup	*Journal for the Study of the Pseudepigrapha*, Supplement Series
JSS	*Journal of Semitic Studies*
JTS	*Journal of Theological Studies*
KAI	*Kanaanäische und Aramäische Inschriften*, eds. H. Donner and W. Röllig
KAT	Kommentaar zum Alten Testament
LCL	Loeb Classical Library
LDSS	Literature of the Dead Sea Scrolls
LEC	Library of Early Christianity
MDOG	Mitteilungen der Deutschen Orient-Gesellschaft
MSU	Mitteilungen des Septuaginta-Unternehmens
NCB	New Century Bible
NEA	*Near Eastern Archaeology*
NHS	Nag Hammadi Studies
NJBC	*The New Jerome Biblical Commentary*, ed. R. E. Brown et al.

NovT	*Novum Testamentum*
NovTSup	*Novum Testamentum*, Supplements
NRSV	*The New Revised Standard Version*
ATD	Das Alte Testament Deutsch
NTOA	*Novum Testamentum et Orbis Antiquus*
NTS	*New Testament Studies*
OBO	Orbis biblicus et orientalis
Or	*Orientalia* (n.s.)
OTL	Old Testament Library
OTP	*The Old Testament Pseudepigrapha*, ed. J. Charlesworth (2 vols., New York: Doubleday, 1983, 1985)
OTS	*Oudtestamentische Studiën*
PEQ	*Palestine Exploration Quarterly*
PL	*Patrologia latina*, ed. J. Migne
PTSDSS	The Princeton Theological Seminary Dead Sea Scrolls Project
QD	Quaestiones disputatae
RA	*Revue d'assyriologie et d'archeologie orientale*
RB	*Revue biblique*
RBib	Recherches Bibliques
REJ	*Revue des études juives*
RevQ	*Revue de Qumran*
RHR	*Revue de l'histoire des religions*
RivB	*Rivista biblica italiana*
RLA	*Reallexikon der Assyriologie*
RNT	Regensburger Neues Testament
SAA	State Archives of Assyria
SANT	Studien zum Alten und Neuen Testament
SB	Sources bibliques
SBLDS	Society of Biblical Literature Dissertation Series
SBLEJL	Society of Biblical Literature Early Judaism and Its Literature
SBLMasS	Society of Biblical Literature Masoretic Studies
SBLMS	Society of Biblical Literature Monograph Series
SBLSBS	Society of Biblical Literature Sources for Biblical Study
SBLSCS	Society of Biblical Literature Septuagint and Cognate Studies
SBLSP	*Society of Biblical Literature Seminar Papers*
SBLSS	Society of Biblical Literature Semeia Studies
SBLSym	Society of Biblical Literature Symposium Series
SBLTT	Society of Biblical Literature Texts and Translations
SBS	Stuttgarter Bibelstudien
SC	Sources chrétiennes
ScrHier	*Scripta hierosolymitana*
SDSRL	Studies in the Dead Sea Scrolls and Related Literature

Sem	*Semitica*
SFSHJ	South Florida Studies in the History of Judaism
SJLA	Studies in Judaism in Late Antiquity
SNTS	Society for New Testament Studies
SNTSMS	Society for New Testament Studies Monograph Series
ST	*Studia theologica*
STDJ	Studies on the Texts of the Desert of Judah
TSJTSA	Theological Studies of the Jewish Theological Seminary of America
TB	Theologische Bucherei: Neudrucke und Berichte aus dem 20. Jahrhundert
TCL	Textes cuneiformes, Musee de Louvre
TCL	Translations of Christian Literature
THKNT	Theologischer Handkommentar zum Neuen Testament
ThWAT	*Thologisches Worterbuch zum Alten Testament* (Stuttgart, 1970-), ed. G. J. Botterweck and H. Ringgren
TLZ	*Theologische Literaturzeitung*
TRE	*Theologische Realenzyklopadie* (Berlin: de Gruyter, 1977-), ed. G. Krause and G. Müller
TSAJ	Texte und Studien zum antiken Judentum
TSK	*Theologische Studien und Kritiken*
TThZ	*Trierer theologische Zeitschrift*
TTZ	*Trierer theologische Zeitschrift*
TUAT	Texte aus der Umwelt des Alten Testaments
TWNT	*Theologisches Wörterbuch zum Neuen Testament*
TZ	*Theologische Zeitschrift*
UF	Ugarit-Forschungen
Ug	*Ugaritica*
VT	*Vetus Testamentum*
VTSup	*Vetus Testamentum*, Supplements
WBC	Word Biblical Commentary
WMANT	Wissenschaftliche Monographien zum Alten und Neuen Testament
WO	Die Welt des Orients
WUNT	Wissenschaftliche Untersuchungen zum Neuen Testament
ZA	*Zeitschrift fur Assyriologie*
ZAW	*Zeitschrift für die alttestamentliche Wissenschaft*
ZBK	Zürcher Bibelkommentare
ZNW	*Zeitschrift für die neutestamentliche Wissenschaft*

LIST OF CONTRIBUTORS

Rainer Albertz
Professor of Old Testament, Westfälische Wilhelms-Universität, Münster

John Barton
Oriel and Laing Professor of the Interpretation of Holy Scripture
Oxford University

Stefan Beyerle
Lecturer in Hebrew Bible and Second Temple Judaism
University of Oldenburg, GERMANY

Gabriele Boccaccini
Professor of New Testament and Second Temple Judaism
University of Michigan, Ann Arbor, USA

John J. Collins (Editor)
Holmes Professor of Old Testament Criticism and Interpretation, Yale University

Philip R. Davies
Professor of Biblical Studies, University of Sheffield

Alexander A. Di Lella
Andrews-Kelly-Ryan Professor of Biblical Studies
Catholic University of America, Washington, DC

James D. G. Dunn
Lightfoot Professor of Divinity, University of Durham

Esther Eshel
Department of Bible, Bar–Ilan University, Ramat–Gan, ISRAEL

Craig A. Evans
Professor of Biblical Studies, Trinity Western University, British Columbia

Peter W. Flint (Editor)
Professor of Biblical Studies, Trinity Western University, British Columbia

Uwe Gleßner
Privatdozent for Old Testament and Early Judaism
Universität Hamburg, Fachbereich Evangelische Theologie

John Goldingay
David Allan Hubbard Professor of Old Testament
Fuller Theological Seminary, Pasadena, California

Lester L. Grabbe
Professor of Hebrew ible and Early Judaism, University of Hull

Ernst Haag
Professor of Old Testament, University of Trier

Jan Willem van Henten
Professor of Biblical Studies, University of Amsterdam

Matthias Henze
Assistant Professor of Religious Studies, Rice University, Houston

John F. Hobbins
Ph.D. Candidate, University of Wisconsin-Madison

Konrad D.Jenner
Director, Pehitta Institute Leiden, Leiden University

Michael A. Knibb
Samuel Davidson Professor of Old Testament Studies
King's College London, University of London

Klaus Koch
Professor emeritus of Old Testament and History of Ancient Near Eastern
Religions, Universität Hamburg

Reinhard G. Kratz
Professor of Old Testament Studies, Georg-August Universität, Göttingen

André LaCocque
Professor of Hebrew Scripture (emeritus), Chicago Theological Seminary

Johan Lust
Professor of Old Testament Exegesis and Chair of Biblical Studies
Katholieke Universiteit Leuven

Shalom M. Paul
Professor of Bible, Hebrew University, Jerusalem

Christopher Rowland
Professor of the Exegesis of Holy Scripture, Oxford University

Daniel Smith-Christopher
Professor of Theological Studies (Old Testament), Loyola Marymount University,
California

Loren T. Stuckenbruck
Reader in New Testament and Early Judaism, University of Durham

Eugene Ulrich
John O'Brien Professor of Hebrew Scriptures, University of Notre Dame

Karel van der Toorn
Professor of Religions of Antiquity and Dean, Faculty of Humanities
Universiteit van Amsterdam

John H. Walton
Professor of Old Testament, Moody Bible Institute, Chicago

Jan-Wim Wesselius
Associate Professor of Hebrew and Aramaic, Universiteit van Amsterdam

PART ONE

GENERAL TOPICS

CURRENT ISSUES IN THE STUDY OF DANIEL

JOHN J. COLLINS

Daniel was probably composed latest of the books in the Hebrew Bible, but few books have been more influential in western history. This is the only book of the Hebrew Bible that speaks clearly of individual resurrection. Its vision of "one like a son of man" coming with the clouds of heaven provided the imagery for prophecies of the Second Coming in the New Testament. Daniel was read for centuries as a guide to political history and messianic chronology. As late as the eighteenth century no less an intellectual than Isaac Newton still read Daniel's visions as coded predictions of western history.

The history of Daniel's influence has been chronicled by Klaus Koch, who has also noted the decline of that influence in modern times.[1] Since the Enlightenment, scholars have increasingly come to view the book not as a reliable guide to history, past or future, but as a collection of imaginative tales and visions that reflect the fears and hopes of beleaguered Jews in the Hellenistic period. In fact, this change of academic perspective was hard won — one need only think of the Fundamentalist crisis that divided American Protestantism at the beginning of the twentieth century.[2] In academic circles, that crisis is generally viewed as having ended in the defeat of the Fundamentalists. Robert Dick Wilson, one of the scholars who consequently left Princeton Theological Seminary to found the more conservative Westminster Seminary, has been called "the last great defender of Daniel's traditional authorship."[3] Fundamentalist read-

---

[1] K. Koch, *Europa, Rom und der Kaiser vor dem Hintergrund von zwei Jahrtausenden Rezeption des Buches Daniel* (Hamburg: Joachim Jungius-Gesellschaft der Wissenschaften, 1997). See also the papers of the colloquium, *Europa, Tausendjähriges Reich und Neue Welt. Zwei Jahrtausende Geschichte und Utopie in der Rezeption des Danielbuches* (Freiburg, Schweiz, 15-18 March, 2000) to be edited by M. Delgado, K. Koch and E. Marsch.

[2] See George M. Marsden, *Fundamentalism and American Culture. The Shaping of Twentieth-Century Evangelicalism: 1870-1925* (New York: Oxford, 1980).

[3] B. S. Childs, *Introduction to the Old Testament as Scripture* (Philadelphia: Fortress, 1979) 612. Cf. R. D. Wilson, *Studies in the Book of Daniel* (New York: Revell, 1917); idem, *Studies in the Book of Daniel. Second Series* (New York: Revell, 1938).

ings of Daniel continue to flourish in the popular culture, as can be
seen from the best-selling writings of Hal Lindsey,[4] and conservative
scholars have continued to fight rear-guard actions in defence of the
reliability of the book.[5] In mainline scholarship, however, the great
issues that made Daniel the focus of controversy for centuries were
laid to rest in the late 19th and early 20th centuries.[6] A broad consensus on several key issues has existed since then. It is agreed that
Daniel is pseudepigraphic: the stories in chapters 1–6 are legendary
in character, and the visions in chapters 7–12 were composed by
persons unknown in the Maccabean era. The stories are almost
certainly older than the visions, but the book itself was put together
shortly after the Maccabean crisis. It must be read, then, as a witness
to the religiosity of that time, not as a prophecy of western political
history or of the eschatological future.

The issues that have engaged scholars in the last century are less
momentous than the great debates of earlier centuries, but are of
considerable interest nonetheless. In some part they have been fuelled
by new discoveries of ancient texts: first the tablets from Mesopotamia unearthed in the 19th century, then the Canaanite texts from
Ugarit and finally the Dead Sea Scrolls, which include fragments of
the Book of Daniel and several closely related compositions. In this
introductory essay I will outline several areas where Daniel continues to be the focus of lively discussion: text, composition, literary
genre, social setting, history of interpretation and modern relevance,
especially in the areas of theology and ethics.

1. TEXT

The fragments of Daniel found at Qumran on the whole confirm
the antiquity of the text preserved by the Masoretes, including the

---

[4] See especially H. Lindsey, *The Late Great Planet Earth* (Grand Rapids:
Zondervan, 1970).

[5] For a critical review of such attempts see L. L. Grabbe, "Fundamentalism and
Scholarship: The Case of Daniel," in Barry P. Thompson (ed.), *Scripture: Meaning
and Method. Essays presented to Anthony Tyrrell Hanson* (Hull, UK: Hull
University Press, 1987) 133–52.

[6] The commentary of J. A. Montgomery, *A Critical and Exegetical Commentary on the Book of Daniel* (ICC; Edinburgh: T. & T. Clark, 1927) is regarded
as the definitive culmination of this process.

transitions between Hebrew and Aramaic.[7] They shed no light, however, on the most puzzling aspect of the textual history: the wide discrepancy between the Old Greek translation of chapters 4–6 and the corresponding Aramaic text.[8] This discrepancy is so striking that from an early time the Old Greek of these chapters was replaced in Church usage by the translation of Theodotion, which conformed closely to the Masoretic text. It is now clear that the Old Greek was not simply an errant translation of the text preserved by the Masoretes. It was based on a different Aramaic Vorlage, and the relationship of that Vorlage to the text now found in the MT is disputed. It is not apparent that either text can be derived simply from the other.[9] The existence of such variant texts suggests that these chapters once circulated apart from the rest of the book, and that the tales may have been transmitted orally for a period.

Related to the phenomenon of divergent texts in Daniel 4–6 is the existence of additional material in the Greek translations, for which there is no equivalent in the Hebrew-Aramaic texts. The Additions to Daniel (Bel and the Serpent, Susanna, the Prayer of Azariah, and the Song of the Three Young Men) all appear to have been translated from Semitic originals,[10] yet no trace of these originals has been found in the Dead Sea Scrolls. The Scrolls do include, however, other examples of Danielic literature, in Aramaic, that were not

---

[7] See P. W. Flint, "The Daniel Tradition at Qumran," in C. A. Evans and P. W. Flint, (eds.), *Eschatology, Messianism, and the Dead Sea Scrolls* (Grand Rapids: Eerdmans, 1997) 42–43. The main editions are by Eugene C. Ulrich, "Daniel Manuscripts from Qumran. Part 1: A Preliminary Edition of 4QDan^a," *BASOR* 268 (1987) 17–37; "Part 2: A Preliminary Edition of 4QDan^b and 4QDan^c," *BASOR* 274 (1989) 3–26. See also K. Koch and M. Rösel, *Polyglotten-synopse zum Buch Daniel* (Neukirchen-Vluyn: Neukirchener Verlag, 2000).

[8] See the essay of A. A. DiLella in this volume.

[9] See J. J. Collins, *Daniel: A Commentary on the Book of Daniel* (Hermeneia; Minneapolis: Fortress Press, 1993) 6–7; E. Ulrich, "Double Literary Editions of Biblical Narratives and Reflections on Determining the Form to be Translated," in idem, *The Dead Sea Scrolls and the Origins of the Bible* (SDSRL; Grand Rapids: Eerdmans, 1999) 43–44.

[10] See now I. Kottsieper, "Zusätze zu Daniel," in O. H. Steck, R. G. Kratz and I. Kottsieper, *Das Buch Baruch, Der Brief des Jeremia, Zusätze zu Ester und Daniel* (ATD Apokryphen 5; Göttingen: Vandenhoeck & Ruprecht, 1998) and the comments of Michael Knibb in the present volume.

included in the Hebrew Bible.[11] There are at least two such pseudo-Danielic compositions (4Q243–44 and 4Q245), which take the form of overviews of history, with eschatological conclusions.[12] These texts resemble parts of the Hebrew-Aramaic Bible much more closely than is the case with the Greek Additions, and for this reason scholars were initially inclined to assume that they depended on the biblical text. This view has been brought into question, however, and the texts are now more properly viewed as independent compositions in the name of Daniel. A further Aramaic composition (4Q246, the so-called Aramaic Apocalypse or Son of God text)[13] recalls Daniel, especially chapter 7, in some of its language and imagery.[14] Whether this text is dependent on Daniel, or even an interpretation of it, or is an independent composition of a similar type, remains a highly controversial question.

The existence of the Greek Additions and of the Pseudo-Daniel literature from Qumran shows that the stories and visions that make up the Masoretic Book of Daniel were selected from a wider corpus of Danielic literature. Variant texts of some chapters of Daniel (4–6) were also part of this wider corpus. It is important, however, to distinguish the two phenomena. In the case of Daniel 4–6 we have variant texts of essentially the same stories. The Greek Additions and the Aramaic Pseudo-Daniel literature from Qumran are not textual variants of anything in the Masoretic texts; they are independent compositions. Their relevance, then, is not strictly to the textual

---

[11]   See the essay of P. W. Flint later in this volume.

[12]   J. Collins and P. Flint, "243–245. 4Qpseudo-Daniel[a-c] ar," in J. C. Vander-Kam (consulting editor), *Qumran Cave 4.XVII: Parabiblical Texts, Part 3* (DJD 22; Oxford: Clarendon, 1996) 95–164; Collins, "Pseudo-Daniel Revisited," *RevQ* 65–68 (Milik Festschrift, 1996) 111–35; idem, "New Light on the Book of Daniel from the Dead Sea Scrolls," in F. García Martínez and E. Noort (eds.), *Perspectives in the Study of the Old Testament and Early Judaism. A Symposium in Honour of Adam S. van der Woude on the Occasion of His 70th Birthday* (VTSup 73; Leiden: Brill, 1998) 180–96; P. Flint, "4Qpseudo-Daniel ar[c] (4Q245) and the Restoration of the Priesthood," *RevQ* 65–68 (Milik Festschrift, 1996) 137–50.

[13]   É. Puech, "246. 4Qapocryphe de Daniel ar," in DJD 22.165–84.

[14]   J. J. Collins, "The Son of God Text from Qumran," in M. C. de Boer (ed.), *From Jesus to John: Essays on Jesus and New Testament Christology in Honour of Marinus de Jonge* (JSNTSup 84; Sheffield: Sheffield Academic Press, 1993) 65–82, esp. 69–70.

history of Daniel, but to the history of the composition of Danielic literature. It should of course be remembered that other writings were composed and attributed to Daniel down into the Middle Ages.[15] While the authors of these later compositions were surely aware of the biblical book, their new compositions were only loosely related to it. It is certainly not possible to ascribe all compositions in the name of Daniel to a single on-going "scribal school."

The textual variety of the book of Daniel is also of some significance for its canonical status. Daniel attained authoritative status very shortly after its composition, as can be seen from the citations in the Dead Sea Scrolls.[16] Yet it shows more clearly than most books the arbitrary and variable nature of the canon. Daniel is located in the Prophets in the Greek Bible, and there is some reason to think that this placement was original, in view of Daniel's reputation as a prophet in antiquity.[17] Yet the book is found among the Writings in the Hebrew Bible, a fact which is often taken to show that the prophetic canon was already closed when it was composed, but which may be due to deliberate displacement. Moreover, the presence of the Additions in the Greek Bible, and the existence of variant texts of chapters 4–6, show that there is considerable variety between the various canonical texts of Daniel. Canonicity, in short, is a status conferred on different forms of the book by different religious communities. The inclusion of Daniel in the canon, moreover, does not negate the fact that its closest literary relationships are with non-canonical Jewish writings of the Hellenistic age.

2. COMPOSITION AND GENRE

It is generally agreed that the tales in Daniel 1–6 are older than the visions in chapters 7–12, and are traditional tales that may have evolved over centuries. Scholars had long suspected that the story of Nebuchadnezzar's madness in chapter 4 had its origin in traditions about the Babylonian king Nabonidus rather than Nebuchadnezzar.[18] This suspicion has been confirmed by the discovery of the *Prayer of*

---

[15] Collins, *Daniel*, 117–18; F. García Martínez, *Qumran and Apocalyptic* (Leiden: Brill, 1992) 149–60.

[16] 4QFlor frg. 1 ii.3; 11QMelch 2:18; Collins, *Daniel*, 73.

[17] See K. Koch, "Is Daniel also among the Prophets?" *Int* 39(1985) 117–30.

[18] See Collins, *Daniel*, 217–18.

Nabonidus at Qumran.[19] While this fragmentary Aramaic text is clearly related to Daniel, it cannot be shown to be a direct source of Daniel 4. Rather it provides a glimpse of the evolution of a legend, which evidently circulated in different forms at different times. Just how closely the *Prayer* is related to Daniel depends on the reconstruction of the very fragmentary text.[20] At the very least the *Prayer* tells how a Babylonian king was smitten with disease and how a Jewish diviner explained to him that his recovery should be credited not to idols but to the Most High God.

All the stories in Daniel 1–6 are explicitly set in the Babylonian court. Conservative scholars such as Robert Dick Wilson labored mightily to establish the authenticity of these stories in light of the Akkadian sources. In large part this effort was misguided. Correct use of local color does not prove that the events in question actually happened. The fact remains, however, that much light can be shed on these tales from Akkadian sources—a point illustrated in this volume by the essays of Karel van der Toorn and Shalom Paul. The survival of authentic Babylonian details in Daniel does not require that the book was written in the Exile, as conservatives have been wont to claim. Rather these details attest to the persistent cultural legacy of Assyria and Babylon in the Hellenistic period, a phenomenon that is only now being explored in a systematic way.[21]

The visions of Daniel, in chapters 7–12, are generally attributed to the Maccabean period, although some scholars suppose that a form of chapter 7 is older than this.[22] These visions are notoriously difficult, in the sense that they go over the same material in different ways and often deviate from sequential logic. Scholars have tried to deal with

---

[19]   J. J. Collins, "242. 4QPrayer of Nabonidus ar," in DJD 22.83–93.

[20]   See Collins, "New Light on the Book of Daniel from the Dead Sea Scrolls," in García Martínez and Noort (eds.), *Perspectives in the Study of the Old Testament and Early Judaism*, 181–87. For important alternative reconstructions see F. M. Cross, "Fragments of the Prayer of Nabonidus," *IEJ* 34 (1984) 260–64; F. García Martínez, "The Prayer of Nabonidus: A New Synthesis," in idem, *Qumran and Apocalyptic*, 116–36; and É. Puech, "La prière de Nabonide (4Q242)," in K. J. Cathcart and M. Maher (eds.), *Targumic and Cognate Studies: Essays in Honor of Martin McNamara* (Sheffield: Sheffield Academic Press, 1996) 208–27.

[21]   See S. Aro and R. M. Whiting (eds.), *The Heirs of Assyria. Melammu Symposia I* (Helsinki: The Neo-Assyrian Text Corpus Project, 2000).

[22]   See the essay of Rainer Albertz in this volume.

these difficulties in two ways. One tradition posits multiple redactional insertions and additions and tries to reconstruct a complex history of composition. This tradition is favored especially by German scholars, although one of its classic exponents was an American, H. L. Ginsberg.[23]

The second tradition attributes the repetitiveness and the breaks in sequential logic to the dream-like nature of myth, and looks to ancient Near Eastern models to explain the configuration.[24] The great pioneer of this approach was the German scholar Hermann Gunkel.[25] In more recent times it has figured prominently in English-language scholarship. It is not implausible that editorial insertions should have been made in the text. Efforts to identify these insertions in minute detail, however, are largely hypothetical and often strain credibility. Inner-biblical exegesis is sometimes thought to be a factor in the composition of the visions.[26] There is at least one explicit case of inner-biblical exegesis in Daniel 9. In this vein R. G. Kratz attempts to explain the imagery of the beasts in Daniel 7 as a combination of Daniel 4 with Hosea 13:7-8. But while allusions to these and other biblical texts can certainly be recognized in Daniel 7, it is difficult to see how they can account for the shape of the vision as a whole, which is precisely what is illuminated by the analogies from ancient Near Eastern myth.[27]

---

[23] H. L. Ginsberg, *Studies in Daniel* (New York: Jewish Theological Seminary of America, 1948). The essay of R. G. Kratz in this volume is a good example of the German tradition.

[24] In recent years, scholars have looked primarily to Ugaritic myth. See Collins, *Daniel*, 286–94, and the essay of André Lacocque in this volume. For attempts to find models in Akkadian literature, see H. S. Kvanvig, *Roots of Apocalyptic. The Mesopotamian Background of the Enoch Figure and of the Son of Man* (WMANT 61; Neukirchen-Vluyn: Neukirchener Verlag, 1988), and the essay of John Walton in this volume.

[25] H. Gunkel, *Schöpfung und Chaos in Urzeit und Endzeit: Eine religionsgeschichtliche Untersuchung über Gen 1 und Ap Joh 12* (Göttingen: Vandenhoeck & Ruprecht, 1895).

[26] The role of inner-biblical exegesis in Daniel is also noted in this volume by Michael Knibb.

[27] See J. J. Collins, "Stirring Up the Great Sea. The Religio-Historical Background of Daniel 7," in idem, *Seers, Sibyls and Sages in Hellenistic-Roman Judaism* (Leiden: Brill, 1997) 139–55.

The debate about the composition of the visions of Daniel reflects different views of their literary genre. On the one hand, some scholars view them a kind of midrash, woven by scribes whose thought world was constituted by the corpus of texts that we now have in the Hebrew Bible. On the other hand, other scholars assume that the authors of these visions had access to many traditions that are now only dimly known to us, and that they wove their visions from fragments of ancient myths that were still alive in oral tradition. Moreover, further light is shed on the nature of these visions by comparison with the roughly contemporary apocalypses of Enoch and with the Dead Sea Scrolls than with the older biblical texts, which served admittedly as source material but were very different in genre. In this regard, attention should be paid to the articles of Loren Stuckenbruck and Esti Eshel in this volume, which claim to identify sources of the Book of Daniel in non-canonical Jewish writings of the Hellenistic period. The significance of the apocalyptic genre for the understanding of Daniel, however, does not lie only in specific motifs, such as those addressed by Stuckenbruck and Eshel, but in the shape of the visions as a whole, which is clearly distinct from (although related to) that of older biblical prophecy.[28]

The differing weight given to biblical or non-biblical contextual material is often reflected in the interpretation of specific passages. No passage in Daniel has been more controversial than the vision of "one like a son of man" coming on the clouds of heaven in Daniel 7. In the last half-century or so, scholarly opinion has been divided between those who identify this figure as an angel (usually Michael) and those who see it as "only" a symbol for Israel. The angelic interpretation has been defended in several recent commentaries on Daniel,[29] but the "merely symbolic" interpretation is often assumed by scholars who make incidental reference to the passage.[30] In general, the latter interpretation seems almost self-evident to scholars

---

[28] Collins, *Daniel*, 52–61.

[29] C. Gaide, *Le Livre de Daniel* (Paris: Mame, 1969) 101–102; A. Lacocque, *The Book of Daniel* (Atlanta: John Knox, 1976) 133; J. E. Goldingay, *Daniel* (WBC 30; Dallas: Word, 1989) 172; Collins, *Daniel*, 318.

[30] The Anchor Bible commentary of L. F. Hartman and A. A. DiLella, *The Book of Daniel* (AB 23; New York: Doubleday, 1978) 85–102, is exceptional among recent commentaries in defending the "merely symbolic" interpretation.

who take the Hebrew Bible as the primary context for the interpretation of Daniel. Scholars who read Daniel in the context of ancient myth, and of the non-canonical apocalypses and Dead Sea Scrolls, generally find the angelic interpretation more persuasive.[31] At issue is the nature of the symbolism one may expect to encounter in a visionary text.

3. SOCIAL SETTING

As Stefan Beyerle remarks in his article in this volume, "the sociological approach is a major tool for the historical-critical investigation of apocalyptic texts." There have been numerous attempts to identify the circles in which Daniel was written, beginning with the commentary of G. Behrmann in 1894.[32] Most have focused on the *maskilim* mentioned in Daniel 11 and the Hasidim known from the books of Maccabees,[33] an identification that has been shown to be problematic.[34] The problem with any attempt to reconstruct the social setting is that the book of Daniel is pseud-epigraphic, and so the explicit setting in the Babylonian exile is known to be fictional. Scholars then have to infer information about the actual settings in which it was composed, from literature that attempts to hide those very settings.

It is generally agreed that the setting of the tales is different from that of the visions. (Some scholars, including Rainer Albertz in this volume, take Daniel 7 with the tales to constitute an "Aramaic Daniel" despite the clear differences in genre and imagery. This attempt requires textual surgery to remove the references to Antiochus Epiphanes, which provide the clearest indication of the

---

[31] For example, J. A. Emerton, "The Origin of the Son of Man Imagery," *JTS* 9 (1958) 225–42; C. Rowland, *The Open Heaven. A Study of Apocalyptic in Judaism and Early Christianity* (New York: Crossroad, 1982) 182; J. Day, *God's Conflict with the Dragon and the Sea* (Cambridge: Cambridge University Press, 1985) 172.

[32] G. Behrmann, *Das Buch Daniel* (HKAT 3/2.2; Göttingen: Vandenhoeck & Ruprecht, 1894) xxv–xxvi.

[33] So especially, O. Plöger, *Theocracy and Eschatology* (Richmond, VA: John Knox, 1968); M. Hengel, *Judaism and Hellenism* (Philadelphia: Fortress, 1974) 1.175–218.

[34] See Collins, *Daniel*, 66–69, and the literature there cited.

setting of Daniel 7.) The tales describe the adventures of Jews at the courts of foreign (Babylonian and Persian) kings. This circumstance invites the conjecture that the actual authors or tradents of these tales worked in the service of foreign kings, most probably the Seleucids.[35] Hence they display a certain knowledge of court protocol. This hypothesis is not implausible, but it is, of course, completely unverifiable, and by no means necessary. Speculation about the setting of the visions, in the Maccabean era, inevitably centers on the *maskilim*, who are presented as wise teachers. The book of Daniel itself is presumably representative of their wisdom. It is greatly concerned with mysteries, and uses the interpretation of older texts as well as dreams as means of arriving at revelation. The *maskilim* are evidently literate, and are often supposed to be scribes. Whether they are at all related to the Ḥasidim of the Maccabean books remains doubtful. The Ḥasidim were scribes, but they were also militant supporters of the Maccabees. There is no evidence of such militancy in the Book of Daniel.

Albertz, in this volume, makes an ingenious argument that there was a split in the apocalyptic movement. One group, whose views are reflected in the Animal Apocalypse of *1 Enoch*, supported the Maccabees. These are the people who are said in Dan 11:35 to "stumble," which Albertz takes to mean "fall away" from the true path. (Most scholars take this reference to mean that some of the *maskilim* meet their deaths, "to test and purify them and make them white.") Even if we allow that the verb may refer to falling away, however, Albertz's brilliant suggestion remains very hypothetical. The Animal Apocalypse in *1 Enoch* stands in a quite different tradition, with a different range of interests from what we find in Daniel. The books of Maccabees give no hint of the apocalyptic interests of the Ḥasidim. Of course the Maccabean authors are only interested in the Ḥasidim from the viewpoint of the Maccabees, and do not give a full account of their motives or beliefs. Nonetheless, we are dependent on the accounts that we actually have. The suggestion by Albertz will remain an interesting hypothesis until and unless some additional

---

[35] For example, R. R. Wilson, "From Prophecy to Apocalyptic: Reflections on the Shape of Israelite Religion," *Semeia* 21 (1981) 79–95, esp. 88. See also P. L. Redditt, "Daniel 11 and the Sociohistorical Setting of the Book of Daniel," *CBQ* 60 (1998) 463–74, esp. 467.

confirmatory evidence is found.

The attempt to infer historical events, such as the supposed split in the Hasidean movement, are inevitably risky. We are on somewhat sounder ground when we focus on the "belief-system" and attitudes reflected in the texts, in the manner proposed by Stefan Beyerle. In the case of the tales, most scholars have seen a fundamental acceptance of foreign rule, at least for the present. To be sure, these tales are critical of the Gentile kings, but they entertain hope for their conversion, not to Judaism but to the veneration of the Most High God and respect for the Jews. In this respect, the paired stories of Nebuchadnezzar's madness and Belshazzar's feast are paradigmatic: the older king repents and is reinstated; the younger ruler persists in his arrogance and is destroyed. The portrayal of Darius in the last of the tales is quite sympathetic. This understanding of the tales is challenged, however, by Daniel Smith-Christopher, both in his recent commentary in the *New Interpreters' Bible*[36] and in his essay in this volume. Smith-Christopher argues that the dreams of Nebuchadnezzar are not after all the dreams of a Babylonian king but the fantasies of a Jewish author. They are, in effect, "dreams of the disenfranchised."[37] The portrayal of Nebuchadnezzar and Belshazzar, and even that of Darius, are by no means flattering to the Gentile kings.[38] They are presented as arrogant buffoons, even if they sometimes come to their senses. Smith-Christopher, then, sees the tales as resistance literature, even if they are more subtle in their depiction of the rulers than are the apocalyptic visions in the second half of the book. It should be granted that there is a critical element in these tales which has often been overlooked, but the attitude to Gentile rule is still very different from what we find in the visions. There is an eschatological perspective in these stories, but it is deferred eschatology, which allows for the viability of Gentile rule for the present.[39]

---

[36] D. L. Smith-Christopher, "The Book of Daniel," in L. Keck (general editor), *The New Interpreter's Bible* (Nashville: Abingdon, 1996) 7.19–152.

[37] *Ibidem*, 57.

[38] See also H. I. Avalos, "The Comedic Function of the Enumerations of the Officials and Instruments in Daniel 3," *CBQ* 53 (1991) 580–88.

[39] J. J. Collins, "Nebuchadnezzar and the Kingdom of God. Deferred Eschatology in the Jewish Diaspora," in idem, *Seers, Sibyls and Sages*, 131–37.

In contrast, the visions portray Gentile rule as utterly unacceptable. In this they reflect the persecution under Antiochus Epiphanes.[40] In Daniel 7–12, there is no interaction between Daniel and the kings; they only appear as (demonic) actors within the visions. In this respect, Daniel 7 clearly belongs with the visions, not with the tales. The stories in 1–6 entertain the promotion of Daniel and his friends at court as a desirable development. There is no such prospect in the visions. While the language of kingdoms is retained in chapter 7, nothing is said of the way in which the final kingdom would be administered. When the personal aspirations of the *maskilim* are expressed in Daniel 11–12, it is the hope for eternal life with the stars or angels. It would seem then that chapters 7–12 are disillusioned with earthly politics. Gentile rule can no longer be reformed, it can only be destroyed. The hope of the righteous is not for power and influence on earth but for heavenly life after death.

This sketch of the differing attitudes in the two halves of the book is of some significance for the "social world" of Daniel, but we remain hampered by the lack of specific information about the authors.

4. THE HISTORY OF INTERPRETATION

The history of interpretation of Daniel is a rich field that has only recently begun to attract serious attention, and perhaps for that reason has not given rise to much controversy.[41] One area that has been very controversial, however, concerns the influence of Daniel 7 in the New Testament.[42] It is quite clear that some passages in the Gospels speak of the Son of Man coming on the clouds of heaven in terms that allude to Daniel 7 (e.g. Mark 13 and parallels). The debate has centered on whether Jesus himself is likely to have used Daniel in this way, or whether these passages are entirely compositions of the Gospel writers. The arguments are complex and cannot be repeated here. One wonders if some scholars are not engaged in what Klaus

---

[40] Cf. Redditt, "Daniel 11," 474.

[41] See the essays of van Henten, Koch, Rowland, Gleßmer, Evans, Dunn and Henze in this volume.

[42] See Adela Yarbro Collins, "The Influence of Daniel on the New Testament," in Collins, *Daniel*, 90–105, and the essays of Craig Evans and James Dunn in this volume.

Koch has called "the agonized attempt to save Jesus from apocalyptic."[43] But questions relating to the historical Jesus are notoriously difficult to resolve and the controversy is likely to continue.

Most of the later history of interpretation, while fascinating in its own right, is important for the understanding of later Judaism and Christianity rather than of the Book of Daniel in its historical context. Nonetheless, the variety of ways in which Daniel came to be interpreted often sheds light on potential meanings embedded in the original text. At various times, interpreters have focused on Daniel as a model of piety, on his loyalty to the Babylonian king, on his radical critique of empire (the phrase of Christopher Rowland), or on the identification of figures mentioned in his prophecies and the calculation of the end. All of these interpretations have some basis in the text, and remind us of the composite character of that text and of the variety of perspectives enshrined within it.

5. THEOLOGY AND ETHICS

Daniel, however, is not only a document of ancient Judaism. It is also part of Jewish and Christian Scripture, and as such is a book to which people continue to look for guidance. Many of the people who take the book most seriously in this regard remain unaffected by critical scholarship, and continue to be fascinated with it as predictive prophecy. For those who accept the results of historical criticism, however, the status of the book as Scripture becomes more problematic. The theology of Daniel is most succinctly expressed in the doxologies that punctuate the first six chapters.[44] The God of Israel is "god of gods and lord of kings and a revealer of mysteries" (2:47). He is "the living God, enduring forever. His kingdom shall never be destroyed and his dominion has no end. He delivers and rescues, he works signs and wonders in heaven and on earth...." (6:26-27). The stories that illustrate these affirmations, however, are

---

[43] K. Koch, *The Rediscovery of Apocalyptic* (SBT 2/22; Naperville: Allenson, 1972) 57.

[44] On the theology of Daniel, see the reflections of John Goldingay in this volume, and those of Stefan Beyerle, "Von der Löwengrube ins himmlische Jerusalem," in *Glaube und Lernen. Zeitschrift für theologische Urteilsbildung* 14 (1999) 23–34, esp. 24–28.

fictions, and one may question how accurately they represent history. It is a notorious fact that the final deliverance promised by apocalyptic visions never comes. This fact does not negate their value, but reminds us that they are expressions of hope rather than statements of fact. The book of Daniel is emphatic that God ultimately rewards the just and punishes the wicked. In the end, however, this retribution is referred to a realm after death, where it is a subject of faith but not of verification.

Short of eschatological verification, the theology of Daniel cannot be confirmed or disproven. The ethics of the book, however, are more amenable to discussion. John Barton, in this volume, emphasizes that much of what is called for in Daniel was not extraordinary. Daniel and his companions avoid pollution in the matter of food, presumably because of the Jewish laws of kashrut. Daniel says his prayers towards Jerusalem. He is a loyal servant of the king, but makes no compromise with idolatry. There is nothing specifically apocalyptic about any of this. Yet the most striking aspect of the ethic of the Book of Daniel is surely the willingness of its heroes to sacrifice their lives rather than compromise their convictions. The confession of the three young men is especially striking in this regard:

> O Nebuchadnezzar, we have no need to present a defense to you in this matter. If our God whom we serve is able to deliver us from the furnace of blazing fire and out of your hand, O king, let him deliver us. But if not, be it known to you, O king, that we will not serve your gods and we will not worship the golden statue that you have set up (Dan 3:16-18).

This confession is remarkable because it seems to say that their willingness to die is not contingent on the hope of rescue. The prohibition of idolatry is simply an ethical imperative. The tales, of course, insist that the righteous are rescued, and so the point is moot, but the acknowledgment that God might not choose to rescue them is nonetheless significant.[45]

The resolution of the visions puts this problem in a different perspective. In light of the persecution of the Maccabean era, fantasies of deliverance from a fiery furnace could not be taken literally, if they ever were. It was necessary to find a theology that

---

[45] See further J. J. Collins, "Inspiration or Illusion: Biblical Theology and the Book of Daniel," *ExAud* 6 (1990) 29-38.

could accept the deaths of the righteous. The explanation was provided by the belief in resurrection, which finds its first clear biblical attestation here, although it is presupposed in the pre-Maccabean Enoch literature.[46] The logic of Daniel 11–12 argues powerfully that the "stumbling" of some of the *maskilim* does not refer to their falling away, but to their deaths. It is precisely the death of the martyrs that makes necessary the affirmation of their resurrection.[47] There is clear continuity between the ethic of the visions and that of the tales. In fact, the stories of the fiery furnace and the lions' den were often read as paradigms of martyrdom in later centuries.[48] Nonetheless, the visions have a more strongly other-worldly character. Their logic requires the importance of hidden realities, the belief that things are not as they seem. The present world is not the end. This would seem to be a considerable modification of the rather this-worldly ethic of the tales. It was a modification that had enormous importance for the later development of western religion.

---

[46] See the essays of Ernst Haag and John Hobbins in this volume.

[47] J. J. Collins, "Apocalyptic Eschatology as the Transcendence of Death," in idem, *Seers, Sibyls and Sages*, 75–97.

[48] See the essay of Jan Willem van Henten in this volume.

THE BOOK OF DANIEL IN ITS CONTEXT

MICHAEL A. KNIBB

1. THE FORMATION OF THE BOOK OF DANIEL

The Book of Daniel in the canonical form known to us from the Hebrew Bible represents the crystallisation in a particular location and at a quite precise point in time—Jerusalem or its immediate surroundings shortly before the rededication of the temple in 165 BCE—of the traditions concerning Daniel and his companions that were then in circulation. It appears from Dan 12:11-12 that the book that we possess was subject to revision very shortly after its completion, and it is in any case widely recognised that the book has a complex history of development, and in particular that the individual stories of which chapters 2–6 are composed belong in a different location—the eastern diaspora—and go back to the early Hellenistic or the Persian period. The fact that Daniel appears as the hero of the stories on which this collection is built remains something of an enigma in that there are no traditions outside of the Book of Daniel which provide a clue as to why he might have been made the hero of them. At best a connection has been suggested with the traditions preserved in Ezek 28:3 and 14:14, 20 concerning the Daniel who was famed for his wisdom and piety[1]—as if, somehow, he was regarded as a younger contemporary of Ezekiel. But the fact that in Ezek 14:14, 20 Daniel is mentioned alongside Noah and Job indicates that he belongs in the remote past,[2] and a link has frequently been made with the tradition, recorded in *Aqhat*, concerning the pious chief Daniel, who is said to have "judged the cause of the widow, tried the case of the orphan."[3] The exile Daniel is a very different figure and belongs in

---

[1] Cf., for example, J. J. Collins, *Daniel: A Commentary on the Book of Daniel* (Hermeneia; Minneapolis: Fortress, 1993) 1–2.

[2] Cf. W. Zimmerli, *Ezechiel* (2 vols., BKAT 13/1–2; Neukirchen-Vluyn: Neukirchener Verlag, 1969) 1.321; 2.670 [ET, *Ezekiel: A Commentary on the Book of the Prophet Ezekiel* (2 vols., Hermeneia; Philadelphia: Fortress, 1979, 1983) 1.314–15; 2.79–80].

[3] Aqhat 17 col. v 7-8, 19 i 23-25; cf. J. C. L. Gibson, *Canaanite Myths and Legends* (2nd ed., Edinburgh: T. & T. Clark, 1978) 107, 114.

a very different context.

It is in fact commonly accepted that the Daniel of the Book of Daniel is presented as a wise man of a mantic type, and that the stories about him and his three companions in chapters 2–6 are court tales which depict the activities and rivalries of courtiers in the service of the king. Of the four stories about Daniel himself, three exploit as a major element in the narrative the theme of Daniel's ability as a mantic, and it was no doubt because Daniel is presented in chapters 2–6 as a mantic that it should have seemed natural that he himself should be made the recipient of divine revelations in the four narratives that follow in chapters 7–12.

In an earlier study I have drawn attention to the importance of inner-biblical exegesis in the formation of Daniel 7–12, and I argued that this points to the essentially scholarly character of this material.[4] So far as Daniel 9–12 is concerned, the significance of inner-biblical exegesis has long been recognised, but here reference should particularly be made to the discussion of these chapters by M. Fishbane, under the rubric "The Mantological Exegesis of Oracles," in his comprehensive treatment of inner-biblical exegesis entitled *Biblical Interpretation in Ancient Israel*.[5] The presupposition of the mantological exegesis of oracles is that the meaning of the prophecy is unclear, and that it requires decoding or explanation in the same way that visions and omens also require explanation. The reason for this may be that the prophecy was regarded as failed or unfulfilled, or that it was thought to have relevance in any case to an age later than that of the original prophecy, and the effect of such exegesis was to reapply the original prophecy to a new situation.[6] The reinterpretation of Jer 25:9-12 (cf. 29:10) in Daniel 9 represents a very obvious example of this kind of mantological exegesis. But the reuse of earlier prophecy is also a prominent feature of Daniel 10–12, and although not all the

---

[4] See Knibb, "'You are indeed wiser than Daniel': Reflections on the Character of the Book of Daniel," in A. S. van der Woude (ed.), *The Book of Daniel in the Light of New Findings* (BETL 106; Leuven: Leuven University Press and Peeters, 1993) 399–411.

[5] See M. Fishbane, *Biblical Interpretation in Ancient Israel* (New York: Oxford University Press, 1985) 441–524. Fishbane discusses the mantological exegesis of prophetic oracles as a second basic type of mantological exegesis alongside that of dreams, visions and omens.

[6] For references and more details for what follows, see Fishbane, *Biblical Interpretation*, 479–95; Knibb, "'You are indeed wiser than Daniel,'" 404–11.

allusions to prophetic texts that have been identified in these chapters are equally significant, there are four texts or groups of texts that do seem important. First, the application of the prophecy of judgment on the Assyrians in Isa 10:24-27 to the Syrians, and particularly to Antiochus Epiphanes, through the allusion to Isa 10:23 (כלה ונחרצה) and 25 (כלה זעם) in Dan 11:36: והצליח עד כלה זעם כי נחרצה נעשתה, "He shall prosper until the period of wrath is completed for what is determined shall be done." Second, the application of the Fourth Servant Song to the group described in Dan 12:3 as "the wise" (המשכילים) and as "those who lead many to righteousness" (מצדיקי הרבים) through the allusion to Isa 53:11 (יצדיק צדיק עבדי לרבים, "the righteous one, my servant will make many righteous") and Isa 52:12 (הנה ישכיל עבדי, "See, my servant shall prosper" or "See, my servant shall be wise"). Third, the direct allusion to Num 24:24 ("But ships shall come from Kittim and shall afflict Asshur and Eber; and he also shall perish for ever," וצים מיד כתים וענו אשור וענו עבר וגם הוא עדי אבד) in Dan 11:30 ("Ships of Kittim will come against him, and he will lose heart," ובאו בו ציים כתים ונכאה), through which it seems likely that the references to Asshur and Eber in Num 24:24 were interpreted in relation to the Syrians and the eastern part of the Seleucid empire, and that the final clause of Num 24:24 ("and he also shall perish for ever") was interpreted in relation to Antiochus Epiphanes. Finally, the use of Hab. 2:3a ("For there is still a vision for the appointed time; it testifies of the end, and does not lie," כי עוד חזון למועד ויפיח לקץ ולא יכזב), three, or perhaps four, times in Daniel 10–12 (see 10:14; 11:27, 35, and perhaps 11:29) as well as in 8:17, 19 as a means of explaining the delay in the defeat of Antiochus and the arrival of the end time. However, in addition to these examples from Daniel 9–12, Daniel 8 may be regarded as a reinterpretaion and actualisation of Daniel 7, and particularly of what is said in Daniel 7 concerning the "little horn" (cf. 7:8; 8:9).

In the precise historical context in which the Book of Daniel achieved its present form it represented a reaction to the crisis of faith caused by the measures taken by Antiochus Epiphanes against the practice of the Jewish religion and as such may be regarded as crisis literature. But the book in its canonical form stems from the circles of those described in the book as "the wise" (המשכילים, 11:33, 35; 12: 3, 10) and—as the kind of scholarly exegesis of scripture that we have just been discussing shows—has something of a scholarly character. It is just those sections of the book that belong directly in the moment of crisis, particularly chapters (8)9–12, that can be seen to have been written on the basis of scholarly reflection on, and reinterpretation of, the scriptures.

2. THE BOOK OF DANIEL AND OTHER DANIELIC WRITINGS

The Book of Daniel belongs in a quite precise historical context, but it also belongs in a literary context consisting on the one hand of related Daniel literature from more or less the same period and on the other of works that have a similar genre. My main concern in what follows is to consider the significance of these two groups of texts in relation to the biblical book.

The Daniel literature outside the Book of Daniel consists both of the Daniel texts from Qumran (4Q242–46) and the Additions to the Greek Book of Daniel. So far as the Daniel texts from Qumran are concerned, they all, apart from the *Prayer of Nabonidus* (4Q242), presuppose the existence of a well developed Daniel tradition and apparently of the Book of Daniel itself.

4Q243–45 (4Qpseudo-Daniel[a-c] ar) were originally thought to be manuscripts of the same work, but the two editors responsible for these scrolls in the DJD series (Collins and Flint) have made a plausible case for the view that they contain two different texts, one represented by 4Q243–44, the other by 4Q245.[7] There is considerable difficulty in interpreting these texts because they survive only as a series of small fragments. But both works mention Daniel by name,[8] 4Q243–44 presupposes a court situation[9] (and the same is probably true of 4Q245), and both works refer to a writing,[10] the contents of which are apparently expounded by Daniel and form an apocalyptic revelation. In the case of 4Q243–44 this revelation consists of a

---

[7] J. Collins and P. Flint, "243–245. 4Qpseudo-Daniel[a-c] ar," in J. C. VanderKam (consulting ed.), *Qumran Cave 4.XVII: Parabiblical Texts, Part 3* (DJD 22; Oxford: Clarendon Press, 1996) 95–164 + pls. VII–X (esp. 154–55).

[8] See 4Q243 1.1; 2.1; 5.1; 6.3; 4Q244 4.2; 4Q245 1 i.3.

[9] See 4Q243, fragments 1, 2, and 3; 4Q244, fragments 1–3, and 4.

[10] See 4Q243 6.2, 4; 4Q245 1 i.4. Perhaps "the book of truth" (Dan 10:21) provides the most likely basis for the reference to the "writing" (cf. Collins and Flint, "243–245. 4Qpseudo-Daniel[a-c] ar," 155–56). But mention should also be made of "the books" from which Enoch, in the introduction to the Apocalypse of Weeks, is said to speak (*1 Enoch* 93:1); these books are identified with "the tablets of heaven" in *1 Enoch* 93:2-3 (cf. 81:2).

survey of history which stretches from the primeval period to the Hellenistic age and reaches a climax in the eschatological era. In 4Q245 the revelation—in the few fragments that we have—consists primarily of two lists of names, of priests (ending with the Hasmonean leaders Jonathan and Simon) and of kings (beginning with David and Solomon). It has commonly been assumed that 4Q243–44 and 4Q245 were dependent on the Book of Daniel, but in relation to 4Q243–44 the editors comment: "Whether it depended on the biblical book at all no longer seems clear as it did when we relied on Milik's construction"—and the same appears to be their view of 4Q245.[11] The doubts of the editors are based on the one hand on whether 4Q243–44 refers to the "seventy years" and the four-kingdom schema of the Book of Daniel, and on the other on whether 4Q245 contains a reference to resurrection based on Dan 12:2.

So far as 4Q245 is concerned, it is clear, by virtue of the reference to Jonathan and Simon, that this text dates from after the completion of the canonical Book of Daniel,[12] and in view of this it is extremely unlikely that it was composed in isolation from the biblical book. The fragment that has been thought to allude to resurrection (4Q245 2 i) is quite small:

2   ]to exterminate wickedness
3   ]these (אלן) in blindness, and they have gone astray
4   th]ese (אלן) then will arise
5   ]the [h]oly [ ], and they will return
6   ]. wickedness[13]

It is impossible to be certain whether there is here an allusion to Dan 12:2, and thus to resurrection, or whether the fragment should be given an historical interpretation along the lines suggested by the editors;[14] but the repetition of "these (אלן)" does seem to make it likely that an allusion to Dan 12:2, where אלה is similarly repeated, was intended, as a number of scholars have suggested.[15]

---

[11] Collins and Flint, "243–245. 4Qpseudo-Daniel[a–c] ar," 136, cf. 133–34.

[12] The script of 4Q245 itself dates from the early first century CE.

[13] Translated by Collins and Flint, "243–245. 4Qpseudo-Daniel[a–c] ar," 163.

[14] See Collins and Flint, "243–245. 4Qpseudo-Daniel[a–c] ar," 157–58, 163; Collins, *Daniel*, 76; Flint, "4QPseudo-Daniel ar[c] (4Q245) and the Restoration of the Priesthood," *RevQ* 17/65–68 (Milik Festschrift, 1996) 137–50, esp. 142–43, 148.

[15] Cf. F. García Martínez, *Qumran and Apocalyptic: Studies on the Aramaic*

The text represented by 4Q243–44 cannot be dated precisely. The script of both manuscripts is Herodian (early first century CE), but the work itself is no doubt significantly older than this. There is, however, no reason to think that the text dates from before the time at which the biblical Book of Daniel achieved its present form. One passage, represented by two fragments (4Q243 13 + 4Q244 12), clearly refers to the giving of the Israelites into the hand of Nebuchadnezzar, and it has commonly been assumed that this was followed by a passage in a fragment (4Q243 16) which referred to "seventy years" and to "the first kingdom" (and hence, by implication, to the four-kingdom schema of the Book of Daniel):[16]

1   [כ] [שנין [עין]שב] אין[
2   ק [אנ]רה רבחא ויושע[בי
3   יא [חסינין ומלכות עממ]
4   [היא מלכותא קד]מיתא

1   ]oppressed(?) for [seven]ty(?) years [ ] k[
2   with] his great [ha]nd and he will save th[em
3   ]powerful[ ]and the kingdoms of [the] people[s
4   ]it is the f[irst] kingdom[[17]

However, both the phrase "seventy years" and the phrase "the first kingdom" have to be restored in the text, and while the restoration [שב]עין שנין is plausible, the restoration מלכותא קד[מיתא] is uncertain, and for this the editors suggest מלכותא קד[ישתא], "the holy kingdom". They point out, quite properly, that the seventy years might not necessarily refer to the length of the exile in that *4Qpseudo-Moses* mentions two periods of seventy years (4Q390 1.2; 2 i.6), which are not references to the exile; and they maintain that the reconstruction "the first kingdom" is difficult because it would be strange for the act

---

Texts from Qumran (STDJ 9; Leiden: Brill, 1992) 146; É. Puech, *La croyance des Esséniens en la vie future: Immortalité, résurrection, vie éternelle?* (2 vols., Études bibliques, n.s. 21-22; Paris: Gabalda, 1993) 569–70. See further Knibb, "Eschatology and Messianism in the Dead Sea Scrolls," in P. W. Flint and J. C. VanderKam (eds.), *The Dead Sea Scrolls after Fifty Years: A Comprehensive Assessment* (2 vols., Leiden: Brill, 1998-99) 2.382–84.

[16] So already J. T. Milik, "'Prière de Nabonide' et autres écrits d'un cycle de Daniel," *RB* 63 (1956) 407–15, esp. 413.

[17] Text and translation based on that given in Collins and Flint, "243–245. 4Qpseudo-Daniel[a–c] ar," 108–109, 144, 148, but with a different reconstruction of line 4, and with [שב]עין (line 1) explicitly reconstructed.

of salvation indicated in line 2 to be followed by the inauguration of the first of a series of Gentile kingdoms, and because this would be the only instance where the four-kingdom sequence begins after the deliverance from exile. They suggest rather that the statement "and with his great hand and he will save them" could more appropriately be applied to God's eschatological salvation; the holy kingdom is the eschatological kingdom.[18]

The difficulty in the interpretation of this fragment stems not only from its small size and the fact that two key words have to be reconstructed, but also from the fact that the order of the fragments cannot be established with certainty except insofar as it is determined by the historical sequence. Collins and Flint may be correct in the interpretation they offer of this fragment. On the other hand the restoration "[seven]ty years" remains the most likely in line 1, and in a Danielic text it seems hard to believe that the phrase was not intended as a conscious allusion to the seventy-year prophecy as it occurs in Daniel 9—unless it is to be assumed that the text antedates the composition of Daniel 9, which seems to me unlikely. In line 4 the restoration "the f[irst] kingdom" is as plausible on textual grounds as the restoration "the h[oly] kingdom," and in a Danielic text a reinterpretation of the four-kingdom schema of the biblical book would not be surprising, particularly in the light of the reuse of this schema in 4Q552–53 and in 2 Esdras 11–12.

Whether 4Q243–44 is or is not dependent on the biblical Book of Daniel, it does seem likely that Daniel is presented in both 4Q243–44 and in 4Q245 in much the same way as he is in Daniel 2, 4 and 5, namely as a seer or mantic attached to the royal court, the mediator of a divine revelation. This also appears to be the case in 4Q246, the so-called *Aramaic Apocalypse*,[19] which has attracted considerable attention because of its references to an individual described as the "son of God" and the "son of the Most High." Only one complete column and half of the preceding column have survived, but it is clear that the first three lines of the fragmentary column presuppose a court scene: an individual is brought in before a king, who is disturbed by what he has seen; the individual then inteprets "your vision, and everything that shall come for ever" (א חזוך וכלא אתה עד עלמא .[, col.

---

[18] Collins and Flint, "243–245. 4Qpseudo-Daniel[a–c] ar," 133–34, 150–51.

[19] For the text, see É. Puech, "246. 4QApocryphe de Daniel ar," in VanderKam (consulting ed.), DJD 22.165–184 + pl. XI.

1:3).[20] The individual is not named, but the similarities with the role of Daniel in Daniel 2, 4 and 5 are obvious, and, as É. Puech, the editor of 4Q246 in the DJD series, notes, it is plausible to believe that the individual is Daniel.[21]

Interpretations of the references to the "son of God" and the "son of the Most High" have tended to follow two main lines, on the one hand a historicising interpretation according to which the titles are to be understood as part of a polemic directed against a Seleucid king—most probably Antiochus Epiphanes—and on the other a messianic interpretation.[22] I have argued elsewhere that, despite the difficulties, the messianic interpretation on balance makes most sense of the text.[23] For our present purposes it is more important to note that the text draws on the language of the Book of Daniel. Thus the phrase מלכותה מלכות עלם (2:5) has apparently been quoted from Dan 7:27 and שלטנה שלטן עלם (2:9) from Dan 7:14.[24] Collins tentatively put forward the view that the text represents a reinterpretation in messianic terms of the "one like a son of man" of Daniel 7, and if so, this text, which at least goes back to the first century BCE and is no doubt older, probably represents the oldest surviving messianic interpretation of Daniel 7.[25]

In contrast to the above, the *Prayer of Nabonidus* (4Q242)[26] does

---

[20] Translation from F. García Martínez and E. J. C. Tigchelaar, *The Dead Sea Scrolls Study Edition* (2 vols., Leiden: Brill, 1997, 1998) 1.493; cf. F. M. Cross, *The Ancient Library of Qumran* (3rd ed., The Biblical Seminar 30; Sheffield: Sheffield Academic Press, 1995) 188–91. The text is understood differently by Puech ("246. 4QApocryphe de Daniel ar," 168–71).

[21] Puech, "246. 4QApocryphe de Daniel ar," 180–81.

[22] For a survey of research and a defence of a historicising interpretation, see A. Steudel, "The Eternal Reign of the People of God—Collective Expectations in Qumran Texts (4Q246 and 1QM)," *RevQ* 17/65–68 (Milik Festschrift, 1996) 509–21.

[23] Knibb, "Eschatology and Messianism," 393–96.

[24] But see also Dan 4:3, 34 (MT 3:33; 4:31). For other evidence of dependence on the text of the biblical book, see Collins, "The *Son of God* Text from Qumran," in M. C. de Boer (ed.), *From Jesus to John: Essays on Jesus and New Testament Christology in Honour of Marinus de Jonge* (JSNTSup 84; Sheffield: Sheffield Academic Press, 1993) 65–82, esp. 69–70.

[25] Collins, "The *Son of God* Text from Qumran," 76–82, esp. 80–81.

[26] For the text, see Collins, "242. 4QPrayer of Nabonidus ar," in DJD 22.83–93 + pl. VI.

not presuppose the existence of the Book of Daniel. Rather it has been widely recognised that the *Prayer* represents an earlier form of the tradition contained in Daniel 4 whereby the story of the illness of Nabonidus has been transferred to the much better known figure of Nebuchadnezzar. The Jewish hero of the story, who is described in the Aramaic text as a גזר (frgs. 1–3.4, "diviner"),[27] is not named in the surviving fragments, and it may well be that he remained anonymous throughout the narrative.[28]

Whatever view is taken on the relationship of 4Q243–44, 4Q245, and 4Q246 to the biblical Book of Daniel, the Additions to the Greek Book of Daniel in their present form and context self-evidently presuppose its existence. However, the relationship of the three Additions to the biblical book varies from case to case. There are reasonable grounds for thinking that all three of the Additions, with the exception perhaps of the prose material in the Addition to chapter 3 (vv. 24-25, 46-50), are translations of Semitic, probably Hebrew, originals,[29] but somewhat surprisingly no trace of these has been found amongst the Scrolls.[30]

The Prayer of Azariah and the Song of the Three form a clear insertion in the story of the three friends in the fiery furnace; the insertion was made somewhat abruptly within the Old Greek, and in Theodotion the attempt was made to smooth over the awkwardness of the transition. The inserted material consists of three elements: the Prayer, a prose narrative describing how the friends were rescued

---

[27] For this title, cf. Dan. 2:27; 4:7 (MT 4:4); 5:7, 11.

[28] Cf. Collins, "242. 4QPrayer of Nabonidus ar," 86–87.

[29] Cf., for example, C. A. Moore, *Daniel, Esther, and Jeremiah: The Additions* (AB 44; Garden City, NY: Doubleday, 1977) 44–49, 81–84, 119–20; Collins, *Daniel*, 199, 202–205, 410–11, 427–28; I. Kottsieper, "Zusätze zu Daniel," in O. H. Steck, R. G. Kratz und I. Kottsieper (eds.), *Das Buch Baruch, Der Brief des Jeremia, Zusätze zu Ester und Daniel* (ATD Apokryphen Band 5; Göttingen: Vandenhoeck & Ruprecht, 1998) 222–23, 254–55, 292. Hebrew is commonly assumed as the original language except in the case of Bel and the Dragon. Moore suggests that the stories in Bel originally circulated in Aramaic, and Kottsieper has argued that the story of Bel and the story of the slaying of the Dragon circulated in Aramaic, but that it is uncertain whether the Habakkuk episode was composed in Aramaic or Hebrew.

[30] 4Q551 (4QDaniel-Susanna? ar) does not belong to an Aramaic version of Susanna; see K. Beyer, *Die aramäischen Texte vom Toten Meer* (Göttingen: Vandenhoeck & Ruprecht, 1984) 224–25.

from the heat of the furnace by the angel, and the Song. It is widely recognised that the first and the third of these, whose language of composition was almost certainly Hebrew, were taken over by the author(s) of the inserted material as pre-existent pieces, but that the prose narrative, which may have been composed in Greek, has a much closer relationship to the narrative of chapter 3 of the book. The Prayer of Azariah—or rather, of Azariah and his friends—conforms broadly to the type of the communal lament in the Psalms and can be dated, from the reference to being handed over into the power of lawless enemies and of "an unjust king, the most villainous on the whole earth" (v. 32), and from the reference to the absence of sacrifice and of a place to sacrifice (v. 38), to the reign of Antiochus Epiphanes, and specifically to the period 168-165.[31] The Song belongs to the type of the hymn and could date from any time in the Second Temple period; it has been adapted to its context by the reference to Hananiah, Azariah and Mishael in v. 88,[32] but neither it nor the Prayer originally had any connection with the Book of Daniel. In their present context they serve to shift attention away from Nebuchadnezzar onto the friends, and to emphasize the piety of the friends and the majesty and power of the God of Israel. The Prayer in particular presents the friends as models of piety,[33] and in the Old Greek their sacrifice of their lives appears to have atoning effect (v. 40). In contrast the prose narrative (vv. 24-25, 46-50 of the Greek), which serves as an introduction to the Song, appears to have been written in dependence on the narrative in chapter 3.[34] It repeats motifs from chapter 3: the overwhelming heat of the furnace, the destruction of those involved in

---

[31] Cf., for example, Collins, *Daniel*, 203; Kottsieper, "Zusätze zu Daniel," 222, 231–32.

[32] Cf., for example, Collins, *Daniel*, 207; Kottsieper,"Zusätze zu Daniel," 223, 240.

[33] Cf. Moore, *Daniel, Esther, and Jeremiah: The Additions*, 44. Kottsieper ("Zusätze zu Daniel," 223) suggests, in the light of the reference in 1 Macc. 2:59, that the friends were models for the Maccabean movement, and that the incorporation of the Prayer into Daniel 3 was intended to make a connection between the friends, who prayed and were delivered, and the Maccabees, and indirectly to legitimize the Maccabees; but it is not clear that there is sufficient evidence for such a view.

[34] So, for example, Collins, *Daniel*, 204. Kottsieper ("Zusätze zu Daniel," 222, 225–27) argues that the prose section is a fragment of an originally independent narrative, but this seems unlikely.

carrying out the king's orders—here described as "those of the Chaldeans that [the flame] found around the furnace." And in its description of the descent of the angel who extinguished the heat and saved the friends, it serves to resolve a difficulty found in the Aramaic text, the abrupt mention in v. 25 of the mysterious fourth figure in the furnace whose appearance was like that of a son of the gods.

The hero of the story of Susanna is represented as being at the start of his career: he is described as a "young man" (νεώτερος) in the Old Greek and as "a young boy" (παιδάριον, v. 45) in Theodotion. The story is remarkable in a number of respects, but my concern is with its relationship to the biblical book. In fact the story of Susanna shows very little connection with, or knowledge of, the biblical book, and the view that it was not in origin a Daniel story at all has a good deal to commend it.[35] Here two points seem to me of particular relevance. First, according to v. 1 of the Theodotionic version, the story of Susanna, like the stories in Daniel 2–6, is set in Babylon, and this setting has often been assumed also for the Old Greek. But in the Old Greek the evidence is unclear. Verses 1–5a are obelised in the Syro-Hexaplar as not part of the Old Greek, and papyrus 967, the prime representative of the Old Greek, begins (pg. 191) with a heading corresponding to v. 5b of Theodotion: "Concerning what (περὶ ὧν) the Lord said, that lawlessness came forth from Babylon, from elders, judges, who seemed to guide the people." The editor of papyrus 967 (A. Geissen) argued that περὶ ὧν must have had an antecendent, and that the Old Greek began at the missing bottom of the previous side (pg. 190) with the equivalent of v. 5a of Theodotion,[36] but it is also conceivable that some other statement, which identified the location of the story, stood before v. 5b. H. Engel has, however, made a very strong case for the view that the Old Greek did begin with v. 5b.[37] If this is correct, all that can be concluded with certainty from the

---

[35] Cf., for example, Moore, *Daniel, Esther, and Jeremiah: The Additions*, 80, 109; and L. M. Wills, *The Jew in the Court of the Foreign King: Ancient Jewish Court Legends* (Harvard Dissertations in Religion 26; Minneapolis: Fortress, 1990) 76–79.

[36] A. Geissen, *Der Septuaginta-Text des Buches Daniel 5–12 sowie Esther 1–2,15* (Papyrologische Texte und Abhandlungen 5; Bonn: Rudolf Habelt Verlag, 1968) 33–37, 280–81.

[37] H. Engel, *Die Susanna-Erzählung* (OBO 61; Freiburg: Universitätsverlag Freiburg; Göttingen: Vandenhoeck & Ruprecht, 1985) 12–15.

heading is that the judges came from Babylon, not that the story is set there, and a Palestinian setting cannot be excluded. The provenance of the story has in any case often been assumed to be Palestinian.

Secondly, the figure of Daniel in the story of Susanna has very little connection with the hero of the biblical book, and this is the element of truth that lies behind Kottsieper's claim that the original story had in mind, not the exile Daniel, but the wise Daniel of the Book of Ezekiel,[38] although it may be doubted whether even this view accurately reflects the character of the hero of Susanna.

One of the major concerns of the story of Susanna in its Old Greek version is the contrast between the corrupt elders and the shrewd young man,[39] and the story ends with the exhortation: "Let us also watch out for capable young sons, for (if) young men are pious, there will be in them a spirit of knowledge and understanding for ever and ever (v. 62b)." Daniel is mentioned by name only five times (vv. 45, 48, 51a, 52, 59) in the Old Greek version, and it must be doubted whether his name originally belonged in the story. Rather we should envisage that the hero of the story—like the hero of the *Prayer of Nabonidus*—was originally anonymous. The reference at the end of the Old Greek version to the endowment of young men with a "spirit of knowledge and understanding" (πνεῦμα ἐπιστήμης καὶ συνέσεως) links up with the statement that the angel gave the "young man called Daniel" a "spirit of understanding" (πνεῦμα συνέσεως, v. 45), and knowledge and understanding (מדע והשכל, Old Greek ἐπιστήμην καὶ σύνεσιν) are exactly the qualities attributed to Daniel and his companions in Dan 1:17. In the form in which the story of Susanna exists in both the Old Greek and Theodotion, it serves to explain how the young man Daniel came to prominence and was thus an appropriate figure to be trained at the court of Nebuchadnezzar. It is in accordance with this understanding of the story's purpose that in Theodotion it has been placed before the Book of Daniel, and that it

---

[38] Kottsieper, "Zusätze zu Daniel," 288–89. Kottsieper argues that a link is made with the exile Daniel in a later redactional layer he identifies in which, through his mantic-prophetic ability, Daniel knows in advance the true character of the elders (vv. 52b-53, 56b-57). But the complex redactional history of the narrative proposed by Kottsieper is unconvincing.

[39] For this contrast, cf. Engel, *Die Susanna-Erzählung*, 177–81, and note the repeated use of the terms πρεσβύτεροι (vv. 5b, 13, 29, 34, 36, 41, 51a, 52) and νεώτερος (vv. 44-45, 52, 55, 60-62, 62a, 62b).

ends with the statement: "And Daniel became great before the people
from that day on." But the inconsistency remains in Theodotion that
the story is already set in Babylon, whereas in chapter 1 of the biblical
book Daniel is one of the exiles taken to Babylon. In view of the lack
of connection with, and knowlege of, the biblical book, the story itself
may be assumed to be older than the formation of the Book of Daniel,
and it may well go back to the early Hellenistic or the Persian period.

The story of Bel and the Dragon consists of two main elements, the
story of the priests of Bel and the story of the killing of the dragon.
But integrated into the latter is a version of the tradition concerning
Daniel in the lions's den according to which Daniel was kept in the
den for six days and was miraculously fed by Habakkuk, who was
transported for this purpose to Babylon and back by an angel.[40] The
different elements in the narrative probably have separate origins, but,
as Nickelsburg and Collins have pointed out,[41] they have been
integrated together, and the narrative as a whole reads as a unity with
a common theme, the attack on idolatry.

The story obviously has some similarities with the stories
concerning Daniel and his companions in Daniel 2–6: the story is set
in Babylon at the court of the king; the attack on idolatry has a general
similarity with the themes of the stories in Daniel 2–6; the confession
of the king which concludes the story: "Great is the Lord God, and
there is none other except him" (v. 41, Old Greek), can be compared
with the confessions of Nebuchanezzar in 2:47; 3:28-29; 4:34-35, and
of Darius in 6:26-27; the hostility of the native population is
reminiscent of the hostility of the officials in the stories of Daniel 2–6;
and finally the motif of imprisonment in the lions's den occurs both in
Daniel 6 and in Bel and the Dragon.[42] However, there are also some
significant points of difference: Daniel himself courts the controversy
with the king instead of being put into a situation of controversy by

---

[40] A version of the tradition that Daniel was fed in Babylon by Habakkuk also
occurs in the *Life of Habakkuk* 4–8, but it is likely that the version in the *Life of
Habakkuk* and the version in Bel and the Dragon are independent of one another
and based on a common older tradition.

[41] G. W. E. Nickelsburg, *Jewish Literature Between the Bible and the
Mishnah* (Philadelphia: Fortress, 1981) 26–27; Collins, *Daniel*, 409.

[42] Wills (*The Jew in the Court of the Foreign King*, 134–38) has argued for
the dependency of Daniel 6 on Bel and the Dragon, but it seems more likely that
the two are separately dependent on an older tradition concerning Daniel and a
den of lions; cf. Collins, *Daniel*, 263–64.

his opponents;[43] the attack on idolatry is quite different in character from anything in Daniel 2–6; above all Daniel is presented at the beginning of the narrative in a quite different way from his presentation in the biblical book: "From the prophecy of Habakkuk the son of Joshua from the tribe of Levi. There was a certain man, a priest, named Daniel, the son of Abal, a companion of the king of Babylon" (so the Old Greek of vv. 1-2; in Theodotion the introduction has been adjusted to link the story with the biblical book).

This heading is somewhat surprising. Daniel is here introduced as if he were an unknown figure. He is furthermore described as a priest, and the story about him is said to be from the prophecy of Habakkuk. The reference to the prophecy of Habakkuk is clearly based on the inclusion of the tradition about Habakkuk and, as Collins notes, is hardly original.[44] But the description of Daniel as a priest is significant; it may suggest that the hero of Bel and the Dragon was identified with the Daniel mentioned in the lists of priests in Ezra 8:2 and Neh 10:7,[45] but may be conditioned by the character of the story—his rivals are priests. In the light of this heading, and of the character of the narrative, it is clear that Bel and the Dragon had an origin quite different from that of the stories in Daniel 2–6, even if the author(s) had some vague knowledge of the traditions concerning the exile Daniel. This point is reinforced by a consideration of the place of origin of the narrative.

The composition of Bel and the Dragon has been placed in the eastern diaspora, in Palestine, and even in Egypt.[46] Recently Kottsieper has argued that the story of the killing of the dragon is a testimony to controversy with the Babylonian religion, specifically the worship of Marduk, in the Babylonian diaspora, and dates the origins of this story to the end of the sixth or the beginning of the fifth century, although he suggests a slightly later origin and a Palestinian provenance for the remaining elements in the narrative. He argues that the tradition of the killing of the dragon goes back to an even older source, namely the tradition concerning Lu-Nanna, the fourth in the series of wise men after the flood, who, in the incantation series *bīt*

---

[43] Cf. Moore, *Daniel, Esther, and Jeremiah: The Additions*, 148.

[44] Collins, *Daniel*, 409.

[45] Cf. Wills, *The Jew in the Court of the Foreign King*, 129.

[46] Cf. Moore, *Daniel, Esther, and Jeremiah: The Additions*, 127–28; Collins, *Daniel*, 418–19.

mēseri, is said to have driven a dragon out of a temple of Ishtar.[47]
Kottsieper finds support for this suggestion in that in his view it offers
an explanation for certain otherwise inexplicable features of Susanna.
The Akkadian term used to refer to Lu-Nanna in *bīt mēseri* (and
elsewhere) is *apkallu*, but in Aramaic, in some dialects, *apkallu* occurs
with the meaning "priest." Furthermore, each of the ante- and
postdiluvian series of wise men was associated with a particular
ruler.[48] Kottsiper suggests that these two facts might explain how
Daniel could be described as a priest and companion of the king.
Kottsieper also claims that the motif that Daniel kills the dragon by a
trick rather than a weapon has no point in the context of Susanna, but
argues that the motif can be explained on the assumption of the use of
the tradition concerning Lu-Nanna in which the fact that the dragon
was expelled by a wise man, and not a warrior, would have been
significant.[49]

It may be argued, however, that these last points are too contrived to
provide a convincing explanation for the particular features in
Susanna that they are supposed to explain. It must also be doubted
whether the tradition concerning Lu-Nanna, which merely reports that
he expelled a dragon from the temple of Ishtar, provides a plausible
basis for the development of the story of Daniel's killing of the
dragon. In any case it is generally thought that the story of the
"dragon" really alludes to the worship of live snakes, for which there
is no evidence in Babylon, although there is evidence for sacred
snakes in the Greek world.[50] In view of this, and of the quite different
character of the Daniel traditions in Bel and the Dragon from those in
Daniel 2–6, it seems more plausible to locate the composition of Bel
and the Dragon in Palestine or, less probably, Egypt.[51] In view of its
character it is difficult to believe that Bel and the Dragon was
composed after the formation of the biblical book, but a date in the
third or early second century would seem plausible. In its present

---

[47] For the text, see E. Reiner, "The Etiological Myth of the 'Seven Sages',"
Orientalia n.s. 30 (1961) 1–11; R. Borger, "Die Beschwörungsserie BĪT MĒSERI
und die Himmelfahrt Henochs," *JNES* 33 (1974) 183–96, esp. 192–94.

[48] Cf. Reiner, "Etiological Myth of the 'Seven Sages'," 7.

[49] Cf. Kottsieper, "Zusätze zu Daniel," 251–52.

[50] Cf. Collins, *Daniel*, 414.

[51] The lack of any Egyptian background in the story makes an Egyptian
provenance much less likely than an origin in Palestine.

context attached to the Book of Daniel, the story serves as a further illustration of Daniel's shrewdness and ability at the Babylonian court, and it belongs with the court tales in Daniel 2–6; but its origins are different, and it belongs much more with the polemical attacks on idolatry that begin in Isaiah 40–55.

In summary, if we leave on one side the *Prayer of Nabonidus* and the Prayer of Azariah and the Song of the Three, which are both special cases, the Daniel literature outside the Book of Daniel falls into two groups. On the one hand the texts preserved in 4Q243–44, 4Q245, and 4Q246 all appear to represent a continuation of the tradition according to which Daniel was a mantic attached to the royal court, the mediator of divine revelations, just as he is in Daniel 2, 4, and 5, and all probably are dependent on the biblical book. On the other hand, although Susanna and Bel and the Dragon are in their present context linked with the court tales of Daniel 2–6, they have an origin quite different from these tales and present Daniel in a different way. The fact that these stories came to be attached to the Daniel corpus no doubt reflects the influence of the biblical book, while at the same time they serve to reinforce the depiction of the piety and shrewdness of Daniel—just as the Prayer of Azariah and the Song of the Three reinforce the depiction of the piety of the three friends. But the very different character of Susanna and of Bel and the Dragon, and the loose way in which these stories have been attached to the biblical book, underlines the way in which the narratives and vision reports in Daniel 1–12 have been skillfully woven together so that the biblical book can be read as an entity, despite the fact that it is the outcome of a long history of development.

3. THE BOOK OF DANIEL AND THE WIDER LITERARY CONTEXT

The Book of Daniel belongs not only in the context of related Daniel literature from more or less the same period but also in the wider context of works that have a similar genre, on the one hand that provided by similar stories of court officials, such as Esther or Ahiqar, on the other that provided by similar apocalyptic writings, such as the *Book of Enoch*. These writings are obviously important for the comparative material they provide for the interpretation of Daniel as a collection of court stories and apocalyptic visions. But in addition to these familiar texts, the material available for comparison with Daniel has been increased over the last few years by the publication of the sapiential texts from Qumran Cave 4,[52] particularly the closely related works *4QInstruction* (*Mûsār lĕ Mēbîn*)[53] and *4QMysteries*.[54] These texts are of interest in relation to Daniel not least because of the attention given within them to the concept of the "mysteries" (רזים) in the light of the occurrence of the term רז in Daniel,[55] and because of the relationship that exists within them between wisdom reflection and instruction and expectation concerning the end of the era; cf. 4Q416 (*4QInstruction*[b]) frg. 1. Here, by way of example, I would like briefly to discuss *4QMysteries*.

According to Schiffmann, the editor of *4QMysteries*, the term רזים is used in the text to refer both "to the mysteries of creation, i.e. the natural order of things which depend on God's wisdom, and to the mysteries of the divine role in the processes of history."[56] In one key text, which is represented by, and can be reconstructed from,

---

[52] For these texts, see D. J. Harrington, *Wisdom Texts from Qumran* (LDSS; London and New York: Routledge, 1996); J. I. Kampen, "The Diverse Aspects of Wisdom in the Qumran Texts," in P. W. Flint and J. C. VanderKam (eds.), *The Dead Sea Scrolls after Fifty Years: A Comprehensive Assessment* (2 vols., Leiden: Brill, 1998-99) 1.211–43, esp. 226–41; Collins, *Jewish Wisdom in the Hellenistic Age* (Edinburgh: T. & T. Clark, 1998) 112–31.

[53] The text survives in 1Q26 and 4Q415ff.; for the texts, see J. Strugnell, D. J. Harrington and T. Elgvin (eds.), *Qumran Cave 4. XXIV: Sapiential Texts, Part 2. 4QInstruction* (Mûsār lĕ Mēbîn): *4Q415ff.* (DJD 34; Oxford: Clarendon Press, 1999). For discussion of this text, see, for example, Harrington, *Wisdom Texts from Qumran*, 40–59; T. Elgvin, "The Mystery to Come: Early Essene Theology of Revelation," in F. H. Cryer and T. L. Thompson (eds.), *Qumran between the Old and New Testaments* (JSOTSup 290; Sheffield: Sheffield Academic Press, 1998) 113–50.

[54] The text survives in 1Q27, 4Q299 and 4Q300, but it is no longer clear, as was originally suggested, that 4Q301 is a further copy of the same work. For the texts, see J. T. Milik, "27. 'Livre des mystères'," in R. de Vaux et al. (eds.), *Qumran Cave 1* (DJD 1; Oxford: Clarendon Press, 1955) 102–107 + pl. XXI–XXII; L. Schiffman, "299–301. 4QMysteries[a–b, c?]," in J. A. Fitzmyer (consulting ed.), *Qumran Cave 4.XV: Sapiential Texts, Part 1* (DJD 20; Oxford: Clarendon Press, 1997) 31–123 + pls. III–IX.

[55] Elgvin ("The Mystery to Come," 115) notes a number of connections between *4QInstruction* and Daniel and suggests that the "circles behind *4QInstruction* might be related to the *maskilim* of the book of Daniel." He also observes that both books reflect "scribal activity and a quest for divine communication."

[56] Schiffman, "299–301. 4QMysteries[a–b, c?]," 31.

fragments in all three manuscripts of *4QMysteries* (1Q27 1, 4Q299 1, 4Q300 3), it is said that wisdom was given to men in order that they might recognise the difference between good and evil, but that despite this they failed to understand "the mystery of that which was coming into being" (רז נהיה)[57] because they failed to understand the significance of events from the past. The text then goes on to describe the sign that the end of the age is imminent:

03　But they did not know the mystery of that which was coming into being, and the former things they did not consider.

04　Nor did they know what should befall them. And they did not save their lives from the mystery that was coming into being.

05　And this shall be the sign to you that it is taking place ...[58]

Other fragments speak of the mysteries of creation which are beyond men's understanding (cf. 4Q299 3a ii-b.9-16, 4Q299 5, 4Q299 6 i-ii) and one passage, which invites comparison with Daniel, speaks of the failure of the magicians to understand the vision (4Q300 1a ii-b):

1　[ ] [the mag]icians who are skilled in transgression utter the parable and relate the riddle before it is discussed, and then you will know whether you have considered [

2　and the signs of the heav[ens]your foolishness, for the [s]eal of the vision is sealed from you, and you have not considered the eternal mysteries, and you have not come to understand wisdom.

3　The[n]you will say [ ] for you have not considered the root of wisdom, and if you open the vision

4　it will be kept secr[et from you[59]

The fragment begins with a challenge to the magicians (חרטמים, cf. Dan 1:20 and 2:2) to "utter the parable and relate the riddle before it is discussed," and this inevitably reminds us of one of the themes of the story of Daniel 2, the ability, or rather inability, of the wise men to tell the king his dream and provide an interpretation. The fragment also alludes to the language of Daniel 9. It states in line 2 "for the seal of the vision is sealed from you," which appears to be an allusion to Dan 9:24 "to seal up vision and prophecy." And it adds that those addres-

---

[57]　רז נהיה is a key concept in *4QInstruction* and *4QMysteries*. Milik ("27. 'Livre des mystères'," 103–104) translated the phrase as "le mystère futur," but it has increasingly been recognised that the phrase embraces God's mysterious deeds in the past and present as well as his plan for the future. The translation of ר נהיה given here follows that of Schiffman (cf. "299–301. 4QMysteries[a–b, c?]," 37), but see also the recent study by Elgvin ("The Mystery to Come," 131–39).

[58]　Translation from Schiffman, "299–301. 4QMysteries[a–b, c?]," 36.

[59]　*Ibidem*, 103.

sed "have not come to understand wisdom (ובבינה לא השכלתם)," and this contrasts with Dan 9:22 where the angel states: "Now I have come to give you understanding of wisdom (להשכילך בינה)."[60]

In contrast to the above passage, another fragment (4Q299 8) speaks of God giving understanding to a select group "who pursue knowledge":

5   ] And how can a ma[n] understand who did not know and did not
        hear [
6   the]discernment, the inclination of our heart. With great
        intelligence He opened our ear so that we would h[ear
7   ] the inclination of understanding for all who pursue knowledge[61]

Taken as a whole, the fragments of *4QMysteries* provide interesting connections with Daniel, where in chapter 2 the term רזא is used to refer to the interpretation of Nebuchadnezzar's dream, which is revealed to Daniel by God, and whose contents concern the course of world history, the four-kingdom schema.

In a preliminary publication of one of the manuscripts of this text, Schiffmann commented: "What we have here is a wedding of wisdom and prophecy, not only a new literary genre, but further testimony to the creativity of Second Temple Judaism."[62] *4QMysteries* is a very different kind of writing from the book of Daniel, but the connections that can be observed underline the point made earlier that the Book of Daniel belongs in a sapiential tradition.

In conclusion, the Book of Daniel belongs in the context of a range of writings of diverse kinds, a context that has now been enlarged by the sapiential literature from Qumran. The comparisons that can be drawn with these different kind of writings are helpful for the understanding and interpretation of the book, but comparison with these other writings serves also to remind us of the fact that the Book of Daniel is in the end *sui generis*.

4. SELECT BIBLIOGRAPHY

Collins, J. J. *Daniel: A Commentary on the Book of Daniel* (Hermeneia; Minneapolis: Fortress Press, 1993).

—. *Jewish Wisdom in the Hellenistic Age* (Edinburgh: T. & T. Clark, 1998).

---

[60] *Ibidem*, 102.

[61] *Ibidem*, 50.

[62] L. Schiffman, "4QMysteries[b], A Preliminary Edition," *RevQ* 16/62 (1993) 203–23, esp. 223.

Collins, J. J. and P. Flint. "4Qpseudo-Daniel[a-c] ar," in J. C. VanderKam (consulting ed.), *Qumran Cave 4.XVII: Parabiblical Texts, Part 3* (DJD 22; Oxford: Clarendon Press, 1996) 95–164 + pls. VII–X.

Elgvin, T. "The Mystery to Come: Early Essene Theology of Revelation," in F. H. Cryer and T. L. Thompson (eds.), *Qumran between the Old and New Testaments* (JSOTSup 290; Sheffield: Sheffield Academic Press, 1998) 113–50.

Engel, H. *Die Susanna-Erzählung* (Orbis Biblicus et Orientalis 61; Freiburg: Universitätsverlag Freiburg; Göttingen: Vandenhoeck & Ruprecht, 1985).

Fishbane, M. *Biblical Interpretation in Ancient Israel* (New York: Oxford University Press, 1985).

García Martínez, F., and E. J. C. Tigchelaar. *The Dead Sea Scrolls Study Edition* (2 vols., Leiden: Brill, 1997-98).

Harrington, D. J. *Wisdom Texts from Qumran* (The Literature of the Dead Sea Scrolls; London and New York: Routledge, 1996).

Kampen, J. I. "The Diverse Aspects of Wisdom in the Qumran Texts," in P. W. Flint and J. C. VanderKam (eds.), *The Dead Sea Scrolls after Fifty Years: A Comprehensive Assessment* (2 vols., Leiden: Brill, 1998-99) 1.211–43.

Knibb, M. A. "'You are indeed wiser than Daniel': Reflections on the Character of the Book of Daniel," in A. S. van der Woude (ed.), *The Book of Daniel in the Light of New Findings* (BETL 106; Leuven: Leuven University Press and Peeters, 1993) 399–411.

—. "Eschatology and Messianism in the Dead Sea Scrolls," in P. W. Flint and J. C. VanderKam (eds.), *The Dead Sea Scrolls after Fifty Years: A Comprehensive Assessment* (2 vols., Leiden: Brill, 1998-99) 2.379–402.

Kottsieper, I. "Zusätze zu Daniel," in O. H. Steck, R. G. Kratz und I. Kottsieper (eds.), *Das Buch Baruch, Der Brief des Jeremia, Zusätze zu Ester und Daniel* (ATD Apokryphen Band 5; Göttingen: Vandenhoeck & Ruprecht, 1998).

Milik, J. T. "27. 'Livre des mystères'," in R. de Vaux et al. (eds.), *Qumran Cave 1* (DJD 1; Oxford: Clarendon Press, 1955) 102–107 + pls. XXI–XXII.

Moore, C. A. *Daniel, Esther, and Jeremiah: The Additions* (AB 44; Garden City, NY: Doubleday, 1977).

Puech, É. "246. 4QApocryphe de Daniel ar," in J. C. VanderKam (consulting ed.), *Qumran Cave 4.XVII: Parabiblical Texts, Part 3* (DJD 22; Oxford: Clarendon Press, 1996) 165–184 + pl. XI.

Schiffman, L. "299–301. 4QMysteries[a-b, c?]," in J. A. Fitzmyer (consulting ed.), *Qumran Cave 4.XV: Sapiential Texts, Part 1* (DJD 20; Oxford: Clarendon Press, 1997) 31–123 + pls. III–IX.

Steudel, A. "The Eternal Reign of the People of God—Collective Expectations in Qumran Texts (4Q246 and 1QM)," *RevQ* 17/65–68 (Milik Festschrift, 1996) 507–25.

Strugnell, J., D. J. Harrington and T. Elgvin (eds.), *Qumran Cave 4. XXIV: Sapiential Texts, Part 2. 4QInstruction* (Mûsār lĕ Mēbîn): *4Q415ff.* (DJD 34; Oxford: Clarendon Press, 1999).

Wills, L. M. *The Jew in the Court of the Foreign King: Ancient Jewish Court Legends* (Harvard Dissertations in Religion 26; Minneapolis: Fortress, 1990).

PART TWO

DANIEL IN ITS NEAR EASTERN MILIEU

SCHOLARS AT THE ORIENTAL COURT: THE FIGURE OF DANIEL AGAINST ITS MESOPOTAMIAN BACKGROUND

KAREL VAN DER TOORN

1. INTRODUCTION

The protagonist of the Book of Daniel is a deported Jew who makes a career as a scholar and administrator at court, serving under various Babyonian and Persian kings. The land of Shinar (Dan 1:2), that is Babylonia, is the setting of his activities. Such data would seem to call for an investigation into the Mesopotamian background of the book and its main character. Despite this requirement, however, many of the standard introductions to the book deal with this background only summarily. According to a widely-shared opinion "Daniel is not a historical person but a figure of legend,"[1] and the book that bears his name is a product that reached its present form in the 2nd century BCE. The Babylonian background would thus belong to the realm of fiction. Various errors of fact seem to corroborate this view.[2]

Without contesting the legendary nature of Daniel and his adventures, however, it is doubtful whether one can dismiss the question of a Mesopotamian background all that easily. It is generally recognized that the story of Nebuchadnezzar's madness in Daniel 4 derives from a Mesopotamian tradition about Nabonidus, known from the *Persian Verse Account of Nabonidus*[3] and the Qumran

---

[1] J. J. Collins, "Daniel, Book of," *ABD* 2.30.

[2] Daniel would have served under Nebuchadnezzar (604-562), Belshazzar (542-539), and Darius the Mede. No mention is made of Nabonidus (556-539), presumaby because the author confuses him with Nebuchadnezzar (cf. R. H. Sack, "Nebuchadnezzar," *ABD* 4.1058–59). A king by the name of Darius the Mede does not figure in the historical records (for suggestions as to his identification, see K. Koch, "Darius the Mede," *ABD* 2.38–39).

[3] S. Smith, *Babylonian Historical Texts Relating to the Capture and Downfall of Babylon* (London: Methuen, 1924; repr. Hildesheim and New York: Georg Olms, 1975), 27–97; B. Landsberger and Th. Bauer, "Zu neuveröffentlichen Geschichtsquellen der Zeit von Asarhaddon bis Nabonid," *ZA* 37 (1927), 61–98, esp. 88ff.; W. von Soden, "Kyros und Nabonid: Propaganda und Gegenpropa-

Prayer of Nabonidus (4QPrNab). The genre of the apocalypse, so characteristic of Daniel 7–12, may likewise be traced back to Mesopotamia.[4] On the strength of these and other indications, various commentators assume that the tales of Daniel 1–6 were composed in the Eastern (i.e. Babylonian) diaspora.[5] Babylonian influence remains a distinct possibility, even if the book as a whole is a product of Jewish Hellenism.

In searching for a Mesopotamian background of the Book of Daniel, one must distinguish between a historical and a literary background. The political history of Babylonia and Persia sheds little light on the biblical narratives, merely showing that the legends are oblivious of historical verisimilitude. A more promising avenue of research focuses on the position of Daniel as a scholar at court. Cuneiform correspondence between scholars and the Neo-Assyrian kings discloses a world of competing court sages, offering a background to the Book of Daniel that adds to its understanding. Here I shall highlight some of the more striking facets of this oriental scholarship in an effort to put Daniel's role in a comparative perspective.

The principal contribution of this essay, however, lies in the realm of literary dependences. Taking my cue from the story of Daniel in the lions' den, I shall demonstrate the likelihood of the author having used a Mesopotamian prototype for his tale. Similar dependences, which were earlier identified for the legend about Nebuchadnezzar's madness, must be reckoned with for much of the other materials in Daniel 1–6.

2. SCHOLARS AT THE ORIENTAL COURT

The tales of Daniel 1–6 picture Daniel as a gifted scholar who made a brilliant career at the courts of the Neo-Babylonian and Persian kings, owing to his supernatural wisdom. Born from families

---

ganda," in H. Koch and D. N. MacKenzie (eds.), *Kunst, Kultur und Geschichte der Achämenidenzeit und ihr Fortleben* (Archäologische Mitteilungen aus Iran, Ergänzungsband 10; Berlin: Reimer, 1983), 61–68, repr. in *Aus Sprache, Geschichte und Religion Babyloniens*, eds. L. Cagni and H. P. Müller (Naples: Istituto universitario orientale, 1989) 285–92.

[4] See W. G. Lambert, *The Background of Jewish Apocalyptic* (London: Athlone Press, 1978); H. S. Kvanvig, *Roots of Apocalyptic: The Mesopotamian Background of the Enoch Figure and of the Son of Man* (WMANT 61; Neukirchen-Vluyn: Neukirchener Verlag, 1988).

[5] So, for example, Collins, "Daniel, Book of," 33.

of the Jewish aristocracy (פרתמים, from the Old-Iranian *fratama*, "first, pre-eminent," see *HALAT* 920, and cf. Est 1:3; 6:9), Daniel and his companions were selected as "youths without blemish, handsome, skilful in all wisdom (חכמה), endowed with knowledge (דעת), and understanding learning (מדע)." They received a three-year training in Babylonian "letters and language" (ספר ולשון), after which they were fit to serve in Nebuchadnezzar's palace (Dan 1:3-5). Daniel and his friends thus became members of the scholarly elite known as "the wise men of Babylon" (חכימי בבל, 2:12, 14, 18, 24, 48; 4:3[6]; 5:7). These "sages" might be subdivided into "magicians" (חרטמים\ן, from Egyptian *ḥry-tp*; Dan 1:20; 2:2, 10, 27; 4:4[7]; 6[9]; 5:11),[6] "exorcists" (אשפים\אשפין, from Akk. *āšipu*; Dan 1:20; 2:2, 10, 27; 4:4[7]; 5:7, 11, 15), "sorcerers" (מכשפים; Dan 2:2), "diviners" (גזרין 2:27; 4:4[7]; 5:7, 11), and "astrologers" (כשדים\כשדאין; 2:2, 4, 5, 10; 4:4[7]; 5:7, 11).

Daniel proved to be a man of such remarkable qualities, that he rose to the position of chief prefect (רב־סגנין) over all the wise men of Babylon (2:48), viz. "chief (רב) of the magicians, exorcists, astrologers, and diviners" (5:11). After the death of Nebuchadnezzar, however, his reputation fell victim to oblivion. A change of rule is often a turning-point in the career of the court scholar, as the story of Joseph shows (Exod 1:8). A new feat of divination was required for Daniel to recover his former post of glory. The writing on the wall in Belshazzar's palace provided him with the occasion. Whereas the exorcists, the astrologers, and the diviners at court (Dan 5:7) were unable to decipher the ominous writing, Daniel read and interpreted the mysterious signs. In reward he was clothed with purple, decked with a chain of gold about his neck, and made third ruler in the kingdom (Dan 5:29).

The description of Daniel's career under Kings Nebuchadnezzar and Belshazzar, though historically unreliable, conveys a fair idea of

---

[6] See J. Vergote, *Joseph en Egypte. Genèse 37–40 à la lumière des études égyptologiques récentes* (Louvain: Publications Universitaires, 1959) 67–73. The etymology of *ḥarṭummîm* is also discussed by H. Goedicke, "*Ḥarṭummîm*," *Or* 65 (1996) 24–30. Goedicke derives the Hebrew term from Egyp. *ḥry-tmꜥ*, "One (sitting) on a reed-mat," an idiomatic designation of the civil servant. Note that Assyrian texts also refer to *ḥarṭibī* in the service of the king; see, for example, J. M. Fales and J. N. Postgate, *Imperial Administrative Records, Part I: Palace and Temple Administration* (State Archives of Assyria [henceforth: SAA] 7; Helsinki: Helsinki Universiy Press, 1992) no. 1 r.ii 2.

the situation obtaining at the courts in Babylon and Asshur. Owing to the discovery of a wealth of letters from Assyrian and Babylonian scholars to the Assyrian kings Esarhaddon and Assurbanipal, we are especially well informed about the situation in Assyria. The Neo-Assyrian kings were constantly making inquiries from groups of religious experts in their service. These men referred to themselves as sages (*enqūtu*) and scholars (*ummânū*); their number consisted of astrologers (*ṭupšarrū Enūma Anu Enlil*), exorcists (*āšipū*), lamentation priests (*kalû*), physicians (*asû*), and diviners (*bārû*). The various groups of scholars were led by a *rab ṭupšarrīa* (chief of the astrologers), a *rab āšipī* (chief of the exorcists), a *rab bārê*, and the like.[7] Such a chief (רב) was clad in a purple garment (*argamannu*, written with the Sumerogram síg.za.gìn.sa₅).[8] Daniel, too, is described as a chief (*rab*) who was dressed in a purple garment in reward of his services. Though clearly exceptional, his career follows the model of a successful Mesopotamian scholar at the king's court.

The correspondence of the scholars that advised the Neo-Assyrian kings contains many allusions to, and descriptions of, the reversal of fortune of individual sages. Court scholars were very much dependent upon the favor of the king for their position, prestige, and livelihood. The king, in his turn, depended on them, but he could choose from a large supply of learned experts. The latter, however, had no other patron to turn to, or at least none so powerful as the king.

The competititon for jobs and the best positions did not foster a spirit of mutual goodwill and collegiality among the scholars. Their letters to the king strike an apologetic note when the writers are discussing their own advice, whereas the work of rival scholars is often the object of critique and ridicule.

> [He who] wrote to the king, my lord, "The planet Venus is visible, it is visible [in the month Ad]ar," is a vile man, an ignoramus, a cheat! (...) Who is this person [that] so deceit[fully] se[nds] such reports to the king, my lord? [Tom]orrow they should let me scrutinize th[em], every single one of them. (...) Why does someone tell lies and boast about it? [I]f he does

---

[7] See Simo Parpola, *Letters from Assyrian Scholars to the Kings Esarhaddon and Assurbanipal. Part II: Commentary and Appendices* (AOAT 5/2; Kevelaer: Butzon and Bercker; Neukirchen-Vluyn: Neukirchener Verlag, 1983) XIV–XXI.

[8] Simo Parpola, *Letters from Assyrian and Babylonian Scholars* (SAA 10; Helsinki: Helsinki University Press, 1993) no. 182:12 r.5.

not know, [he should] keep his mouth shut. The [ki]ng, my lord, should not hesitate but promote him [at once]![9]

In the climate of intrigue reigning at the Assyrian court, the king had to be circumspect in his choice of advisors. With some kings, such as Ashurbanipal, such circumspection turned into outright suspicion. In this respect the biblical description of Nebuchadnezzar, who mistrusts his experts to the point where he does not even want to tell them his dream (Dan 2:5), is true to type. Kings often proved receptive to allegations of fraud and incompetence, which led them to make frequent readjustments in their circle of advisors. To the persons concerned, this could mean a dramatic loss of influence and income.

In various respects, then, the tales about Daniel preserve the atmosphere of the oriental court as it can be reconstructed from the letters of Assyrian and Babylonian scholars. At the same time, however, one must be cautious not to overestimate the strength of the parallels as though the stories could only have been written by someone with intimate personal knowledge of the Neo-Babylonian court. The enumeration of the various branches of scholarship remains schematic. It is reminiscent of the designation of the servants of Pharoah as the חכמים מכשפים חרטמי מצרים (Exod 7:11, 22; 8:7, 18-19; 9:11). Some of the more important specialists at the Assyrian and Babylonian courts go unmentioned, such as the physicians and the lamentation priests. The *couleur locale* of the stories is convincing in its general outline, but falls short when it comes to detail.

One aspect of the Daniel stories that can hardly be called a detail is the proficiency of the protagonist in the interpretation of dreams. In this respect, the tales about Daniel seem to depart from the customs at the Assyrian and Babylonian courts. Although a Neo-Assyrian prayer to the sun-god speaks of the oneiromancer (*šāʾilu*) explaining a dream to the king,[10] there is no mention of oneiromancers among the court sages, nor does any of their letters deal with the interpretation of royal dreams. It is not beyond the realm of possibility that the interpretation of dreams belonged to the expertise of the

---

[9] Parpola, *Letters from Assyrian and Babylonian Scholars*, no. 72:6-10, 24 r.6, 13–9.

[10] R. C. Thompson, *Assyrian Medical Texts* (London: Humphrey Milford and Oxford: Oxford University Press, 1923), nos. 71/1+72/1:40, [*ina balika*] *šāʾilu* ([lú]en-me-li) *ana šarri qība ul išakkan.*

bārû[11] or the—at least originally Egyptian—*ḫarṭibu*,[12] but even if this were the case, difficult dreams play a minor to non-existent role in their correspondence. And in spite of the existence of an Assyrian *Dream-Book*, the modern editor of that text concludes that the Assyrian kings were averse to having dream interpreters at their courts.[13]

Things may have been slightly different at the Babylonian court, but the only evidence that might be adduced to this effect is the very Book of Daniel.[14] It seems more prudent to assume that the biblical author drew upon his imperfect knowledge of the Babyonian court to throw his protagonist into sharper relief: first and foremost as a supernaturally gifted dream interpreter. In doing so he was led by the conviction that dreams were a legitimate mode of revelation—whereas extispicy and astrology were not.

3. DANIEL IN THE LION'S DEN

Whereas the Mesopotamian background of Daniel as a scholar at the Babylonian court remains rather sketchy, a more convincing case can be made for the thesis that the author of the Book of Daniel used literary motifs from Babylonia in order to put his hero in a favorable light. A good instance is furnished by the story of Daniel in the lions' den.

The tale of Daniel in the lions' den (Daniel 6) is both powerful and puzzling. The narrator implies that confinement into a pit of lions (for the Aramaic term refers to a pit rather than a den) was a generally practiced punitive measure among the Medes and Persians. As most commentaries observe, there is no extrabiblical evidence

---

[11] Note W. G. Lambert, *Babylonian Wisdom Literature* (Oxford: Clarendon Press, 1960) 128:53–54 [*ina*] *mākalti bārûti ana rikis* [gis]*erīni*, [*atta*] *mušimmi šāʾilī pāšerū šunāti*: "[In] the seer's bowl with the cedar-wood appurtenance, [You] enlighten the oneiromancers that interpret dreams." On the use of cedar-wood and a bowl by the *bārû*, see also W. G. Lambert, "Enmeduranki and Related Matters," *JCS* 21 (1967), 126–38, esp. 132.

[12] Basing himself on A. Gardiner, *Ancient Egyptian Onomastica* (London: Oxford University Press, 1947) 1:56, A. L. Oppenheim interprets the *ḫarṭibu* as as primarily a dream interpreter; see idem, *The Interpretation of Dreams in the Ancient Near East* (Philadelphia: The American Philosophical Society, 1956), 238. On the etymology of *ḫarṭibu* see also note 6 above.

[13] Oppenheim, *The Interpretation of Dreams*, 238.

[14] *Ibidem*, 239.

whatsoever that would verify this implication.[15] Does this mean that the author invented Daniel's trial from scratch?

Cuneiform sources show that the lions' den is not just a fantasy on the part of the author of the biblical tale. The story of Daniel's fall from grace, the period of his tribulations, and his eventual return to court conforms to the traditional narrative pattern of what might be called the *Tale of the Vindicated Courtier*. Such tales tell the story of an esteemed royal counselor who suffers disgrace and misery at the hands of envious colleagues, but who is eventually restored to his former glory owing to the intervention of a friendly god. The pattern belongs to the literature of the sages; its protagonist is a sage who enjoys the confidence of the king. The stories of Joseph and Ahiqar can be adduced as examples.

The biblical variant of the *Tale of the Vindicated Courtier* extant in the story of Daniel follows a Babylonian narrative tradition. The vicissitudes of Daniel are patterned after those of the protagonist of a classic of Babylonian wisdom literature, viz. *Ludlul bēl nēmeqi*, "I shall praise the Lord of Wisdom."[16] Close study of *Ludlul bēl nēmeqi* reveals that the motif of the pit of lions goes back to Babylonia as well. In the Babylonian tradition, however, the lions are not real lions; they stand for human adversaries. The single time that a "pit of lions" is mentioned in a cuneiform scholarly text, it serves as a metaphor for the hostility and competition among the court sages. The biblical author inherited the motif of the lions' pit from the Babylonian tradition, but when incorporating this into the Daniel narrative he interpreted the metaphor as though it were a literal description.

The protagonist of *Ludlul* is called *Šubši-mešrê-Šakkan* (III 43). A person with almost the same name (*Šubši-mašrê-Šakkan*) is known to

---

[15] See for example, L. F. Hartman and A. A. DiLella, *Daniel* (AB 23; Garden City, NY: Doubleday, 1978) 199.

[16] Edition: Lambert, *Babylonian Wisdom Literature*, 21–62, 343–45. For additions see D. J. Wiseman, "A New Text of the Babylonian Poem of the Righteous Sufferer," *Anatolian Studies* 30 (1980), 101–107; A. R. George and F. N. H. al-Rawi, "Tablets from the Sippar Library, VII: Three Wisdom Texts," *Iraq* 60 (1998), 187–206, esp. 187–201. For recent translations, including references to relevant literature, see W. von Soden, "Der leidende Gerechte," *TUAT* III/1 (1990) 110–35; B. R. Foster, *Before the Muses: An Anthology of Akkadian Literature* (Bethesda, MD: CDL Press, 1993) 1.308–25. Excerpts of the text will be given with reference to the tablet and lines of the composition.

have been a deputy (*šakin māti*) of the Kassite king Nazimaruttaš (ca. 1307-1282 BCE).[17] It is possible that this man served as a model for the central personage of *Ludlul*. Names such as Laluralimma and Ur-Nintinugga—belonging to persons with supporting parts in *Ludlul*—would equally fit in the Kassite period.[18] The composition could be tentatively dated to the 12th century BCE. The author of *Ludlul* did not invent the genre of the biographical description of the unlucky court scholar. An Akkadian text from Ugarit contains the fragments of a narrative that is very similar, both in its story-line and in its formulations.[19] Since it is older than *Ludlul*, the latter composition must be regarded as a variation on a traditional theme in Babylonian literature: the fall of the successful sage, eschewed by his colleagues and friends, and his eventual delivery by his god. The quality of *Ludlul* is such, however, that it came to stand as the canonical model of its genre. When interpreting their life in light of the career of the righteous sufferer, people referred primarily to *Ludlul*.

The plot of *Ludlul* is simple and straightforward: *Šubši-mešrê-Šakkan*, trusted servant of the king, loses his position at court, falls ill, and sees no way out of his misery, until Marduk reveals to him in a series of dreams that he will be healed and attain greater glory than before. The narrative has the form of a monologue in which the sufferer rehearses his vicissitudes and the god's intervention; it is designed "to praise the Lord of Wisdom," viz. Marduk. The exposition of the protagonist's downfall opens with a description of the conditions that paved the way for evil powers to exert their influence on his life:

> My god rejected me, and went far away.
> My goddess left me, and kept at a distance.
> My good genius, always at my side, was filled [with rage],
> My guardian angel panicked, and looked for someone else.[20]

From a theological perspective, the source of the misfortunes that would befall the sufferer was the departure of his personal gods.

---

17   See O. R. Gurney, "Note brève," *RA* 80 (1986) 190.

18   See W. van Soden ,"Der leidende Gerechte," *TUAT* III/1, 111.

19   J. Nougayrol, "(Juste) souffrant (R. S. 25.460)," *Ug* 5 (1968) 265–73, 435; W. von Soden, "Bemerkungen zu einigen literarischen Texten in akkadischer Sprache aus Ugarit," *UF* 1 (1969) 189–95, esp. 191–93; idem, "Klage eines Dulders mit Gebet an Marduk," *TUAT* III/1 (1990) 140–43.

20   *Ludlul* I 43–46.

From a more mundane vantage-point, however, everything started to go wrong as he lost the goodwill of the king. The reason for the king's disfavor is not stated, but it seems to have been caused—and was certainly exacerbated—by slander and enmities by other men at court.

> The king, the very flesh of the gods and the sun of his subjects,
> developed a grudge against me, impossible to dissolve.
> The courtiers were exchanging depreciating comments about me,
> they gathered into a clique to spread treachery.
> If one said: "I will make him end his life,"
> a second says: "I will make him vacate his post."
> Just so the third: "I shall grab his office,"
> The fourth declared: "I shall take over his estate."
> The fifth turns against (me) the opinion of fifty,
> as the sixth and the seventh follow hard on his heels.
> The gang of seven have joined their forces against me,
> merciless as demons, the image of devils.
> One is their flesh, united in purpose,
> their hearts rage against me, they are ablaze like fire.
> They combine against me in slander and lies.[21]

The dismissal from court triggers a series of disasters: the unfortunate dignitary loses all social esteem. Friends and family fail him; they treat him as an alien. People have diverted the irrigation canal from his field, so that the soil has become parched and unproductive.[22] Even though the sufferer has been a paragon of virtue and loyalty, his fall is inexorable.

In the midst of his sorrow the sufferer recalls the days when he was still a respected counselor in the service of the king:

> The homage to the king, that was my joy,
> and his festive meal was my happiness.
> I instructed my countrymen to observe the god's rites,
> and made my people venerate the name of the goddess.
> I made my praises of the king as though he were a god,
> and taught the populace respect for the palace (*puluḫti ekalli*).[23]

It is clear from these lines that the protagonist was at home in the

---

[21] *Ludlul* I 55–69, on the basis of George and al-Rawi, "Tablets from the Sippar Library," 7.196.

[22] See W. G. Lambert, review of W. von Soden, *Akkadisches Handwörterbuch*, Lieferungen 7 and 8, *JSS* 14 (1969) 247–51, esp. 250 (*Ludlul* I 100, where *umaddidu* is to be read).

[23] *Ludlul* II 27–32.

royal administration. The description of his physical decay (he is stricken with a headache, debility, fever, convulsions, bowel disorders, coughing and hacking, eventually turns blind and deaf, and is on the verge of dying) should not make us overlook the fact that this chain of untoward events was set in motion by the sudden end of his career at court.

After three premonitory dreams, the sufferer regains his health through the intervention of Marduk. The god takes away the various illnesses from which his servant has been suffering. The physical recovery, described in detail in tablet III, is the prelude to the restoration of respect and social prestige. By means of the river ordeal, it seems, the man is cleared of all blame; the suspicions of the king prove to have been unfounded.[24] Restored to the king's favor, the protagonist proceeds to the temple of Marduk to bring an offering of thanksgiving. The words with which he summarizes the god's intervention on his behalf deserve particular attention.

> [ša] imḫaṣanni [^{d}Mard]uk ušaqi rīši
> imḫaṣ ritti māḫiṣiya ušaddi kakkašu ^{d}Marduk
> ina pī girra ākiliya iddi napsama ^{d}Marduk
> ^{d}Marduk ša mukaššidiya īkim aspašu assukkašu usaḫḫir

> [He who] smote me, [Mard]uk he restored me.
> He smote the hand of my smiter, Marduk made him drop his weapon.
> Marduk put a muzzle on the mouth of the lion that was devouring me.
> Marduk despoiled my pursuer of his sling, and deflected his slingstone.[25]

These poetic images refer to an enemy, presented as though he were single, that is human in nature. Considering the context of the poem of *Ludlul* as a whole, the reference is to the hostile courtiers whose allegations eroded the confidence of the king. They are his smiters and pursuers; they are the lions that were devouring him.

The poem of *Ludlul* uses the image of the lion to convey the ferocity with which colleagues at court attack the baffled counselor. The vindication of the protagonist, his triumph over his detractors

---

[24] Lambert, *Babylonian Wisdom Literature*, 54, k-l: *ina itê nāri* (commentary: ḫuršān) ašar dēn nišī ibbirru muttutu ammašid abbuttum appašir, "At the bank of the river (commentary: river ordeal), where the law cases of the people are examined, I was struck on the forehead (?), my slavemark was removed."

[25] For the reconstruction of the text, see the suggestion by W. von Soden, "Das Fragen nach der Gerechtigkeit Gottes im Alten Orient," *MDOG* 96 (1965) 41–59, esp. 51 n.5, elaborated in *TUAT* III/1, 111, 133–4. See also E. Reiner, *Poetry from Babylonia and Assyria* (Ann Arbor: University of Michigan, 1985) 118 n.13.

and calumniators, is pictured as a delivery by Marduk from the mouth of the lion. The importance of the metaphor is borne out by the fact that a mid-first millennium text from Babylon containing selected lines from literary texts quotes precisely this line from *Ludlul*: "Marduk put a muzzle on the mouth of the lion."[26] The line is also quoted and explained in a commentary text from the Ashurbanipal library in Nineveh.[27] It must be assumed that many who had received their scribal training in first millennium Mesopotamia would recognize the line and know that it came from *Ludlul*. The "Poem of the Righteous Sufferer" (as the text is often referred to in the Assyriological literature) was apparently part of the scribal curriculum, and thus belonged to the literary culture of the intellectual elite.

The author of Daniel 6 was not the first to make use of the plot of *Ludlul*. Faced with the hostility of colleagues and dismissal from the king's presence, Assyrian and Babylonian scholars turned to *Ludlul* as well in order to understand their own experience. A case in point is provided by one Urad-Gula. Being the son of the royal exorcist Adad-šumu-uṣur, Urad-Gula was promised to a brilliant career at the Assyrian court. He started as a deputy of the chief of physicians (*rab asî*) under Sennacherib (704-681), and continued as a court exorcist under Esarhaddon (680-669), but was dismissed from court after the accession of Ashurbanipal (668).[28] His father, who continued to serve the crown, pleaded the case of his son in various letters.

> Nobody has reminded the king about Urad-Gula, the servant of the king, my lord. He is dying of a broken heart, and is shattered from falling out of the hands of the king, my lord. The king, my lord, has revived many people.[29]

Urad-Gula's misery made a gloomy contrast with the happy

---

[26] J. van Dijk, *Literarische Texte aus Babylon* (Vorderasiatische Schriftdenkmäler 24; Berlin: Akademie-Verlag, 1987) no. 124:6-8 *ina pi-i gir-ri i-di nap-sa-am* ^dAMAR.UTU. Note especially the dingiršadibba quotation in ll. 4–5 (*minû annū²ama ki²am epšēku*) and the *Enūma eliš* quotation in ll. 8–11 (*bēlum ša takluka napištašu gimilma*).

[27] K 3291 r. line q: *gir-ra:* ur.maḫ *nap-sa-mu: ma-ak-ṣa-ru ša pî sīsî*, "*girra*: lion, *napsamu*: muzzle of the mouth of a horse"; see Lambert, *Babylonian Wisdom Literature*, 56.

[28] S. Parpola, "The Forlorn Scholar," in F. Rochberg-Halton (ed.), *Language, Literature and History: Philological and Historical Studies Presented to Erica Reiner* (AOS 67; New Haven, CT: American Oriental Society, 1987) 257–78, esp. 269.

[29] Parpola, *Letters from Assyrian and Babylonian Scholars*, no. 224:16-r.8.

conditions that marked—or were supposed to mark—the first year
of Ashurbanipal's reign. It was the custom for the new king to
release political prisoners and to provide special charity for the
needy among his subjects in a public display of gentleness and goodwill. This was also the time, however, at which positions in the royal
administration were redistributed; many of the old elite rested in
place, but some were vacated from their post. Urad-Gula was a
victim of this change of ruler; the position of Adad-šumu-uṣur, was
apparently affected by the downfall of his son as well.

> The king, my lord, has revived the one who was guilty and condemned to
> death; you have released the one who was imprisoned for many [ye]ars.
> Those who were sick for many days have got well, the hungry have been
> sated, the parched have been anointed with oil, the needy have been covered
> with garments. Why then must I and Urad-Gula, amidst them, be restless
> and depressed? The king, my lord, has now displayed his love for Nineveh
> to all the people, in saying to the family heads: "Bring your sons to stay in
> my entourage!" Urad-Gula is my son; he too should stay with them in the
> entourage of the king, my lord. We too should, together with all the people,
> be merry, dance, and bless the king, my lord!
>
> My eyes are fixed on the king, my lord. None of those who serve in the
> palace likes me; there is not a single friend of mine among them to whom I
> could give a present, and who would accept it from me and speak in my
> favor. May the king, my lord, have mercy on his servant; May I not di[e]
> amidst all the people! May those who wish me ill not attain their heart's
> desire with regard to me![30]

It is clear from the last lines that a scholar who had fallen into the
king's disfavor could rarely count on solidarity from his colleagues.
The rivalry was such that the unemployed scholar would inevitably
stand alone.

Two letters from Urad-Gula himself reveal his feelings as he was
still suffering from his unexpected fall from grace.[31] These letters
have an unmistakable literary quality; they strikingly illustrate how
Urad-Gula perceived his predicament. The following quotations are
from most elaborate letter, edited and discussed by Simo Parpola
in the *Festschrift* for Erica Reiner.[32]

> Initially, in the days of the king's father, I was a poor man, son of a poor
> man, a dead dog, a vile and limited person. He lifted me from the dung

---

[30] *Ibidem*, no. 226:21-r.23.

[31] *Ibidem*, nos. 289 and 294.

[32] *Ibidem*, no. 294; see also Parpola, "The Forlorn Scholar," 258–65.

heap; I got to receive gifts from him, and my name was mentioned among men of good fortune.

Such phrases of self-humiliation are not unusual in letters addressed to kings: they are meant to show the addressee that the writer is fully aware of the fact that he owns his fortune to the generosity of his benefactor. In reality, neither Urad-Gula nor his father were particularly "poor" under the reign of Esarhaddon. The rise from rags to riches was simply a traditional topos in the career of the successful scholar.

Urad-Gula continues with a reminder of his faithful service for Ashurbanipal when the latter was yet a crown-prince. At that time he was still regarded as a trusted servant. After Ashurbanipal's accession, however, Urad-Gula has not been treated in accordance with his deeds. Although he guarded the secrets of the king, he has had to suffer like never before. In spite of this he has continued to teach the king's servants, non-eunuchs and eunuchs alike, "submission, toil, and fear of the palace" (kanāšu kadāru u puluḫtu ša ekalli, line 29, note the parallel with Ludlul II 32). but his efforts were apparently not appreciated, for the king removed him from his presence. His former pleas for help went unheeded. Whereas Urad-Gula feels he deserved to receive a necklace (kišādu) from the hands of the king (rev. 10-11)—a detail which reminds one of Daniel who was given a golden chain about his neck (Dan 5:29)—he has only met with indifference. First-ranking scholars should be riding a donkey, but Urad-Gula has to go on foot: "People pass my house, the mighty on palanquins, the assistants in carts, even the juniors on mules, and I have to walk!"[33] Urad-Gula's services are no longer required; the king has summoned other exorcists in his stead. The spurned scholar has been reduced to such poverty that he cannot even afford a pair of sandals. What will become of him in his old age? The prophet (raggimu) whom Urad-Gula consulted did not predict happy prospects.

In the midst of Urad-Gula's detailed complaints there is one reference of special relevance to the story of Daniel in the lions' den. Though the passage occurs in a broken context, enough has been preserved to allow the following reconstruction.

39 [x x x x x ū]mu u mūšu ina pān gabʾi ša nēši šarra ūṣal[la]
40 [x x x x x x x x x x x]x-ni ina libbi ukalāti lā sammûn[i (x)]
41 [x x x x x x x x]x libbī bīrti miḫrīya [x]x [x x x]

---

33 Parpola, Letters from Assyrian and Babylonian Scholars, no. 294 r.18–19.

39   [... D]ay and night I pray to the king in front of the lions' pit
40   [... that] .. are not finicky[34] about the morsels [...]
41   [....] my heart amidst my colleagues [....]

In discussing this passage, Parpola did not fail to note the parallel with the Daniel story.[35] But what exactly does it mean to be "in front of the lions' pit?" Earlier on, Urad-Gula writes that he once used to be regarded "as one who eats lion's morsels" (*ākil ukalāti ša nēši attadgil*, line 22). This, apparently, was something to be happy about, whereas he now deplores his position "in front of the lions' pit."

The references to the food of lions and to the lions' pit can be elucidated once we abandon a literal reading of these passages. Urad-Gula can hardly be expected to have received the same food as the lions. In fact, he has just stated that he used to receive "leftovers" (*rēḫāti*) with the king's exorcists (line 19). These leftovers were the remains of the offerings given to the gods; it was quality food since only the best was good enough for the gods. By comparison with the ordinary population, court scholars ate quite well. Since his dismissal from court, however, Urad-Gula finds himself "in front of" the lions' pit. This lions' pit, I suggest, is the circle of his former colleagues from which he has been ousted. He no longer enjoys his food in their midst; for him they have turned into lions indeed, now eager to devour him.

The literary quality of Urad-Gula's letter of complaint shows that its author was a man of letters. Familiar with the classics of the Mesopotamian literary tradition, he interpreted his personal experiences in the light of the texts he knew. In the Urad-Gula letter, the image of the lion has developed into a pit of lions. Such a pit was a traditional device in Mesopotamia for capturing lions. Compare the following account in an Old Babylonian letter from Mari:

> A lion was devouring the sheep of Ḫabdu-Ammi in the pen, so he opened a pit (*šaḫātu*, cf. Heb. שחת) in his pen, in Bīt-Akkaka, and the lion, as it was making its attack on the pen, fell into the pit. The lion tried to get out, but the shepherds gathered wood, filled the pit, and set fire to the pit.[36]

There is also other—and later—evidence for the use of the pit

---

[34] Translation based on the analysis of the verbal form as belonging to *samû* II, with the basic meaning "to be undecided, to waver," see *AHW* 1020.

[35] Parpola, "The Forlorn Scholar," 274.

[36] George Dossin, "Documents de Mari," *Syria* 48 (1971) 1–19, A. 717 (pp. 16-19) = ARM 14 no. 2:5-17. The translation follows *CAD* Ṣ 54 s.v. *saḫātu* A.

(normally ḫaštu or būru, cf. Heb. בּוֹר and the Akk. fem. būrtu) as a trap for catching beasts of prey.[37] It is known that the Assyrian kings kept wild animals. For this purpose they created zoological gardens; pits were not used to house lions.[38] Lions that ended up in a pit were bound to die there from starvation if they were not killed by human hand. The image of a group of lions in a pit, therefore, evokes the idea of famished animals fighting one another for the slightest morsel of food. Such was, in the experience of Urad-Gula, the situation among the sages and scholars at the Assyrian court.

Although *Ludlul* has often been compared to the biblical Book of Job, its plot runs closer to the story of Daniel. The protagonist is an advisor to the king; his misfortune is the result of the jealousy of his colleagues; his misery begins with the loss of his position at court. The prominence to which Daniel had risen triggered the envy of his colleagues. Qualified as satraps in Daniel 6 (אֲחַשְׁדַּרְפְּנַיָּא), they connived with the counselors and the governors to oust Daniel from his position. Profiting from a change of rule, they then set a trap for Daniel which the new king failed to see through. Thus the latter was eventually forced to have Daniel thrown into the pit of lions (גֻּבָּא דִי אַרְיָוָתָא, Dan 6:17 [16]) because the man persisted in his daily devotions to his God. To prevent Daniel from escaping, the mouth of this pit was covered with a stone sealed with the signet of the king and the signet of his lords. Daniel thus seemed to be doomed.

After a fitful night, the king hurried to the pit hoping for a miracle. And a miracle it was indeed, for God had sent an angel to shut the lions' mouths (סְגַר פֻּם אַרְיָוָתָא). Thrilled with joy, the king ordered Daniel's release and commanded that the men who had accused Daniel be thrown into the pit of the lions in his stead. They were cast into the pit together with their families; "and before they reached the bottom of the pit the lions overpowered them and broke all their bones in pieces" (Dan 6:25 [24]). Having thus been avenged, Daniel

---

[37] See the dictionaries s.v. *būru, būrtu,* and *ḫaštu.* See also W. Heimpel, "Jagd. A.Philologisch," *Reallexikon der Assyriologie und vorderasiatische Archäologie* 5 (Berlin: de Gruyter, 1976-80) 234–36, esp. 235; Note Lambert, *Babylonian Wisdom Literature,* 74:62, *gillat nēšu īpušu petâssu ḫaštu,* "For the crime which the lion committed the open pit awaits him."

[38] See L. Trümpelmann, "Jagd. B.Archäologisch," *Reallexikon der Assyriologie,* 5.236–38, esp. 237 §5. There is no connection between a zoological garden and a pit for lions, *pace* K. Marti, *Das Buch Daniel* (Kurzer Hand-Commentar AT 18; Tübingen: Mohr-Siebeck, 1901) 44.

returned to his erstwhile position as principal counselor of the king.

The author of the story of Daniel's career at the Babylonian and Persian courts exhibits a knowledge, however imperfect, of the milieu in which his protagonist moves.[39] It may be assumed that he was familiar as well with the tale of the slandered and vindicated courtier, as found in *Ludlul* and *Ahiqar*. Its plot offered him the outline for his description of Daniel's career at court: risen to prominence owing to his extraordinary wisdom, the Jewish court sage was condemned to the lions' den through the plotting of his colleagues. The part of the lions' den goes back, ultimately, to the Babylonian model as well. Our biblical author, however, took a metaphor for a literal description. The Mesopotamian authors had intimated that the competition among the king's scholars was such that life at court compared to a pit of lions. The author of the biblical story had somehow caught on to the expression, but took it to be a description of the punishment of the sage. In his eagerness to portray the protagonist in a heroic situation, his imagination had little difficulty in picturing Daniel in the pit. This is a classical case of the misrecognition of a metaphor, the type of misunderstanding that is not uncommon in accounts of foreign cultures.

In defense of our author, it may be said that there are elements in the biblical tradition which lend a certain plausibility to his interpretation of the lions' den. Lions were a relatively frequent phenomenon in Palestine; they threatened the safety of small cattle, so that shepherds had to take measures to protect their flock (Jer 50:17; Amos 3:12).

As in Babylonia, lions could be trapped in a pit (שחת, Ezek 19:4, 8; cf. Jer 48:43-44) or a cistern (באר, var. בור, 2 Sam 23:20 = 1 Chr 11:22). Such subterranean cavities were also used as places of detention for humans; Jeremiah, for instance, was confined to a cistern (בור, Jer 38:6).[40] King David, who had been a shepherd in his youth, claimed that Yahweh had deliverd him "from the paw of the lion and the paw of the bear" (1 Sam 17:37). The author of the Daniel story, then, bred on the Bible, knew that victims of jealousy and royal disfavor might expect to be cast into a pit; that many a lion had ended up in a pit as well; and that God had delivered his servants from the attacks of lions before. When we mix these ingredients and

---

[39] Cf. Parpola, *Letters from Assyrian and Babylonian Scholars*, XIV–XV.

[40] Cf. K. van der Toorn, "Prison," *ABD* (1992) 5.468–69.

add some imagination, we may very well get a story not unlike that of Daniel in the lions' den.

The author of Daniel 6 is not alone in having taken a metaphor literally. In 1988 A. Hilhorst published a somewhat neglected article on "biblical metaphors taken literally," in which he discusses seven metaphors in the Bible that have been erroneously read as literal descriptions.[41] A prime example is Num 24:17 (LXX) as interpreted by Matt 2:2, where the "star from Jacob" has become a real star. Other examples of a literalist reading of figurative language may be found elsewhere in the Book of Daniel. Thus the delivery of the three men from the fiery furnace (אתון נורא) in Daniel 3 might be understood as an edifying tale drawing its inspiration from the image of the exodus as a deliverance from "the iron blast furnace" (כור הברזל, Deut 4:20, cf. 1 Kgs 8:51; Jer 11:4). Although it cannot be excluded that the author believed he was referring to a real type of punishment, "this punishing by burning remains unusual," as one commentator rightly notes.[42] Thus a metaphor taken literally presents itself also as an attractive solution to the tale of the fiery furnace as well.

4. CONCLUSION

The example of Daniel in the lions' den demonstrates that we have to reckon, more than has been customary in the past, with elements in the narratives of Daniel that can be traced back to a Mesopotamian background. Existing traditions and expressions have been used by the author(s) of the book to cast Daniel in the role of a visionary hero of faith. It should come as no surprise that in the melting pot of the Hellenistic Age, Jews from the Eastern diaspora made use of Mesopotamia's cultural heritage to offer Jews in the diaspora new models of Jewish identity. One of the procedures used to this effect was the literary elaboration of metaphors into tales of the miraculous.

---

[41] A. Hilhorst, "Biblical Metaphors Taken Literally," in T. Baarda et al. (eds.), *Text and Testimony. Essays on New Testament and Apocryphal Literature in Honour of A. F. J. Klein* (Kampen: Kok, 1988) 123–31. I owe this reference to Dr. E. Smelik (Kampen).

[42] O. Plöger, *Das Buch Daniel* (KAT 18; Gütersloh: Mohn, 1965) 63 ("Diese Strafe durch Verbrennen bleibt ungewöhnlich ..."). For the most plausible parallel of burning as a method of execution in antiquity, see 2 Macc 13:4-8 and cf. Ktesias, *Persae*, 48, 51, 58.

5. SELECT BIBLIOGRAPHY

Hilhorst, A. "Biblical Metaphors Taken Literally," in T. Baarda et al. (eds.), *Text and Testimony. Essays on New Testament and Apocryphal Literature in Honour of A. F. J. Klein* (Kampen: Kok, 1988) 123–31.

Lambert, W. G. *Babylonian Wisdom Literature* (Oxford: Clarendon Press, 1960).

—. *The Background of Jewish Apocalyptic* (London: Athlone Press, 1978).

Parpola, S. *Letters from Assyrian Scholars to the Kings Esarhaddon and Assurbanipal. Part II: Commentary and Appendices* (AOAT 5/2; Kevelaer: Butzon and Bercker; Neukirchen-Vluyn: Neukirchener Verlag, 1983).

—. "The Forlorn Scholar," in F. Rochberg-Halton (ed.), *Language, Literature and History: Philological and Historical Studies Presented to Erica Reiner* (AOS 67; New Haven, CT: American Oriental Society, 1987) 257–78.

van der Toorn, K. "In the Lions' Den: the Babylonian Background of a Biblical Motif," *CBQ* 60 (1998) 626–40.

THE MESOPOTAMIAN BACKGROUND OF DANIEL 1–6

SHALOM M. PAUL

INTRODUCTION

The book of Daniel, though authored and compiled at a very late date (with Dan 1–6 dating from the Hellenistic period and chapters 7–12 from the eve of the Maccabbean revolt),[1] nevertheless bears noticeable linguistic, philological, and typological Mesopotamian imprints. The following examples, several of which are drawn from my own prior research,[2] shed interesting light on this relatively neglected field of study.

1. DANIEL 3:29[3]

The literary genre of the martyr tale is exemplified in chapter 3 by the miraculous rescue of Shadrach, Meshach, and Abednego from the fiery furnace to which they had been condemned when they refused to worship the golden image erected by Nebuchadrezzar. The Babylonian king, upon personally witnessing this miracle, utters praises to their God and issues a decree to the effect that anyone who יֵאמַר שָׁלָה [שָׁלוּ qere] against their God shall be severely punished by dismemberment.[4] The Aramaic expression in question is the interdialectal semantic and (partial) etymological equivalent of the Akkadian *šillata(m) qabû/dabābu*,[5] "to speak" *šillatu(m)*, which is one of a number of words that are utilized to express improper

---

[1] From the wealth of recent commentaries and studies in Daniel, much can be especially culled from L. F. Hartman and A. A. Di Lella, *The Book of Daniel* (AB 23; Garden City, NY: Doubleday, 1978); and J. J. Collins, *Daniel: A Commentary on the Book of Daniel* (Hermeneia; Minneapolis: Fortress, 1993).

[2] For a complete discussion of the issues involved, along with the corroborative evidence drawn from the cuneiform material, one must consult the articles themselves.

[3] See S. M. Paul, "Daniel 3:29—A Case Study of 'Neglected' Blasphemy," *JNES* 42 (1983) 291–94.

[4] Such a punishment is very well attested in Mesopotamian sources. See B. Meissner, *Babylonien und Assyrien* (Heidelberg: C. Winters, 1920) 1.176–77.

[5] See *CAD*, Š/2.445–46.

speech,[6] and when uttered against a deity designates blasphemy.
Compare the following examples: *ana ištarišina iqabbâ šillatu rabītu*,
"They utter grievous blasphemy against their goddesses;"[7] and *ša ina
muḫḫi Aššur ilija bānija iqbû šillatu rabītu lišānšunu ašluq ašḫuṭ
mašakšunu*, "(Those Babylonians) who spoke gross blasphemy
against Assur, my god, who has created me, I split their tongues and
skinned them alive."[8] Thus, here too in Daniel, the correct
translation is "to utter blasphemy."

2. DANIEL 6:5

When this verbal offense is directed against human beings,
moreover, it connotes slander, insolence, impudence, and/or
effrontery. Such a case may be reflected in Dan 6:5, when the chief
ministers and satraps were unsuccessful in finding any grounds for
accusation against Daniel, "since he was trustworthy, no שָׁלוּ or שְׁחִיתָה
could be discovered against him."

It is possible to interpret the Aramaic שָׁלוּ as "negligence" (which is
well attested in the Targum as the translation for Hebrew שָׁכַח, "to
neglect, forget" [Ps 9:13; Job 8:13; 39:15] and שָׁגָה/שָׁגַג, "to err, make
a mistake" [Lev 4:2; 5:18; Job 6:24; 12:16]), a word which enters
neo- and late Babylonian texts as a verb, *šelû*, "to be negligent,
careless,"[9] and as a noun, *šilûtu*, "negligence."[10] However, in its
present context the term may also reflect Akkadian *šillatu*, and thus
the two nouns שָׁלוּ and שְׁחִיתָה would be the cognate equivalents of
Akkadian *arnu u šillatu*, "crime and/or improper speech."[11]
Compare, for example, *šumma mimma arnam u šillatam teppaša*, "If
she (i.e. the slave woman) commits any offense or insult (the buyer
may sell her)."[12] The intention in Daniel, then, would be that all

---

[6] W. G. Lambert, *Babylonian Wisdom Literature* (Oxford: Clarendon Press,
1960) 312 n.28.

[7] L. Cagni, *L'Epopea di Erra* (Studi Semitici 34; Rome: Università di Roma,
1969) 92, III:12. English translation: *The Poem of Erra* (Malibu: Undena, 1977) 42.

[8] E. F. Weidner, "Assyrische Beschreibungen der Kriegs-Relief Aššurbâni-
palis," *AfO* 8 (1932-34) 175–203, esp. 184, line 28.

[9] W. von Soden, "Aramäische Wörter in neuassyrischen und neu- und spät-
babylonischen Texten: Ein Vorbericht II," *Or* 37 (1968) 261–71, esp. 268.

[10] *CAD*, Š/2.274–75.

[11] *Ibidem*, 2.453.

[12] H. Hirsch, *Untersuchungen zur altassyrischen Religion* (AfO Beih. 13/14;

those who conspired against Daniel were unsuccessful in discovering any "improper speech" or "corruption" against him. The two substantives would thereby constitute a merism—in both speech and deed Daniel remained a loyal and trustworthy servant to his king.

3. DANIEL 6:8[13]

Chapter 6 reports the collusion of the political and administrative hierarchy of the Persian government to persuade king Darius[14] to publish an edict prohibiting the entire population from addressing any request or prayer to any human being or god, except to the king himself, upon the penalty of being hurled into the lions' den. The wording of the Aramaic, לקימה קים מלכא ולתקפה אסר, exemplifies the literary phenomenon of parallel phrases in prose passages of Daniel (cf. 4:16; 5:10).[15] The first half of the expression, לקימה קים מלכא, means "to establish/ confirm/publish a royal edict."

For the legal nuance of the Aramaic term לקימה, compare its occurrence in an Aramaic inscription from Assyria from the middle of the seventh century BCE[16] and in the Qumran Targum (11Qtg Job) to Job 40:28-9 (col. 35:6-7), where the Hebrew היכרת ברית עמך, "Will he make a covenant with you?," is translated היקים קים עמך[17] (For the Hebrew, compare similarly the use of לקים in Ruth 4:7; Esth 29:31).

However, the nuance of the second half of the expression, ולתקפה אסר, has usually been misinterpreted by commentators. The Aramaic pa'ēl infinitive, לְתַקָּפָה, is none other than the interdialectal cognate equivalent of the Akkadian verb dunnunu,[18] which parallels

---

Graz: Selbstverlage, 1961) 74.

[13] S. M. Paul, "Dan 6, 8: An Aramaic Reflex of Assyrian Legal Terminology," *Bib* 65 (1984) 106–110.

[14] On the identification of this non-existent "Median" Darius, see the various commentaries.

[15] J. C. Greenfield, "Early Aramaic Poetry," *JANESCU* 11 (1979) [=*Near Eastern Studies in Memory of M. M. Braumann*] 45–51, esp. 47.

[16] H. Donner and W. Röllig, *Kanaanäische und Aramäische Inschriften* (Wiesbaden: Harrassowitz, 1962) text 233:9 (pg. 46).

[17] J. A. Fitzmyer and D. J. Harrington, *A Manual of Palestinian Aramaic Texts* (Rome: Biblical Institute, 1978) 42; M. Sokoloff, *The Targum to Job from Qumran Cave XI* (Ramat Gan: Bar Ilan University Press, 1974) 96.

[18] *CAD*, D.90–91.

the semantic development of its nominal form, *dannatu*, and its Aramaic loan translation, דנת, which appears in ninth-century neo-Assyrian legal dockets with the meaning "a valid deed/tablet."[19] A similar development from this root, which primarily denotes "strength," to that which is legitimate, valid, and binding, is evidenced both in the corresponding adjective *dannu*,[20] and in the feminine plural tantum, *dannātu*,[21] "binding agreement."

The verb *dunnunu*, as well, also carries the legal connotation "to make valid and binding."[22] This is already documented from Old Assyrian *tuppūšu ludanninma*, "Let him make his tablets binding,"[23] through the Neo-Assyrian *adê ... udannina*, "He made the treaty binding."[24]

In the light of this linguistic evidence, the expression לתקפה אסר should now be understood as the Aramaic calque of Assyrian *riksa dunnunu*, in which both the nouns אסר and *riksu*,[25] which derive from the root meaning "to bind," represent technical legal terms for "obligatory bonds," and the verbs תקף and *dunnunu* signify "to ratify"—i.e. to make a document legally binding. Compare also the Nabatean תקף[26] and Hebrew תֹּקֶף (Esth 9:29), both meaning a valid deed.[27]

---

[19] Y. Muffs, *Studies in the Aramaic Legal Papyri from Elephantine* (Leiden: Brill, 1969) 187.

[20] *CAD*, D.95.

[21] *Ibidem*, 91.

[22] *Ibidem*, 85.

[23] *Ibidem*, 85.

[24] D. J. Wiseman, *The Vassal Treaties of Esarhaddon* (London: British School of Archaeology in Iraq, 1958) 33, lines 64–65; see also lines 23–24 and 286–87 for the same usage of the verb.

[25] See *AHw*, 984.

[26] C. F. Jean and J. Hoftijzer, *Dictionnaire des Inscriptions Sémitiques de l'Ouest* (DISO; Leiden: Brill, 1965) 258, 333. See also Muffs, *Aramaic Legal Papyri*, 208; S. E. Loewenstamm, "Esther 9:29-32: The Genesis of a Late Addition," *HUCA* 42 (1971) 117–24, esp. 119–20; J. C. Greenfield, "Studies in the Legal Terminology of the Nabatean Funerary Inscriptions," *Sefer Hanoch Levin* (Ramat Gan: Kiryat Sefer, 1974) 73 n.49 (Hebrew); S. A. Kaufman, *The Akkadian Influences on Aramaic* (Chicago: University of Chicago Press, 1974) 46 n.72.

[27] See Lowenstamm, "Esther"; Kaufman, *Akkadian Influences*; and Paul, "Daniel 6, 8," 107–8.

4. DANIEL 9:27[28]

Another reflex of this very same expression, in a Hebrew guise, appears in the section describing the religious persecutions of Antiochus IV and the profanation of the Temple during the last "week of years": "For one week he [Antiochus] הגביר ברית with the many." The Hebrew verb, whose root גבר in the *qal* means "to be strong" and in the *hip'il*, as here, means "to make strong," is none other than the semantic equivalent of the Akkadian *dunnunu* and Aramaic תקף, and shares with its cognates the legal meaning "to make valid and binding." Thus what is meant in 9:27 is that Antiochus "contracted a legally binding contract with the many," referring most likely to his relations with the Hellenizers of the period as echoed in 1 Macc 1:11-14.

5. DANIEL 5:6, 16[29]

This chapter recounts how Belshazzar received a supernatural forewarning when "the fingers of a human hand appeared and wrote on the plaster of the wall of the king's palace opposite the lampstand" (5:5). Upon witnessing this foreboding revelation and realizing that "once the moving finger having writ ...," he becomes panic-stricken and immediately summons his coterie of mantic professionals to read and decipher the written omen. The king's trepidation and perturbation are vividly described in imagery drawn from the familiar ancient Near Eastern *topos* of physiological reactions to alarming news. This literary convention, which has been studied in reference to both Ugaritic and Biblical literature,[30] can also be documented from Mesopotamian texts, some of whose expressions are precisely the same as those in the Aramaic passage of Daniel. The bodily symptoms of overwhelming fear and trembling which attack Belshazzar are detailed in a corporeal *wasf*-like descending order.

---

[28] S. M. Paul, "Gleanings from the Biblical and Talmudic Lexica in Light of Akkadian," in M. Brettler and M. Fishbane (eds.), *Minḥah le-Naḥum: Biblical and Other Studies Presented to Nahum M. Sarna in Honour of His 70th Birthday* (JSOTSup 154; Sheffield: JSOT Press, 1993) 242–56, esp. 251–53.

[29] S. M. Paul, "Decoding a 'Joint' Expression in Dan 5:6, 16," *JANESCU* 22 (E. L. Greenstein and D. Marcus [eds.], *Comparative Studies in Honor of Yochanan Muffs*, 1993) 121–27.

[30] D. R. Hillers, "A Convention in Hebrew Literature: The Reaction to Bad News," *ZAW* 77 (1965) 86–89.

First it is reported that זיוהי שנוהי[31] (cf. also 5:9, 10; 7:28). The
Aramaic זיו is a loan-word from the Akkadian *zīmu*, "appearance,
looks, countenance, luster,"[32] which appears with several verbs
signifying a "changed countenance[33]—one of which, *ewû*, "to
change,"[34] is the exact semantic equivalent of Aramaic שנה. Thus
zīmūšu (the *šapᶜel* of *ewû*) means "his countenance changed."[35] This
exact expression still appears in Rabbinic Hebrew, זיוו שנשתנה,[36] and
for its corresponding Biblical Hebrew interdialectal cognate
equivalents, compare שנה פנים, Job 14:20; Eccl 8:1; Sir 12:18; and
הודי נהפך, Dan 10:8.[37] In sum: "change of face" means that his
countenance blanched.

As the text goes on to detail the "terrible" effects of his condition,
between his "terrified thoughts" and "his knees knocking together,"[38]
it is written that וקטרי חרצה משתרין, "the joints[39] of his loins were
loosened." The identical physiological phenomenon is expressed in
Mesopotamian documents by the Akkadian interdialectal cognate
equivalents, *kaslū* (or) *riksū*, (both in the plural) *puṭṭuru*. The
Aramaic קטרין, similar to the Akkadian *riksū*, literally means
"bound, knotted together." The former refers to "joints," while the
latter, along with *kaslū*, designates "sinews, tendons."[40] And the

---

31 Many exegetes read שְׁנוֹ עֲלוֹהִי.

32 *CAD*, Z.119–21; Kaufman, *Akkadian Influences*, 113.

33 Cf. also, for example, *nakāru*, *CAD*, N/1.163; *CAD*, Z.120–21.

34 *CAD*, E.413–14.

35 O. R. Gurney, P. Hulin, and J. J. Finkelstein, *The Sultantepe Tablets*
(London: British Institute of Archeology at Ankara, 1957) I, text 24:6.

36 *Shir ha-Shirim Rabbah* to Song of Songs 2:2.

37 H. L. Ginsberg, *Studies in Daniel* (New York: Jewish Theological Seminary
of America, 1948) 41. For a similar idiom, see Jer 30:6.

38 For the "buckling" of the knees as a sign of extreme fright, cf. Nah 2:11.
Somewhat similarly, see the expression *itarrura išdāšu*, "his legs trembled," which
is just one of the many physical reactions of the panic of a king upon hearing
Esarhaddon's royal message. In addition, it is recorded that "his hips collapsed, his
heart was seized (by fear) (or, 'his insides were affected'), and his countenance
looked bad." See R. Borger, *Die Inscriften Asarhaddons, Königs von Assyrien*
(AfO Beih. 9; Graz: Selbstverlage, 1956) ii 1–4 (pg. 102).

39 For the Aramaic קטר (Hebrew קשר), "knot," meaning "joint," see *y.Maᶜaś.*
4.51b, "the joints of his fingers."

40 Compare the terrified reaction of the goddess Anat to the ill tidings reported
in the Baal epic (KTU 2nd edition 1, 3, iii:32-35): "Her feet wobble. Behind, her

Akkadian *puṭṭuru* (D-form of *paṭāru*)[41] is the semantic cognate of the Aramaic שרי, "to loosen, untie."[42] Compare, for example, "If a ... baby's sinews are loosened (*kaslūšu puṭṭurū*) from its neck to its backbone, it will die."[43] For the use of the verb with *riksū*, compare the description of the anguished sufferer: "Through twisting, my sinews are loosened" (*puṭṭurū riksūa*).[44]

This specific picturesque imagery was deftly chosen, moreover, in order to recall what was referred to earlier in the chapter. There, after the frustrating impotence of all the court personnel—magicians, exorcists, diviners, and astrologers—to read and decipher the ominous handwriting, the queen (mother) enters and reminds the king that during the reign of Nebucharezzar, his father, there was found a man who possessed an "extraordinary spirit, knowledge, and understanding, which enabled him to interpret dreams, to explain riddles, and משרא קטרין" (vv. 11-12). The king then immediately summons Daniel and requests him פשרין למפשר (= Akkadian *pašāru*, "to release, loosen, solve," very similar in usage to *paṭāru/puṭṭuru*), and קטרין למשרא, which is the identical phrase employed to describe the king's panic. Here, however, it does not describe Daniel's physiological condition but rather his mantic expertise in "untying, unraveling, loosening knots," which refers either to his ability to break spells and charms, where "knots" in magical texts and incantations, tied by the sorcerer (or by his apprentice) to bind the victim symbolically, had to be untied by corresponding counter-magic (Akkadian *kiṣru paṭāru/puṭṭuru/pašāru*);[45] or "untying knots" refers simply to solving knotty difficulties. And, as so often happens,

---

tendons (*ksl*) break; above her face sweats. Bent are the joints [lit., 'corners'] of her sinews (*kslh*); weakened are those [i.e., tendons] of her back." For the Ugaritic *ksl* = Akkadian; *kislu* = Hebrew כֶּסֶל, "sinew, tendon," see M. Held, "Studies in Comparative Semitic Lexicography," in H. G. Güterbock and T. Jacobsen (eds.), *Studies In Honor of Benno Landsberger On His Seventy-Fifth Birthday, April 21, 1965* (Chicago: University of Chicago Press, 1965) 395–406, esp. 401–406.

[41] See *AHw*, 849–51.

[42] Contrast Dan 3:24, מְכַפְּתִין ("bound") with 3:25, שְׁרַיִן ("untied, loosen").

[43] Cited by Held, "Studies," 402–403, from R. Labat, *Traité akkadien de diagnostics et pronostics médicaux* (Leiden: Brill, 1951) 222:41.

[44] Lambert, *Babylonian Wisdom Literature*, 44:104 (*Ludlul*).

[45] For the textual citations of *kiṣru*; see *CAD*, K.437, and for *pašāru* see *AHw*, 842, G.9b, Š.3, N.7c. For the Aramaic שרי, "to release from a spell," see *y.Moʿed Qaṭ.* 3.81d; *y. Sanh.* 7.25d.

it may very well serve as a clever double entendre, whereby the king desired to have the enigmatic code "spelled" out, so that his "charmed" existence would remain unharmed.[46]

6. DANIEL 1[47]

This chapter shares a remarkable stage by stage correlation with a letter from Mari sent to Šibtu, the wife of king Zimrilim, describing the procedure of induction into court service:[48]

(a) In both texts the candidates (female in the Mari letter; male in Daniel: he and his three companions) were selected from among captives taken as war booty and brought to the capital city (Mari in the letter, and Babylon in Daniel).[49]

(b) In both texts the selected candidates already possessed their own unique skills (Mari: weavers; Daniel [v. 4]: "proficient in all wisdom, knowledgeable and intelligent").

(c) Their superiority was evinced also by their outstanding physical features (Mari [lines 12-15]: *damqātim ša ištu ṣuprim adi šārti ša qaqqadim šummannam la išâ,*[50] "Beautiful women who, from the tip of their toe to the hair on their head, have no blemish;" Daniel [v. 4]: "youths without blemish and handsome").

(d) The names of the officials appointed to supervise them are specifically mentioned (Mari: first Waradilišum and then Mukannišum; Daniel: אַשְׁפְּנַז [v. 3] and then הַמֶּלְצַר [vv. 11, 16], itself a loan-word from the Akkadian *maṣṣaru/maṣṣartu,* "watcher, supervisor").[51]

(e) The purpose of the selection, in both cases, was to instruct

---

[46] See also A. Wolters, "Untying the King's Knots: Physiology and Wordplay in Daniel 5," *JBL* 110 (1991) 117–22.

[47] S. M. Paul, "From Mari to Daniel: Instructions for the Acceptance of Servants into the Royal Court," *ErIsr* 24 (Abraham Malamat Volume, eds. S. Aḥituv and B. A. Levine, 1993) 161–63 (Hebrew).

[48] For the text, see G. Dossin, *Archives royales de Mari: La correspondance féminine* (= ARM X; Paris: Imprimerie Nationale, 1967) text 126. For the translation and transliteration, see G. Dossin and A. Finet, *Correspondance féminine* (Paris: P. Geuthner, 1976). For the latest study of these texts, in addition to those cited in my article, see now N. Ziegler, *Le harem de Zimri-Lîm = Florilegium marianum* (Paris: Sepoa, 1999).

[49] See text ARM X, 125:4-6, 9-10; cf. lines 15, 17; and Dan 1:1ff.

[50] *CAD,* Š/3.280. For the corporeal merism, see Paul, "From Mari to Daniel," 162 n.15.

[51] *CAD,* M/1.333–34, 341–42.

(Akkadian *šūḫuzu*, Hebrew ללמד) the youthful candidates in a new profession (Mari [lines 17-18]: "to become adept at singing Subarean music"; Daniel [vv. 3-4]: "to teach them the writings and the language of the Chaldeans").

(f) Afterwards their status was officially changed (Mari [lines 18-19]: *temmanūšina lu nukkurū*,[52] i.e. from weavers to singers; Daniel [v. 5]: "they entered the king's service").[53]

(g) During their "residency" training period, explicit mention is made of the specific food portions they were to be given. Compare Mari: *ana kurummatišina nuʾidima*, "pay heed to their food allotment;" and Daniel (v. 5): they were initially to receive "daily rations from the king's food" (Hebrew פתבג is a loan word from Persian *patibaga*, "portions of food provided by the authorities") "and from the wine he drank." However, since they wished to avoid becoming polluted cultically, they requested and received lentils as their culinary substitute (v. 12).

(h) The stated purpose, in both texts, for their special food allotments was to enable them to maintain their "healthy appearance." Compare Mari: *zīmūšina la inakkirū*, literally, "so that their countenance does not change;" and Daniel (v. 10): the supervisor feared that if they became vegetarians, "their face would be less healthy" (זועפים),[54] and this would eventually cost him his life. The results, however, were very positive. Though maintaining their strict diet, Daniel and his friends nevertheless "looked better and healthier than all the youths who were eating of the king's food" (v. 15).

The following additional analogues should also be noted:

*The formula "O king, live forever!" (Dan 2:4; 3:9; 5:10; 6:7, 22) is well documented in Ancient Near Eastern literature.[55]

---

[52] Von Soden (*AHw*, 1346) refers to W. H. Ph. Römer (*Frauenbriefe über Religion, Politik und Privatleben in Mari* [AOAT 12; Neukirchen-Vluyn: Kevelaer, Butzon & Bercker, 1971] 71 n.5), who questions whether the Akkadian *te/immenu(m)* may be explained by a semantic development from "Grundstein > Gründungsurkunde > Urkunde," and thus von Soden translates, "Beurkundungspfahl." However, *CAD*, T (not yet published; courtesy of Prof. Martha Roth) states that the meaning of this word is "uncertain."

[53] For the Hebrew idiom, its analogues, and Akkadian cognates, see Paul, "From Mari to Daniel," 162 n.14.

[54] For this word, compare Gen 40:6, 7. It is cognate to Arabic *daʿif, daʿafa*, "to be lean."

[55] See S. M. Paul, "A Traditional Blessing for the Long Life of the King,"

*The two references to heavenly books (Dan 7:10; 12:1) are ultimately traceable to Mesopotamian origins.[56]

*The Babylonian provenance of chapters 1–6 is evidenced by many Akkadianisms.[57]

*The Aramaic מלך מלכיא (Dan 2:37) is a calque of Akkadian šar šarrāni, "king of kings," referring here to Nebuchadnezzar.[58]

*The fact that the name of Belshazzar, which was not preserved in classical sources, is found in Daniel 5 strongly suggests that the ultimate origin of this story comes from a neo-Babylonian milieu.[59] This is irrespective of the erroneous data, since he was not the son of Nebuchadnezzar, but of Nabonidus, and never was actually king of the empire, but rather co-regent while his father was abiding in Teima. It might also be added that the plot of chapter 4 ultimately harks back to the reign of Nabonidus (rather than to Nebuchadnezzar, as the text states), as is now seen from the *Prayer of Nabonidus* discovered at Qumran.[60]

*Mention should also be made of the composition called the "Dynastic Prophecy," which contains *vaticinia ex eventu*, pseudo-prophecies which refer to the rise and fall of kings (and empires) from neo-Babylonian times until the Seleucid period, and which is very similar both in its literary style and thematically to Dan 8:23-25 and 11:2-45 (whose relation to apocalyptic literature has been well discussed).[61] Both the Akkadian text and the Book of Daniel (11:45) also conclude with a real attempt to predict future events: the former foretelling the downfall of the Seleucid dynasty, and the latter the demise of Antiochus.[62] The colophon at the end of the "Dynastic

---

JNES 31 (1972) 351–55.

[56] S. M. Paul, "Heavenly Tablets and the Book of Life," *JANESCU* 5 (D. Marcus [ed.], *T. H. Gaster Festschrift*, 1973) 345–53.

[57] See K. A. Kitchen, "The Aramaic of Daniel," in D. J. Wiseman, T. C. Mitchell, R. Joyce, W. J. Martin, and K. A. Kitchen (eds.), *Notes on Some Problems in the Book of Daniel* (London: Tyndale, 1965) 31–79, esp. 34–35.

[58] M.-J. Seux, *Epithètes royales Akkadiennes et Sumériennes* (Paris: Letouzey et Ané, 1967) 318–39; S. M. Paul, "Hosea 8:8-10 and Ancient Near Eastern Royal Epithets," *ScrHier* 31 (*Studies in Bible*, ed. S. Japhet, 1986) 193–204. For the Hebrew equivalent, מלך מלכים, referring to the Babylonian king, see Ezek 26:7. For another example of the Aramaic, see Ezra 7:12.

[59] Collins, *Daniel*, 32–33, 48.

[60] For a discussion of this work, see Collins, *Daniel*, 51, 217–19.

[61] A. K. Grayson, *Babylonian Historical-Literary Texts* (Toronto: University of Toronto Press, 1975) 24–37. For discussion, see pp. 17–24.

[62] For the most recent attempts to find analogues between Mesopotamian literature and Daniel, see H. Avalos, "Dan 9:24-25 and Mesopotamian Temple Rededications," *JBL* 117 (1998) 507–11; E. C. Lucas, "Daniel: Resolving the

Prophecy" (col. IV:7-9), though mostly broken, refers to the secret nature of this work: "You must not show it [to the uninitiat]ed," and may be compared to the command given to Daniel to keep his book sealed, וחתם הספר סתם הדברים (12:4).

7. CONCLUSION

The question naturally arises as to how one can account for the above reflexes in such a late biblical composition. These influences on Daniel, however, are just one facet of the remarkable continuity of Babylonian cultural, societal, and linguistic norms that were preserved and maintained not only in their original cuneiform garb, but were also transferred and transformed into Aramaic, the new *lingua franca*.[63] There was no break in the vitality of the cultural milieu after Cyrus' conquest of the neo-Babylonian empire, as the ever-expanding documentation of texts through the Hellenistic period so amply demonstrates. Some have even called the Seleucid period the "final flowering of Babylonian culture." This late period, from Cyrus through the Seleucid period, witnessed the composition and/or copying in cuneiform of historiographical sources (chronicles and royal inscriptions), astronomical texts (the latest known tablet is an astronomical almanac dated to 75 CE), business documents, juridical and administrative contracts, letters, omens, incantations, lexical lists, ritual texts, and even *belles lettres*: a collection of Emesal hymns in the Berlin Museum which, according to the colophon, were

---

Enigma," *VT* 50 (2000) 66–80.

[63] For a complete discussion and documentation, with extensive bibliography of all the documents cited, see A. Kuhrt, "Survey of Written Sources Available for the History of Babylonia under the Later Achaemenids," in H. Sancisi-Weerdenburg and A. Kuhrt (eds.), *Achaemenid History* I: *Sources, Structures and Synthesis* (Leiden: Brill, 1987) 147–57; G. van Driel, "Continuity or Decay in the Late Achaemenid Period: Evidence from Southern Mesopotamia," in *Achaemenid History* I, 159–81; A. Kuhrt, "Achaemenid Babylonia: Sources and Problems," in H. Sancisi-Weerdenburg and A. Kuhrt (eds.), *Achaemenid History* IV: *Centre and Periphery* (Leiden: Brill, 1996) 177–94; M. J. Geller, "The Last Wedge," *ZA* 87 (1997) 43–95. Cf. also J. Oelsner, "Kontinuität und Wandel in Gesellschaft und Kultur Babyloniens in hellenistischer Zeit," *Klio* 60 (1978) 101–16; L. Cagni, "La fonti mesopotamischi dei periodi neo-babilonese, achemenide e seleucide (VI-VII sec. a. C.)," *RivB* 34 (1986) 11–53; A. Kuhrt, "Babylonia from Cyrus to Xerxes," *Cambridge Ancient History* (2nd ed., Cambridge: Cambridge University Press, 1988) 4.112–38; idem, "The Achaemenid Empire: A Babylonian Perspective," *Proceedings of the Cambridge Philological Society* 214 (n.s. 34; 1988) 60–76.

copied in the first century BCE. The best description of the Akitu festival celebrated in Babylon comes from the Seleucid period. And the temples in Babylon, Borsippa, Uruk, Kish, and Nippur were still functioning well into the period with a fully staffed personnel.

To cite just a few examples: the Cyrus cylinder, the Persian Verse Account (containing the vilification of Nabonidus and the adulation of Cyrus), and Bisitun inscriptions all reflect a Babylonian ideological framework and show that the Achaemenid kings did not usher in a new imperial policy; the Uruk King List ends with Seleucus II; a British Museum text refers to Arses and possibly to Alexander; astronomical diaries contain lunar eclipse reports and relate long-term observation of specific planets (600-300 BCE); horoscopes are developed (the earliest from the late fifth century BCE); terrestrial (*šumma ālu*) and astral omens (*enūma Anu Enlil*) appear in Buddhist texts in the fourth and third centuries BCE, exemplifying widespread cultural penetration between distant geographical areas. A vast quantity of business documents exist, in particular the Murashu archive from the second half of the fifth century BCE, from year 10 of Artaxerxes I to year 8 of Darius II, recording the family firm's purchase and sale of real estate and moveable property, lease of land, and payment of feudal dues. Other collections include the transactions of the Egibi family and family and private archives from Babylon, Dilibat, Ur, Borsippa, as well as Sippar, Uruk, and Nippur.

In addition to all the above written in Akkadian, one must also take into serious account the Aramaic conduit, so starkly evidenced in the cuneiform legal traditions (clauses, terms, and vocabulary) preserved in the Aramaic formulary of Elephantine, which reads like a palimpsest of earlier cuneiform texts. These documents contain a late and provincial reflex of the neo-Assyrian docket tradition[64] (i.e. ninth century neo-Assyrian deeds were provided with short Aramaic summary dockets introduced by דנת, which is a loan-translation from the Akkadian *dannatu*, "valid deed/tablet").[65] As for *belles lettres*,

---

[64] Y. Muffs, *Aramaic Legal Papyri* (Leiden, 1969), 13–15, 179–189. See already M. San Nicolò, *Beiträge zur Rechtsgeschichte im Bereich der Keilschriftlichen Rechtsquellen* (Oslo: H. Aschehoug, 1931) 53; E. Ebeling (*Das aramäisch-mittelpersische Glossar* [Leipzig, 1941] 86–112) pointed out a long time ago that a late Aramaic-Persian glossary was based on HAR.RA = *ḫubullu* and SIG.ALAM = *nabnītu* lists, and still combined Assyrian terms.

[65] See above, n.19.

witness in particular the framework story of Elephantine Ahiqar, which, for all its folkloristic features, is most likely based on a historical personality. According to Mesopotamian tradition, Ahiqar was the last of the *ummānu* (counselors, scholars, authors, high officials) who served in the Assyrian court of Sennacherib and Esarhaddon.[66] Then, in the 1959-60 excavations of Warka (Uruk), a document from the Seleucid period (but reflecting an older tradition) containing a list of court scholars was discovered, in which it was recorded that "in the time of king Assurahiddina, Abaʾenlildari, whom the Ahlameans [= Arameans] call Ahiqar (*ᵐa-ḫu-ʾu-qa-a-ri*), was *ummānu*."[67] In the prose framework of this composition, written in "official" Aramaic and whose very theme of the disgrace and rehabilitation of a cabinet minister (combined with an "ungrateful nephew") appears in Akkadian "bilingual proverbs,"[68] there are Akkadianisms as well as Akkadian proper names. And the background of one of the proverbs (line 156) reflects a well-attested Mesopotamian penalty clause—the mutilation of the tongue.[69]

Thus, as now can be readily appreciated, the millennia-old cuneiform stream of tradition continued to flow and be diffused throughout the last centuries before the Common Era, exerting its influence upon various literary works, including the book of Daniel.

8. SELECT BIBLIOGRAPHY

Avalos, H. "Dan 9:24-25 and Mesopotamian Temple Rededications," *JBL* 117 (1998) 507–11.

Collins, J. J. *Daniel: A Commentary on the Book of Daniel* (Hermeneia; Minneapolis: Fortress, 1993).

Driel, G. van. "Continuity or Decay in the Late Achaemenid Period: Evidence from Southern Mesopotamia," in H. Sancisi-Weerdenburg and A. Kuhrt (eds.), *Achaemenid History* I: *Sources, Structures and Synthesis* (Leiden: Brill, 1987) 159–81.

---

[66] See E. Reiner, "The Etiological Myth of the 'Seven Sages' Zweisprachig," *Or* 30 (1961) 1–11.

[67] J. C. Greenfield, "The Background and Parallel to a Proverb of Ahiqar," in A. Caquot and M. Philonenko (eds.), *Hommages à André Dupont-Sommer* (Paris: Librairie d'Amérique et d'Orient Adrien-Masionneuve, 1971) 49–59.

[68] Reiner, "Etiological Myth," referring to Lambert, *Babylonian Wisdom Literature*, 239–40, ii:50–63.

[69] Greenfield, "Ahiqar," 58. See also above, n. 8.

Geller, M. J. "The Last Wedge," ZA 87 (1997) 43–95.

Kuhrt, A. "Survey of Written Sources Available for the History of Babylonia under the Later Achaemenids," in Sancisi-Weerdenburg and Kuhrt (eds.), Achaemenid History I, 147–57. [see under Driel.]

—. "Achaemenid Babylonia: Sources and Problems," in H. Sancisi-Weerdenburg and A. Kuhrt (eds.), Achaemenid History IV: Centre and Periphery (Leiden: Brill, 1996) 177–94.

Lucas, E. C. "Daniel: Resolving the Enigma," VT 50 (2000) 66–80.

Oelsner, J. "Kontinuität und Wandel in Gesellschaft und Kultur Babyloniens in hellenistischer Zeit," Klio 60 (1978) 101–16.

Paul, S. M. "Daniel 3:29—A Case Study of 'Neglected' Blasphemy," JNES 42 (1983) 291–94.

—. "Dan 6, 8: An Aramaic Reflex of Assyrian Legal Terminology," Bib 65 (1984) 106–110.

—. "Decoding a 'Joint' Expression in Dan 5:6, 16," in E. L. Greenstein and D. Marcus (eds.), JANESCU 22 (Comparative Studies in Honor of Yochanan Muffs, 1993) 121–27.

—. "From Mari to Daniel: Instructions for the Acceptance of Servants into the Royal Court," ErIsr 24 (Abraham Malamat Volume, eds. S. Ahituv and B. A. Levine, 1993) 161–63 (Hebrew).

Wolters, A. "Untying the King's Knots: Physiology and Wordplay in Daniel 5," JBL 110 (1991) 117–22.

THE *ANZU* MYTH AS RELEVANT BACKGROUND FOR DANIEL 7?

JOHN H. WALTON

1. INTRODUCTION

The premise of the Book of Daniel is that Daniel was trained in the language and literature of the Babylonians (1:4) with the intention that he join the ranks of the wise men of the court. Indeed, he not only takes his place in that vocation but excels, to the extent that he advances to the very top of the profession and distinguishes himself in his discipline. The attainment of such a position could admittedly be an embarrassment in the vita of a supposedly faithful Israelite, but any complaints about his virtual assimilation are mitigated by the insistence of the narratives that the arts in which Daniel was trained served only as the fodder for the revelation that enabled his success. As he had refused the king's packaged diet in chapter 1, preferring his own concoctions from the "seeds,"[1] so the divinatory and mythological literature of Babylon provided but the raw materials for Daniel's career as a sage and prophet in the court of Babylon.

Chapter 7 of Daniel has received much attention from scholars interested in demonstrating the influence of Akkadian (as well as West Semitic) literature on the Book of Daniel. The following provides a sampling of the identified influences:

1. The initial churning of the sea (7:2) has been recognized as the typical mythical scene in which the churning of the cosmic ocean disturbs the creatures (monsters, beasts) that represent the forces of chaos and disorder. In *Enuma Elish*, Anu creates the four winds that stir up Tiamat.[2]

2. The similarity of the description of the beasts (7:4-6) to some of the descriptions of birth anomalies that occur in the omen series *šumma izbu* and portend significant events.[3]

---

[1] The Hebrew term for the king's food, פתבג, is understood in later Greek literature as a prepared dish, whereas Daniel's choice, זרעים, is not usually food at all. We could therefore conclude that he is perhaps asking for the rations from which he would prepare his own meals.

[2] *Enuma Elish* I:105-10.

[3] P. Porter, *Metaphors and Monsters: A Literary-Critical Study of Daniel 7 and*

3. The prominence of winged lions (7:4) in Mesopotamian iconography.[4]

4. The common occurrence of stacks of horns (7:7, 20, 24) on the crowns of Mesopotamian kings and deities.[5]

5. The association of El with the Ancient of Days (7:9-10).[6]

6. The thrones equipped with wheels (7:9) used in divine processions.[7]

7. The motif of riding on the clouds (7:13).[8]

8. The periodization of history into four empires (7:17).[9]

Many of these, intriguing as they are, have only a single point of contact and offer no help in understanding the larger genre issues in the chapter. It has long been recognized, however, that the basic outline of the chapter follows the course of the chaos combat myths whose varying exemplars are widely attested in the literature of the Ancient Near East.[10] In Akkadian literature the chief representative, though one of the last in the line of permutations, is *Enuma Elish*. The connection cited in (1) above is only the beginning of this familiar sequence. After the chaos monster is disturbed by the churning of the sea, it leads a revolt against the gods, which includes procuring the Tablet of Destinies. The gods consequently seek out and appoint a champion who defeats the enemy and is therefore granted dominion. A few of these elements have also been identified

---

8 (ConB 20; Lund: Gleerup, 1983) 17–22.

[4] J. J. Collins, *Daniel. A Commentary on the Book of Daniel* (Hermeneia; Minneapolis: Fortress, 1993) 297.

[5] For an example see *ANEP* #646.

[6] E. T. Mullen, *The Assembly of the Gods* (HSM 24; Chico, CA: Scholars Press, 1980) 160–61; F. M. Cross, *Canaanite Myth and Hebrew Epic* (Cambridge, MA: Harvard University Press, 1973) 16; J. Day, *God's Conflict With the Dragon and the Sea* (Cambridge: Cambridge University Press, 1985) 161; Collins, *Daniel*, 290; and J. Goldingay, *Daniel* (Dallas: Word, 1989; Milton Keynes, UK: Word, 1991) 151.

[7] D. Collon, *First Impressions: Cylinder Seals in the Ancient Near East* (Chicago: University of Chicago Press, 1987) 160, #725–26.

[8] One of the epithets of Baal is "Cloudrider," for example in the Baal Cycle, "Baal and Yamm," IV:7-8. See S. B. Parker, *Ugaritic Narrative Poetry* (Writings from the Ancient World 9; Atlanta: Scholars Press, 1997) 103; and Goldingay, *Daniel*, 151.

[9] D. Flusser, "The Four Empires in the Fourth Sibyl and in the Book of Daniel," *IOS* 2 (1972) 148–75; Collins, *Daniel*, 166–70.

[10] For presentation of a number of examples see N. Forsyth, *The Old Enemy: Satan and the Combat Myth* (Princeton: Princeton University Press, 1987) 44–66.

in the Baal Cycle in Ugaritic literature,[11] and as early as J. A. Emerton's work there have been those that have argued for a Canaanite origin for Daniel 7.[12] Some of the exemplars serve as the foundation for cosmic origins (as does *Enuma Elish*), because the initial subduing of the forces of chaos enabled the creation and organization of the cosmos. As N. Forsyth demonstrates, however, the creation element is just one of the variables, not the defining characteristic of the genre.[13] Since Daniel 7 has not generally been considered to contain a cosmogony, it may be instructive to examine some of the other exemplars of the chaos revolt paradigm to see what parallels they offer, especially the *Anzu* Myth, which has been neglected by the interpreters of Daniel 7.

2. THE *ANZU* MYTH[14]

The *Anzu* Myth is also in the category of chaos combat myths,[15]

---

[11] Day, *God's Conflict With the Dragon and the Sea*; for comparisons to Daniel 7 see esp. 151–78; idem, "Dragon and Sea, Gos's Conflict With," in *ABD* 2.228–31; Forsyth, *The Old Enemy*, 46–48;

[12] J. A. Emerton, "The origin of the Son of Man imagery," *JTS* 9 n.s. (1958) 225–42.

[13] Forsyth, *The Old Enemy*, 44.

[14] The text is published in E. Reiner, "K7257," *RA* 51 (1957) 107–108; idem, "K3454+3935," *RA* 48 (1954) 146–49; Blahoslav Hruska, *Der Mythenadler Anzu in Literatur und Vorstellung des alten Mesopotamien* (Budapest: Eötvòs Loránd Tudományegyetem, Ókori Történeti Tanzékek, 1975); W. W. Hallo and W. Moran, "The first tablet of the SB recension of the Anzu Myth," *JCS* 31 (1979) 65–115; H. W. F. Saggs, "Additions to Anzu," *AfO* 33 (1986) 1–29. Translations may be found in the standard collections including: "The Myth of Zu,"*ANET*, 111–13; "The Myth of Zu,"*ANET*, 514–17; S. Dalley, *Myths From Mesopotamia* (Oxford: Cambridge University Press, 1991) 205–27; B. R. Foster, *From Distant Days* (Bethesda, MD: CDL, 1995) 115–31. Helpful studies include: the *Reallexikon der Assyriologie*; *CAD*, A/2.153–55; A. George, "Sennacherib and the Tablet of Destinies," *Iraq* 48 (1986) 133–46; and M. Mallowan, *Nimrud and Its Remains* (London: Routledge and Kegan Paul, 1966).

[15] It is commonly recognized that *Enuma Elish* and *Anzu* are in the same category; see B. Batto, *Slaying the Dragon* (Louisville, KY: Westminster/John Knox Press, 1992) 33–37; and Forsyth, *The Old Enemy*, 48–54. W. G. Lambert has suggested that *Enuma Elish* is dependent on the Anzu Myth in "Ninurta Mythology in the Babylonian Epic of Creation," in K. Hecker and W. Sommerfeld (eds.), *Keilschriftliche Literaturen. Ausgewälte Vorträge der XXXII. Rencontre assyriologique internationale* (Berliner Beiträge zum Vorderen Orient 6; Berlin: Dietrich

and has versions in both Old Babylonian and Standard Babylonian
with exemplars dating from the early second millennium to the
seventh century. Its main character in the former is Ningirsu, and in
the latter, Ninurta who by that time had supplanted Ningirsu. The
basic story line can be briefly summarized as follows:

Anzu is a fierce beast who is a combination of eagle and lion. His
appearance intimidates even the gods. The chief god, Enlil, enlists
the creature as a guardian, hoping to benefit from its vicious male-
volence. This offers Anzu the opportunity to observe Enlil wielding
the Tablet of Destinies to enforce his rule over the gods. When the
chance presents itself, he absconds with the tablet and threatens to
wreck havoc among the gods. This initiates a search for a champion
who will conquer Anzu and recover the tablet. Several candidates
(Adad, Gibil, and Shara) are offered the opportunity, but decline,
terrified by the possibilities of facing a renegade armed with the
power of the tablet.

Finally, the gods enlist the help of Mami, the creatrix and mother
goddess, urging her to persuade Ninurta (son of Mami and Enlil) to
take on the task for the sake of his father's honor. She is successful
and Ninurta proceeds to engage Anzu. The invulnerability of the
beast proves to be as big a problem as all had anticipated. His possession of the Tablet of Destinies gives Anzu the ability to counteract
any weapon used against him. Finally, Ea is consulted to provide a
strategy that will succeed. He suggests that if Ninurta can manage to
pluck Anzu's wing feathers, the creature will summon them back to
him. As the summons is voiced, Ninurta is to loose an arrow. The
summons for feathers will draw the arrow to its mark.[16] Thus Anzu
is slain and the tablet is recovered. For unknown reasons (due at least
in part to the fragmentary nature of the text at this point), there is a
delay in Ninurta's return of the tablet, but after some negotiation it is
restored to the gods. Subsequently, Ninurta is honored and declared
the greatest among the gods.

Reimer, 1986). The basis for the proposed dependence is conveniently summarized
in R. J. Clifford, *Creation Accounts in the Ancient Near East and in the Bible*
(CBQMS 26; Washington DC: Catholic Biblical Association, 1994) 84–86.

[16] This follows Foster's interpretation of the events in *From Distant Days*, 115.
E. Reiner sees Anzu being reduced to birdcalls by the clipping of his feathers in
*Your Thwarts in Pieces, Your Mooring Rope Cut: Poetry from Babylonia and
Assyria* (Michigan Studies in the Humanities 5; Ann Arbor, MI: University of
Michigan Press, 1985) 64–65.

3. MOTIFS

Daniel 7 exhibits a number of the major motifs that are found in the chaos combat myth paradigm, though there are many elements in the vision that have no point of contact with the known exemplars of the paradigm. In the following paragraphs the story-line of Daniel 7 will be compared with the chaos combat myth paradigm primarily as it occurs in *Baal and Yamm*, *Enuma Elish* (*Ee*), and *Anzu*. Based on this comparison, the extent of literary interrelationship will then be discussed.

3.1 Monster from the Sea

The first three beasts in Daniel 7 do not coincide with any of the standard monsters from Akkadian literary traditions,[17] showing instead more affinity to the animal abnormalities typical of *šumma izbu*.[18] There is little physical description of the fourth beast. Only the iron teeth, bronze claws and ten horns are referred to. It is not compared to any known animal, nor is it explicitly given composite features as the first and third beast are. This beast comes out of the cosmic sea that has been churned up by the four winds of heaven.

In *Ee* the opponent is Tiamat, the deity of the primeval cosmic ocean. She is a creatrix and is paired with Apsu. She is identified with the sea, but does not come forth from the sea. Tiamat is not like the sea monsters that simply inhabit the sea. In Ugaritic literature Yamm is the sea god, yet he is sometimes identified with the chaos monsters such as Lotan.[19] In *Ee* I:105-109 Anu forms the four winds and gives them to his son, Marduk, to play with. By them Tiamat is roiled and churned up. She is never described as a monster,[20] but in *Ee* I:133-143 creates various fearsome creatures to serve her cause.

---

[17] W. G. Lambert ("Ninurta Mythology," 57) lists the eight specific monsters of *Ee* as *bašmu, mušḫuššu, laḫamu, ugallu, uridimmu, girtablullû, kullulû,* and *kusarikku,* translated respectively as "snake," "savage snake," "hairy hero," "big demon," "savage dog," "scorpion-man," "fish-man," and "bull-man."

[18] Porter, *Metaphors and Monsters*, 17–22. Comparison has also been made to the fifteen *mischwesen* identified in a seventh century Assyrian text; see H. S. Kvanvig, "An Akkadian vision as background for Daniel 7," *ST* 35 (1981) 85–89.

[19] See F. Stolz, "Sea," in *DDD*, 1390–1401, esp. 1396.

[20] A cylinder seal that is thought to represent a scene from the Creation Epic may depict Tiamat in sea serpent form; see Collon, *First Impressions: Cylinder Seals in the Ancient Near East*, 180, #850.

In *Baal and Yamm* the antagonist is Yamm, but he is not portrayed in this text as a monster. Yamm is the personified Sea in much the same way as Tiamat is; he is anthropomorphic.[21]

In *Anzu*, the opponent is the monstrous beast for whom the myth is named. He is considered to have been conceived in the flood waters (I:50-52), so to that extent, he emerged from the sea. However, this beast is not portrayed as representative of the chaotic forces associated with the sea as Tiamat and Yamm are. Additionally, the motif of four winds churning up the sea does not occur here, nor is the actual emergence from the sea described. Though there is no physical description of Anzu in the text, there are many representations of him in Mesopotamian iconography. Early texts, especially, portray him in bird shape (IM.DUGUD) or as a bird with a human head, or even as a human with bird posture (wings slanting along side from shoulder).[22] The ninth-century reliefs at Kalah (where Ninurta was the chief deity) portray Anzu as a feathered creature with lion's feet and legs, eagle wings and torso, and a lion-like face with gaping jaws and a horn.[23] Its claws/talons are among the most notable characteristics.[24]

In this category, then, Daniel 7 is closer to *Ee* with regard to the churning of the sea, but is closer to *Anzu* in the description of the antagonist as a fearsome beast. It differs from both in the idea of the beast as part of the sequence of beasts arising from the churned up sea. There is no mythological tradition in the ancient Near East that clearly has a chaos monster emerging from the sea to do battle.[25]

---

[21] Stolz, "Sea," 1395.

[22] See the brief discussion in *CANE* 3.1851–52.

[23] The identification of the face is problematic. Early on, B. Landsberger associated it with the vampire bat (cf. Hallo and Moran, "The first tablet of the SB recension," 70 n.14), but that suggestion has not gained consensus. For numerous comparisons to the face of Anzu, see *CAD*, A/2.154–55. Despite the common identification of the opponent in the Kalah relief as Anzu, T. J. Lewis's study of the lion-dragon combination certainly opens up that possibility as well ("CT 13.33-34 and Ezekiel 32: Lion-dragon myths," *JAOS* 116 [1996] 28–47).

[24] *CAD*, A/2.155.

[25] The sea emergence motif occurs with the seven *apkallus*, the *puradu* fish, who are seen as responsible for teaching mankind many of the arts of civilization. Also intriguing is the fact that they have a significant connection to the Tablet of Destinies. In passing it is interesting to note, as my colleague A. Schmutzer pointed out to me, that Rev 13:1 follows Daniel in having the beast emerge from the sea,

The closest may be the fragmentary *Labbu Myth*, which W. G. Lambert also identifies as one of the precursors of *Enuma Elish*.[26] The chaos monster, Labbu, is serpentine, and possibly also leonine,[27] and is said to have been created by the Sea (*tamtu*).

3.2 Revolt and the Tablet of Destinies

In Daniel 7, the fourth beast crushes, devours and tramples his unidentified victims. The revolt aspect appears only in the king represented by the little horn who wages war against the קַדִּישׁיִן (vv. 21-27). The identification of this group has proved controversial. Traditional interpretation has favored relating them to godly Israel,[28] while recent commentators have made a persuasive case for understanding them to be the angelic agents who are executing God's plans.[29] In either case, they fill the role of the gods of the chaos combat myths who temporarily lose control of their authority, but regain it after the enemy has been vanquished. This passage does not establish a revolt scenario as clearly as the Ancient Near Eastern tales do. Yet persecution and oppression are clear enough, and when those are added to the comment that he sets himself up as an antagonist to the Most High (v. 25), the revolt pattern is recognizable. It is further bolstered by the boastful words that he speaks (vv. 8, 20).

The threat that is posed by the boastful king's attempt to change the "sacred seasons and the law" (זְמְנִין וְדָת) brings the Tablet of Destinies (*tuppi šīmāti*) immediately to mind. The Tablet of Destinies is the means by which the cosmic functions were established and regulated,[30] and is described in an inscription of Sennacherib as follows:

> The Tablet of Destinies, the bond of supreme power, dominion over the
> gods of heaven and the underworld, and kingship of the Igigi and

---

and goes the next step in eliminating the sea (chaos) entirely in the New Heaven and the New Earth (21:1).

[26] Lambert, "Ninurta Mythology," 55.

[27] Lewis, "CT 13.33-34 and Ezekiel 32," 28–47.

[28] For example, L. F. Hartmann und A. A. DiLella, *The Book of Daniel* (AB 23; New York: Doubleday, 1978) 207; A. LaCocque, *The Book of Daniel* (Atlanta: John Knox, 1979) 126–27; J. A. Montgomery, *The Book of Daniel* (ICC; Edinburgh: T & T Clark, 1927) 307.

[29] See especially Collins, *Daniel*, 312–18.

[30] *CAD*, Š/3.11–19

Anunnaki, the secret of the heavens and the netherworld, the link of the
Canopy of Anu and Gansir, the leash of [multitudes(?)].[31]

The fundamental operations of the cosmos, the areas of jurisdiction
of the gods, the foundational skills, arts and structure of civilization,
and the decisions guiding human history and destiny, are all
governed by means of the Tablet of Destinies. That which is
governed is referred to in Sumerian as *me.gal.gal an.ki.a*, "the great
offices of heaven and earth" (Akk. *uṣurāt/parṣu šamê u erṣeti*). These
are at times mediated by the gods,[32] but at other times, by the
apkallu.[33] They are sometimes in the hands of the Assembly of the
gods, whereas at other times they are administered on behalf of the
assembly by a particular god (for example, Nabu).[34] The calendar
and the laws and customs of society were two of the major aspects of
civilization that were believed to have been established by the Tablet
of Destinies.[35] Of course, in Daniel no object is acknowledged as a
mechanism, so there is nothing to be stolen, but usurpation of the
prerogatives usually associated with the Tablet of Destinies is in
evidence.

In *Ee*, there is clearly a revolt that is led by Tiamat and her
consort, Qingu. It is a revolt against the gods, attempting to seize

---

[31]   Translated by A. R. George, "Sennacherib and the Tablet of Destinies," *Iraq*
48 (1986) 133–46, esp. 134.

[32]   *Cattle and Grain*, lines 53–55.

[33]   J. Tigay, *The Evolution of the Gilgamesh Epic* (Philadelphia: University of
Pennsylvania Press, 1982) 205; E. Reiner, "The Etiological Myth of the 'Seven
Sages'," *Or* 30 (1961) 1–11.

[34]   A. R. Millard, "Nabû," in *DDD*, 1141–47, esp. 1142.

[35]   Aspects of culture and civilization are designated as ME in Akkadian, and are
among the things to be determined when destinies are established. Likewise, the
attributes and areas of jurisdiction of the gods are among the destinies that are
determined (as *Enuma Elish* I:8 makes clear). It is possible, therefore, to see the
destinies operating on several different levels. Human beings have their own fixed
destiny; cities have a destiny; civilization has its destiny; and the gods have their
destinies. Discussion of these can be found in A. L. Oppenheim, *Ancient Mesopotamia* (Chicago: University of Chicago Press, 1977) 201–204; and J. Bottéro,
Mesopotamia (Chicago: University of Chicago Press, 1992) 237–39. In contrast,
S. Paul (*Studies in the Book of the Covenant in the Light of Cuneiform and Biblical
Law* [VTSup 18, Leiden: Brill, 1970]), places the law (*kittum*) in the category of
the metadivine (pp. 6–7). The connection of the calendar to the Tablet of Destinies
can be seen clearly in *Enuma Elish* V:1-25, where Marduk sets up the operation of
the heavenly bodies as one of his first tasks after regaining the tablet (IV:121).

power from them, and is characterized by rumbling, raging and hostility (II:11-18). The accusation that is eventually made against Tiamat is that she "attempted wicked deeds against Anshar, sovereign of the gods (IV:83). The Tablet of Destinies is involved, but Tiamat is not portrayed as stealing it; she simply entrusts the tablet to the care of Qingu, whom she has appointed as her commander-in-chief (*Ee* I:148-62). No indication is given about how Tiamat has procured the tablet, or whether she has obtained it illegitimately. Nevertheless, the authority that Tiamat proclaims for Qingu is based on his possession of the tablet. He is elevated over all the gods and put in control of their destinies (III:102-11). Tiamat utters boastful words in her declaration of Qingu's supreme station. Later, after both Tiamat and Qingu are destroyed, Marduk retrieves the tablet (IV:119-22), presumably uses it in his reorganization of the cosmos (V:1-68), and turns it over to Anu (V:69-70).

In the Baal Cycle, Yamm is the antagonist who sets himself up against the divine assembly. He claims supremacy and demands that Baal be handed over to him (*CTA* 2.i.18-19). This brings to mind the statement in Dan 7:25 that the holy ones will be handed over for a time. Again, boastful words characterize the antagonist's speech as he makes his demands before the divine assembly.

In *Anzu*, there is no general revolt against the gods, only the greedy desire for power by an individual. Anzu's theft of the Tablet of Destinies is more an act of treachery than rebellion, though he does desire to control the responsibilities of the gods (I:71-73).[36] Anzu also has boastful words, both when he decides to steal the tablet (I:70-73) and when he is confronted by Ninurta (II:40-42). Unlike the emphasis on revolt and overthrow in *Ee*, the prominent threat in *Anzu* concerns how the Tablet of Destinies will be wielded by the creature. He does not speak of change as the king in Dan 7:25 does, but he speaks of gaining control of the Destinies.[37]

One of the most striking elements of the comparison concerns

---

[36] The attempt to procure control of the Destinies by devious means is known not only from Anzu, where it is by outright theft, but also in the Sumerian myth called *Inanna and Enki*, in which Inanna seeks to wrest them from Enki by getting him drunk. For a convenient abridged version, see *CS* I:522-26.

[37] The expression of a desire by a human to change the *šīmātu* is found in the Gilgamesh Epic, where Enkidu declares his intention to alter the destiny of the city of Uruk by challenging Gilgamesh (I.v:1-2).

v. 25. There the enemy is (1) speaking against the Most High (paralleled most strikingly in *Ee*); (2) oppressing the holy ones (paralleled in both *Ee* and *Anzu*; and (3) threatening to change the set times and laws (paralleled in *Anzu*). Daniel 7 splits the roles (fourth beast, little horn) as *Ee* does (Tiamat, Qingu), but at the same time features oppressive threats more than revolt, as *Anzu* does.

Another remarkable point of comparison is that the fourth beast in Daniel is represented by the ten horns that have an eleventh (the little horn) added. In *Ee* Tiamat is accompanied by eleven monsters that she has created to serve her cause. W. G. Lambert has demonstrated, however, that the set of eleven monsters of *Ee* is a reflection of that myth's dependence on the Ninurta tales, including *Anzu*.[38] Daniel's use of the eleven reflects a conflation of *Ee* and *Anzu*. On the one hand, since the eleven operate under the auspices of the fourth beast, there would be a closer connection to *Ee* where Tiamat commands the eleven. In the Ninurta tradition the eleven are separate and individual conquests, rather than compatriots in the chaos combat. This would be a closer parallel to the likelihood that Daniel 7 views the eleven as successive kings.

3.3 Ancient Gods and The Champion

In the chaos combat paradigm, the protagonists can be divided into three categories. First is the group that is threatened by the revolt. Often the chief god is in this group and representative of it. This is generally made up of the older, more established gods and focuses on the gods in the Assembly. The second category is made up of the individual or individuals that are delegated to devise a solution. This process is directed by the chief god, who typically does not succeed in finding someone. The crafty god of wisdom, Enki/Ea, often steps in at that point. The third category is occupied by the potential deliverers. It is not uncommon for several candidates to either decline the offer, or fail in the attempt before the real hero comes on the scene.

Category 1: At Risk and Terrified

One of the consistent features of the paradigm is the fear generated among the gods under the threats or attacks of the monster. This fact undermines what may otherwise have appeared as a most logical role

---

[38] Lambert, "Ninurta Mythology," 56–58.

for the Ancient of Days in Daniel 7, for in contrast there is nothing but calm and confidence as the Ancient of Days and the Son of Man make their appearance. As mentioned earlier, the ones at risk from the threats of the antagonist in Daniel 7 are identified as the holy ones, and in that role they are comparable to the divine assembly, whether they should be identified in Daniel as supernatural creatures or not.

In *Ee*, Anu (II:106) and Ea (II:82) are specifically cited as being terrified, and the entire assembly of Igigi and Anunnaki are stunned and in mourning (II:121-24; III:127). They are joined by the ancient Lahmu and Lahamu (III:126). Anshar, who is treated as the one in charge, is distressed and angry (II:49-51), but not in a panic.

In *Baal and Yamm*, the assembly of the gods does not express fear, but appears totally cowed by Yamm and readily submits to his demands (*CTA* 2.i.22-27). Baal, when ordered to submit to Yamm, is described as shaken or angry, and begins to attack his messengers (*CTA* 2.i.38-41).

In *Anzu*, the chief god, Enlil, registers the first distraught reaction, since the tablet has been taken away from him (I:82). After three candidates refuse to accept the mission against Anzu, the assembly of Igigi gods is in turmoil (I:154).

Category 2: Source of the Solution

In Daniel 7, the Ancient of Days has always been an intriguing yet obscure figure, though there is little doubt that in Daniel he can represent none other than Yahweh. He is seated on the throne of dominion (v. 9), grants authority (vv. 13-14), and passes judgment (v. 22). The only mitigation of this identification is that there is grammatical cause to draw a distinction in v. 22 between the "Ancient of Days" and the "Most High" (an epithet generally used for Yahweh).[39] Since the Most High, (עֶלְיוֹנִין)[40] does not occur until after the introduction of the "Son of Man," it is alternatively possible that as a result of the Son of Man being granted authority (v. 14), he thereby qualifies for the epithet "Most High." This creates the expected correspondence between the kingdom being given to the son

---

[39] If the two were the same, it would have been easier to have the Ancient of Days pronounce judgment in favor of *his* holy ones.

[40] For the use of the plural form as an imitation of the Hebrew אלהים, see Collins, *Daniel*, 312.

of man in v. 14 and to the Most High and his holy ones in v. 27.

Regardless of what name we attach to the Ancient of Days and of what connections can be drawn between the description of him and descriptions in other biblical or extra-biblical texts,[41] what is important for our study is the role that he plays. The Ancient of Days is the one who is responsible for responding to the threat. He shows no anger, distress, turmoil or confusion, but convenes the assembly (of which he is the head) to address the problem. In this he is most comparable to Anshar in *Ee* and Anu in *Anzu*.

In *Ee*, the solution sequence is mediated first by Anshar, who fails to find a champion, and then by Ea, who selects Marduk to play the role of champion.

In *Anzu*, the solution sequence is mediated first by Anu, who fails to find a champion, but then accepts Ea's offer to find one (I:157-62). Ea selects Ninurta, but enlists Mami (Belet-ili) to persuade her son. Mami is not near as close a match for the "Ancient of Days" imagery as El is in the Ugaritic material, though her status as the ancient creatrix puts her in a similar category.

In Daniel 7, the Ancient of Days rolls all of these into one as the head of the assembly and the one who both mediates the solution sequence and designates a champion.

Category 3: The Champion

In Daniel 7 the champion position is filled by one who is identified as "like the son of man." J. Day has built a convincing case that this individual is best identified as Michael,[42] which is in contrast to the traditional interpretation, which had seen here a Messianic figure. The designation of this individual as a cloud rider (v. 13) has drawn the comparison with Baal in the Ugaritic texts. When Kothar-wa-Hasis prepares Baal's weapons, he designates him cloudrider and proclaims his kingship and dominion (*CTA* 2.iv.8-10). An important caveat, however, is that in Daniel 7 the son of man does no battle and is therfore not a champion comparable to those found in the other exemplars. Likewise, in *Baal and Yamm* El is not clearly on the side of Baal, and thus cannot be blended with Baal in the champion role.

---

[41] All of these options have been thoroughly presented by Collins.

[42] J. Day, *God's Conflict With the Dragon and the Sea*, 167–77. Of Day's many points of evidence, one of the most intriguing (pg. 173) is that in Revelation 12 it is Michael who defeats the dragon, suggesting that this had become part of Jewish tradition and understanding.

In *Ee*, Anshar has been seeking a champion with no success. The first candidate, Ea, cannot vanquish Tiamat (II:72-94), and neither can his father, Anu (II:96-115). Marduk is eventually identified and is successful. Marduk is armed for battle with thunderbolts (IV:39) and deploys the four winds (IV:42-45), but is not designated as one who rides on the clouds.

In *Anzu*, Ninurta is the chosen champion. Though "Son of Man" would seem intrinsically inappropriate in Mesopotamian literature to describe a deity, his status as "son" of the ancient ones is very much in focus.[43] The hymn of praise that opens the first tablet recognizes that there are other beasts that Ninurta has defeated (lines 10-14),[44] but there is certainly no sequence of beasts like that which occurs in Daniel 7. Ninurta is a storm god, or, as T. Jacobsen puts it, "a thundercloud warrior,"[45] so the portrayal of him as a rider on the clouds would not be out of place (though he is not so described in *Anzu*). S. Parpola considers Ninurta a savior figure and compares him both to Christ and to Michael.[46]

3.4 Victory over The Monster

In Daniel 7 the Son of Man is given authority and dominion, but, as mentioned above, there is no battle with the beast. Instead, the authority of the beast is simply stripped away. The Son of Man is not even mentioned as having a role in the court that carries out the verdict. It is at this point in the ancient Near Eastern exemplars that the magical element emerges most clearly. Baal uses magical clubs manufactured by Kothar-wa-Ḥasis and then "drank sea" as his ritual of capture. In *Ee* Marduk is likewise provided with special weapons including the storm winds and magical spells (IV:35-62, 95-104). His ritual of destruction is to cut Tiamat in half (IV:135-40).

In *Anzu*, Ninurta approaches the beast with the winds as weapons (II:31-34), yet the initial battle involves arrows, which Anzu easily turns aside (II:61-69). In the eventual victory, the winds are used to

---

[43] Hallo and Moran, "The first tablet of the SB recension," 71.

[44] *Lugal-e*, lines 129–39; T. Jacobsen, *The Harps that Once ...* (New Haven, CT: Yale University Press, 1987) 243.

[45] T. Jacobsen, *Treasures of Darkness* (New Haven, CT: Yale University Press, 1976) 129; O. Keel and C. Uehlinger, *Gods, Goddesses and Images of God in Ancient Israel* (Minneapolis: Fortress, 1998) 291.

[46] S. Parpola, "The Assyrian Tree of Life: Tracing the Origins of Jewish Monotheism and Greek Philosophy," *JNES* 52 (1993) 161–208, esp. 204–205.

carry away Anzu's feathers so that when he summons them, Ninurta's arrows will be drawn (magically) to Anzu as well. The text becomes fragmentary at this point, so there is no record of any ritual acts to dispose of the defeated Anzu. In this category, Daniel has taken his departure from any known exemplars of chaos combat. The magical weapons and rituals of conquest of the champion are replaced by the sovereign decision of the assembly (v. 26). The role of champion is thereby eliminated from the characterization of the one who receives the kingdom. It is precisely at this point that the author of Daniel would have startled the readers who were familiar with the literary pattern of the chaos conflict genre. Since in the Ancient Near Eastern exemplars the champion is the focus of the narrative and his victory is the centerpiece of the account of his elevation, Daniel's version would appear to have the heart cut out of it. The resulting vacuum is filled with emphasis on the kingdom itself rather than on a new king.

3.5 Honoring of The Champion

In all ancient Near Eastern exemplars the champion is granted kingship and sovereignty. In Daniel 7 the kingdom is handed over to the קדשׁין, identified as the People of the Most High, but it is the Most High who is seen as having possession of the everlasting kingdom and who is obeyed and served (7:27). It is clear from the comparison of the wording of v. 27 with v. 14 that the Most High must be identified with the son of man. The argument has been made that the one like the son of man is most easily identified as Michael.[47] If this is so, the text thus avoids setting up a second divine king succeeding to the head of the pantheon as portrayed in the ancient Near Eastern exemplars. At the same time, if this is so, it is the only place in the OT where the kingdom is ruled by an angelic figure rather than a messianic figure.

The question we have thus far attempted to address is whether there are elements of Daniel 7 that can be understood most easily against the background of *Anzu* in contrast to the other exemplars of the chaos combat myth. That is, is there evidence that the author of

---

[47] Day, *God's Conflict With the Dragon and the Sea*, 167–77. J. Collins (*Daniel*, 311) points out that the description of the kingdom that is turned over to the son of man here is similar to that of the kingdom entrusted to Nebuchadnezzar in Dan 2:37 and 5:18.

Daniel demonstrates specific use of the elements of *Anzu* as one of many exemplars of the chaos combat pattern, or does he simply reflect *Anzu* secondarily because of its use in *Ee*? Is there sufficient basis to suggest a particular and primary use of *Anzu* by identifying motifs that are not present in other exemplars? To determine this, we must identify which elements in Daniel 7 suggest specific knowledge of any of the various exemplars.

4. EXEMPLARS

4.1 Baal and Yamm

The portrait of the Ancient of Days in Daniel 7 is more likely to have been drawn from a West Semitic exemplar than from Mesopotamia. The Mesopotamian exemplars fill the role of the Ancient of Days with a series of gods brought forth to designate a champion. There is nothing to match the description the text offers of this august figure. Even the Ugaritic material, however, does not contain many points of contact with the text of Daniel 7. The description of El as the "father of years" occurs only four times,[48] none of which are in the tale of the conflict between Baal and Yamm. It is supplied, however, with good reason, at the end of column iii, line 6.[49] El is occasionally described as having gray hair,[50] but not white. If the author of Daniel is drawing on Canaanite literary traditions for the Ancient of Days, it is not just the chaos conflict material that he is using. There is very little in the Baal and Yamm account specifically that is reflected in Daniel. The cloudrider designation of the champion is also most closely associated with the Canaanite material.

4.2 Enuma Elish

Elements of Daniel 7 that show closest association to *Enuma Elish* include the churning of the waters and the eleven associates of Tiamat, corresponding to the eleven horns connected to the fourth beast in Daniel 7. The representation of the enemy in two figures (the fourth beast and the little horn) is also most closely paralleled

---

[48] *CTA* 1.iii.24; 4.iv.24; 6.i.36; 17.vi.49; see A. J. Ferch, "Daniel 7 and Ugarit: A Reconsideration," *JBL* 99 (1980) 75–86, esp. 82.

[49] J. Gibson, *Canaanite Myths and Legends* (Edinburgh: T&T Clark, 1977) 37.

[50] Day, *God's Conflict With the Dragon and the Sea*, 161.

here (Tiamat and Qingu). The fact that Qingu, rather than Tiamat, has possession of the Tablet of Destinies, would be most closely reflected in the little horn rather than the fourth beast trying to change the sacred seasons and the law.

4.3 Anzu

The element that most evokes the tale of Anzu is the monster. Besides his portrayal, the boastful words in Daniel 7 are probably more closely related to Anzu than to the other exemplars in that they center on speaking against his opponents and wielding the Tablet of Destinies. In Daniel 7, there are no demands being made as in *Baal and Yamm*, and there is no bragging of high status as Tiamat does on behalf of Qingu.

4.4 Daniel

There are, of course, also elements in Daniel 7 that are not represented in any of the exemplars. These could be classified into three categories. First would be those elements that have good cause to be considered representatives of Daniel's creativity. As an example, we have already mentioned the vacuum surrounding the issue of the champion. Perhaps in the same category would be elements such as the three kings that are deposed (7:24). The second category would be comprised of motifs that are recognizable from ancient Near Eastern sources, but drawn from outside the exemplars of the chaos conflict genre. In this category would be the sequence of four beasts. A third category contains those minor details that would hardly have served as an occasion for the author's creative energy. These might include the river of fire flowing from the throne and the great throng that attends the Ancient of Days (7:10). Perhaps these details are drawn from sources that are no longer extant. Despite the existence of these three categories, however, the author's originality is most frequently evident not in what motifs he includes or does not include, but the way he arranges and adapts the various motifs to his use.

The chart on the facing page will summarize the points of comparison of these four exemplars that emerge from the sea of ancient literature:

ELEMENT/MOTIF	BAAL & YAMM	ENUMA ELISH	ANZU	DANIEL 7
Monster	None (Yamm is personified sea)	Tiamat with Qingu	Anzu	4th beast and the little horn
From sea	Personified sea	Waters churned, primordial sea	Derived from sea	Emerges from sea
Revolt	Challenge and demand	Seeks to overthrow gods	Seeks to control gods	Wages war against holy ones
Tablet	none	Entrusted to Qingu by Tiamat	Stolen by Anzu	Little horn attempts to wield power of the sort often connected to a Tablet
Boastful words	Makes demands	Naming Qingu king	Against the gods	Speaks boastfully against Most High
Eleven	none	11 monsters	Former opponents	11 horns
Ancient gods	El (but no description in this text)	Anshar/Ea	Enlil/Ea/Belet-ili	Ancient of Days
Champion	Baal	Marduk	Ninurta	One like a son of man/Most High
Victory	Two divine weapons cast out Yamm	Divine weapons and spells kill Tiamat	Trick used to draw arrow to Anzu	Little horn judicially stripped of power
Honor	Promised everlasting kingdom	Chief of the gods	Chief of the gods	Everlasting kingdom

5. CONCLUSIONS

None of the exemplars of the chaos conflict genre are capable of offering an explanation for all of the elements in Daniel 7. Instead we have seen evidence that the author of Daniel was familiar with and used a number of the exemplars in putting this chapter together. If Daniel 7 is not borrowed whole from a single known tradition, we must either assume that it reflects a single exemplar that is not extant, or that it is drawing liberally from several traditions. It would be useless speculation to suggest a non-extant single source, for then we would have to attribute to that hypothetical source the same kind of creativity that we could just as easily consider for Daniel itself. If we have no evidence to conclude that Daniel was taken whole from a known or unknown exemplar, then we can begin to investigate Daniel's use of his sources. There is no need to attempt to build a case for a unilateral and exclusive stream of tradition. All evidence points to Daniel 7 being a conflated and eclectic account. If this is true, it is useless to deny the influence of one exemplar or another because of differences between it and Daniel.[51] Differences would naturally occur when the author chose to use motifs from one tradition over another. The differences only demonstrate that Daniel 7 is not just a recension of some other ancient work.

Conflation is evidenced in a number of places in Daniel 7. Examples would include: (1) Characterization of the rebellion featuring both speaking against the Most High (with *Ee*) and oppressive threats (with *Anzu*). (2) The eleven as being under the fourth beast (with Tiamat and her crew) and successive opponents (Ninurta's conquests). (3) A characterization of the Ancient of Days in terms that show some similarity to the El traditions—but this characterization also combines several roles into one, mostly from the Mesopotamian traditions, as he serves as head of the Assembly, mediator of the solution, and brings about the defeat of the rebel.

Although many the elements of Daniel 7 suggest its conflated and eclectic nature vis à vis the ancient Near Eastern materials, the eclectic use of motifs traceable to various exemplars of the chaos combat myth is only the beginning of the shaping of chapter 7. The parallels that exist, whatever the list includes, cannot be used to read between the lines of Daniel 7 because there is such extensive repackaging in Daniel. While topoi, motifs, and patterns from the mythology are all used, the complexity of Daniel 7's reflection of the chaos combat paradigm, added to its own unique features and admixtures, demands that it be treated as an independent exemplar. This is expressed also in the conclusions of J. J. Collins:

> We must bear in mind that whoever composed Daniel 7 was a creative author, not merely a copyist of ancient sources. It should be no surprise that his composition is a new entity, discontinuous in some respects with all its sources. What is significant is whether there are also aspects of the text that are rendered more intelligible when considered in the context of the proposed background.[52]

---

[51] Consequently, Ferch ("Daniel 7 and Ugarit," 75–86) may have succeeded in demonstrating that Daniel 7 shows considerable independence from the Ugaritic traditions, but has not ruled out some usage of Ugaritic traditions intermixed with a number of other traditions in Daniel 7.

[52] See Collins, *Daniel*, 281–82. This direction is consistent with Collins' earlier

To the parallels previously adduced in commentaries (from *Baal and Yamm* and *Ee*) we may now add the precursors of *Ee*, *Anzu* (and possibly even *Labbu*). Previously Daniel has converted mythological motifs to historical contexts (for example, the world tree in Nebuchadnezzar's dream in chapter 4), but now his conversion has moved through history into visions of the future, where apocalypticism is going to standardize the transformation of mythological imagery. This eschatologization of myth[53] is accomplished not by depending solely on a single exemplar, but by an eclectic use of exemplars that were creatively merged into Daniel's own theologically unique chaos combat myth.

It is not unprecedented for a biblical author to turn mythological traditions into historical expectations. For instance, the biblical Day of YHWH motif represents an expectation (at times imminent, at times eschatological) that Yahweh will right wrongs and establish justice, ushering in a time of stability and security, though his judgment of the wicked will involve significant disruption of society, and even the cosmos. Similar concepts and concerns are represented in the myth and ritual that surrounds the New Year's enthronement festival in Babylon.[54] Examples such as Isaiah 27 and Ezekiel 32 could also be given to demonstrate the Bible's conversion of mythological motif to historical expectation established through prophetic proclamation.[55] There is no reason to think that Daniel has simply tried to rework something like *Enuma Elish* or *Anzu*. He has rather used them, and probably several others, to enrich the apocalyptic imagery that becomes his own visionary masterpiece. This has long

---

contention that our understanding of the sources of apocalypticism should favor a generic approach rather than a genetic one: *The Apocalyptic Imagination* (2nd ed., Grand Rapids: Eerdmans, 1998) 19–20.

[53] Day, *God's Conflict With the Dragon and the Sea*, 177.

[54] Though I agree with Mowinckel's identification of similarities, I am not thereby adopting his view of the Day of the Lord as an integral part of an Israelite New Year's or Enthronement celebration.

[55] It is likely that ancient Myth may also have a historical connection, but it is more inclined to represent and even celebrate historical realities of the past—and perhaps even hopes for the present—rather than to frame specific historical expectations of the future. So in *DDD* ("Nimrod," 1181–86, esp. 1182–83), C. Uehlinger remarks that Ninurta's exploits and conquests mirror "the political and cultural antagonism between Mesopotamia and the northeastern mountain regions, ... claiming divine protection and superiority for the Mesopotamian civilization."

been recognized as a *modus operandi* of apocalypticism.[56] R. Bauckham in his masterful studies on the Book of Revelation notes that John

> often uses common apocalyptic traditions in highly creative ways and develops the conventions of the literary genre for his own purposes and by means of his own literary genius.[57]

We could observe the same for Daniel as he works in the chaos conflict genre. As Collins notes, "Ultimately the meaning of any given work is constituted not by the sources from which it draws but by the way in which they are combined."[58]

What is the relevance of Anzu to Daniel 7? It has alerted us to yet another level of literary awareness on the part of the author of Daniel. Far from suggesting that other alleged sources be abandoned with Anzu being posited as the source from which Daniel 7 has been derived, this study has hopefully shown us once and for all that Daniel 7 ought not be dismissed as an example of cheap plagiarism or vitiated as an ill-disguised and haphazard patchwork quilt. Instead, it ought to be recognized as an informed and articulate literary mosaic whose author has assimilated and mastered a wide spectrum of literary traditions in order to transform them to his own theological will and purpose. Perhaps the insight of D. Damrosch could also appropriately apply to Daniel:

> Ordinarily, the literary history of a major text provides a ringing affirmation of the greatness of the text and its author; our appreciation of Shakespeare's creativity is only enhanced by the study of his sources, whose material seems to us to have been lying inertly, awaiting the quickening force of his art.[59]

6. SELECT BIBLIOGRAPHY

Batto, B. *Slaying the Dragon* (Louisville, KY: Westminster/John Knox Press, 1992).

Clifford, R. J. *Creation Accounts in the Ancient Near East and in the Bible* (CBQMS 26; Washington, DC: Catholic Biblical Association, 1994).

---

[56] So, for instance, its elaboration in D. S. Russell, *The Method and Message of Jewish Apocalyptic* (Philadelphia: Westminster, 1964) 122–27.

[57] R. Bauckham, *The Climax of Prophecy* (Edinburgh: T & T Clark, 1993) xii.

[58] Collins, *The Apocalyptic Imagination*, 20.

[59] D. Damrosch, *The Narrative Covenant* (San Francisco: Harper and Row, 1987) 298.

Cross, F. M. *Canaanite Myth and Hebrew Epic* (Cambridge, MA: Harvard University Press, 1973).

Day, J. *God's Conflict With the Dragon and the Sea* (Cambridge: Cambridge University Press, 1985).

Emerton, J. A. "The origin of the Son of Man imagery" *JTS* 9 n.s. (1958) 225–42.

Ferch, A. J. "Daniel 7 and Ugarit: A Reconsideration," *JBL* 99 (1980) 75–86.

Forsyth, N. *The Old Enemy: Satan and the Combat Myth* (Princeton: Princeton University Press, 1987) 48–54.

George, A. "Sennacherib and the Tablet of Destinies," *Iraq* 48 (1986) 133–46.

Hallo, W. W. and Moran, W. "The first tablet of the SB recension of the Anzu Myth," *Journal of Cuneiform Studies* 31 (1979) 65–115.

Lewis, T. J. "CT 13.33-34 and Ezekiel 32: Lion-dragon myths," *JAOS* 116 (1996) 28–47.

Lambert, W. G. "Ninurta Mythology in the Babylonian Epic of Creation," in K. Hecker and W. Sommerfeld (eds.), *Keilschriftliche Literaturen. Ausgewälte Vorträge der XXXII. Rencontre assyriologique internationale* (Berliner Beiträge zum Vorderen Orient 6; Berlin: Dietrich Reimer, 1986).

Porter, P. *Metaphors and Monsters: A Literary-Critical Study of Daniel 7 and 8* (ConB 20; Lund: Gleerup, 1983).

PART THREE

ISSUES IN INTERPRETATION OF SPECIFIC PASSAGES

THE VISIONS OF DANIEL

REINHARD G. KRATZ

1. THE COMPOSITION OF THE BOOK OF DANIEL

The book of Daniel divides stylistically into two halves: the third-person narratives of chapters 1–6 and the first-person visions of chapters 7–12. Whereas in the first part Daniel is able to guess and interpret dreams and to decipher the writing on the wall, in the second part he becomes a recipient of visions which he does not understand and for whose meaning he is dependent upon the *angelus interpres*. According to the chronology of the book, however, Daniel does both at the same time. 7:1 and 8:1 run parallel with chapter 5; 9:1 and 11:1 with chapter 6; and 10:1 with 1:21 and 6:29. Nevertheless, in the first part as a rule he converts gentile kings whom he serves to the highest God, while in the second part he foresees their downfall. This role-change represents more than just the story's dramatization. Here, just as in the shift from Hebrew to Aramaic in 2:4 and in the transition from chapter 7 to chapter 8, the formation of the book of Daniel begins to reveal itself.[1]

If change of style is used as the criterion, it is clear that the visions form a supplement to the older collection of narratives. Complicating the matter somewhat is the fact that this does not correspond with the shift in language. The situation is least problematic in chapters 7–8, where the boundaries of the language coincide with the boundaries of the textual units. Chapter 7 is accordingly the initial supplement which looks back chronologically behind chapter 6 for the first time and changes Daniel's role while retaining the language of the narrative. Chapters 8–12 likewise form the second supplement, which presupposes the role change and contains additional visions in the language of Scripture. In contrast, the language in 2:4a changes quite abruptly in the middle of the sentence as indicated by

---

[1] See G. Hölscher, "Die Entstehung des Buches Daniel," *TSK* 92 (1919) 113–38; R. G. Kratz, *Translatio imperii. Untersuchungen zu den aramäischen Danielerzählungen und ihrem theologiegeschichtlichen Umfeld* (WMANT 63; Neukirchen-Vluyn: Neukirchener Verlag, 1987) 11–76.

the gloss אַרְמִית.[2] Thus we do not have here a case of a redactional interpolation, but rather one of a secondary alteration. The most plausible explanation is that 1–2:4a represents a translation from the Aramaic (and partial glossing) in connection with the addition of the Hebrew visions of chapters 8–12.[3]

The addition of the visions has left its traces not only in the language in 1:1-2:4a. As in chapter 7, Nebuchadnezzar's dream in chapter 2 is about the four kingdoms and their replacement by the kingdom of God. As are all the visions in chapters 7–12, chapter 2 is dated exactly to the year (2:1) and continues until "the end of days" (2:28). When considered on internal grounds, these references as a whole prove to be secondary.[4] The dating in 2:1aα is calculated from the statement in 1:1 and 5 (Joiakim's 3rd year + 3 years), but also contradicts the three years in 1:5 and is not necessary before the beginning of the story in 2:1aβ. In anticipation of v. 29, Dan 2:28 aβγb (or vv. 27b-28) turns the simple phrases מה די להוא אחרי דנה and מה די להוא into the eschatological expression מה די להוא באחרית יומיא. Finally, the stone in 2:34-35, which smites the statue and grows there into a mountain that fills the whole earth, has in vv. 31-45 two competing interpretations: (a) the two succeeding kingdoms in v. 39, the first of which is smaller than Nebuchadnezzar, and the second which "rules over the whole earth;" and (b) the kingdom of God in v. 44, which destroys all preceding kingdoms and rules for eternity. According to the first interpretation, the statue represents the Babylonian kingdom, and the individual body parts and metals represent the Babylonian kings; according to the second interpretation, the metals symbolize the kingdoms of the world. The first interpretation (v. 39) agrees with v. 37 and continues in v. 45 without seams. This is the original interpretation, which runs hand in hand with the doctrine of the three kingdoms[5] in the framework of the collection Daniel 1–6 (cf. 1:1, 21; 5:25-28; 6:29). The second interpretation completely alters the symbols. It adds the numeration and interpretation of the empires to the individual metals in 2:39 in

---

[2] Omitted in 1QDan[a]; cf. Ezra 4:7.

[3] See H. Preiswerk, *Der Sprachenwechsel im Buche Daniel* (Dissertation, Bern; 1902-3).

[4] See Kratz, *Translatio*, 55–70.

[5] For this and for the origin of the doctrine of four/five kingdoms, see Kratz, *Translatio*, 197–222.

order to prepare for the insertion of a fourth kingdom in vv. 40-43, and of the kingdom of God (in v. 44), which puts an end to the excesses to the former. The opposition of the fourth empire and the kingdom of God also dominates the vision in chapter 7, and both the horns in chapters 7–8 and the kings of the North and South in chapter 11 correspond to the toes in 2:40-44.

The existing form of the book is thus based on an extensive revision and completion of the older, also redacted, collection of Aramaic Daniel tales in chapters 1–6.[6] The additions in chapter 2 and supplements in chapters 7–12 have one thing in common: all are oriented to the end-time during the reign of King Antiochus IV Epiphanes. The toes in 2:41-43, the horns in chapters 7 and 8, the calculation of the 70 years in chapter 9, and the outline of history in chapter 11 all relate to this king and the sacrilege that he committed against the people of God and the Temple in Jerusalem between 169-164 BCE. In specific details the descriptions certainly deviate from one another, which is partly determined by traditio-historical factors.[7] Nevertheless, this factor does not account for all details, such as why in the visions almost the same thing is repeated successively in three or four different ways. Jürgen-Christian Lebram investigated this question with reference to the character of King Antiochus. In doing so he discovered various typologies, which in his commentary he assigned to Antiochus III and IV and to three literary layers.[8] Other before and after Lebram have arrived at different literary solutions. These differ from one another in that some reckon with extensive redactional expansions in the same

---

[6] What I mean here is developed further in my *Translatio*; "Reich Gottes und Gesetz im Danielbuch und im werdenden Judentum," in A. S. van der Woude (ed.), *The Book of Daniel in the Light of New Findings* (BETL 56, Leuven: Leuven University Press and Peeters, 1993) 435–79. As far as the dating is concerned, I gladly concede to O. Kaiser the half century; see his *Grundriß der Einleitung in die kanonischen und deuterokanonischen Schriften des Alten Testaments 2* (Gütersloh: Gütersloher Verlagshaus, 1994) 167–68.

[7] For example, J. J. Collins, *The Apocalyptic Vision of the Book of Daniel* (HSM 16; Missoula, MT: Scholars Press, 1977) 95–122. K. Koch offers a survey in *Das Buch Daniel* (EdF 144; Darmstadt: Wissenschaftliche Buchgesellschaft, 1980) 113–18.

[8] J. C. H. Lebram, "König Antiochus im Buch Daniel," *VT* 25 (1975) 737–72; idem, *Das Buch Daniel* (ZBK.AT 23; Zürich: Theologischer Verlag Zurich, 1984) 18–25, 84, 92–93.

book,[9] and others with the insertion of separate pieces from foreign contexts.[10] Closer examination reveals that the visions are redactional expansions which need to be more strongly differentiated. When this is done, the traditio-historical differentiation will actually be seen as indicative of literary differentiation. As a kind of midrash to the Daniel narratives, the visions accumulate successively. The whole work is a textbook example of inner-Biblical exegesis, which always feeds from two sources: the direct literary context and the other authoritative writings of the later canon.[11]

2. THE FOUR BEASTS AND THE SON OF MAN (DANIEL 2 AND 7)

The narratives Daniel 1–6,[12] which depict the career of Daniel and his friends in the courts of Babylonian, Median and Persian kings, form the point of departure for our analysis. As members of the Gola they are trained in Chaldean sciences and made fit for service in the royal court. They withstand their probationary tests due to divine help, and this in spite of the difficulties caused by kosher restrictions. Proving themselves to be so superior, these Jewish men incur the envy of their gentile competitors. This cannot, however, prevent their success with the gentile king. They win royal affection

---

[9] Hölscher, "Entstehung," 133–34; M. Noth, "Zur Komposition des Buches Daniel," *TSK* 89/99 (1926) 143–63, repr. in his *Gesammelte Studien zum Alten Testament II* (TB 39; München: Kaiser, 1969) 11–28; Kratz, *Translatio*, 41–42. For a different description of the development, see J. G. Gammie, "The Classification, Stages of Growth and Changing Intentions in the Book of Daniel," *JBL* (1976) 191–204; B. Hasslberger, *Hoffnung in der Bedrängnis. Eine form-kritische Untersuchung zu Dan 8 und 10–12* (ATAT 4; St Ottilien: EOS, 1977).

[10] H. Junker, *Untersuchungen über literarische und exegetische Probleme des Buches Daniel* (Bonn: Peter Hanstein, 1932); H. L. Ginsberg, *Studies in Daniel* (TSJTSA 14; New York: Jewish Theological Seminary, 1948); idem, "The Composition of the Book of Daniel," *VT* 4 (1954) 246–75; A. Jepsen, "Bemerkungen zum Danielbuch," *VT* 11 (1961) 386–91; L. F. Hartman and A. A. Di Lella, *The Book of Daniel* (AB 23; New York: Doubleday, 1978) 11–14.

[11] Cf. I. L. Seeligmann, "Voraussetzungen der Midraschexegese," *Congress Volume, Copenhagen 1953* (VTSup 1; Leiden: Brill, 1953) 150–81, esp. 170–71; L. M. Fishbane, *Biblical Interpretation in the Bible* (Oxford: University Press, 1985) 479–95; M. A. Knibb, "'You are indeed wiser than Daniel.' Reflections on the Character of the Book of Daniel," in van der Woude (ed.), *Daniel in the Light of New Findings*, 399–411.

[12] 1:1-2:4a Aramaic and without the additions 2:1aα, (27b-) 28aβγb, 39 (only תליתיא and נחשא ד׳), 40–44.

and patronage both in the competition for the interpretation of dreams and riddles, which depends on wisdom (chapters 2, 4 and 5), as also in the contentious questions of Jewish confession, which depends upon loyalty to God and the king (chapters 3 and 6). Not just the life and confession of the four Jewish heroes are at stake here, but also the life of the king and the survival of his empire; for in working for themselves and the kingdom of God, the Jews of the Gola also work for the kingdom of the world. Provided that this is realized by the gentile rulers, whom the God of heaven has ordained to rule for the well-being of all people and especially for the Jews, the empire and the kingdom of God will coexist in perfect harmony. The spirit of this narrative collection is summed up by the hymnic pieces: the prayer of thanksgiving on the lips of Daniel (2:20-23); the confession to the highest God on the lips of the gentile kings (2:47; 3:28-29; 3:31-33/4:31-34 [5:18ff.]); and also the summarizing edict in 6:26-28, which brings the prolonged conflict between the "law of the Medes and Persians" and the "law of God" to a satisfying end for all sides concerned. In keeping with this, the collection concludes in 6:29 as it began in 1:21 with a reference to Cyrus of Persia representing redemption to the Babylonian Gola. It is taken from 2 Chr 36:22-23/Ezra 1: "So this Daniel prospered in the reign of Darius the Mede and in the reign of Cyrus the Persian."

The collection Daniel 1–6 contains two exceptions which confirm the rule: the hubris of Nebuchadnezzar in chapter 4 and the sacrilege of Belshazzar in chapter 5. Then in chapter 7 the exceptions suddenly become the rule. The reader is taken back once more to the first year of Belshazzar's reign (7:1), and not without reason, for the beginning of the end of the Babylonian rule heralds the end of the kingdoms of the world.

Much energy has been devoted, although without much success, to finding analogies between ancient Near Eastern mythology and the strange list of beasts 7:4-8 and the "Son of man" 7:13-14. Yet in devoting attention to the book itself, one discovers that the imagery actually derives from chapter 4, and that most of the formulations were borrowed from chapters 1–6.[13] The list of beasts can be explained via the combination of Daniel 4 with Hos 13:7-8. While Nebuchadnezzar is only temporarily transformed into a beast (4:12-

---

[13] For the following compare the individual proofs in Kratz, *Translatio*, 43–48; idem, "Reich Gottes und Gesetz," 449–50.

13, 20, 22, 29-30), the empires in Daniel 7 assume a lasting beastly form (cf. Prov 28:15). The *passivum divinum* in 7:4-6 makes it clear that these empires do not operate through their own strength but rather through God's dispensation; this is why they assume the form of the divine likenesses in Hos 13:7-8 (lion, panther, bear). They are then embellished with features from Daniel 2 and 4, distributed to the first three beasts or empires: the process of removal from power and reinstatement based on chapter 4; the eagle based on 4:30; the heart of man based on 4:13; 5:21; flesh instead of grass for food based on 4:9, 22, 29-30;[14] and the four wings and four heads together with the bestowal of reign based on 2:37-39.

The fourth beast is not identified, and is completely different from the first three (7:7). The description is nonetheless also informed from chapters 1–6: It demands fear as did the statue in 2:31, the king in 5:19, and Daniel's God in 6:27—yet it is even more terrifying. This beast is just as strong as God's miracle in 3:33 and the divinely-bestowed reign in 2:37; 4:19. Its strength, however, manifests itself —as in 2:40—in the hardness of iron and in destructive action. The qualities of the fourth beast are those of the empire itself, yet in perverted form. What had served the order and welfare of the whole earth in Daniel 1–6[15] raises itself in the character of the fourth beast against the whole earth and therefore against the highest God, who bestows or withdraws dominion for the well-being of the entire earth. And it is not until the fourth beast and empire, respectively, that the first three empires become evil and suffer more or less the same fate in the eschatological judgment (7:11-12, 17-18, 26). The historical succession of the empires merges together into a unified world power, which is withdrawn not only temporarily (as in chapter 4), or in a single case (as in chapter 5), but rather collectively and definitively. The differences in the depiction of the first three beasts (7:4-6) and their fate (7:12), when compared with that of the fourth beast (7:7, 11, 19ff.), take into account the positive experiences of Daniel and his friends with the world empires in chapters 1–6. However, due to the character of the fourth empire,

---

[14] The voracity of the second beast (Media) is perhaps an allusion to the lions' den in Daniel 6; the strange raising up "on one side"—in contrast to the full raising of the first beast in 7:5—corresponds to the relation of the second kingdom with the first in 2:39a.

[15] Cf. 2:37-39; 3:31-33; 4:7-9, 17-19, 27, 31-34; 5:18-19.

the other empires also end up in the eschatological judgment.

The judgment holds session in heaven, the divine court is assembled and presided over by the "Ancient of days," and books are opened (7:9-10). This scene depicts the heavenly resolution of chapter 4. The designation for the deity corresponds to the "end of days" of 2:28 and presents him as the Lord of time (cf. 2:21 and 4:13, 20, 22, 29, 31); accordingly, with features recalling Ezekiel 1, it could have been created ad hoc. After the judgment the kingdom of God arrives, and it is entrusted to one "like a human being" (7:13-14). The human countenance of this divine reign stems also from Daniel 4, esp. v. 13 (5:21), and is nothing other than the opposite of the bestial countenance of the world empires. The "Son of man" as an eschatological figure is yet in formation; here he is merely a symbol that emerges from this opposition and completely represents the kingdom of God. According to the vision's interpretation, he is identical with the "saints of the Most High" (7:18, 27). On the basis of 4:10, 14, 20, 22 and the scene in 7:9-10, 16, the "Son of man" is to be identified as an angelic creature.[16] Those who in chapter 4 judge Nebuchadnezzar's fate become themselves inheritors of the kingdom in chapter 7. The wording has been taken from 2:37-38; 4:19, 33; 5:18-19 and 2:44; 3:33; 4:31; 6:27.

Moreover, Daniel becomes in chapter 7 a visionary whose night dreams are not enlightening (2:19) but confusing, and who does not handle inquiries but rather must inquire. The formulation of the vision's frame in 7:1-2, 15-16, 28 cites relevant phrases from chapters 2 and 4, esp. 4:2, 16 and 2:45b (for 7:16). Dreams and visions, which to this point have plagued Nebuchadnezzar, now plague Daniel himself. The role which Daniel once played for the king is now played for Daniel himself by someone from the heavenly scene.

It is apparent that chapter 7 was never an independent text, not even in parts, but was in its substance and from the beginning composed with the context of chapters 1–6 in mind. But chapter 7 is also not the original continuation of chapters 1–6; even the literary connections prove that the original narrative collection was newly understood and interpreted in chapter 7. Chapters 1–6 and 7 relate to one another as text and commentary, except that the commentary in narrative form is added as a flashback to the time of chapter 5. What stands historically behind this postscript is the downfall of the

---

[16] For more reasons see Kratz, *Translatio*, 27–31.

Persian empire, Alexander's final expedition and the division of his empire into the rival states of the Diadochi; this historical reality has shattered the theological conception of chapters 1–6. The author of the supplement condemns the world empires and relegates the kingdom of God to eschatology. Thus he allows the king's document in 6:26-28 to be followed by Daniel's document that had been drafted in the first person (7:1, 28a). This document introduces a knowledge of Daniel which the Daniel of chapters 1–6 does not yet have, and which lends the narratives a new meaning. In order not to make Daniel and the reader wait too long and to inform them immediately, the additions considered above are introduced in chapter 2: the dating in v. 1; the eschatological crisis in v. 28; and the completion of vv. 40-44, which relates the metals of the statue to the empires and numbers them consecutively (2:39) and explains the stone from heaven as the eternal kingdom of God. The tensions generated by the writer of these additions, in order to harmonize the mix of iron and clay with the hardness of the fourth kingdom, plainly show that a secondary point was added to the vision scene.[17] In so doing the division of the states of the Diadochi came to the writer's aid. The literary and material contacts of these additions with chapter 7 are so tight that it is easy to think them to have the same author,[18] who intimates already in chapter 2 what he is formulating independently in chapter 7 in accordance with the model of chapter 4.

Of course, everything in 2:40-44 and chapter 7 cannot be charged to this author's account. For example, the (ten) toes and their mixing in 2:41-43 are an addition to an addition.[19] For the author of the first supplement, the iron and clay feet are only a matter of the durability and striking power of iron (as in 7:7, 19, 23):

And a fourth kingdom will arise … (2:40).
It will be a divided kingdom, yet there will be in it the strength of iron, forasmuch as you saw the feet partly of iron and partly of clay" (2:41aβ-bα, 42a).

The author of the second supplement inserted the toes and interprets the mix of metals after chapter 11 as denoting the unstable marriage

---

[17] In connection with this the dream report may have also been glossed. In particular, vv. 34-35 seem to be somewhat overfilled. The feet of iron and clay, however, cannot be removed (v. 34). For a different opinion, see Noth, "Zur Komposition," 23–24.

[18] Cf. especially 2:40 with 7:7, 19, 23; and Kratz, *Translatio*, 48–55.

[19] Kratz, *Translatio*, 32–35.

politics of the Diadochi (2:41aα, bβγ, 42a "and the toes," 42b, 43).

As G. Hölscher and many others recognized long ago, the ten horns and the little horn in Daniel 7 likewise drop out of the structural and literary framework of the vision of the four beasts and the Son of man.[20] The elimination of the additions to the vision in 7:7bβ, 8, 11a is clear-cut. As to the interpretation of the vision, the question may be posed whether the entire section 7:19-27, which seems superfluous after 7:17-18, was subsequently inserted. However, the separate interpretation of the beast in 7:19, 23, 26-27 is anticipated in the vision, and originally had nothing to do with the horns. It is certainly feasible that there was once an original form which concluded with 7:17-18, 28a, and which did not yet contain the separate interpretation of the fourth beast. This could have then been sparked by the confusion that, while the beasts successively enter and exit, they are mentioned in one breath at the beginning (7:2-3) and in the interpretation at 7:17. Yet in the judgment scene just the opposite occurs. Here the fate of the first three beasts in 7:12 could have been subsequently inserted on the basis of the collective interpretation 7:17, and according to the model of the simultaneous destruction of all worldly kingdoms in 2:34-35, 44-45. In any case, the horn-revision in 7:7bβ, 8, 11a, 20-22, 24-25, which is similar to the supplement of the toes in 2:41-43, is younger than the expanded original text of chapter 7 (vv. 1-7bα, 9-10, 11b, 12, 13-14, 15-16, 17-18, 19, 23, 26-27, 28a) which belongs to the same stratum as the first supplement in 2:1, 28, 39-44.

The distinctive character of the fourth beast (7:7bα) is passed on to the little horn (7:24) which, like the fourth kingdom, surpasses three of its ten predecessors. Presumably this revision also stems from more than one hand. Only vv. 20, 24, 25aα, 26 agree with 7bβ, 8, 11a, while the remaining verses 21-22, 25aβb stand alone. The saints, on whom the little horn wages war, are interpreted as the representatives of God's people. The horn-revision does not derive from the literary context with chapters 1-6; but is related to the addition in chapter 8, just as the toes in 2:41-43 are related to chapter 11.

3. THE HORNS AND THE LITTLE HORN (DANIEL 8)

Daniel's first-person written report, introduced in 7:1 in narrative form, concludes with 7:28a. As the second introduction after 7:1 in

---

[20] *Ibidem*, 21–32.

7:2aα and the afterthought in 7:28b indicate, the first-person report should continue, and this is what happens in chapter 8 in Hebrew: Daniel is still anxious after the interpretation and retains the matter in his heart. Two years later, in the third year of Belshazzar, he becomes the recipient of another vision which he expressly relates to the first. The scheme is the same as that of the first vision: after the introduction (8:1-2), the vision (8:3-12) follows in several scenes; after Daniel's expression of horror and request for understanding (8:15-19) a detailed two-part interpretation in 8:20-22, 23-25 is revealed; and two concluding remarks are made in 8:26 and 8:27.

It already becomes obvious that chapter 8 was thought of as a supplement and was conceived according to the pattern of chapter 7; the hinge made especially with this in mind is found at 7:28b. Basically we have here a case of a Hebrew targum to the first vision, to which we should perhaps already connect the translation of 1:1–2:4. Both of these give the Aramaic book of Daniel chapters 1–7 a new Hebrew framework. The second vision expressly states what chapter 7 says only cryptically: that the vision concerns the change from the Medo-Persian empire to Alexander's empire and its division into the individual states of the Diadochi (8:20-22 according to 8:3-8). What is said about the little horn in 8:9-14, 23-25, which corresponds to the horn revision in 7:7-8, 20-22, 24-25, remains cryptic; yet several additional details are disclosed. The kingdom of God is no longer the topic; everything is about the identity, the actions and the fate of both last world powers which mark the "end."

Several additional details seem to have accrued only after time. With respect to the framing sections we must presume that such is the case for vv. 2, 16, 18-19 and 27b. Verse 2 goes to the trouble of adapting the localization of the vision to the contents, and of fixing the appearance of the vision here to the more precisely-specified locale of vv. 3 and 6. In v. 16 Gabriel appears quite unexpectedly on the scene with Daniel and the one who "looks like a man" developed from 7:15-16. Verses 18-19 allow Daniel to fall unconscious, prostrate on the ground for the second time, so as to afterwards place him again on his feet and to qualify the information that follows—the distant time of the end (vv. 17, 26) is the time of the end of wrath. Finally, v. 27b imitates the transition in 7:28b and needs to be resumed. The original conclusion is to be found in 8:26b, 27a, which likewise imitates 7:28 but does not require a continuation. With the exception of v. 2, all of the additions exhibit deviations from the language usage that pre-dominates in chapter 8, and point forward to chapters 9–12,[21] as also do the contents.

In the relationship between vision and interpretation, the calculation of the end precisely to the day in vv. 13-14 and again in v. 26a (according to 2:45b; 7:16) are out of place. This calculation stipulates the indefinite statement in v. 26b numerically, and is secondary to the time-period in 7:25; 9:27 and 12:7 (see also 12:11, 12). Moreover, verses 8:9-12 strike us as overfilled. The masculine form in vv. 11-12a indicates a later insertion, with v. 12b being the resumption of v. 10. This insertion identifies the war of the little horn against the host of heaven with the abolition of the sacrifice by Antiochus IV. The abolition of this sacrifice does not reappear in the interpretation in vv. 23-25, but is the main point in Daniel 9 and 11.

To be sure, without vv. 11-12 the vision and the interpretation in vv. 9-10, 23-25 do not really agree. In vv. 9-10 the two-fold גדל is conspicuous, being directed first against specific geographical regions, including the Holy Land, and secondly against the host of heaven. Corresponding to this is the sacrilege against the strong and the many (vv. 23-25), based on Deut 28:50, and the insurrection against the "Prince of princes" (v. 25b). The text in vv. 23-25 is so crammed and disfigured that it is not possible to reconstruct a fitting interpretation. This is a rare case of a vision that is clearer and more concrete than its explanation. One notices here strong points of contact both with the horn-revision in chapter 7 and with the sketch of history in chapter 11. Dan 8:9-12, 23-25 thus differs significantly from vv. 3-8, 20-22 where vision and interpretation are perfectly matched; their only function is to make the vision of chapter 7 more precise with another beast-vision. My only explanation for this is that the little horn was added later in chapter 8. Whoever is not satisfied with the ending in v. 8 = 22 will not find much more in vv. 9-10, 11-12, 23-25. The nice allusion to 2:34, 45 in 8:25bβ contains no more information about the little horn than 8:22 contains about the great one, namely, that it is broken. Here, as in the relationship of vv. 7, 10, 12 (רמס, ארצה השליך \ הפיל) and in other places;[22] this is a matter

---

[21] Compare 8:16 with 9:21; 8:18-19 with 10:9-11, 15; and 8:27b with 9:21-23; 10:1, 12ff.

[22] Compare גדל and עצם in v. 8 (of the ram v. 4) and vv. 9-10, 24-25; ולא בכחו in v. 22 (of the ram v. 7) and v. 24; also v. 4 with v. 9; and בחמת כחו in v. 6 (transferred to Antiochus IV in 11:30) with v. 19.

of literary resumption. Like the horn-revision in chapter 7, it applies the characteristics of the fourth beast to the little horn.

Let us now attempt to reconstruct the literary development and to place in perspective the many later insertions. If we may assume that the original text in chapter 8 comprises just 8:1, (2), 3-8, 15, 17, 20-22, 26b, 27a, then it is clear that the reference in v. 8 can only relate in the first instance to the (expanded) original layer of chapter 7 with the transition in v. 28. As in chapter 7 the emphasis in chapter 8 is also placed on the image section. The exchange of the beasts takes into account the anonymity of the fourth beast in chapter 7, and indicates the move toward historical refinement already in the metaphor. The ram and he-goat represent Persia and Syria in astrological geography.[23] In Daniel 8 the three beasts/kingdoms from chapter 7—which follow the first kingdom (cf. 7:1; 8:1)—are replaced with the antagonism of the two states (Media-Persia and Jawan), symbolized by the ram and the he-goat, and their rulers, symbolized by horns. The differences in the description of the beasts/kingdoms in chapter 7 are transferred to the horns in chapter 8.

The transition to the interpretation in 8:15, 17 follows quite precisely the model of 7:15-16. It is worth noting that just as the attribute "like a human being" in 7:13-14 becomes the attribute of the *angelus interpres*, so the designation "Son of man" is transferred to the seer according to the model of Ezekiel. Moreover, the new focus on the time of the end may have been inspired by Ezekiel (cf. Ezek 7:2, 3, 6; 21:30, 34).

The terse interpretation in 8:20-22 is patterned on 7:17-18, and perhaps does not yet know of the particular explanation of the fourth beast in 7:19, 23, 26-27. In place of the beasts in Daniel 7, which have become two animals with three horns in Daniel 8, the four horns appear and disperse themselves towards the four winds whence have come the four beasts of 7:2-3. The influence of Zech 2:1-4, 10 and 6:5 is possibly present here. The historical reference, of course, is to the split of Alexander's empire into the (three) states of the Diadochi. Apparently the number four has yet another purpose: with it the oversized power of the great horn is broken, and a new danger is introduced. The dénouement is missing, yet the reader knows what is happening with the four simultaneous king-doms in chapter 7, and

---

23 Cf. F. Cumont, "La plus ancienne géographie astrologique," *Klio* 9 (1909) 263–73.

what is to be expected afterwards. For this reason the vision can end at this point. The concluding note 8:26b, 27a, which imitates 7:28, attributes the literary record of the vision (7:1, 28a) to divine instructions and has Daniel returning to the business of Daniel 1–6.

The several additions to the original text in chapter 8 can be separated into two categories, the first being the additions to the vision reception in vv. 16, 18-19 and 27b, which are connected with the continuation in Daniel 9–12. The second category is the addition of the little horn together with the calculation of the end in vv. 9-12, 13-14 and vv. 23-25, 26a, which are connected with the horn-revision in chapter 7 and exhibit contacts with Daniel 9 12. It is hardly possible to make out which of these categories is earlier and which is later; I tend to regard the additions to the mode of the vision's reception as the first link to Daniel 9–12, and the horn additions as the second.

We can also not be sure about the sequence of the horn additions in chapter 7–8. The small horn is surely an extrapolation of the horns of the ram and he-goat. So much is clear and commends the assumption that it was first introduced in chapter 8, and was transposed from there to chapter 7. But an opposing scenario is also conceivable. In chapter 7 the horn has not five, but rather ten, predecessors of which three are separately named (7:7-8, 20, 24). The number 10 agrees with the toes in 2:41-43; the crushing of the three predecessors is obviously oriented to the 3 + 1 beasts in chapter 7 and to 8:7-8. Furthermore, the little horn in chapter 7 has human eyes and a mouth with which it contrasts the human countenance of the empire and the divine reign (cf. 7:4, 13-14). With its mouth the little horn blasphemes the Most High. In 7:21-22, 25 references are added describing war against the saints of the Most High (7:13-14, 18, 27) and the interference with the cosmic order—the alteration of times and laws (2:21; 6:6)—both being limited to three and one half times. These statements in vv. 7:7bβ, 8, 20, 24, 25aα manifest few points of contact with the additions in 8:9-12, 23-25, whereas 7:21-22, 25 manifest many points of contact. Vice versa, 8:24 was adapted to 7:21, 25; and 8:11-12, 13-14 were added according to 7:25. The war against the saints is the war against the holy people; the interference with the times and laws signifies the cessation of the sacrifices under Antiochus IV; the limitation to three and one-half times amounts to 2,300 evening-mornings.

The impression gained above, that the horn-revision is not homogenous, is confirmed. The additions were reciprocally touched up. Yet it remains open as to whether the little horn grew and became ever larger (cf. 8:3, 8) first in 7:7-8, 20, 24-25, or in 8:9-10, and whether the crushing of the three predecessors and the great blasphemies against the Most High in chapter 7 or the war against the three regions of the earth and the stars in 8:9-10, 23-25 (cf. Isaiah 14) form the point of departure from which everything else developed.

At any rate, both possibilities presuppose chapter 11. It is obvious that whereas we cannot understand the additions in chapters 2, 7 and 8 without chapter 11, the latter can be interpreted independently. In chapter 11 the visions of the four kingdoms (chapters 2 and 7) and of the four Diadochi (chapter 8) are taken up and brought up-to-date. On the other hand, the additions in chapters 2, 7 and 8 anticipate these expansions in both matters of content and language. For example, 2:41-43 combines the iron-clay mixture with 11:6, 17, and thus insert the toes. Moreover, seven of the ten horns in 7:7, 20-24 are possibly identical with the active kings of chapter 11: together with the three individually named predecessors, they complete the number ten.[24] The blasphemies are evidenced in 11:36. Features taken from Antiochus III[25] and IV from chapter 11, especially vv. 21, 23-24, 25, 26, 33, 36ff., are brought together with the additions in 8:9-12, 23-25, predominantly in a typological manner, so that both the celestial and mundane worlds are merged with one another.[26] The anticipation hardly stems from one and the same hand, for the differences and ambiguities, which came to be through the interpolations, are too great. Furthermore, the additions cannot be older than Daniel 10–12, since they are in themselves unintelligible, the relation of vision to interpretation is too unbalanced, and in chapter 11 it is not sufficiently clear that they are used as models. In short, the additions are not only "to be interpreted from the

---

[24] R. Hanhart, "Kriterien geschichtlicher Wahrheit in der Makkabäerzeit. Zur geschichtlichen Bedeutung der danielischen Weltreichelehre," (Theologische Existenz Heute 140; München: Kaiser, 1967, 7–22); repr. in his *Studien zur Septuaginta und zum hellenistischen Judentum* (FAT; Tübingen: Mohr-Siebeck, 1999) 137–50, esp. 142–43.

[25] Compare 8:9 with 11:16, 41, 45 (ארץ הצבי); 8:25 with 11:14, 18 (רבים), also 11:11-12.

[26] Compare, for example, 8:10, 11-12 as an interpretation of 11:33-39, 31 in view of the "prince" of 10:13, 21; 12:1.

perspective of the story of the eleventh chapter."[27] Instead, they have also been entered from there into the text of the second, seventh and eighth chapters. These additions impart the visionary appearance to the historical outline, and contribute to the theological homogeneity of Daniel 8–12 and of the "Maccabean" book of Daniel.[28]

4. THE KING OF THE SOUTH AND THE KING OF THE NORTH (DANIEL 10–12)

Dan 8:27b makes the transition from chapters 1–8 to chapters 9–12. Since G. Hölscher the relationship is usually defined in terms of chapter 9 first being added on, and chapters 10–12 somewhat later.[29] The reason for this is that in the present form of the text chapters 10–12 appear as a detailed recapitulation of Daniel (7)8–9. In reality, however, chapter 9 *intrudes* into the context of chapters 8–12. Both complexes, chapters 9 and 10–12, attribute the insight to Daniel, which is denied to him in chapter 8 (9:2, 22-23; 10:1, 11, 12, 14). In doing so, chapter 9 does not link itself directly to chapter 8, but rather via a detour through Jeremiah's 70 years, which Daniel does not understand. On the other hand, chapters 10–12 offer straightforward information on the understanding of chapter 8, while the main points in chapter 9—the 70 years and the sins—do not appear in 10–12. In the relationships between chapters 9 and 10–12,[30] the latter seems to me to be the source and the former derivative. As in the case of the relationship between chapters 10–12 and the additions in chapters 2, 7 and 8, so in chapter 11 we are at a loss for literary allusions which presuppose the preceding chapter. Yet when the relationship is construed in reverse, i.e. so that chapter 11 has directly influenced the selection of expressions in chapter 9, it is quite enlightening. Furthermore, with the expectation of the cleansing of the sanctuary (cf. 8:14), chapter 9 presupposes an advanced

---

[27] Hanhart, *Studien zur Septuaginta*, 142.

[28] See O. H. Steck, "Weltgeschehen und Gottesvolk im Buche Daniel," in D. Lührmann and G. Strecker (eds.), *Kirche. Festschrift G. Bornkamm* (Tübingen: Mohr-Siebeck, 1980) 53–78; repr. in his *Wahrnehmungen Gottes im Alten Testament. Gesammelte Studien* (TB 70; München: Kaiser, 1982) 262–90, esp. 272ff.

[29] See Kratz, *Translatio*, 41–42, 73.

[30] Compare 9:21-23 with 10:11-12, 14, 20-21; 11:2a; also 9:24 with 11:14; 9:26b with 11:10, 22, 26, 40; and 9:27 with 11:30, 32-34, 31, 36.

stage of the religious struggle. This leads to the conclusion that chapters 10–12 form the first answer to the lack of understanding in 8:27b, while chapter 9 forms the second answer.[31]

The connection of chapters 10–12 to 8 is to be found either in 10:1 or 10:2. Dan 10:1 imitates 7:1 and harks back thematically to chapter 1 (especially 1:6-7, 21), as well as to 6:29. Unlike chapters 8 and 9 and the continuation in 10:2ff., the dating is retained in narrative style. It should mark then a clear insertion corresponding to chapter 7, which does not fit as well with the continuation of chapter 8 in 10–12, and should thus probably be attributed to the interpolation in chapter 9. Dan 9:1 connects to chapter 8 in the first person, while 10:1 is a kind of resumption, re-establishing the older contact with 8:26-27 after the insertion of chapter 9 and the chronological anticipation in 9:27. The apparent intention is that the visions in chapters 7–9 should be situated before, and those in chapters 10–12 after, the end of the 70 years in the first year of Cyrus (2 Chronicles 36/Ezra 1), which has long passed, and in chapter 9 is thus temporally extended. The beginning in 10:2, on the other hand, connects without seams to 8:27: Daniel fasts because he did not understand chapter 8 (cf. 10:12).

However, this is not the only addition to chapters 10–12. The oversized vision in chapter 10, which introduces chapter 11, contains a doublet to 10:2-14 in 10:15-11:2a.[32] Like 8:18-19, 10:15ff. depicts Daniel reacting for the second time to the appearance. The awe for the *angelus interpres* increases each time: in 7:15 Daniel approaches him; in 8:15 he approaches Daniel who falls to the ground; and in 9:21-23 (8:16) and 10:2ff. the angel himself becomes the apparition and his speaking provokes intense reactions (8:18-19; 10:9, 15ff.). In accordance with the appearance in 10:2ff. and the reaction in vv. 9-11, a second reaction in 8:18-19 was inserted, and in accordance with this, 10:15ff. is once again supplemented. Within the course of the first part of the vision 10:2-14, the interjection 10:7-8, 9a, which breaks the connection of vv. 6 and 9b, may also be an addition. Per-

---

[31] See Ginsberg, "Composition," 273–75; Hasslberger, *Hoffnung in der Bedrängnis*, 397–400; also J. J. Collins, *Daniel. A Commentary on the Book of Daniel* (Hermeneia; Minneapolis: Fortress, 1993) 343: "We find this vision (i.e. Daniel 8) more fully elaborated in the angel's revelation in chaps. 10–12."

[32] According to P. David, "Daniel 11:1: A Gloss?," in van der Woude (ed.), *Daniel in the Light of New Findings*, 505–14.

haps it is on the same level of the addition of 10:15ff. (cf. vv. 8, 16).

Finally, the passages which make the *angelus interpres* into a national angel are also interpolated. The national angel, who fights side by side with Michael against the (angel-) princes of Persia and Greece, does not (yet) have a name here, whereas in 8:16 and 9:21 he is called Gabriel. Dan 10:13 disrupts the first announcement of the revelation of history of 11:2ff. in 10:12, 14, while 10:14 could also be a secondary resumption. In 10:20-11:2a the double ועתה and the double announcement of the following revelation in 10:20a and 11:2a indicate the literary seams. Either 10:20aβ-21a and 10:21-11:2a were successively added, or 10:20aβ-11:1 was stuck into 10:15-20aα; 11:2a. Moreover, the prophecy of deliverance in 12:1-3 belongs to the same level. The notion of the fight of the national angel in chapters 10 and 12 transfers the historical drama of chapter 11 to heaven and thereby agrees with additions in chapters 7 and 8— especially 7:21-22, 25; 8:9-10, 11, 24-25 (ועל שׂר שׂרים יעמד)—which, being dependent upon chapter 11, blend mundane and celestial elements. Not only Antiochus IV but also the combined world powers wage war on two levels: in heaven and on earth, against God and against the people of God.

The original conclusion of the interpretation of history is found in 12:4 and is formulated in imitation of 8:26b. Dan 12:5-12 contains supplements which concern themselves with the calculation of the end. The scene is depicted according to 8:1-2, 15ff., 26b; 10:4ff.; 12:4; and the conversation between the two angels in Zech 1:10-13. The time period in 12:7 originates in 7:25 (9:27); and in 12:11-12 the days are counted as in 8:13-14. Dan 12:5-9 is the first, 12:10, 13 the second, 12:11 the third, and 12:12 the fourth supplement, and 12:10, 12 presupposes the interpolation of 12:1-3.

According to this, the following passages form the original continuation of chapter 8: 10:2-6, 9b-12 (14) + 11:2-45 + 12:4. Because of the lack of understanding in 8:27b, Daniel begins to fast and receives another vision, again by a river (this time the Tigris). However, the vision does not repeat what was previously witnessed, what Daniel does not understand; instead, it has as its object the *angelus interpres*, who is known from 7:15-16; 8:15, 17 and who is embellished with features from Ezekiel. This means that the interpretation, which has become incomprehensible, is now itself the object of the vision. The vision occurs only in order to explain what was previously witnessed: cf, 10:11-12 (14). The contents of the

vision are the words which the angel delivers; in mind is the drama
of history in chapter 11 which chapter 8 does not newly interpret but
continues. The historical background to the lack of understanding in
8:27b, which leads to the further writing of the history, is the time
of Antiochus IV. The disturbances to the cult and the Maccabean
revolt are already in view (11:31, 34)—occurences temporally and
factually so unexpected in relation to the predictions in chapters 7–8
that they require an individual portrayal.

It is a widely-held view that an older source was incorporated into
chapter 11. J. Lebram[33] presumes also that there are additions, above
all in 11:14, 30ff., which were inserted at the moment the source was
brought into the book of Daniel. That, however, is quite improbable.
Independent from all other information in the book of Daniel,
chapter 11 is the oldest depiction of history of the Ptolemies and
Seleucids up to Antiochus IV, but presupposes the visions in chapters
7 and 8. However, the visions are not presupposed in their present
form, but in their original version, which is easy to see in that the
content of the original version of chapter 8 is recapitulated in 11:2-4
in phrases that sound almost exactly alike. The four beasts in chapter
7 and the two horns of the ram in 8:3 become the four Persian kings;
these precede Alexander's empire and the four Diadochi of 8:5-8, 22
who are scattered to the four winds. What follows is a continuation
of the history in two of the four directions of heaven, in the South
and in the North, and into the author's time when the end of
Antiochus IV is prophesied (11:40ff.). The almost simultaneous
reconsecration of the sanctuary is not (yet) mentioned.

It is not possible here to enter into a detailed discussion of the
text's formulations and statements about the Diadochi and their
significance for Palestine in the 3rd and 2nd centuries BCE. Suffice it
to say that the quite monotonous diction of the portrayal of history
may have been guided by (e.g. Egyptian) models, yet must have been
composed in one stroke and with the context of the book of Daniel in
mind. Not only do the literary connections in 10 and 11:2-4 give
reason to believe this, but also the allusions to other biblical writings,
notably Isaiah.[34] These allusions serve the purpose of reciprocal ex-

---

33 *Das Buch Daniel*, 112.

34 Compare the use of (ועבר) שׁטף in Dan 11:10, 22, 26, 40 (9:27) according
to Isa 8:8; 28:2, 15ff.; Dan 11:36 with Isa 10:22-27; Dan 10:14; 11:27, 35 with
Hab 2:3; also Dan 11:30 with Num 24:24 and above n. 11.

planation of the biblical texts: what Isaiah foretells can clarify the vision of Daniel 8, and Daniel 11 clarifies who and what is meant in the Isaianic prophecy about Asshur and Egypt. Chapters 10–12 are thus a pesher not only to chapter 8, but latently also to several predictions of older prophets that were highly relevant for the author.

5. THE SEVENTY YEARS OF JEREMIAH (DANIEL 9)

Far from being latent, the pesher in chapter 9, which was later placed between chapters 8 and 10–12, refers by name to the passage which Daniel considers: the 70 years of Jer 25:11-12; 29:10. Dan 9:1-2 quotes this passage, and 9:24, 25-27 explains it. Daniel's prayer in v. 3, which is answered in vv. 21-23 and is recited word-for-word in vv. 4-20, serves as the means of transition. The prayer does not represent a piece of tradition, as is often presumed, but is rather a literary formation that was either written simultaneously with 9:1-3, 21-27, or was written subsequently into the context.

In addition to both of the Jeremiah passages, there are allusions to Zech 1:12 (7:5) and 2 Chr 36:21 (cf. Lev 26:31ff.). The Jerusalem ruins refer back to the first passage, while the "fulfillment" of prophecy and the following qualification of the time period as Sabbath years in 9:24-27 refer back to the second passage. The occasion for the petition is an equation of the events during the reign of Antiochus IV with the year 587 BCE. Due to this equation the number of the 70 years becomes a problem. In Jeremiah they refer to the time of the Babylonian empire, and in 2 Chr 36:22-23/Ezra 1 the end of this time coincides with the "first year of Cyrus" and with the beginning of the reconstruction of the temple as predicted in Zech 1:12; 7:5. The problem arises because Daniel 1 (and 6:29) also presuppose the Chronicler's period of 70 years for Babylon until the first year of Cyrus.[35] The ever-longer delay of the restoration makes itself felt in the dating 9:1: According to the literary fiction, Daniel lives between the end of Babylon, which has already passed away, and the first year of Cyrus, which is directly at hand.

Daniel 9 solves the problem by both requalifying as well as recalculating the 70 years. In requalifying the 70 years, the time period in the meaning of Deuteronomistic theology is related to Israel herself, and is viewed as a time of sin and prolonged wrath. This is evidenced in 9:24 and elaborated upon in the prayer 9:4-20.

---

[35] See Kratz, *Translatio*, 38–40, 261–67.

In recalculating the 70 years, the time period in the meaning of
Sabbath years is stretched out to 70 weeks of years. The division into
7 + 62 + 1 is made up of 49 years for Babylon (the original "70
years" of 587 till 539 BCE), the 62 years of the Median Darius in
6:1, and the remaining final week-year. The latter period is divided
once more, yet it is not clear whether the cessation of the sacrifices
falls in the first or second half of week. The "covenant with many"
must be strong for a whole week. However one calculates it, the time
between 167-164 BCE, which dominates chapter 9, is never exactly
arrived at. The events during the reign of Antiochus IV, which are
foretold in chapters 7–8 and 10–12, cited in 9:26-27 from 11:31-35,
36, and correlated with the date of destruction of the temple in 587
BCE, have obviously a temporal significance beyond themselves for
chap-ter 9. We can even ask ourselves whether the reconsecration of
the temple, which 8:14 and 9:24 (unlike chapter 11) have as a prospect, already belongs to the past, yet with the end as still pending. In
any case, the deliverance in 12:1-3, 13 is broader in its horizon.

Moreover, chapter 9 was written as a continuation of the vision in
chapter(s) (7)–8 to which 9:21 expressly refers. The supplement of
Gabriel in 8:16 is presupposed; both passages mention the *angelus
intepres* of chapter 10 by name. In contrast to chapters 11–12,
however, it is not a question here of the historical events of the end
time, but rather of the destruction of Jerusalem and the sanctuary
and the prolongation of the judgment. The question is sparked by the
vague information in 8:26b. As in 12:8, the writer of chapter 9
relates the lack of understanding of 8:27b to the date of the end. In
search of an answer he comes across the 70 years of Jeremiah
(suggested by Daniel 1), which are are not intelligible by themselves
and whose interpretation requires an additional revelation. The
enigma of Yahweh's word in Jeremiah (9:2) can only be cleared up
by an additional, current "word" (9:21-23). "Word and vision" in
9:23, which are also here an answer to the fasting and supplications,
take the place of the verbal revelation in chapters 10–12. For this
reason they are given both a new heading in 10:1, corresponding to
chapter 9, and a new function for the full context of the visions. Both
of the headings in 9:1 and 10:1 resume the scheme of the four
kingdoms from Daniel 1–6 and are responsible for the chronological
division of the book into chapters 1–6 and 7–12. Thematically they
express the difficulty of the delay of the 70 years inasmuch as 9:1
dates shortly before, and 10:1 shortly after, the Chronicler's first

year of Cyrus. The stylistic break in 10:1, which corresponds to 7:1, divides the visions into two phases: chapters 7–9 and chapters 10–12. Chapter 9 concludes the first phase with the calculation of the end of what was seen before in chapters 7–8, and chapters 10–12 fill in substantively this period of time. The anticipation of chapters 10–12 in 9:21-27[36] contribute to the creation of an adequate replacement for the original explanation of chapter 8 in 10–12, and prepare for the following foretelling of history.

With this, both the visions in 7–8 as well as the view of history in 10–12 are stamped with a new theology. It is prompted by the exegesis of Isa 10:22-27 in Dan 11:36, which is cited not without reason in 9:27. Moreover, 8:13, 19, 23 indicate that the theology of the visions in chapter 9 is coming to a head. Not until and only in chapter 9, however, does the Deuteronomistic-shaped Jewish theology of the 2nd century BCE—which dominates the final form of the book of Daniel and is tangible in Ezra 9, Nehemiah 1 and 9 and in many other passages—assert itself in the interpretation of the time period of four kingdoms (including Antiochus IV).[37]

6. CONCLUSION

Let us recapitulate the results of our investigation of the formation of the visions of Daniel. Little by little and one after another the pieces were woven together: Daniel 1–6 is first expanded by the addition of chapter 7,[38] in the course of which the older collection of Danielic narratives is changed into an eschatological work. Chapter 8,[39] which translates the Aramaic vision of chapter 7 into Hebrew and updates it, is then made to follow upon chapters 1–7. Chapters 10–12[40] thus continue the editing of the book into the 2nd century BCE. What is particularly striking is the ever-increasing interest in the simple course of history. While Daniel 7 is still completely similar to Daniel 1–6 in both imagery and language and opposes the world empire to the kingdom of God, chapter 8 directs its attention

---

[36] See above n. 30.

[37] See Steck, "Weltgeschehen und Gottesvolk," 278–86. For a different opinion, see Collins, *Daniel*, 360.

[38] 7:1-7bα, 9-10, 11b (12), 13-14, 15-16, 17-18 (19, 23, 26, 27), 28a; 2:1aα, (27-) 28aβγb, (34-35) 39 (only תליתיא and נחשא ד), 40, 41aβ-bα, 42a, 44.

[39] 8:1 (2) 3-8, 15, 17, 20-22, 26b, 27a.

[40] 10:2-6:9b-12 (14) + 11:2-45 + 12:4.

to the world powers, and chapters 10–12 devote themselves to the politics of the day. Hand in hand with this is the increasing significance of the heavenly mediation of the vision and its interpretation. In chapters 10–12 the heavenly agent himself becomes the subject of the vision, and the mediated word takes the place of the vision and interpretation. The increasing historical precision does not pursue antiquarian novelties, but rather theological interests. Because the kingdom of God is not to be noticed in either history, as chapters 1–6 would have it, nor in the addendum to the history of the four kingdoms, as chapter 7 would have it, the ever more unbearable history itself was attributed in every detail to God's foreordination. The world kingdoms do as they please and witness success, which occurs exactly in accordance with God's plan. Everything that takes place on earth is predestined. Everything takes places just as witnessed by the seer and explained by the *angelus interpres*. And everything, when it takes place, indicates the expected end.

Dan 9:1–10:1 shares this view of things, but offers a new reason and a new calculation of the end. The course of history is as it is because Israel is still in a state of sin, and because the judgment of 587 BCE is still being executed. The history of the empires is the continuation of the destruction of Jerusalem and her sanctuary and thus God's penalty for the committed sins of his people. Chapter 9 splits the original context between chapters 8 and 10–12, and brings both visions in 7–8 to an end. After this chapters 10–12 merely fill in the details that are foreseen and foretold in 7–9. This was possibly the occasion for further additions to the text, which may have been made before or after the interpolation of chapter 9 but only after the addendum of 10–12. These additions fill out the description of the vision's reception,[41] carry back into the visions themselves the historical details of the last, decisive phase of history before the expected end,[42] transport the events on earth to heaven,[43] and count the days until the end.[44] Why almost the same thing is said

---

[41] 8:16, 18-19; 10:7-9a, 15-20aα, 21a (or 11:2a). The influence of chap. 9 is probable in 8:16, 18-19.

[42] 2:41aα, bβγ, 42a (only ואצבעת), 42b, 43; 7:7bβ, 8, 11a, 20-22, 24-25; 8:9-12, 23-25. The influence of chap. 9 is probable in 7:21-22, 25 and 8:11-12, 23.

[43] 10:13; 10:20-11:1; 12:1-3.

[44] 7:25; 8:13-14, 12:5-13. The time-period in 7:25; 12:7 is dependant upon 9:27, and the counting of the days is dependant upon the three and one-half times.

successively in four different ways is explained by this redaction of the narratives and the gradual increase of the visions. The many additions assimilate both the visions to one another, bring the two sections in chapters 7–9 and 10–12 together after the interpolation of chapter 9, and give the revealed course of history in chapters 10–12 a supplementary theological profile.

7. SELECT BIBLIOGRAPHY

Collins, J. J. *The Apocalyptic Vision of the Book of Daniel* (HSM 16; Missoula, MT: Scholars Press, 1977).

—. *Daniel. A Commentary on the Book of Daniel* (Hermeneia; Minneapolis: Fortress, 1993).

Gammie, J. G. "The Classification, Stages of Growth and Changing Intentions in the Book of Daniel," *JBL* (1976) 191–204.

Ginsberg, H. L. *Studies in Daniel* (TSJTSA 14; New York: Jewish Theological Seminary, 1948).

—. "The Composition of the Book of Daniel," *VT* 4 (1954) 246–75.

Hartman, L. F. and A. A. Di Lella. *The Book of Daniel* (AB 23; New York: Doubleday, 1978).

Hasslberger, B. *Hoffnung in der Bedrängnis. Eine form-kritische Untersuchung zu Dan 8 und 10–12* (ATAT 4; St Ottilien: EOS, 1977).

Hölscher, G. "Die Entstehung des Buches Daniel," *TSK* 92 (1919) 113–38.

Jepsen, A. "Bemerkungen zum Danielbuch," *VT* 11 (1961) 386–91.

Junker, H. *Untersuchungen über literarische und exegetische Probleme des Buches Daniel* (Bonn: Peter Hanstein, 1932).

Koch, K. *Das Buch Daniel* (EdF 144; Darmstadt: Wissenschaftliche Buchgesellschaft, 1980).

Kratz, R. G. *Translatio imperii. Untersuchungen zu den aramäischen Daniel-erzählungen und ihrem theologiegeschichtlichen Umfeld* (WMANT 63; Neukirchen-Vluyn: Neukirchener Verlag, 1987).

—. "Reich Gottes und Gesetz im Danielbuch und im werdenden Judentum," in A. S. van der Woude (ed.), *The Book of Daniel in the Light of New Findings* (BETL 56, Leuven: Leuven University Press and Peeters, 1993) 435–79.

Lebram, J. C. H. "König Antiochus im Buch Daniel," *VT* 25 (1975) 737–72.

Noth, M. "Zur Komposition des Buches Daniel," *TSK* 89/99 (1926) 143–63, repr. in his *Gesammelte Studien zum Alten Testament II* (TB 39; München: Kaiser, 1969) 11–28.

Steck, O. H. "Weltgeschehen und Gottesvolk im Buche Daniel," in D. Lührmann and G. Strecker (eds.), *Kirche. Festschrift G. Bornkamm* (Tübingen: Mohr-Siebeck, 1980) 53–78; repr. in his *Wahrnehmungen Gottes im Alten Testament. Gesammelte Studien* (TB 70; München: Kaiser, 1982) 262–90.

ALLUSIONS TO CREATION IN DANIEL 7

ANDRÉ LACOCQUE

1. THE SETTING AND THE CHARACTERS

This paper addresses itself to the theme of creation in Daniel 7. A thesis will be proposed that concurs with what Loren Fisher wrote more than 30 years ago:

> ... conflict, kingship, ordering of chaos, and temple building are all related to an overarching theme that I would call "creation." However, this is not a theogony or creation of the El type. Rather it is cosmogonic and is of the Baal type."[1]

To this, it is appropriate to add, with Richard Clifford,[2] that for the ancient world the "product" of the cosmogony is all important. "... what emerges ... [is] an ordered human society" (cf. *Enuma elish*; Psalms 77:16-20; 89:10-15; 104), not just a "cosmos." Furthermore, the cosmogony is reported in terms of a drama, one that is wont to focus upon one element at a time and appears therefore to be incomplete. But it must be realised that "the part stands for the whole," it is "a kind of synecdoche."[3] Thus, singled out is a palace, for example, or the erection of a throne. The final triumph of Marduk or of Baal is consecrated by the building of a palace for the god. This inaugurates the cosmogony.

The phenomenon of synecdoche is also present in Daniel 7. However, here an important shift of interest has occurred. The motif of palace-building is only implicitly or allusively present, the reason being that, as is so characteristic of biblical literature, the concern with time/history has superseded all interest in space. All the same, the presence of thrones (v. 9) demands location, as is expressly stated in Exod 15:17. The palace-sanctuary is implicitly present in Daniel 7:9ff. because the nature of the throne(s) is celestial, but its epiphanic location seems understood (as also by the book of Revelation) as set

---

[1] See L. Fisher, "Creation at Ugarit and in the OT," *VT* 15 (1965) 313–24, esp. 316.

[2] R. J. Clifford, "Cosmogonies in the Ugaritic Texts," *Or* 53 (1984) 183–201, esp. 186.

[3] *Ibidem*, 188.

up on earth. In Rev 21:1-5, as a matter of fact, the one enthroned proclaims, "Now at last God has his dwelling among men! He will dwell among them and they shall be his people, and God himself will be with them." As Norman Cohn writes, "By the descent of the heavenly Jerusalem earth and heaven are made undissolubly one."[4]

In this respect, it is interesting to turn to another cosmological evocation, this time in Bildad's speech (Job 25:1-6 + 26:5-14). Here both the motifs of God's throne and the clouds are also associated (26:9) and God's victory over chaos is celebrated (26:12-13). One will also note the cultic theme that accompanies the cosmogony in Job 38:4-7. In biblical conception the world is a temple and its creation amounts to a dedication (cf. Exodus 25ff.). In Daniel 7, God's retinue is mentioned (v. 10, cf. v. 27) for that very purpose. The divine judgment is re-creation. Now the parallelism between temple-building/cult, and creation is very old;[5] already in Sumero-Akkadian creation material the temple is the site of creation. In Akkadian, the verb *banû* describes the creation of the universe as well as the building of temples. R. Clifford writes, "[in the temple] the gods receive the services and goods for which they created the human race ... [this is] the finality of creation."[6]

Let us further note that the emphasized element of fire in Dan 7:9b-10 may be indicative of the composition of God's palace as well as of God's throne. In other words, as intimated above, the throne here might be a synecdoche for the whole physical setting. This is supported by the Ugaritic myth of the building of a palace for Baal. "The house was made of silver and gold, lapis lazuli, and perhaps some other kind(s) of precious stone(s) (*ilqsm*) and the materials were apparently fused by a fire set inside the structure (cf. II AB iv-v, pp. 75–81)," writes Marvin Pope.[7] In II AB vi, pp. 22–35, a fire

---

[4] N. Cohn, *Cosmos, Chaos and the World to Come. The Ancient Roots of Apocalyptic Faith* (New Haven, CT: Yale University Press, 1993) 218.

[5] R. Clifford writes (*Creation Accounts in the Ancient Near East and in the Bible* [CBQMS 26; Washington, DC: Catholic Biblical Association, 1994] 26, 30): "Temple building is associated with creation; a part of the temple of Nippur was called *ki-ùr* ['foundation ... the primeval ground before its fertilization by An, high Heaven'] and bore the epithet 'the great land.' ... Enki builds his house on the very day of creation" [reference is made to the *Hymn to E'engura* li.4–6].

[6] *Ibidem*, 60–61.

[7] M. Pope, *El in the Ugaritic Texts* (Leiden: Brill, 1955) 100.

burns "in the palace" for seven days, so that, "the silver turns into plates, the gold is turned to bricks." Pope judiciously refers to Umberto Cassuto, tallying the אַבְנֵי־אֵשׁ of Ezek 28:14-16 with the Ugaritic *abn brq*. He explains that the fantastic stones appeared as lightning, as spitting flames of fire (cf. Ezek 1:13).[8]

Be that as it may as to the scenery, it is without surprise that we find in Daniel 7 a process of historicization of the myth. While the Akkadian and the Ugaritic literatures are concerned with space/power and thus are anxious to state that Marduk or Baal have received their worthy residences, Daniel 7 is eschatological and concerned with the last judgment.

Furthermore, Baal's palace symbolizes his autonomy vis à vis El, the head god. Such a shift in the supreme authority was, needless to say, unusable in Daniel 7. What remains of the mythological environment is an enthronement ceremony (whose *Sitz im Leben* is the Autumn festival of *Sukkot* with a תְּרוּעָה acknowledging God as creator/judge/savior/King). Israel's king is, during the feast, enthroned as Lord of the universe, an illustration of which is found in Psalm 47. For the ancient world this amounts to a veritable cosmogony. In Daniel 7, the "Son of Man"[9] replaces the human king, enthroned with his God to judge (i.e. bring order, create) the world.[10]

Thus the setting of the thrones in Daniel 7, as well as the scene of judgment that ensues, bring us to detect a mythological background to the chapter. True, scholars are divided regarding such a possible origin to the imagery in Daniel 7. First proposed by J. A. Emerton, it has been forcefully supported by F. M. Cross, J. J. Collins, E. W. Nicholson, J. Day, C. Colpe, and myself, among others.[11] This is

---

[8] See U. Cassuto, *From Adam to Noah* (Jerusalem: Magnes, 1944) 42–43; idem, *The Goddess Anath* (Jerusalem: Magnes, 1951) 81; Pope, *El in the Ugaritic Texts*, 99.

[9] Here and in what follows, "Son of Man" is in quotes to indicate the abbreviation of "the-one-who-is-like-a-son-of-man" in the Aramaic text of Daniel 7.

[10] Cf. W. H. Schmidt, *Königtum Gottes in Ugarit und Israel* (Berlin: Töpelmann, 1961) 51–54: the kingship of El and the one of Baal are complementary; they are not in mutual opposition. This is important for our understanding of the same relationship expressed in the transposed image of the Ancient of Days and the One-like-a-Son-of-man. In *1 Enoch* also, the Chosen One, who is also the Son of Man, sits on a throne. Compare *1 Enoch* 45:3: "The Chosen One will sit on the throne of glory," cf. also 51:3.

[11] J. A. Emerton, "The origin of the Son of Man Imagery," *JTS* 9 n.s. (1958)

because, in spite of some 1200 years elapsing between the Ugaritic version of the myth (14th century) and the book of Daniel (2nd century), the Canaanite influence on Daniel 7 is, I believe, undeniable. A roughly contemporary text like Isa 27:1 (and Isaiah 24–27 in general)[12] shows that God's fight with the Dragon or Mot was very much on the minds of second century Israelites (or of an intellectual elite?). It is not utterly surprising to find a resurgence of mythological elements of the myth in the Isaiah apocalypse or in the book of Daniel. For, in contrast to the evolution of the mythic narrative toward systematic sapiential doctrine, the "apocalypses retain much more of the narrative form of the older creation traditions," as say Clifford and Collins.[13]

As mentioned above, the ancient accounts of creation report it as drama and, frequently, as "a conflict of wills," with the good divinities triumphing over the evil ones.[14] Thus creation is also *cosmo*-gony, that is, the advent of an ordered universe. The apocalypses consider, however, that wickedness has so deeply corrupted the world that the latter is doomed to destruction, and a new creation must take place.

That is why the scene of judgment in Daniel 7 is also a scene of war. The Judge is also the Great Warrior, and he vindicates the righteous (cf. Pss 7:6-8; 9:19; 35:23; 43:1, etc.). The condemnation of the culprit (the killing of the Beast) is his victorious feat. He takes

---

225–42; F. M. Cross, *Canaanite Myth and Hebrew Epic* (Cambridge, MA: Harvard University Press, 1973) 345 n.8; J. J. Collins, *Daniel: A Commentary on the Book of Daniel* (Hermeneia; Minneapolis: Fortress, 1993) passim; E. W. Nicholson, "Apocalyptic," in G. W. Anderson (ed.), *Tradition and Interpretation* (Oxford: Oxford University Press, 1979) 189–213, esp. 206; J. Day, *God's Conflict with the Dragon and the Sea. Echoes of a Canaanite Myth in the OT* (Cambridge: Cambridge University Press, 1985) 157ff.; C. Colpe, "huios tou anthropou," *TWNT* 8 (1969) 403–81; A. LaCocque, *The Book of Daniel* (Atlanta: John Knox, 1979) on Daniel 7.

[12] Cf. Day, *God's Conflict with the Dragon and the Sea*. Reference should also be made to F. M. Cross, *Canaanite Myth*, 20–21 and 114–21, in particular, where relevant Ugaritic texts are presented with their translation. See also other late texts such as Isa 51:9 (perhaps by a redactor around 400 BCE); Isa 44:27 (where YHWH dries up the rivers that fill the abyss [צוּלָה]); 51:9-10 (תְּהוֹם); and Ps 66:6 (יָם).

[13] R. J. Clifford and J. J. Collins (eds.), *Creation in Biblical Traditions* (CBQMS 24; Washington, DC: Catholic Biblical Association, 1992) 14.

[14] *Ibidem*, 10.

vengeance on his enemies (Pss 31:17; 35:1, 4-6; 55:9, 15; 69:22-28; 109:9-15, 28-29), as he *ab origine* overcame the chaotic monsters.[15] The wicked in Daniel 7 are the historical personifications of Yam/Mot/Chaos. When it is realized that those who belong to that category are a mix of foreign Syrians and "inside" Jewish Hellenizers, the depiction in Daniel is certainly not toothless!

Daniel 7 is not by far the first witness of the Canaanite influence upon Israelite literature. Elsewhere in the Bible, the Baal-Yam struggle is reflected in texts like Exod 15:1-18; Pss 74:12-17; 77:14-21; 89:10-11; 114; and the Baal-Mot confrontation is echoed, *inter alia*, in Deut 32:7-14 and Isa 43:16-21. Of particular importance is Psalm 89 which, according to Ernst Haag, constitutes an intermediary link between the Zion-David tradition, itself a reflection of Canaanite ideology, and Daniel 7.[16] YHWH is enthroned in the midst of the Holy Ones (v. 6, 8), then he chooses a man as representative of his universal kingship (v. 26), promotes him to the first place among the powerful of the earth (v. 28) and establishes his throne for ever (vv. 37-38). Already in 1986, Paul Mosca had insisted on the derivation of Psalm 89 from Ugarit. This Psalm, he says, presents the Jerusalem king as playing the role of the Most High himself vis-à-vis the other kings. His cosmic dimensions recall those of Baal: David's throne is comparable to the sun and moon (vv. 37-38), and obliquely to the heavens (v. 30b); it stands constantly in the divine presence (v. 37b, נֶגְדִּי); it is firm for ever (v. 38a) and on a par with the ones of the בְּנֵי אֵלִם and the קְדֹשִׁים, the heavenly beings and the holy ones (vv. 7-8, NRSV). Such a hyperbolic description of the Davidic throne recalls the divinized thrones in Ugarit (*CTA* 38.2; 45.4, 5; 47.7).[17]

Let us further note the presence in Daniel 7 of the Ugaritic cosmological pattern, which follows the following sequence: battle/victory/kingship/judgment/recreation.[18]

---

[15] Moreover, the telescopage of the themes of judging and fighting is found in Ugaritic literature (cf. I AB vi, pp. 16–29, concerning Mot).

[16] E. Haag, "Der Menschensohn und die Heiligen (des) Höchsten. Eine literar-, form-, und traditionsgeschichtliche Studie zu Daniel 7," in A. S. van der Woude (ed.), *The Book of Daniel in the Light of New Findings* (BETL 56, Leuven: Leuven University Press and Peeters, 1993) 137–86.

[17] P. Mosca, "Ugarit and Daniel 7: A Missing Link," *Bib* 67 (1986) 496–517; idem, "Once Again the Heavenly Witness of Psalm 89:38," *JBL* 105 (1986) 27–37.

[18] See L. G. Perdue, *Wisdom in Revolt: Metaphorical Theology in the Book of*

If such is the background of Daniel 7, we should probably see in the fourth beast a reminiscence of the goddess Anat, the Canaanite patron of war. Like the Dragon in Daniel 7, Anat is described as trampling upon everything and uttering enormities (cf. Dan 7:17, 23, 25 with *CTA* V AB, E, III D i: Anat threatens El of wreaking havoc if he withdraws permission to build a palace for Baal). This identification of Anat with the fourth Beast (that is, Antiochus IV) makes it much clearer why the latter is described as wallowing in blood (Dan 7:7, 19, 23). So also is Anat in Canaanite myth (cf. V AB, B).

It is true that here Anat is the ally (sister, spouse) of Baal,[19] so that the analogy of Baal with the "Son of Man" (see below) and of Anat with the Monster does not fit the cosmological model. However, the model is never purely duplicated. Clifford calls the anthological free rearrangements of the borrowed features, a "kaleidoscopic reuse of traditional details ... [A]ncient authors evidently liked to put familiar objects in new contexts."[20]

The author of Daniel 7 has recourse to mythological motifs and to the model of the cosmogonies to describe an eschatological event. The historical character Antiochus IV is but the last avatar of the chaotic monsters. Hence, the primeval imagery was the only one fitting such a pattern of *Urzeit wird Endzeit*. Mircea Eliade writes:

> "*in illo tempore* is situated not only at the beginning of time but also at its end.... The only difference is that this victory over the forces of darkness and chaos no longer occurs regularly every year but is projected into a future and Messianic *illud tempus*."[21]

Thus the eschatological events need not occur as a mere duplication of those in the original Canaanite model, neither do the relations between the protagonists. A case in point is the unusual denomination of God in Daniel 7. This surprising name of God, the "Ancient of Days," recalls unmistakably El's title *ᶜab snm* in Ugarit

---

Job (Sheffield: Sheffield Academic Press, 1991). This contrasts with the anthological pattern, whose sequence is: judgment (slavery)/slavery and toil/revolt/fall/judgment culminating in redemption. See also Psalm 74, where the sequence is salvation/destruction of dragons/creation/vindication of the just.

[19] *CTA* V AB, D, pg. 83; I AB ii, pg. 12.

[20] Clifford, *Creation Accounts*, 148.

[21] M. Eliade, *Cosmos and history: The Myth of the Eternal Return* (New York: Pantheon, 1959) 106.

(I AB i, pg. 10; II AB iv–v, pg. 24; III AB C, pg. 6; V AB E, pg. 16; VI AB iii, pp. 21-25). His gray hair is mentioned in II AB iv–v, pg. 66; V AB, E, pp. 32-33; IV D vi, pp. 11-12. The situation seems to me comparable with the one found in Psalm 19, where, in a no less a unique way, the cosmos is said to proclaim כְּבוֹד־אֵל. As Gerhard von Rad comments, "The most colourless possible word has been chosen."[22] In Daniel 7, the "colorlessness" of the title "Ancient of Days" is also intentional, since the scene in this chapter is one of the passing of powers (to the "one-like-a-Son of Man," see below). It would have been totally inappropriate to have YHWH stripping himself from his very attributes. But there is, as seen above, a striking precedent to this "deference" in the Canaanite myth.[23] So much so that the "Ancient of Days" is transparently the god El of Canaanite pantheon, creator of the world and of humanity, an aged

---

[22]   G. von Rad, "The Theological Problem of the OT Doctrine of Creation," in his *The Problem of the Hexateuch* (New York: McGraw-Hill, 1966) 131–43, esp. 139. Note that, according to von Rad (pg. 140), Psalm 19 is "an ancient Canaanitish hymn subsequently adapted to Yahwistic beliefs."

[23]   And prior to that, in the Akkadian predecessor. Thorkild Jacobsen cites the description of the god An from the Isin-Larsa period: "The exalted lord, the leader ... ascended step by step the pure mountain of (his) office, took his seat on the great throne-dais, An, king of the gods. (From) afar he looked firmly toward him, looked firmly toward Prince Lipit-Eshtar, granted ... [and] granted ... the kingship ... great An granted as a gift" (*The Treasures of Darkness: A History of Mesopotamian Religion* [New Haven, CT: Yale University Press, 1976] pg. 98). By the way, I take exception to John Day's sharp distinction between Cannanite mythology, which he rightly sees as influential upon Daniel 7, and Babylonian myth, which he wrongly discards as out of the picture in Daniel 7. In reality, such an exclusion is misleading. The Mesopotamian influence upon Israel remained strong all through Israel's history (and was revived during the exile in Babylon). Besides, much of the Caananite tradition is the outcome of its appropriation of further eastern material. The biblical parallels are too many and too strong with, say, the *Enuma elish*, to dismiss it with respect to Daniel 7 (and, according to Day, such texts as Genesis 1, etc.). As Cohn writes (*Cosmos, Chaos*, 123): "Baal's initial adventure has much in common with the exploits of that other youthful storm-god, Marduk of Babylon." One of the apocalyptic roots leads back to Mesopotamia; cf. Dan 10:4, etc.; see also Pss 29:10; 89:25 (on which, see F. M. Cross, *Canaanite Myth*, 261–62). J. W. van Henten ("Antiochus IV as a Typhonic Figure in Daniel 7," in van Woude [ed.], *The Book of Daniel*, 223–243) defends the thesis that Daniel 7's description of Antiochus is dependent upon the Egyptian identification of their enemies with the mythological Typhon/Seth, "the enemy of the gods."

deity, "father of the years."[24] A closely-related text is Gen 14:19 where God is called אֵל עֶלְיוֹן קֹנֵה שָׁמַיִם וָאָרֶץ. El, says the Hittite-Canaanite myth *Elkunirsa* [= El, creator of the earth?], dwells at the source of the Euphrates river (cf. Gen 2:10-14, the very location of Eden)!

In an article written in 1956, "El and YHWH,"[25] Otto Eissfeldt showed that El, as a figure and a name, continued to be honored in Israel, either as a designation of YHWH—sometimes passionately claimed, an indication that the two were originally distinguished—or in texts where El is "an entity different from, and originally superior to, YHWH" (pg. 27). Among texts of the latter category, Psalm 82 shows YHWH in the congregation of El; and in Deut 32:8-9, in its LXX rendering which is confirmed by a Qumran version,[26] YHWH is said to have received Israel as his portion from Elyon. Eissfeldt writes:

> [T]he El cult was conceived of as an older form of belief, and although it was lifted to a higher level by the YHWH epiphany, it continued.... [El] was identified in His essence with YHWH ... [YHWH] appropiated the function of Creator of the world and King of the gods, which according to the evidence of the Ugaritic texts are especially peculiar to El.[27]

The pair "Ancient of Days" and "The One like a Son of Man" parallels very closely El and Baal in Ugaritic Literature. Their judgment/victory recalls the theme of Baal's combat with Yam and Mot, a motif that is omnipresent in the Ancient Near East. In Egypt, for example, Chaos versus Cosmos is symbolized by the confrontation between Ra and Apophis, or between Osiris and Seth. The same applies to Mesopotamian epos.[28] In fact, apocalyptic literature draws its imagery of final cataclysm from mythological evocations of chaotic mayhem. Suffice it here to recall the *Epic of Erra.*[29]

Furthermore, this mythological motif has already been used in J's account of the anthropogony. In the Garden (associated with royalty

---

[24] El is credited with "begetting" the other gods and mankind (II AB iv–v, pg. 48 = V AB E, pp. 42–43; IV AB iii, pp. 5–7). See Deut 32:6; Ps 87:56; Job 31:15.

[25] *JJS* 1 (1956) 25–37.

[26] See Patrick W. Skehan, "A Fragment of the 'Song of Moses'," *BASOR* 136 (Dec. 1954) 12–15.

[27] O. Eissfeldt, "El and Yahweh," *JJS* 1 (1956) 25–37, esp. 35–36.

[28] Cf. Cohn, *Cosmos, Chaos*, 44.

[29] *Ibidem*, 52–53.

in the whole Ancient Near East), the Deus Rex delegates powers to Adam, who accordingly names the animate creatures and is in charge of controlling them. And in the P version, as R. A. Oden writes,[30] "... human authority over the earth is overtly portrayed on the analogy of God's own authority over all of creation (Gen 1:26)." In Daniel 7, the Ancient of Days has the same type of relationship with the "Son of Man," whose final judgment is God's judgment. Remarkably, the same phenomenon of power-shifting is also present in the *Similitudes of Enoch.* In 52:6, for example, what used to be attributed in the prophetic texts to theophanies is now transferred to the Chosen One's appearance at the end of days. This latter figure is frequently described as seated on a throne (cf. 62:5, 9) and is called "Son of Man" sixteen times here (cf. 46:1-6 in particular). He judges and damns the wicked (63:11; 69:26-27).

In summary, the Danielic "Ancient of Days" plays the role of El in mythology, and the "Son of Man" that of Baal. But the author did not detract from monotheism. Under his pen, the "Ancient of Days" is none else than YHWH, and the "Son of Man" is, according to the context (Daniel 8–12), Michael, the patron angel of Israel.[31] "Then," says Emerton, "the Son of Man was degraded to the status of an angel, even though he retained the imagery which was so closely attached to him in tradition."[32] As the heavenly patron of Israel, the "Son of Man" is enthroned as a king and thus occupies the place of the Davidide in the enthronement festival when the Temple was standing. Michael, or Israel as the holy community, is crowned and receives the royal investiture.

But if the Ancient of Days makes us think of the god El, and the One-like-a-Son-of-Man of Baal, there is, however, in Daniel 7 no rivalry between the two and no struggle for prominence. In the mythological lore, the cosmogony is more than once also a theogony and the problem of the pre-eminence among the gods plays a central role. Thus, responding to discrete political-religious ambitions, a local god (for instance, Marduk) emerges as the head of the pantheon at the expense of an older god (for instance, Enki). The latter is "older" because his dominion located elesewhere comes to an end. In

---

[30] *ABD* 1.1166 s.v. "Cosmogony, Cosmology."

[31] Cf. N. Schmidt, "'The Son of Man' in the Book of Daniel," *JBL* 19 (1900), 22–28.

[32] Emerton, "Origin of the Son of Man Imagery," 242.

Daniel 7, however, in spite of the duality of (supreme) characters, there is no such rivalry between "The Venerable" and the presumably younger "Human One." The "Son of Man" is none else than the Archangel Michael and takes the ultimate highest position among the angels.[33] The judgment/victory belongs eternally to God, who *delegates* it to the One-like-a-Son-of-Man. It does not have to be wrenched out by threat from anyone. To the contrary, in several biblical texts such as this one, the mutual relation between "messenger (or angel)" and God is striking; compare, *inter alia*, Gen 16:7-13; Genesis 18–19; Judges 6 [esp. vv. 14, 16]; Exod 24:9-11; 33:23.

The matter of the delegation of power is important. The book of Daniel is consistent in showing that God, throughout history, delegates power to rulers.[34] Daniel 7 befits this conception: the "Son of Man" is displacing all political dominions and replacing them with his own ultimate delegated power. It is true that, in comparison with him, the displaced monarchs are but beasts while the "Son of Man" is human/angelic—but in both cases we are dealing with *kings*. The setting is an enthronement festival (see above).

The character described as "one like a son of man" in Daniel 7 is the ultimate Judge. The mythological narrative in the background shows that the preposition "like" (כְּ/כְּמוֹ) is to be understood as asseverative rather than comparative. When Enkidu, in the Gilgamesh epic, acquires (sexual) wisdom through his commerce with Shamhat the prostitute, he is said to have become *kima muti ibassi*, "like a human."[35] As the motif of the "Son of Man" is dealt with elsewhere in this volume, I shall not elaborate here on it, except to stress that this figure, once again, takes us to the motif of creation. A confirmation can be found, for instance, in a contemporary document, the "Animal Apocalypse" (*1 Enoch* 85–90), which shows the "Son of Man" as a new Adam, more perfect than the first one, and inaugurating a new world, more glorious than the old one. Himself a combination of angelic and Adamic, this personage appears

---

[33] In Daniel, other angels of God are mentioned, as well as the "Prince of Persia" and the "Prince of Greece" (10:20-21).

[34] The verb נתן is used in the book of Daniel in a significant way to mean a shift in the delegation of power; cf. Dan 1:2; 2:21, 37, 38; 8:12a, 13; 7:6, 12b. Incidently, this notion lies in the background of Romans 13.

[35] *Gilgamesh* II.iii.27; Shamhat also declares, "you have become like a god" (I.4.34), and the *kima* retrieves its comparative function.

in Daniel 7 as the "understudy" of God, a phenomenon already found in Ezekiel (for example, chapter 8) and, later, in Qumran and Christian literatures. The *Community Rule* presents the "God of Israel and his Angel of Truth" as, in fact, one and the same person. In Rev 1.14, Christ's "hair of his head is white as snow-white wool, and his eyes are flaming like fire."[36]

Furthermore, since Baal is called at times "son of Dagan" (son of Wheat?),[37] Daniel 7 transforms the phrase into "son of Adam." This is particularly striking, for the great god El is called *ʿab ʿadm* in the legend of Keret (i.37, 43, 136, 151, 278, 297)! As for our text harking back to Adam, rather than to David the Messiah (for instance), this represents in the post-exilic period a widespread tendency to leap back beyond the period of Israel come of age—which occurred during the Mosaic period or after the Conquest—to the primordial times of creation. In this manner the "Son of Man's" kingship has its foundation in the event of creation.[38] His kingship is on the model of Adam's kingship: non political, it is a universal, cosmic, humanization process, whose ultimate aim is communication with the Creator (the Ancient of Days, the One who was before the beginning) and with the created, which in the process is transformed (transfigured) into a "people of the saints," that is, a "double nature" people, both human and angelic.[39] Then, truly, *Urzeit wird Endzeit*, and the dynamism of the initial preposition בְּ in the first word of the Bible reaches its goal in the *eschaton* ushered in by the "Son of Man."[40]

---

[36] In Christian ancient art, Christ is sometimes represented as the Ancient of Days, for example, on an ivory diptych of the 6th century now in Berlin's Staatliche Museen, and on a mural painting in Kastoria. See photographs in *Le Monde de la Bible* 114 (Oct. 1998) 21 and 29.

[37] Cf. I AB vi, pg. 24; III AB B, pg. 19, 35, 36; etc. *Dagan* means wheat elsewhere in Ugarit, cf. II K iii, 9, 13.

[38] P's Adam is the first Priest and the first King; cf. also Pss 8:6-9; 2:6; 45:7; 72:8, 17. In Psalm 110, there is a heavenly enthronement of the Davidic Messiah, who is also Priest for ever, after the order of Melchizedek; cf. Heb 8:1-2. But according to Daniel 7's process of "democratization," the hoping one and the one hoped for coincide: Israel as people is kingly/messianic. See 1QM 17:7: God is going "to raise up the rule (משרת) of Michael amongst the angels and the dominion (ממשלת) of Israel amongst all flesh."

[39] Cf. *1 Enoch* 48:7.

[40] In Gen 1:1, בְּרֵאשִׁית does not just signal a beginning, but indicates already

2. A REREADING OF DANIEL 7 IN THE LIGHT OF CREATION MYTH

The theophanic setting of a tribunal in Daniel 7, with the Ancient of Days presiding as the One who rules over space and time, corresponds to other comparable scriptural descriptions within a context of *creation* and its *perfect fulfillment*.[41] With the scene of Daniel 7, history is present from its beginning (creation) to its end (eschaton), a fact already signified by the first part of the chapter with its succession of world empires. These now occupy the place filled in other biblical literary genres by events in Israel's history. Such a substitution, by the way, explains the striking absence of "Messiah" in Daniel 7. For the "Anointed One" belongs to *Heilsgeschichte* and only indirectly to universal history. He is here replaced by a universal, "Adamic" figure, whose function transcends (hence also recalls) the one of the Messiah ben David.[42] But his judgment/destruction of foes, and his glory/world dominion, are not confined to Israel (on the model of the prophetic forecast of restoration); they are cosmic (on the pattern of battle/victory/kingship/judgment/recreation).

The grand scene of Daniel 7 takes us to the point where the process reaches its climax: the imperfection in creation, dramatically described in the first part of the chapter as a "persistence of evil," or of chaos, is about to be absorbed into perfection through the divine judgment of the earth. Judgment is thus crisis and purification; purification by elimination of historical monsters and by introduction from before the Ancient of Days of his lieutenant ("one-like-a-human-being"). The contrast between what is eliminated and what is introduced parallels the ages of imperfection and perfection. The "Son of Man" is embodying the *telos* of creation, its finality, its *plerôma*.

---

the finality of creation: "For the prime/excellence." Also verified in Daniel 7 is von Rad's stance (but which he pushes to the point of exaggeration) that "We found [the doctrine of creation] invariably related ... to soteriological considerations" (The Theological Problem," 142).

[41] Cf. the assembly of the Sons of God: Pss 29:1; 82:1; Job 1:6; 2:1; of the Spirits: 1 Kgs 22:19-22; of the Saints: Ps 89:6, 8; of the Watchers: Dan 4:10, 14.

[42] *1 Enoch* 90:37 refers to a "white bull" in the eschaton. Often interpreted as the Messiah, this is rather the New Adam. As to 4Q246 (the so-called "Son of God Text"), this may be a reinterpretation of Daniel 7's "Son of Man" (by fusion of traditions on the Warrior Messiah) in parallel with *4 Ezra*.

This must be underscored, for it would have been simpler, it would seem, to have God seizing for himself the power usurped by arrogant human kings with monstrous appetites and rules. This alternative move is present in other Jewish apocalypses (cf. Isa 27:1; *1 Enoch* 90:24; 91:12-17; and in *4 Ezra* 13, where the Messiah dies with the rest of humanity before God's kingdom is inaugurated). In Daniel 7, however, "dominion, glory, and kingship" do not bypass humankind. The author of this book wanted to encourage his suffering people and to unveil for them the glorious outcome of their present predicament by showing their enthronement at the imminent end of times (cf. 7:27). As the "Adamic" has become bestial (in the first section of the chapter), so also the "Adamic" is restored in its humanness and, according to its status granted by creation, is "given dominion over the works of God's hands, and all things are put under its feet" (Ps 8:7; cf. Job 7:17; Gen 1:28).

These latter texts, especially Psalm 8, provide the correct perspective for understanding the universal dominion of the one-who-is-human. The Psalm sheds bright light on the reason why Daniel 7 chose to emphasize humanity as the referent for its eschatological figure. Kingship is here exercised by the human *qua* son of Adam, not *qua* son of David. The universalization process allows other shifts toward fulfillement to happen: from chaos to life (chapters 3 and 6); from animality to humanity (chapter 4); from weakness to strength (chapter 10); from dust to stars (chapter 12); from mystery to understanding (chapter 12); and from death to life (chapter 12).[43]

Yet the Messianic mystique is definitely in the background of Daniel 7. The insistence of this chapter on kingship (the setting of thrones; the exercise of judgment; the granting of universal dominion) definitely leads in that direction. During a crowning ceremony, God confers upon the "Son of Man" kingship, the divine kingship, so that the final judgment upon the beasts be imbued with ultimate authority. In other words, the mythic scene of the assembly of the gods conferring royal authority to Marduk or to Baal is here replaced, as may be expected, by the one God charging his lieutenant to wage divine authority.

In the background is King David (cf. Psalms 2 and 110, texts that

---

[43] See J. Doukhan, "Allusions à la création dans le livre de Daniel," in van der Woude (ed.), *The Book of Daniel*, 285–92, esp. 290.

show the Davidic king enthroned alongside with YHWH). Aage Bentzen[44] calls attention to the fact that in the ancient Middle East the king is seen as the Primal Man, a feature that transpires, according to the Danish scholar, in Gen 1:27; Psalm 8 (cf. 80:17); Mic 5:1ff.; cf. Job 15:7-8; Ezek 28:11ff. While it is true that this hypothesis perhaps treads on insecure ground, as J. A. Emerton cautioned,[45] Daniel 7 was straightaway interpreted messianically in Jewish tradition, as *1 Enoch* 48:10; 52:4 already testify, where the term "anointed" is applied to the Son of Man (cf. also 49; 62:2).[46]

What precedes will prove helpful for our rereading of the first part of Daniel 7. For the unique kingship with which the "Son of Man" is invested appears in stark contrast with a multiple kingship that is illegitimately based on crude and cruel power wrought by human potentates. The nature of their rule is bestial. Ambiguously and ominously, however, the power of the great historical empires transcends history. As Collins notes, the emergence of the four kings from the Sea "implies that the kings have a metaphysical status."[47] They proceed from Chaos.[48] The monsters coming from the sea are not creatures to whom a role is allotted "in the structure of creation, as is the Prince of Darkness in the Instruction on the Two Spirits in the *Community Rule*."[49] But this does not detract from the fact that the sea motif is highly mythological, playing even in the Bible a negative role in the process of creation. It belongs to Chaos, which must be subdued by the Creator of life and order. At the beginning and also at the end of time, God must kill Rahab or Leviathan (cf. Job 26:12; Isa 27:1; 51:9; in Canaanite lore, Leviathan is Lotan, enemy of Baal).

The image of the stirred sea in Daniel 7 is a further segment in a trajectory that started with creation in Genesis 1, and continued with the Flood in Genesis 6–8 and the numerous allusions to cosmogonic

---

[44] A. Bentzen, *King and Messiah* (Oxford: Oxford University Press, 1955) 74ff., 109–110. The author refers to Ps 97:2.

[45] J. Emerton, "The Origin of the Son of Man Imagery," *JTS* 9 (1958) 225–42.

[46] See H. Riesenfeld, *Jesus Transfiguré* (Lund: Gleerup, 1947) 134, 308.

[47] J. Collins, *Seers, Sibyls and Sages in Hellenistic-Roman Judaism* (Leiden: Brill, 1997) 144.

[48] Cf. LaCocque, *Daniel*, 138.

[49] J. Collins, *Apocalypticism in the Dead Sea Scrolls* (Literature of the Dead Sea Scrolls; New York: Routledge, 1997) 100. See also 1QM 13.

battles (Psalms 29; 68; 74; 89; 104; Isa 27:1; 51:9-11; Job 3; 7; 26; 40–41). In each case the mythological backdrop makes clear that the Warrior God (Marduk, Baal, YHWH) defeats chaos. There is doubtlessly an intertextual relationship between Dan 7:1ff. and Gen 1:2, which evokes an ominous watery and dark abyss from which, one can surmise, only terrible monsters can emerge. The Danielic scene describes the ultimate victory over the last enemy and the inauguration of the "new" creation (that is, a creation at last freed from the threat of chaos).

However, as Collins rightly reflects, in Daniel God does not wage war against the Sea, which is no personified Satanic figure.[50] Here, I may add, the accent has shifted from the Sea to one of its productions, the fourth animal and, even more specifically, to one of its horns, Antiochus IV. Thus the mythic Chaos is historicized and the historical Epiphanes is concurrently mythicized!

The "Son of Man" slays the four rulers-monsters and inherits from the Ancient of Days the eschatological kingdom. On this score as well, the "Son of Man" is Adam-king glorified.

3. CONCLUSION

While Genesis 1–11 (P and J) have been written under the obvious influence of Mesopotamian lore,[51] Daniel 7 retells the myth in far greater continuity with the Canaanite version of the cosmogony.

Clearly, the resurrection of myth in Israel was not, theologically speaking, exempt of danger. The slaughter of the chaos monster by an angelic "Saint George" tends to exteriorize evil, and hence to demoralize it. Along this line, Tiamat needs to be ritually destroyed annually, during the *Akitu* festival. Daniel 7 escaped, however, that ethical failure thanks to the historicization of the dragon in the person of Antiochus Epiphanes, and of "the one-like-a-son-of-man" in the persons of the saints. In this manner, evil and its opposite, holiness, remain the outcome of contrasting options.

As a matter of fact, there is a taut contrast between Chaos/Sea that

---

[50] As in other biblical texts (for example, Isa 17:12), the Sea represents peoples. In Ps 74:13-15, which was written after 586, we find the imagery of the ancient combat myth and the divine victory over Yam.

[51] Especially the myth *Atrahasis* as regards J, and *Enuma elish* as regards P. Cf. B. F. Batto, "Creation Theology in Genesis," in Clifford and Collins (eds.), *Creation in Biblical Traditions*, 1–38.

has found its historical monstrous incarnation, and the people of the Saints, the slayers of the Dragon (by participation in the divine victory) who discover their heavenly identity in the Human Being par excellence, Adam glorified. The Beast is overcome by the Human; Gen 3:15 is fulfilled. For, while the victory is God's, it is equally Man's as well. As for the hidden identity of the Beast, all ambiguity is lifted in Revelation 12, where "the Dragon" is demonic, the devil himself in person.

The Beasts, simultaneously mythical and historical, recall Behemoth and Leviathan, which are in Ugaritic literature the enemies of Baal and allies of Yam. In the Hebrew Bible Job 40:15-24 and 40:25–41:26 come to mind,[52] as does *1 Enoch* 60:7-9, where both monsters respectively represent the unruly Sea and the immense Desert (that is, Yam and Mot). In Daniel 7, the monsters are four, coming from "the four winds of the world" and emerging from the hostile sea. Daniel 7 zooms in on the latter, which symbolizes Antiochus Epiphanes. This monster is killed by God, as Lotan was in Ugarit by Baal. This amounts in Daniel to the eradication of evil, the eschatological fall of Satan. Now, as in the book of Job "the beasts echo the Satan of chapters 1 and 2,"[53] in Daniel 7 the destruction of the fourth beast builds an "inner" *inclusio* with the appearance of the first beast from the sea, i.e. the Babylonian Nebuchadnezzar, destroyer of Jerusalem and the Temple. It also builds an "outer" *inclusio* as Nebuchadnezzar happens to appear in Dan 1:1 with a mention of his heinous crime. The fourth beast is detroyed by fire (as water would not do, the monster coming from the sea); this brings to mind Amos 7:4, which shows YHWH engulfing in fire the תְּהוֹם רַבָּה.[54]

The features of the beasts assembled from varigated animal species have been generally recognized as inspired by Mesopotamian hybrids. The human features of some are highly surprising at first blush, but, besides the fact that divine representations in Akkad evolved towards the human form, there is a subtle connection between the beasts and the "Son of Man." Offered is a discreet suggestion that the terrible worldly empires *could* have been human

---

[52] See M. Pope, *Job* (AB 15, Garden City, NY: Doubleday, 1952) 320–23.

[53] Clifford, *Creation Accounts*, 196.

[54] Perhaps the sea serpent, cf. H.W. Wolff, *Dodekapropheten 2: Amos und Joel* (BK 14/2; Neukirchen: Neukirchener Verlag, 1969); English translation, *Joel and Amos* (Philadelphia: Fortress, 1977) 292–93.

instead of bestial, and that the summit of evil is reached when it is not pure. The ultimate evil is impure, as the ultimate lie contains some elements of truth.[55]

But this is not the only potential bridge between these two poles. A further link between the beasts and the "Son of Man" is provided by the cloud upon which the "Son of Man" is riding. In Mesopotamian myth (cf. the myth *Lugale*) the cloud is considered as the product of evaporation from the Apsû. So the primeval sea in myth and in Daniel 7 might be ambivalent; it produces chaos monsters and, through the process of evaporation and downpour, irrigates the soil.

The myth of origins, however, delayed all reference to fertility and focused on the awesome primordial war. So according to *Enuma elish*, Marduk mounts a storm-chariot to go into battle with Tiamat, which shows that "riding the cloud" is not, traditionally, a peaceful parading of sorts. Rather, the motif of the cloud borrowed by Daniel 7 is the harbinger of the judgment meted out on the beasts by the Man, a reminder of the widespread myth of the battle between the storm-god and the sea.

Dominion is given to the "Son of Man," who is logically to be credited with the victory or, rather, with the judicial execution of the Evil power.[56] The Messianic expectation is thus reinterpreted in the sense of its universalization. Messianism becomes the eschatological fulfillment of man's humanity; it consists in eradicating evil and ruling over the whole of creation ("sheep, oxen, the beasts of the field, the birds of the air, the fish of the sea, whatever passes along the paths of the seas," says Ps 8:8-9). "Humanity," which certainly also implies humaneness, contrasts with the bestiality of pagan empires, but the texts are not explicit as to just what is meant by dominion over creation. Left only with these two terms, "humanity" and "dominion," we should probably interpret the relationship between the two as did Teilhard de Chardin, namely, the "humanization" of the universe—more properly, a re-creation.

The shift from the particular to the universal is strikingly verified in the shift from YHWH to the "Ancient of Days" (or the Most High, the God of Heaven, etc.); from Jerusalem to Babylon (that is, to the world at large); from human empires to the Kingdom of God; and from the earth to heaven.

---

[55] The primeval lie, the one of the Genesis serpent, is a parade example.

[56] See Collins, *Seers, Sibyls and Sages.*

4. SELECT BIBLIOGRAPHY

Clifford, R. J. "Cosmogonies in the Ugaritic Texts," *Or* 53 (1984) 183–201.

—. *Creation Accounts in the Ancient Near East and in the Bible* (CBQMS 26; Washington, DC: Catholic Biblical Association, 1994).

Clifford, R. J. Clifford and J. J. Collins (eds.). *Creation in Biblical Traditions* (CBQMS 24; Washington, DC: Catholic Biblical Associaition, 1992).

Cohn, N. *Cosmos, Chaos and the World to Come. The Ancient Roots of Apocalyptic Faith* (New Haven, CT: Yale University Press, 1993).

Collins, J. J. "Apocalyptic Genre and Mythic Allusions in Daniel," *JSOT* 21 (1981) 83–100.

—. "Stirring up the Great Sea: The Religio-Historical Background of of Daniel 7," in A. S. van der Woude (ed.), *The Book of Daniel in the Light of New Findings* (BETL 56, Leuven: Leuven University Press and Peeters, 1993) 121–35 (repr. in Collins, *Seers, Sibyls and Sages in Hellenistic-Roman Judaism* [Leiden: Brill, 1997] 139–55).

—. *Daniel: A Commentary on the Book of Daniel* (Hermeneia; Minneapolis: Fortress, 1993).

Cross, F. M. *Canaanite Myth and Hebrew Epic* (Cambridge, MA: Harvard University Press, 1973).

Day, J. *God's Conflict with the Dragon and the Sea. Echoes of a Canaanite Myth in the OT* (Cambridge: Cambridge University Press, 1985).

Doukhan, J. "Allusions à la création dans le livre de Daniel," in van der Woude (ed.), *The Book of Daniel in the Light of New Findings*, 285–92 [see the second entry under Collins].

Emerton, J. A. "The origin of the Son of Man Imagery," *JTS* 9 n.s. (1958) 225–42.

Haag, E. "Der Menschensohn und die Heiligen (des) Höchsten. Eine literar-, form-, und traditionsgeschichtliche Studie zu Daniel 7," in van der Woude (ed.), *The Book of Daniel in the Light of New Findings*, 137–86 [see the second entry under Collins].

Jacobsen, T. *The Treasures of Darkness: A History of Mesopotamian Religion* (New Haven, CT: Yale University Press, 1976).

Pope, M. *El in the Ugaritic Texts* (Leiden: Brill, 1955).

W. H. Schmidt, *Königtum Gottes in Ugarit und Israel* (Berlin: Töpelmann, 1961).

DANIEL 12 UND DIE AUFERSTEHUNG DER TOTEN

ERNST HAAG

Obwohl Dan 12:1-4a als Auferstehungszeugnis unbestrittene Anerkennung genießt, bleibt sein Aussagewert für die Biblische Theologie verhältnismäßig gering. Der Grund hierfür liegt in der noch ungelösten exegetischen Problematik[1] des Textes. Proklamiert Dan 12:1-4a eine allgemeine Auferstehung der Toten für Israel oder nur die einer repräsentativen Auswahl? Zählen zu dieser Auswahl nur die Märtyrer des makkabäischen Religionskampfes oder auch die Abtrünnigen der hellenistischen Reformpartei? Gründen die Aussagen des Textes auf fremdreligiösen Vorstellungen oder auf einer genuin israelitischen Glaubenstradition? Hat die Auferstehungsherrlichkeit der aufgewachten Toten ihren Ort noch auf Erden oder schon im Himmel? Zu der mit diesen Fragen nur in Umrissen aufgezeigten Problematik wollen die folgenden Ausführungen einen Lösungsvorschlag erarbeiten.[2]

1. DAN 12:1-4a: EXEGETISCHE ANALYSE

Im Verlauf einer das Endzeitgeschick Israels aufhellenden Vision (Dan 10:1-12, 13) erhält Daniel, belehrt durch das Offenbarungswort eines Himmlischen, Aufschluß über die Rettung der von Gott

---

[1] Vgl. hierzu den Forschungsbericht von K. Koch (unter Mitwirkung von T. Niewisch und J. Tubach), *Das Buch Daniel* (Darmstadt: Wissenschaftliche Buchgesellschaft, 1980).

[2] Zu Rate gezogen wurden die Kommentare von J. J. Collins, *Daniel: A Commentary on the Book of Daniel*, with an essay "The Influence of Daniel on the New Testament" by A. Y. Collins (Hermeneia Series; Minneapolis: Fortress, 1993); J. C. Lebram, *Das Buch Daniel* (Züricher Bibelkommentare AT 23; Zürich: Theologischer Verlag, 1984); L. F. Hartmann und A. A. DiLella, *The Book of Daniel* (AB 23; New York: Doubleday, 1978); A. Lacoque, *Le Livre de Daniel* (CAT 15b; Neuchâtel/Paris: Delachaux et Niestlé, 1976); M. Delcor, *Le Livre de Daniel* (SB; Paris: Gabalda, 1971); O. Plöger, *Das Buch Daniel* (KAT 18; Gütersloh: Mohn, 1965), N. W. Porteous, *Das Danielbuch* (ATD 23; Göttingen: Vandenhoeck & Ruprecht, 1962); A. Bentzen, *Daniel* (HAT 19; Tübingen: Mohr-Sibeck, 1952); J. A. Montgomery, *The Book of Daniel* (ICC; Edinburgh: T. & T. Clark, 1927).

Auserwählten seines Volkes in der Enddrangsal und über deren Auszeichnung durch Gott nach ihrem Tod (Dan 12:1-4a). Der Text dieses Offenbarungswortes lautet:

12:1 In jener Zeit wird auftreten
Michael, der große (Engel) fürst,
der eintritt für die Söhne deines Volkes.
Und herrschen wird eine Zeit der Not,
wie noch keine, seit es ein Volk gibt,
geherrscht hat bis zu jener Zeit.
In jener Zeit aber wird Rettung finden (dein Volk),
jeder, der sich aufgezeichnet findet in dem Buch.

2 Und viele von denen, die (schon) schlafen
in dem Land des Staubes, werden aufwachen.
Diese haben ewiges Leben zu erwarten,
die anderen (Schmach und) ewige Schande.

3 Und die Verständigen werden aufstrahlen
wie der Strahlenglanz an der Himmelsfeste
und die, welche die Vielen gerecht gemacht haben,
wie die Sterne auf immer und ewig.

4 Du aber, Daniel, halte diese Worte geheim
und versiegele das Buch bis zur Zeit des Endes.

Der Aufbau des im Kontext der Vision als relativ selbständige Aussageeinheit abgegrenzten Offenbarungswortes läßt drei gleich lange Abschnitte zu je sechs Stichen erkennen: Nachdem der erste Abschnitt als Ausgangspunkt der Darstellung die Enddrangsal des Gottesvolkes benannt hat, kündigt der zweite Abschnitt für diese Notzeit die Rettung aller von Gott Auserwählten an, deren Heilszustand der dritte Abschnitt an der Auferstehungsherrlichkeit der Verständigen beispielhaft verdeutlicht. Der von der Enddrangsal bis zur Auferstehungsherrlichkeit der zu Gott Erhöhten reichende Spannungsbogen, dessen Darstellung dem Stil einer visionären Auskunft entsprechend in futurisch formulierten Verbalsätzen ergeht, wird im Zentrum, nämlich auf dem Höhepunkt der Ausführungen des mittleren Abschnittes, von einem als Alternativ-aussage gestalteten Nominalsatz[3] unterbrochen, der das Endschicksal der von Gott

---

[3] B. Hasslberger, *Hoffnung in der Bedrängnis. Eine formkritische Untersuchung zu Dan 8 und Dan 10–12* (St. Ottilien: Eos, 1977) verfälscht die Bedeutung des Nominalsatzes in 12:2b, wenn er, wie viele andere Erklärer, in ihm

Auserwählten dem Los der zu ewiger Schande verurteilten Frevler
gegenübergestellt und als Auferstehungsherrlichkeit beschreibt. Die
Aussageabsicht der Darstellung zielt demnach auf die Auszeichnung
und Belohnung der Verständigen nach ihrem Tod und auf die damit
verbundene Würdigung ihres Glaubenseinsatzes in der Not ihres
Volkes.

Die im ersten Abschnitt dreimal angesprochene "Zeit" meint die
nach dem Vier-Reiche-Schema des Buches Daniel vorgesehene
eschatologische Epoche des "Endes" (8:17,19; 11:35, 40), in der die
Auflehnung der Macht des Bösen im Auftreten des Anti-Jahwe
(11:36-45) ihren Höhepunkt (8:23) erreicht und die Not des
Gottesvolkes sich bis zur Unerträglichkeit steigert (12:1). Für diese
eschatologische Epoche erhofft das Offenbarungswort jedoch, wie
der die Tag-Jahwes-Vorstellung aufgreifende Ausdruck "in jener
Zeit" andeutet, eine Manifestation der Königsherrschaft Gottes, die—
entsprechend der Ambivalenz eines solchen Machterweises auch in
diesem Endgeschehen—die entscheidende Wende zum Heil herbei-
führt und gleichzeitig die Widersacher des Gottesvolkes für immer
bloßstellt und beschämt.

Von dieser Manifestation der Königsherrschaft Gottes handelt der
zweite Abschnitt in drei sich inhaltlich steigernden Aussagen.
Zunächst heißt es, daß "in jener Zeit" alle, die sich im Buch aufgeschrieben finden, Rettung erfahren (12:1b). Von himmlischen
Büchern, in denen Menschen- und Völkerschicksale aufgeschrieben
sind, weiß die alttestamentliche Überlieferung mit Bezug auf Mose
(Ex 32:32-33), die Frommen in Israel (Ps 69:29; 139:16; Mal 3:16)
und das Gottesvolk der Endzeit (Jes 4:3; Ps 87:6) zu berichten. Da in
den himmlischen Büchern jedoch nicht nur Gutes, sondern auch
Böses vermerkt ist, erscheint die Abrechnung mit den Frevlern als
ein aufgeschriebenes Gericht (Ps 149:9), das die Widersacher Gottes
hinwegrafft (Jes 65:6). Im Horizont der endzeitlichen Manifestation
der Königsherrschaft Gottes weist das Aufgeschriebensein der von
Gott Auserwählten jedoch darauf hin, daß das "Gerettetwerden" in

---

noch das Prädikat von 12:2a nachwirken sieht (294–96). Inhaltlich handelt es sich
dann bei den in 12:2b Genannten um zwei Unterabteilungen der aus dem
Todesschlaf aufgewachten "Vielen." Dabei hat B. Hasslberger vorher ausdrücklich
festgestellt, daß die nach 12:1 "in jener Zeit" angesiedelten Ereignisse das in 11:40-
45 dargestellte Geschehen von einem anderen Blickwinkel her ergänzen (292). Dort
aber ist von dem Anti-Jahwe die Rede, zu dessen Anhang die in 12:2b
angesprochenen Frevler aus Israel (vgl. 11:32) gehören.

der Enddrangsal offenbar mehr bedeutet als nur das Überleben in einer innergeschichtlichen Bedrängnis. Das Offenbarungswort hat darum hier die in der Schöpfungs- und Geschichtsplanung Gottes vorgesehene Vollendung aller Auserwählten im Blick, die sich, wie es anschließend heißt, in der ewigen Lebensgemeinschaft mit Gott vollzieht (12:2b).

Weiterhin kündigt das Offenbarungswort an, daß viele von denen, die im Land des Staubes schlafen, kraft dieser Heilsoffenbarung Gottes aufwachen werden (12:2a). Meint "schlafen" (יָשֵׁן)[4] beim Menschen den Vorgang zwischen dem Sich-Hinlegen zur Ruhezeit (1 Kön 19.5, Ps 4:9) und dem Erwachen und Aufstehen danach (1 Sam 26:12; 1 Kön 3:20-21), wobei die Parallelität zu "ruhig liegen, stille sein" (שָׁכַב) und "ohnmächtig, betäubt sein" (עָלַף) innerhalb der gleichen Aussage (1 Sam 26:7; Jer 51:39) die Ausschaltung aller Aktivitäten festhält, so kann, wie man leicht einsieht, der Schlaf als Bild zur Veranschaulichung des Todeszustandes in der Stille des Grabes dienen, wo alle Unruhe und Hast des Lebens ein Ende hat (Ijob 3:13). Bedenkt man, daß bei dem Bild vom Todesschlaf auch die Analogie zu der aus der altkanaanäischen Baalreligion bekannten Vorstellung von einem jährlichen Absterben und Auferstehen der Vegetationsgottheit mitgewirkt hat, dann versteht man, warum man auf der einen Seite den Gedanken des Wiederaufstehens mit diesem Bild vom Todesschlaf in Verbindung gebracht hat, aber auf der anderen Seite zur Unterstreichung der Endgültigkeit des Todes ein Aufwachen aus diesem Schlaf ausdrücklich verneint hat (Jer 51:39; Ijob 14:12). Ähnlich verhält es sich mit dem als Ort des Todesschlafes angegebenen "Land des Staubes."[5] Die Ausdrucksweise greift die Vorstellung des Grabes auf, wo die Gebeine des Menschen zu Staub zerfallen, aber auch, wie die Parallelität der Redewendungen "zum Staub" (Ps 22:30) und "zur Grube hinabfahren" (Jes 38:18) beweist, die Vorstellung der Unterwelt (vgl. Akk. bit epri, "Haus des Staubes") oder Scheol, wo die Toten ein Schattendasein führen. Der Umstand jedoch, daß die Wendung "Land des Staubes" hier den Ort als אדמה und nicht als ארץ bezeichnet, läßt, nicht zuletzt in der sonst ungewöhnlichen Verbindung mit "Staub" auf eine Beziehung zu dem Strafurteil schließen, mit dem Gott im Anschluß an den Sündenfall die Rückkehr des

---

[4]   Vgl. J. Schüpphaus (Art. "יָשֵׁן") ThWAT 3.1032–35.

[5]   Vgl. L. Wächter (Art. "עָפָר") ThWAT 6.275–84.

Menschen zum Staub des Erdbodens verfügt, aus dem er ihn vorher geformt hat (Gen 3:19; vgl. 2:7). All dies unterstreicht die Endgültigkeit des Todes bei den Dahingeschiedenen, aber noch viel mehr das Wunder der Neuschöpfung, das sich in ihrem Aufwachen aus dem Todesschlaf und in ihrer Aufnahme in die ewige Lebensgemeinschaft mit Gott vollzieht.

Die Ankündigung des zweiten Abschnittes, daß bei der Manifestation der Königsherrschaft Gottes am Ende alle, die sich im Buch aufgezeichnet finden, Rettung erfahren und daß viele von den (schon) im Land des Staubes Schlafenden ein Aufwachen erleben, schließt das Offenbarungswort mit der Feststellung ab, daß dann als Lohn den von Gott Auserwählten das ewige Leben, den anderen dagegen Schmach und ewige Schande verbleibt (12:2b). Die Interpretation der als Nominalsatz formulierten und in ihrem Kontext als selbständig geltenden Aussage ist in der Forschung kontrovers. Handelt es sich bei den zwei Gruppen, deren Endschicksal alternativ aufgezeigt wird, um Unterabteilungen der aus dem Todesschlaf aufgewachten "Vielen" (12:2a)?[6] Oder stehen hier die aus der Enddrangsal geretteten Auserwählten den vom Bund abgefallenen (11:32) und darum von der Heilsoffenbarung Gottes am Ende ausgeschlossenen Frevlern gegenüber?[7] Bedenkt man, daß die Intention des Offenbarungswortes im Aufweis des postmortalen Geschicks der Märtyrer aus der Zeit des makkabäischen Religionskampfes besteht und daß die Manifestation der Königsherrschaft Gottes in der Enddrangsal Heil und Unheil bedeutet, wie der Hinweis auf das Auftreten Michaels "in jener Zeit" (12:1a) beweist, dann gehört nach den positiven Ankündigungen zur Rettung der von Gott Auserwählten die negative Feststellung von dem Scheitern der

---

[6] So z. B. Collins, *Daniel*, 393; Lebram, *Das Buch Daniel*, 134; Delcor, *Le Livre de Daniel*, 255; Plöger, *Das Buch Daniel*, 171.

[7] So z. B. B. J. Alfrink, "L'Idée de Résurrection d'après Dan XII, 1-2," *Bib* 40 (1959) 355–71; Hartmann-DiLella, *The Book of Daniel*, 308; Lacoque, *Le Livre de Daniel*, 179; U. Kellermann, "Das Danielbuch und die Märtyrertheologie der Auferstehung," in J. W. van Henten (Hg.), *Die Entstehung der jüdischen Martyrologie* (Leiden: Brill, 1989) 51–75; G. Stemberger, "Das Problem der Auferstehung im Alten Testament," *Kairos* 14 (1972) 273–90. Mit Berufung auf G. F. Moore (*Judaism II* [Cambridge, MA, 1930] 298) weist Stemberger darauf hin, daß diese Auffassung auch schon von jüdischen Exegeten des Mittelalters, nämlich von Saadia Gaon, Ibn Ezra und einem in den rabbinischen Bibeln abgedruckten Kommentar eines Saadia (nicht des Gaon), vertreten worden ist (274–75).

vorher (11:40-45 und 11:32) genannten Frevler als abschreckende
Alternative unbedingt zur Logik der Darstellung. Von einer doppelten Auferstehung kann aber dann nicht mehr die Rede sein, wie nicht
zuletzt auch das aus dem Buch Jesaja entlehnte Bild von der
"Schande" (Jes 66:24) bestätigt, das sich dort auf die Leichen der im
Tod verbleibenden Frevler bezieht. Die Auferstehung gilt vielmehr
nur, und zwar der Intention des Offenbarungswortes gemäß, den von
Gott Auserwählten, und das heißt im vorliegenden Fall: den Mär-
tyrern aus der Zeit des makkabäischen Religionskampfes.

Im dritten und letzten Abschnitt verdeutlicht das Offenbarungswort den Heilszustand der von Gott Auserwählten am Beispiel der
Verständigen, die für die Vielen Wegbegleiter zur Gerechtigkeit
waren: Sie strahlen wie der Strahlenglanz der Himmelsfeste und wie
die Sterne auf immer und ewig (12:3). Die Wortbildung "Verständige" (משכלים) mit dem Partizip *Hifil* von שכל, das im
Kausativstamm die Bedeutung "Einsicht haben, verstehen" hat, aber
auch, weil Einsicht die Fähigkeit zu erfolgreicher Lebensgestaltung
ist, die Bedeutung "Erfolg haben," weist auf zwei Eigenschaften
dieser Menschen hin: Zunächst ist die "Einsicht" der Verständigen als
Glieder des jahwetreuen Israel, das seinen Gott "kennt" (11:32), mit
der Gotteserkenntnis in Verbindung zu bringen, die als Glaubenseinsicht das Wissen von Gottes Offenbarung und dem in ihr
beschlossenen Anspruch an die Gläubigen umfaßt. Da jedoch die
Aneignung, der Besitz und die Weitergabe der Gotteserkenntnis
vornehmlich die Aufgabe der Priester (Dtn 33:10-11; Hos 4:6; Jer
2:8; Mal 2:7) und Schriftgelehrten (Neh 8:4-8; Sir 39:1-11) war,
sind die Verständigen offenbar im Bereich der geistlichen Führungs-
schicht Israels zu Hause. In Anbetracht der Leiden dieser Verständigen in der Zeit des makkabäischen Religionskampfes und ihrer
Bewährung in einer Glaubenshaltung, die zu dem Opportunis-mus
der als "Frevler am Bund" bezeichneten Reformjuden im Gegensatz
stand (11:32-35), hatten diese Zeugen Gottes nach Auffassung der
Jahwetreuen im Endgericht einen Lohn zu erwarten, der ihnen den
"Erfolg" ihrer im Martyrium erprobten Glaubenseinsicht bescherte.
Allem Anschein nach stellt daher die Wortbildung "Verständige," die
schwerlich als offizieller Titel gedient hat, ein wohl erst in der
Makkabäerzeit aufgekommenes und den Autoren des Danielbuches
vertrautes apokalyptisches Motivwort dar, das in Anspielung auf die
Doppelbedeutung des Verbums שכל im *Hifil* sowohl die "Glaubens-
einsicht" wie auch den dafür vorgesehenen "Erfolg" im Endgericht

gleichzeitig zum Ausdruck brachte.[8]

Das Hauptverdienst der Verständigen bestand darin, daß sie für "die Vielen" (הרבים) Wegbegleiter zur Gerechtigkeit waren (12:3b). Mit der durch die Setzung des Artikels hervorgehobenen Bezeichnung "die Vielen" (im Unterschied zu der in 12:2a erwähnten "Vielheit" der Dahingeschiedenen) ist nach Ausweis des Danielbuches das zur Zeit der Verständigen lebende, von ihnen mit der Gotteserkenntnis belehrte (11:33) und zur Gerechtigkeit geführte (12:3) Gottesvolk der Endzeit gemeint, das nach der Verfolgung durch den Anti-Jahwe (11:39) das Übermächtigwerden des Bundes in der siebzigsten Jahrwoche erlebt (9:27). Die Frage, warum man hier ausgerechnet den Rest Israels als "die Vielen" bezeichnet hat, läßt sich, wie es scheint, im Hinblick auf die Nachkommenschaft Abrahams im "Bund" (9:4, 27; 11:22, 28, 30, 32) gemäß der an den Erzvater ergangenen Mehrungsverheißung (Gen 17:4) und mit Bezug auf die Vielheit der Menschen in dem Jerusalem der Heilszeit (Jes 54:1-3; Sach 2:8) beantworten. Eine Vermittlerrolle hat dabei wohl die deuteronomisch/deuteronomistische Paränese gespielt, in der die Volkwerdung Israels aus unscheinbaren Anfängen (Dtn 1:10; 10:22; 26:3) zum Paradigma des Neubeginns nach dem Gericht Gottes geworden ist (Dtn 6:3; 13:18; 30:1-10, 16). Der Ausdruck "die Vielen" ist darum vermutlich ebenso wie die Redeweise von den "Verständigen" ein apokalyptisches Motivwort, mit dem man in der Zeit des makkabäischen Religionskampfes den Rest Israels bezeichnet hat, der in der als Läuterungsgericht erfahrenen Enddrangsal seiner Vollendung gläubig entgegenging.[9]

Diesen Rest Israels haben die Verständigen "gerecht gemacht" (מצדקים) und damit zu jener Gerechtigkeit geführt, die im Deuteronomium als Ausdruck der vollkommenen Gesetzeserfüllung gilt (Dtn 6:25; 24:13). Ohne Zweifel hat dazu die Weitergabe der Gotteserkenntnis gehört (11:33), aber offensichtlich auch ihr als Vorbild und Wegweisung aufgefaßter Glaubenseinsatz im Gottesvolk. Aufschluß darüber gibt eine Parallelaussage der Ebed-Jahwe-Prophetie in Jesaja 53. Dort heißt es in der ebenfalls zur Zeit des makkabäischen Religionskampfes entstandenen Bearbeitungs-schicht,[10] daß

---

[8] Vgl. E. Haag, "Die Hasidäer und das Danielbuch," *TThZ* 102 (1993) 51–63, ders., *Daniel* (EB, Würzburg: Echter, 1993) 78–79.

[9] Vgl. Haag, *Daniel*, 79–80.

[10] Zur Untersuchung und Begründung des Abhängigkeitsverhältnisses vgl. E.

der Gottesknecht dadurch "die Vielen" (הרבים) zur Gerechtigkeit führt (מצדיק), daß er in Stellvertretung für sie ihre Sündenlast trägt (Jes 53:11b). Nun hat man nach Ausweis des deuterokanonischen Asarja-Gebetes im Danielbuch nach der Einstel-lung des Opferkultes im Tempel zu Jerusalem das Hingeschlach-tetwerden der Märtyrer im makkabäischen Religionskampf als ein Gott wohlgefälliges Opfer bezeichnet, das zur Vergebung der Sünden beiträgt und sühnende Kraft besitzt (3:38-40). Es legt sich daher die nicht unbegründete Vermutung nahe, daß zu dem als Vorbild aufgefaßten Glaubens-einsatz der Verständigen auch das in Nachahmung der Idealgestalt des Gottesknechts als Sühneleiden ertragene Martyrium gehört hat und daß nicht zuletzt wegen dieser Hinführung der Vielen zur Gerechtigkeit ihnen als Lohn die Auferstehungsherrlichkeit in der Erhöhung zu Gott geschenkt worden ist.

Über die Auferstehungsherrlichkeit der Verständigen sagt das Offenbarungswort, daß sie aufstrahlen wie der Strahlenglanz der Himmelsfeste und wie die Sterne auf immer und ewig (12:3). Der mit der paronomastischen Konstruktion in dem Vergleich ange-sprochene Lichterglanz des Sternenheeres am Himmel, der ent-sprechend der Doppelbedeutung der Basis זהר "leuchten" und "warnen" die Tätigkeit und die Bedeutung der Verständigen bildhaft hervorhebt, meint schwerlich das astronomische Phänomen des gestirnten Nachthimmels als solchen; denn der hier wahrgenommene Lichterglanz ist nur von mäßiger Intensität. Der apokalyptischen Darstellung und ihrem theologischen Gegenstand entspricht es eher, in dem zum Vergleich herangezogenen Bild eine mythische Vorstellung zu sehen, nämlich die von dem Sternenheer des Himmels als Hinweis auf die Göttersöhne in der Umgebung des auf dem Gottesberg thronenden Höchsten Gottes El (Ri 5:20; Ob 4; Dan 8:10; Ijob 38:7; vgl. auch Jes 14:12-15; Ezek 28:14,16). In diesem Fall aber hat der Vergleich mit dem Strahlenglanz des Sternenheeres die Auferstehungsherrlichkeit der Verständigen im Blick, die ihnen kraft ihrer Erhöhung zu Gott im Himmel geschenkt worden ist. Auf-schlußreich ist auch hier wieder eine Parallelaussage über den Gottesknecht, der offenbar den Verständigen als Vorbild gedient hat. Von dem Gottesknecht heißt es nämlich in der aus der Makkabäerzeit stammenden Bearbeitungsschicht von Jes 53, daß er aufsteigen, erhaben und sehr hoch sein wird (Jes 52:13). In dreifach sich

---

Haag, "Stellvertretung und Sühne nach Jesaja 53," *TThZ* 105 (1996) 1–20.

steigernder Aussage erinnert das Wort an die Hoheit und Erhabenheit Jahwes (Jes 5:16) und seines himmlischen Thrones (Jes 6:1) sowie des endzeitlichen Zion (Jes 2:2). Offensichtlich handelt es sich hier um die Erhöhung des Gottesknechts, durch die Gott ihm Anteil an seiner ewigen Königsherrschaft verleiht. Den gleichen Vorgang der Erhöhung hat auch das Offenbarungswort über das Endschicksal der Verständigen im Blick, und zwar als Ausgleich für die von ihnen bei ihrem Glaubenseinsatz erlittene Erniedrigung und Schmach.

Mit der Aufforderung an Daniel, die Worte geheimzuhalten und das Buch zu versiegeln bis zur Zeit des Endes (12:4a), schließt das Offenbarungswort. Der apokalyptischen Darstellung entsprechend (vgl. auch 8:26) hebt die Aufforderung noch einmal die tröstliche Glaubenswahrheit hervor, daß Gott in seiner Schöpfungs- und Geschichtsplanung auch über die Enddrangsal hinaus für die von ihm Auserwählten die Auferstehungsherrlichkeit in der Lebensgemeinschaft mit ihm bereithält.

2. DAN 12:1-4a: THEOLOGISCHE SYNTHESE

Traditionsgeschichtlich gründet das Offenbarungswort Dan 12:1-4a in einer für das Alte Testament erst spät greifbaren Glaubensüberlieferung, deren Umrisse und Schwerpunkte schon in der Prophetie von der Wiederbelebung der Totengebeine in Ezek 37:1-14 in Erscheinung treten.[11] Obwohl der Text inhaltlich nur von der Wiederherstellung Israels nach dem babylonischen Exil handelt, hat dennoch der dargestellte Vorgang aufgrund seiner eschatologischen Ausrichtung den Rang eines biblischen Modells für den Glauben an die Auferstehung der Toten erlangt. Die literarische Ausgestaltung der Perikope[12] und ihre Rezeptionsgeschichte im Judentum[13] sind

---

[11] Zur Exegese von Ezek 37:1-14 vgl. W. Eichrodt, *Der Prophet Hesekiel* (ATD 22; Göttingen: Vandenhoeck & Ruprecht, 1978); und W. Zimmerli, *Ezechiel* (BK XIII,2; Neukirchen: Neukirchener Verlag, 1969). Zur Einordnung von Ezek 37:1-14 in die alttestamentliche Tradition von der Auferstehung der Toten vgl. den Exkurs "On Resurrection" von J. Collins (*Daniel*, 394–98); E. Haag, "Seele und Unsterblichkeit in biblischer Sicht," in W. Breuning (Hg.), *Seele. Problembegriff christlicher Eschatologie* (QD 106, Freiburg: Herder, 1986) 31–93; R. Martin-Achard, "Résurrection dans l'Ancien Testament et le Judaisme," *DBS* 10 (1985) 437–87.

[12] Vgl. R. Bartelmus "Ez 37:1-14, die Verbform $w^e qatal$ und die Anfänge der Auferstehungshoffnung," *ZAW* 97 (1985) 366–89, der exegetisch überzeugend den Nachweis erbracht hat, daß in Ezek 37:7a, 8b-10a ein Einschub aus der

dafür der Beleg.

Der Aufbau des Textes gestaltet sich so, daß auf den Visionsbericht Ezechiels von der Wiederbelebung der Totengebeine Israels
(37:1-11a) ein Disputationswort folgt, in dem der Prophet der
Hoffnungslosigkeit der Exulanten in Babel (37:11b) die Ankündigung entgegensetzt, daß Gott sein Volk aus der Behausung des
Todes herausführen und, ausgestattet mit seinem Geist, in das Land
Israel bringen werde (37:12-14). Im Zentrum der Textkomposition
steht somit ein nach menschlichem Ermessen unabwendbares Todes-
geschick, zu dessen Aufhebung es nicht nur der Überwindung des
Todes als Unheilsmacht durch Gott, den Schöpfer und Erlöser,
sondern auch noch des Abschlusses der Führungsgeschichte Jahwes
mit Israel im Land der Verheißung bedarf.

Der Visionsbericht beginnt mit der Angabe des Propheten, daß
die Hand Jahwes über ihn kam und ihn im Zustand der Verzückung
in eine Ebene geführt hat, die voll von Totengebeinen war (37:1).
Gemeint ist mit dieser Ebene die Weite Mesopotamiens, die hier—
vermutlich als geographischer Gegensatz zu den Bergen des Landes
Israel—für den Ort des Exils steht. Dort erkennt Ezechiel in den
Totengebeinen die Übermacht des Todes, die nach dem Strafgericht
Gottes Israel eingeholt hat. Die Frage Jahwes: "Können diese
Gebeine wieder lebendig werden?" ist daher eine Provokation; denn
so wird in die Evidenz des triumphierenden Todes hineingefragt. Die
Antwort des Propheten lautet jedoch: "Jahwe, du weißt es" (37:3)!
Die Antwort zeigt, daß Ezechiel mit dem Bekenntnis seiner Ohn-
macht als Mensch den Hinweis auf das Erkennen Jahwes verbindet.
Offenbar will der Prophet damit andeuten, daß die Antwort auf die
Frage nach der Wiederbelebung der Totengebeine in der für alles
Geschaffene konstitutiven Schöpfungs- und Geschichts-planung
Gottes beschlossen ist. Darauf ergeht an ihn das Wort, den Toten-
gebeinen anzukündigen, daß Gott sie wieder mit Sehnen, Fleisch und
Haut ausstatten und mit Lebensgeist erfüllen wird, damit sie erken-
nen, daß er Jahwe ist (Ezek 37:4-6). Bezeichnenderweise ist diese
Ankündigung als Erweiswort gestaltet, dessen formgeschichtliche
Eigenart den Inhalt des Auftrages hier auf die Erkenntnis des Ich-
Geheimnisses Jahwes bezieht. Als Adressat der Ankündigung er-

---

Makkabäerzeit vorliegt.

[13] Vgl. hierzu die Illustration von Ezek 37:1-14 in der Synagoge von Dura
Europos und die Interpretation von W. Zimmerli, *Ezechiel*, 899.

scheinen die Totengebeine des Gottesvolkes, die im Horizont der Vision auf die in der Situation des Endes gefährdete, aber dennoch erhalten gebliebene Identität Israels verweisen. Zur Aufrechterhaltung und Weiterführung dieser Identität offenbart Gott darum in dem Erweiswort seine Identität als "Jahwe" (vgl. Ex 3:14). Das heißt aber: Gottes "Da-sein" bei der Führung seines Volkes in der Situation des Endes äußert sich in der durchgehaltenen Konsequenz seiner in Schöpfung und Auserwählung frei eingegangenen Bindung an den Menschen. Auch im Tod, will der Prophet sagen, besteht noch die Möglichkeit eines Wirksamwerdens der Schöpfermacht Gottes.

Was Ezechiel in der Darstellung des Visionsberichtes hintergründig über die Schöpfermacht Gottes bei der Wiederherstellung seines Volkes gesagt hat, entfaltet er in dem anschließenden Disputationswort im Hinblick auf die Todesnot der Exulanten (37:11b). Danach vollzieht sich der das Schöpfungsgeschehen weiterführende Akt der Vollendung in der Herausführung des Volkes aus der Behausung des Todes und in der Versetzung der Geretteten in das Land der Verheißung, wo ihnen die Ausstattung mit dem Geist Jahwes die Lebensgemeinschaft mit Gott verbürgt (37:12-14).

Strukturell weist die Darstellung eine überraschende Ähnlichkeit mit dem vorpriesterschriftlichen Schöpfungsbericht in Genesis 2 auf, wie nicht nur die neue "Formung" des Menschen aus den verdorrenden Totengebeinen und ihre "Belebung" mit dem Geist (vgl. Gen 2:7), sondern auch die Herausführung der Neugeschaffenen aus ihrer Behausung des Todes und ihre Ansiedelung im Land der Verheißung beweist: ein Vorgang, für den die der Entrückung altorientalischer Heroen nachgestaltete Versetzung des Menschen in den Garten von Eden (Gen 2:15) das Vorbild abgegeben hat.[14] Im Unterschied zu Genesis 2 geht es jedoch in Ezechiel 37 nicht mehr um die Setzung des Anfangs bei der Ersterschaffung des Menschen und der Angabe seiner Bestimmung, sondern um die Einholung dieses Anfangs bei der Neuschöpfung des Menschen und bei dessen Aufnahme in die Lebensgemeinschaft mit Gott.

Zur Makkabäerzeit hat, wie schon gesagt, ein Bearbeiter den Visionsbericht in Ezechiel 37 durch einen Texteinschub (vv. 7a, 8b-

---

[14] Vgl. A. Schmitt, *Entrückung—Aufnahme—Himmelfahrt. Untersuchung zu einem Vorstellungsbereich im AT* (Stuttgart: Katholisches Bibelwerk, 1973) 310–12.

10a) erweitert, der inhaltlich den Glauben an die Auferstehung der Toten bezeugt. Während der Visionsbericht ursprünglich die Wiederbelebung der Totengebeine durch den von Gott mitgeteilten Geist vorgesehen hat (37:5), heißt es jetzt, daß der Prophet den Geist von den vier Winden herbeirufen soll, damit er die Totengebeine zum Leben erweckt (37:9). Diese ganz auf die Naturseite des göttlichen Wirkens bezogene altisraelitische Geistvorstellung (vgl. Ps 104:29; Gen 6:3,17; 7:15, 22; Num 16:22; 27:16; Ijob 10:12; 12:10; 17:1), die sich von den Aussagen über den Geist als Wirkkraft der Heilsgeschichte und als innere Wesensmacht Gottes deutlich unterscheidet, ist mit dem Lebensatem, den Gott dem Menschen bei dessen Erschaffung einhaucht (Gen 2:7), aufs engste verwandt. Während dort aber die Übertragung des Lebensatems durch Gott den Menschen vor allen anderen Lebewesen auszeichnet, geht es hier bei dem Zusammenfluten des Geistes offenbar um einen Großangriff auf die Macht des Todes, der nur mit dem Sieg des Lebens enden kann.[15] Darüber hinaus verdient der Umstand Beachtung, daß hier von den Totengebeinen der "Erschlagenen" (37:9) die Rede ist und damit eine Bezeichnung gebraucht wird, die auf die Märtyrer des makkabäischen Religionskampfes verweist. Damit aber ergibt sich gegenüber dem ursprünglichen Visionsbericht eine nicht unerheb-liche, neue Akzentsetzung: Geht es bei Ezechiel noch um die Frage, ob und wie Jahwe die Wiederherstellung Israels als Kollektiv nach dem im Gottesgericht erlebten Ende bewirkt, so bei dem Bearbeiter um die Frage, ob und wie Jahwe dem einzelnen Frommen, der für seinen Glauben gekämpft und das Martyrium erlitten hat, über dessen Tod hinaus noch zur Seite steht. Mit anderen Worten: An die Stelle der Hoffnung auf eine irdische Restitution Israels als Volk ist die Hoffnung auf eine jenseitige Restitution des einzelnen Frommen getreten.[16]

Vorbereitet wurde die Wende zu dieser individuellen Auferstehungserwartung durch die Konzentration des einzelnen Frommen auf sein postmortales Geschick im Horizont einer das Kollektiv Israel betreffenden Heilseschatologie, wie sie vor allem Deuterojesaja vertreten hat. Als theologischer Denker und Prophet sah Deuterojesaja sich nämlich vor die Aufgabe gestellt, die bisherige Führungsgeschichte Jahwes mit Israel in einer übergreifenden Einheit mit dem

---

15 So W. Eichrodt, *Der Prophet Hesekiel*, 356.

16 So R. Bartelmus, "Ez 37:1-14, die Verbform *weqatal*," 388.

zu seiner Zeit erfahrenen neuen Heil so zu verbinden, daß der durch
das Gottesgericht des Exils bezeichnete Bruch zwischen der sündigen
Vergangenheit und der Setzung eines neuen Anfangs nicht zu über-
sehen war. Diese übergreifende Einheit ergab sich dem Propheten im
Rückgriff auf das von Anfang an heilvolle Handeln Gottes in
Schöpfung und Geschichte. Für Deuterojesaja stellt sich daher die
Erlösung Israels als die schöpferische Einholung jenes Anfangs dar,
den Gott einst mit der Auserwählung dieses Volkes im Hinblick auf
das Heil der Schöpfung gesetzt hat. Hierbei kommt nach Ansicht
Deuterojesajas das Schöpfertum Gottes in einer doppelten Weise zum
Tragen: einmal in der Überwindung der Diskontinuität zwischen
dem Früheren und dem Neuen, einer Aufgabe also, die das am
Nullpunkt seiner Existenz angelangte Gottesvolk niemals aus eigener
Kraft zu bewältigen imstande war, und sodann in der Vollendung der
Führungsgeschichte mit Israel durch eine abschließende Heilstat von
universaler Bedeutung. Im Horizont dieser für die exilisch-
nachexilische Zeit maßgeblichen Heilseschatologie bildeten sich
darauf im Bereich der individuellen Auferstehungserwartung zwei
Schwerpunkte heraus: zunächst die Glaubensauffassung von der
Überwindung des Todesverhängnisses durch Jahwe, den Gott des
Heils (Ps 88:2-19; Jes 25:8), und dann die Hoffnung, daß Gott den
mit ihm verbundenen Frommen in einem als Entrückung vor-
gestellten Akt dem Los der Frevler in der Scheol entreißen und
durch die Aufnahme in die ewige Lebensgemeinschaft mit ihm
vollenden werde (Ps 49:6-21; 73:24).

Ganz auf die endzeitliche Manifestation der ewigen Königsherrschaft Jahwes ist die Große Jesaja-Apokalypse Jesaja 24–27
konzentriert. Die in diesem Horizont nicht fehlende Auferstehungs-
problematik bringt ein Vertrauensbekenntnis Israels zur Sprache, das
zwei hier interessierende Schwerpunkte aufweist: Während der Blick
zunächst auf die Offenbarung der Gerechtigkeit Jahwes und den von
ihm erhofften Frieden gerichtet ist, der als Heilsgut ebenso wie die
Auferstehung der Toten den Frevlern verwehrt bleibt (26:7-14),
wendet sich die Aufmerksamkeit anschließend der Heilsoffenbarung
Jahwes für die Gerechten zu, die ihnen über die Mehrung ihres
Volkes hinaus eine auch das Todesschicksal ihrer Verstorbenen
umwandelnde Vollendung schenkt (26:15-19). So artikuliert auf dem
Höhepunkt des Vertrauensbekenntnisses das Volk seinen Glauben mit
den Worten: "Leben werden deine Toten, meine Leichen auferstehen. Erwacht und frohlockt, ihr Bewohner des Staubes! Denn Tau

der Lichter ist dein Tau, und die Erde gebiert die Verstorbenen"
(26:19). Läßt der auffällige Wechsel der Possessivpronomina bei den
"Toten" und den "Leichen" auf ein Todesschicksal schließen, das
sowohl Gott wie auch sein auserwähltes Volk bewegt, so weist der
von den Staubbewohnern bis zu dem Tau der Lichter reichende
Spannungsbogen auf einen den Gerechten geltenden Akt der
Belohnung hin, der die von Gott bewirkte Mehrung des Volkes und
die Ausweitung seines Lebensraumes mit der Vollendung in der
Herrlichkeit Jahwes krönt. Beachtet man nämlich, daß hier die allem
Anschein nach dem Mythos entlehnte Ausdrucksweise "Tau der
Lichter" eine von den Sternen als Gottessöhnen (Ijob 38:7)
ausgehende Wachstumskraft meint, dann zielt die mit Nachdruck als
Tau Jahwes ("dein Tau") bezeichnete Macht auf eine Heilsoffen-
barung, die nach der Vernichtung des Todes als Unheilsmacht (25:8)
den toten Gerechten die Teilnahme an der Herrlichkeit Jahwes und
seines ewigen Lebens eröffnet.

Direkt mit Bezug auf das postmortale Geschick der jüdischen
Märtyrer aus der Zeit des makkabäischen Religionskampfes und
gleichzeitig in Weiterführung der bisher aufgewiesenen Ansätze für
eine jenseitige Restitution des Frommen hat 2 Makkabäer 7 mit fast
systematischer Präzision eine Theologie der Auferstehung von den
Toten entwickelt, die sich von den Unsterblichkeitsvorstellungen der
hellenistischen Umwelt Israels deutlich abhebt.[17] Ausgangspunkt ist
die Verhaftung einer jüdischen Mutter und ihrer sieben Söhne, die
ein heidnischer König unter Androhung der Todesstrafe zum Abfall
vom Jahweglauben bewegen will. Nachdem die Mutter und ihre
Söhne sich gegenseitig unter Berufung auf die Tora des Mose Mut
zugesprochen und ihr Endgeschick mit dem in der Offenbarung
Gottes beschlossenen Lohn in Verbindung gebracht haben (7:6; vgl.
Dtn 32:36), bekennen die Söhne in zwei antithetisch angeordneten
Aussagereihen zunächst, daß der heidnische König ihnen zwar ihr
gegenwärtiges Leben mit Gewalt nehmen kann, daß aber der König
der Welt seine Getreuen zu einer ewigen Wiedergeburt des Lebens
auferwecken wird (7:9), bei der sie im Zuge der Neuschöpfung des
Menschen ihre verlorenen Gliedmaßen wiederbekommen (7:11) und
wie alle Frommen in Erfüllung der Heilsverheißungen Gottes durch
seine Kraft die Auferstehung erlangen (7:14); diese Äußerung ent-

---

[17] Vgl. U. Kellermann, *Auferstanden in den Himmel. 2 Makkabäer 7 und die
Auferstehung der Märtyrer* (Stuttgart: Katholisches Bibelwerk, 1979).

faltet die zweite Aussagenreihe mit dem Bekenntnis, daß Gott bei der
Offenbarung seiner Rettermacht an Israel den heidnischen König zur
Rechenschaft ziehen (7:17) und seine widergöttliche Auflehnung
(7:19) im Endgericht bestrafen wird (7:34-36).

Nachdem das Bekenntnis der Söhne den Stellenwert der Aufer-
stehung im Rahmen der Führungsgeschichte Jahwes mit Israel zum
Ausdruck gebracht hat, bietet auf dem Höhepunkt der Erzählung das
Bekenntnis der Mutter, die hier das von der Hoffnung auf Gottes
Heil (7:20) getragene Israel repräsentiert, die Lehre von der
Auferstehung der Toten als solche. Hierbei sind zwei von der
Darstellung her getrennte, aber inhaltlich einander ergänzende
Abschnitte zu unterscheiden. Mit deutlichem Rückbezug auf den
vorpriesterschriftlichen Schöpfungsbericht von der Erschaffung des
Menschen (Gen 2:7) und unter Betonung der absoluten Schöpfer-
initiative Jahwes schildert die Mutter in dem ersten Abschnitt, wie
das Dasein ihrer Söhne durch die Mitteilung des Lebensatems von
seiten Gottes und durch die von ihm bewirkte Anordung des
Grundstoffes seinen Anfang genommen hat (7:22-23). Die Erzählung
hat damit das für die ältere Darstellung bezeichnende Bild des
Staubes dem hellenistischen Elementardenken angepaßt. Allein der
Schöpfergott, der den Anfang des Menschen gesetzt hat, besitzt auch
die Macht, in Erfüllung seiner heilsgeschichtlichen Führung die
Vollendung des Menschen selbst über die Todesschwelle hinaus noch
herbeizuführen. Der zweite Abschnitt ist so aufgebaut, daß die
Schilderung der Mutter von der Fürsorge für ihr Kind und dem
Wunsch nach einem Wiedersehen mit ihm nach dessen Tod sachlich
die Vollendung des Menschen zum Gegenstand haben und in dieser
Eigenschaft eine Schöpfungsaussage umschließen, die von der
Wirkmacht Gottes bei der Erschaffung der Welt und des Menschen
handelt (7:27-29).

Der in diesem Zusammenhang geäußerte Hinweis auf das Schaffen
Gottes aus noch nicht bestehenden Dingen (7:28; vgl. Gen 1:2) und
die Aufgliederung des Schöpfungswerkes in die Entstehung von
Himmel und Erde sowie von allem, was diese erfüllt (7:28; vgl. Gen
1:3-28), zeigen unübersehbar, daß diese Schöpfungsaussage im Kern
des Abschnittes auf den priesterschriftlichen Schöpfungsbericht
zurückgreift. Offensichtlich ist dies mit Absicht geschehen, weil der
priesterschriftliche Schöpfungsbericht als Anfangsdarstellung von
der Erschaffung der Welt und des Menschen auch noch deren
Vollendung am siebten Tag als ein eigenes Schöpfungswerk Gottes

kennt (Gen 2:1-3). Auf diese Vollendung aber kommt es der Erzählung an, wenn sie die Mutter von der Zeit des Erbarmens sprechen läßt, in der sie den Sohn nach seinem Tod wiederzusehen hofft (7:29).

Den gleichen Schöpfungsvorgang der Vollendung hat offenbar auch 2 Makkabäer 12 im Blick, wenn es dort heißt, daß es im Hinblick auf die Auferstehung der Toten nicht sinnlos und überflüssig ist, für die Verstorbenen ein Sündopfer darzubringen und für ihr Heil zu beten (12:43-45). Die Aussage bezieht sich nicht auf das Fortleben der Toten in der Scheol, sondern auf das Weitergehen der Führungsgeschichte Gottes mit seinem Volk, insofern in ihr auch nach dem Abschluß des irdischen Lebens noch eine Aufnahme des Menschen in die unzerstörbare Lebensgemeinschaft mit Gott vorgesehen ist, dann nämlich, wenn Gott bei der Manifestation seiner ewigen Königsherrschaft das Schöpfungswerk vollendet.[18]

Auch wenn das Alte Testament noch nicht (wie später das Neue Testament) die Faktizität einer schon erfolgten Auferstehung der Toten und deren prinzipielle Universalität zum Gegenstand haben konnte, so läßt doch die Heilseschatologie der Propheten in Verbindung mit ihrem Echo im deuterokanonischen Schrifttum klar erkennen, daß die jenseitige Restitution des Gerechten und seine Vollendung im Eschaton nicht nur die Überwindung des Todes als Unheilsmacht durch Gott, den Schöpfer und Erlöser, sondern auch den Abschluß der Führungsgeschichte dieses Gottes mit dem Menschen durch dessen Aufnahme in die ewige Heilsgemeinschaft mit ihm, dem lebendigen Gott,[19] wesenhaft zur Voraussetzung haben. Zu dieser Glaubenseinsicht aber hat, wie der Überblick über die

---

[18] Ähnlich urteilt das Buch der Weisheit, wenn es von den Seelen der Gerechten behauptet, daß sie in Gottes Hand sind (3:1). Trotz der terminologischen Nähe zur hellenistischen Anthropologie hat die Aussage, ganz in Übereinstimmung mit der ganzheitlichen Sicht des Menschen im Alten Testament, hier die Personalität der Gerechten im Gegenüber zu Gott, ihrem Schöpfer und Erlöser, im Blick, der, wie die Anspielung auf seine Hand verrät, seine Führungsgeschichte mit diesen Menschen noch nicht vollendet hat.

[19] Vgl. E. Haag, "Söhne des lebendigen Gottes (Hos 2:1)," in: T. Söding (Hg.), *Der lebendige Gott. Studien zur Theologie des Neuen Testamentes* (Festschrift W. Thüsing; Münster: Aschendorff, 1996) 3–24, wo gezeigt wird, daß durch die Fortschreibung der Prophetie des Hosea schon in der deuteronomischen Epoche das Fundament für den Glauben an Jahwe gelegt worden ist, der als Schöpfer und Erlöser den Tod als Unheilsmacht überwindet.

alttestamentliche Tradition von der Auferstehung der Toten gezeigt hat, das Offenbarungswort Dan 12:1-4a einen aufschlußreichen und grundlegenden Beitrag geleistet.

3. AUSGERWÄHLTE BIBLIOGRAPHIE

Alfrink, B. B. J. "L'Idée de Résurrection d'après Dan XII, 1-2," *Bib* 40 (1959) 355–71.

Bartelmus, R. "Ez 37:1-14, die Verbform $w^e qatal$ und die Anfänge der Auferstehungshoffnung," *ZAW* 97 (1985) 366–89.

Haag, E. "Seele und Unsterblichkeit in biblischer Sicht," in W. Breuning (Hg.), *Seele. Problembegriff christlicher Eschatologie* (QD 106, Freiburg: Herder, 1986) 31–93.

—. "Die Hasidäer und das Danielbuch," *TThZ* 102 (1993) 51–63.

—. "Söhne des lebendigen Gottes (Hos 2:1)," in: T. Söding (Hg.), *Der lebendige Gott. Studien zur Theologie des Neuen Testamentes* (Festschrift W. Thüsing; Münster: Aschendorff, 1996) 3–24.

—. "Stellvertretung und Sühne nach Jesaja 53," *TThZ* 105 (1996) 1–20.

Hasslberger, B. *Hoffnung in der Bedrängnis. Eine formkritische Untersuchung zu Dan 8 und Dan 10–12* (St. Ottilien: Eos, 1977).

Kellermann, U. *Auferstanden in den Himmel. 2 Makkabäer 7 und die Auferstehung der Märtyrer* (Stuttgart: Katholisches Bibelwerk, 1979).

Koch, K. (unter Mitwirkung von T. Niewisch und J. Tubach). *Das Buch Daniel* (Darmstadt: Wissenschaftliche Buchgesellschaft, 1980).

Martin-Achard, R. "Résurrection dans l'Ancien Testament et le Judaisme," *DBS* 10 (1985) 437–87.

Schmitt, A. *Entrückung—Aufnahme—Himmelfahrt. Untersuchung zu einem Vorstellungsbereich im AT* (Stuttgart: Katholisches Bibelwerk, 1973).

Stemberger, G. "Das Problem der Auferstehung im Alten Testament," *Kairos* 14 (1972) 273–90.

DANIEL 3 AND 6 IN
EARLY CHRISTIAN LITERATURE

JAN WILLEM VAN HENTEN

1. INTRODUCTION

The dramatic episodes in the careers of Daniel and his three companions as royal administrators (Daniel 3 and 6) were popular among Christians of the first two centuries CE. There is a considerable number of early Christian uses of these tales in their Aramaic or Greek versions, which often focus upon just one the motifs involved.[1] In this contribution I intend to survey most of the explicit references to both tales in early Christian literature up to roughly 200 CE,[2] and to discuss briefly how these references seem to function in their literary contexts. Before that, however, I will offer a few introductory remarks to indicate the direction which my own reading of both chapters of Daniel has taken.

2. RELIGION AND POLITICS IN DANIEL 3 AND 6

In their present Aramaic form the stories of Daniel 3 and 6, to a considerable extent, correspond to a pattern found in so-called ancient Near Eastern wisdom stories that describe the defamation of a sage by other members of the court, his conviction by the king and his mira-

---

[1] On the various versions of Daniel 3 and 6 and their interconnections, see J. J. Collins, *Daniel. A Commentary on the Book of Daniel* (Hermeneia; Minneapolis: Fortress, 1993) 2–12, with references. For the additions, see K. Koch, *Deuterokanonische Zusätze zum Danielbuch. Entstehung und Textgeschichte* (AOAT 38; Neukirchen-Vluyn: Butzon & Bercker/Neukirchener Verlag, 1987). For surveys of Daniel's reception in early Christian literature, see A. Yarbro Collins, "The History of Interpretation: B. The Christian Interpretation," in Collins, *Daniel*, 90–117; R. Bodenmann, *Naissance d'une exégèse: Daniel dans l'église ancienne des trois premiers siècles* (BGBE 28; Tübingen: Mohr-Siebeck, 1986).

[2] Unless specified otherwise, the Greek text of Daniel and its numbering follows the edition of A. Rahlfs, *Septuaginta. Id est Vetus Testamentum graece iuxta LXX interpres* (8th ed., 2 vols.; Stuttgart: Würtembergische Bibelanstalt Stuttgart, 1965).

culous deliverance and rehabilitation.[3] Daniel as well as the three
Judean men of chapter 3, therefore, can be understood as sages (cf. the
references to their wisdom in 1:17; 5:11-12, 14). Furthermore, their
accusation, conviction, execution and miraculous deliverance, comparable to the fate of some sages in wisdom tales, are highlighted in both
stories.

King Nebuchadnezzar's erection of an enormous golden statue and
his command to worship it are the point of departure of the story in
chapter 3 (vv. 1-7).[4] Several times an exhaustive list of officials is
mentioned: these have to worship the statue as representatives of the
various ethnic and language groups of the kingdom. The Aramaic text
mentions separately the god of the statue and the king (3:12, 14, 18),
but the Old Greek translation identifies the two as one, which implies
the veneration of the king (cf. Judith 3:8). The repetitious references
to the musical instruments and officials, and the officials' falling on
their knees as a sign of veneration for the statue, create the impression
of a gigantic manifestation of loyalty to the king. The statue's god
seems to be the principal state god, who protects the king and makes
him triumph. Its veneration, therefore, was a demonstration of loyalty
to Nebuchadnezzar, and any refusal, of course, was a manifest act of
civil disobedience. Next, the story focuses upon the response of the
three young men to this new situation. The accusation against them
(3:8-12), as well as their dialogue with the king (3:13-18), juxtaposes
the veneration of the three men's God on the one hand and the king's
god on the other, which implies a principal conflict of loyalties (cf.
3:17-18).

A similar conflict of loyalties is described in Daniel 6. There
Daniel's behaviour implies that he relativizes the king's authority and
considers it subordinate to the authority of his God. He explains his

---

[3] J. J. Collins, "The Court-Tales of Daniel and the Development of
Apocalyptic," *JBL* 94 (1975) 218–34. Idem (*Daniel*, 38–52) suggests that Daniel
1–6 correspond to the genre of the court tale; see also L. M. Wills, *The Jew in the
Court of the Foreign King: Ancient Jewish Court Legends* (HDR 26; Minneapolis:
Fortress, 1990). While I do not deny that there are important correspondences to
court tales, the alternative suggestion of the wisdom tale, advocated by (among
others) Hans-Peter Müller and Jürgen Lebram seems to account better for some of
the features in Daniel 3 and 6. See esp. H. P. Müller, "Die weisheitliche Lehrerzählung im Alten Testament und seiner Umwelt," *WO* 9 (1977) 77–98.

[4] For details, the study of C. Kuhl, *Die drei Männer im Feuer* (BZAW 55;
Giessen: Töpelmann, 1930), is still useful.

rescue to the king by stating that he has not been found guilty by God and therefore has done nothing wrong against the king (6:23), even though he has transgressed the king's law. The edict which concludes the chapter (6:26-28) can be read as a summary of chapters 1-6, and offers an acknowledgement of the Judeans' God that surpasses that of Dan 3:28-30. King Darius not only recognizes this God as an imperial god among others, but also orders his subjects to pay respect to Daniel's God. The religion of the Judeans seems to be a central element of their identity which limits their loyalty to the state. Daniel's and his companions' monotheism leads to a fundamental relativization of state authority at the moment when the king's policy, and the four men's religious practice, run into conflict with each other. Such a conflict of loyalty seems to underlie many Jewish and Christian traditions about noble death.

The death penalty as sanction against the refusal to worship a state deity is emphasized in Daniel 3 (vv. 6, 11, 15, 19-21, 28). Likewise, Daniel's horrible death penalty is referred to several times (Dan 6:8, 13, 17-18). In both cases there are serious doubts about the historicity of the penalty. The punishment in Daniel 6 may be understood as a creative adoption of biblical and possibly also Babylonian passages.[5] Both the decree and penalty of Daniel 3 are unheard of in a Neo-Babylonian context. However, to a certain extent they do remind us of Greek traditions about *asebeia* trials (trials because of ungodliness).[6] According to these traditions, which date from the classical period onwards, the "ungodliness" of which one could be accused could consist of profanation of holy places or objects, contempt for state deities, or the introduction of new gods who were not recognized by the state. Josephus lists instances of *asebeia* trials in *Against Apion* in order to prove that the Greeks despised the deities of other peoples (2 §§262-67). The attitude of the three young men towards the king's statue can easily be considered a case of contempt for a state deity.

---

5   Ezek 19:4, 8-9; Ps 22:21; 57:4; *Ludlul Bel Nemeqi*. See A. Bentzen, "Daniel 6. Ein Versuch zur Vorgeschichte der Märtyrerlegende," in W. Baumgartner, O. Eißfeldt a.o. (eds.), *Festschrift Alfred Bertholet zum 80.Geburtstag gewidmet* (Tübingen: Mohr-Siebeck, 1950) 58-64; E. Cassin, "Daniel dans la 'fosse' aux lions," *RHR* 139 (1951) 129-61; Collins, *Daniel*, 267; K. van der Toorn, "In the Lions' Den: The Babylonian Background of a Biblical Motif," *CBQ* 60 (1998) 626-40.

6   This view has been advocated by my Doktorvater Jürgen Lebram in a paper which, unfortunately, never has been published.

Compared to other wisdom tales, Daniel 3 and 6 catch the eye, since the religion of the key persons is a focal point in the narratives. We will presently see that this is also true for some Christian re-interpretations of the tales. Besides, as I have argued elsewhere, the narrative structure of Daniel 3 and 6 shows great similarity to the pattern of Jewish stories about noble death which are slightly later than Daniel 3 and 6 in their present form.[7] The formal similarity between Daniel 3 and 6 on the one hand, and stories of martyrdom on the other, may explain—at least in part—the *Nachleben* of Azariah, Hananiah, Mishael and Daniel: they become models and forerunners of Jewish and Christian martyrs, as will be discussed in the last part of this essay.

We should not neglect, however, the political dimension of the stories in Daniel 3 and 6. These not only show a tension between the foreign ruler's authority and the God of his four young administrators, but also between the ethnic identities of these young men and the people who accuse them. The second tension concerns more than professional envy alone. Shadrach, Meshach, and Abednego are accused as Judeans (3:12), a reference that has a double meaning: the three belong to a specific ethnic entity *and* they are worshippers of the God of this people. The Chaldean accusers are their colleagues (3:8). References to the Chaldeans can thus point to a professional class of sages (e.g. 1:4; 2:2, 4, 10; 4:4), but to an ethnic entity as well (5:30; 9:1).[8] Since the Chaldeans belong to the same professional group as Daniel's companions, and the references to those as Judeans or Jews has an ethnic significance, the ethnic connotation of "Chaldeans" in Daniel 3 is obvious. As administrators, they are presented as competitors of the Judeans Shadrach, Meshach and Abednego.

As in Daniel 3, religious practice and politics go hand in hand in Daniel 6.[9] Daniel's being a worshipper of his people's God does not prevent him from acting as a high government official. Envy is an obvious motive for the other satraps and ministers for trying to get rid

---

[7] J.-W. van Henten, *The Maccabean Martyrs as Saviours of the Jewish People: A Study of 2 and 4 Maccabees* (JSJSup 57; Leiden: Brill, 1997) 8–13 + references.

[8] Cf. Ezra 5:12 and the translation of בבל by Χαλδαῖοι in Dan 9:1LXX/Th; see Collins, *Daniel*, 137–39 with references.

[9] Cf. J. Levinger, "Daniel in the Lions' Den: A Model of National Literature of Struggle," *Beth Mikra* 70 (1977) 329–33*; 394–95* (Hebrew).

of Daniel, who was in line for the second position in the kingdom. However, ethnic tensions may be apparent from the accusation as well, since it does not mention Daniel's position at the court[10] but rather refers to him as "one of the exiles of Judah" (6:14). Darius allows himself to be manipulated by "those men" (6:6). In fact, the other satraps knew that only Daniel's religion could serve as a ground to accuse him (6:5). The redundant description of the opposition by all the satraps, united against Daniel, through the repetition of "went in a throng to the king" (6:7, 12, 16), emphasizes the foreigness and particular ethnic identity of Daniel. The king's decree functions as a test case for the recognition of his absolute authority, and has religious implications too. It forbids requests from any god or human being, except the king, for thirty days, which may well hint at a divine status for the king. Of course, all inhabitants have to obey the king's decree; as a worshipper of the God of the Judeans, Daniel is manoeuvred into an extraordinary position. The trap anticipates the confirmation of his double loyalty towards the king and towards his God.

Thus, Daniel and his three companions can be considered exemplary Judean figures. Their identity has two important aspects. The first is religious: they venerate the God of the Judeans, who is the living God and is able to save from death those who remain faithful to him. The second aspect is political-patriotic: they belong to a people of their own, and serve as members of this people in the foreign government in a diaspora situation. They are as loyal to the king as their religion allows them to be (3:12; 6:3-6). If they have to choose between faithfulness to their God and loyalty to the king, they choose to obey their God. In fact, the author of Daniel suggests that the foreign king's authority derives from the sovereignty of God (cf. Daniel 2 and 4). The outcome of Daniel 3 and 6 clearly shows that the king's power is subordinate to that of the God of the Jews. In this way, the stories of Daniel 3 and 6 may have offered religious as well as political guidelines for Judean readers who lived under a foreign government. In the first two centuries, early Christian readers experienced such a conflict of loyalty as well, belonging as they did to an illegal monotheistic religious minority in a society where polytheistic religion was present in an inextricable way. This may partly explain

---

[10] The Old Greek differs from the Aramaic text and refers to Daniel as the king's friend in 6:14, which indicates a high position in the king's service; cf. 2 Macc 7:24.

the popularity of these stories, and the fact that some early Christians saw their fate as analogous to that of the four men in the Daniel account.

3. EARLY CHRISTIAN READINGS OF DANIEL 3

3.1 Matt 13:42, 50: An Image of Punishment

The Matthean *Sondergut* attached to the parables of the kingdom of God contains a double quotation from Dan 3:6LXX: "and they will throw them into the furnace of fire" (Matt 13:42, 50). This quotation is implicit but fairly certain, since the Greek vocabulary of Matt 13:42, 50 is unique to this single passage in the Greek versions of the Old Testament.[11] The change to a plural personal pronoun matches the context of Daniel 3 as well as that of Matthew.

The parables of the weeds (13:36-43)[12] and the fishnet (13:47-50) which contain the quotations have a similar content. Both parables seem to suggest that mankind will be divided into two groups in the divine judgement at the end of times. The Angels of the Son of Man will separate the evil people from the just and throw the evil ones into the burning furnace (13:41-42, 49-50). Matthew probably expected that the evil persons would be burned at the eschaton (cf. 3:12 with Luke 3:17). The furnace appears as a place of execution and may well be an image for hell (cf. Matt 5:22).[13] For both Daniel 3 and Matthew 13 the burning furnace functions as the instrument of punishment, but the contexts are very different, for the tenor in both Matthean parables is contrary to that in Daniel 3. Reading Daniel 3 in the light of Matt 13:42, 50 points to a double contrast with the original text: the

---

[11] Κάμινος ("furnace") occurs only four times in the New Testament (apart from Matt 13:42, 50 only in Rev 1:15 and 9:2). It is rather frequently used in the Septuagint, but the combination (ἐμ-)βάλλω with a personal pronoun as object and the phrase εἰς τὴν κάμινον τοῦ πυρός occurs only at Dan 3:6 (cf. 3:46LXX/Th and the passive forms in Dan 3:6Th; 3:11LXX/Th; 3:15LXX/Th; 3:21LXX/Th and 3:24LXX).

[12] See U. Luz, "Vom Taumellolch im Weizenfeld. Ein Beispiel wirkungsgeschichtlicher Hermeneutik," in H. Frankemölle & K. Kertelge (eds.), *Vom Urchristentum zu Jesus: Für Joachim Gnilka* (Freiburg-Basel-Wien: Herder, 1989) 154–71.

[13] W. C. Allen, *A Critical and Exegetical Commentary on the Gospel According to S. Matthew* (ICC; Edinburgh: T & T. Clark, 1912) 153; W. Grundmann, *Das Evangelium nach Matthäus* (THKNT 1.1; Berlin: Evangelische Verlagsanstalt, 1968) 351. Cf. also *1 Enoch* 98:3 and Rev 9:2.

eschaton versus present time; and punishment of evil versus reward of the just.[14]

3.2 Rev 13:7, 14-15: The Analogy of Fate and Attitude

The vision of the two beasts in Revelation 13, with its description of the first beast's veneration (13:14-15), recalls the veneration of Nebuchadnezzar's statue through a cluster of allusions.[15] The first beast seems to be a creative combination of the four beasts rising out of the sea in Daniel 7 (Rev 13:1-2), and its blasphemous sayings and acts correspond to the utterances and acts of the fourth beast's

---

[14] This does not exclude a reference to Daniel 3, since such a reference can also be made to emphasize a principally different or even contrasting case; see K. Berger & C. Colpe, *Religionsgeschichtliches Textbuch zum Neuen Testament* (NTD Textreihe 1; Göttingen: Vandenhoeck & Ruprecht, 1987) 19–21.

In Paul's discussion of love (ἀγάπη) in 1 Corinthians 13 the reading καυθήσομαι should be preferred to καυχήσωμαι (against B. M. Metzger, *A Textual Commentary on the Greek New Testament* [London: United Bible Societies, 1975] 563–64; J. Smit, "Two Puzzles: 1 Corinthians 12.31 and 13.3, A Rhetorical Solution," *NTS* 39 [1993] 255–64; and many other scholars). Καυθήσομαι can be considered the *lectio difficilior* because of the construction of ἵνα followed by an indicative verbal form and the harsh combination of καυθήσομαι and σῶμα, which presupposes a passive 3rd sing. form. See, among others, J. K. Elliott, "In Favour of καυθήσομαι at I Corinthians 13:3," *ZNW* 62 (1971) 297–98; R. Kieffer, "'Afin que je sois brûlé' ou bien 'Afin que j'en tire orgueil'? (1 Cor. xiii.3)," *NTS* 22 (1976) 95–97. This reading fits the structure and content of Paul's hypothetical statements in vv. 1-3 that lead to a climax. The reasoning that Christian experiences of martyrdom would have led to the change of καυχήσωμαι into καυθήσομαι is not conclusive, since Paul himself may well have referred to Jewish (or Gentile) models of martyrdom or self-cremation. See already A. Plummer & A. Robertson, *First Epistle of St. Paul to the Corinthians* (2nd ed., ICC; Edinburgh: T & T Clark, 1914) 291. The surrender formula in Paul's hypothetical reference is to the most terrible violent death thinkable: "and if I hand over my body (myself) to be burned (καὶ ἐὰν παραδῶ τὸ σῶμά μου ἵνα καυθήσομαι)" is close to a formula in the Greek version of Daniel 3 used by Nebuchadnezzar in his summary of the events of chapter 3: "they handed over their bodies to burning/to the fire" (Dan 3:95LXX: καὶ παρέδωκαν τὰ σώματα αὐτῶν εἰς ἐμπυρισμόν; Th: ... εἰς πῦρ; = 3:28MT ויהבו גשמיהון). But an allusion is far from certain, since the phrase links up with several Jewish and non-Jewish traditions about noble death; see van Henten, *Maccabean Martyrs*, 108.

[15] On the many allusions to Daniel in Revelation, see G. K. Beale, *The Use of Daniel in Jewish Apocalyptic Literature and in the Revelation of St. John* (Lanham, MD: University Press of America, 1984); Yarbro Collins, "History."

eleventh horn in Daniel 7.[16] The allusions to Daniel 3 in Rev 13:14-15 are apparent from a cluster of corresponding phrases and concepts:[17] (1) the combination of προσκυνέω and εἰκών (Dan 3:5-7, 10, 12, 14-15,18LXX; Rev 13:15; cf. 13:4, 8, 12);[18] (2) the death penalty as sanction (Rev 13:15; Dan 3:5-6, 11, 15LXX/Th); and (3) the first beast's power over various categories of groups in Revelation 13 and the various groups that have to venerate Nebuchadnezzar's statue (cf. Rev 13:7: "And it was given power over every tribe and people and language group and nation," καὶ ἐδόθη αὐτῷ ἐξουσία ἐπὶ πᾶσαν φυλὴν καὶ λαὸν καὶ γλῶσσαν καὶ ἔθνος; cf. Dan 3:2 7LXX; Dan 3:4, 7Th; 3:96LXX/Th).[19]

The correspondences between Revelation 13 and Daniel 3 imply an analogous context. The refusal to bestow divine honors upon the image of the beast—which may be associated with the Roman emperors[20]—or upon Nebuchadnezzar's statue results in the death penalty. The rulers force their subjects, directly or indirectly, to decide between being loyal to them or to the God of Israel, or his Messiah, respectively (cf. section 1 above). Thus an analogous situation is suggested for Hanaiah, Azariah and Mishael on the one hand, and for the faithful believers in Jesus Christ on the other (Rev 13:7, 10). In Rev 13:10 a violent death seems to be indicated as the ultimate consequence of the choice to remain loyal to God and his Anointed One.[21]

3.3 The Martyrdom of Polycarp 14-15: The Analogy of Fate, Attitude, and Vindication

The *Martyrdom of Polycarp* contains a cluster of references to

---

[16] Cf. Rev 13:5-7 with Dan 7:8, 11, 20, 25; see also Dan 8:10-12.

[17] Beale, *Use of Daniel*, 229–49; P. Prigent, *L'Apocalypse de Saint Jean* (CNT Serie 2.14; Lausanne: Delachaux et Niestlé, 1981) 210: "L'allusion à Dan 3 est vraisemblable."

[18] Cf. also Dan 7:7, 11-2, 18Th; *Bel et Draco* 4:24LXX/Th.

[19] Beale (*Use of Daniel*, 244) considers Rev 13:16a to be a "paraphrased echo" of Dan 3:2-7.

[20] A. J. Beagley, *The "Sitz im Leben" of the Apocalypse with Particular Reference to the Role of the Church's Enemies* (BZNW 50; New York: De Gruyter, 1987) 72–80; S. J. Scherrer, "Signs and Wonders in the Imperial Cult. A New Look at a Roman Religious Institution in the Light of Rev 13:13-15," *JBL* 103 (1984) 599–610; F. G. Downing, "Pliny's Prosecutions of Christians: Revelation and 1 Peter," *JSNT* 34 (1988) 105–23.

[21] See also Rev 2:10, 13; 3:10-2; 12:11.

Daniel 3 in chapters 14–15. Polycarp's situation at the stake in chapter 14 is similar to that of Hananiah, Mishael and Azariah in the fiery furnace. In both cases death by burning is the punishment for refusing to manifest loyalty to the ruler and state religion. Like Daniel's companions in the Greek versions, Polycarp invokes the Lord in a final prayer which starts with a doxology (*Mart. Pol.* 14.1-2; cf. Dan 3:24-27LXX/Th).[22] An important correspondence between the old bishop and Daniel's companions is that all are compared to a burnt offering:

> Bound like that, with his hands behind him, he was like a noble ram taken out of some great flock for sacrifice: a goodly burnt-offering all ready for God (ὁλοκαύτωμα δεκτὸν τῷ θεῷ ἡτοιμασμένον).[23]

The cultic terminology of *Martyrdom of Polycarp* 14 is strongly reminiscent of Dan 3:39-40: "May I be received among them (scil. the martyrs who died earlier) this day in Thy presence, a sacrifice rich and acceptable" (ἐν οἷς προσδεχθείην ἐνώπιόν σου σήμερον ἐν θυσίᾳ πίονι καὶ προσδεκτῇ).[24]

By weaving a cluster of phrases from Azariah's Prayer into the account of Polycarp's execution, the author of the *Martyrdom of Polycarp* was probably hinting at an analogy of fate between Polycarp and Daniel's companions.[25] The purpose of this analogy does not

---

[22] Cf. *Martyrium Carpi* 41, situated by Eusebius in Marcus Aurelius' reign (*Hist. Eccl.* 4.15.48).

[23] Cf. the double ὡς in Dan 3:39bc and in the beginning of v. 40a: οὕτω γενέσθω ἡμῶν ἡ θυσία.

[24] *Mart. Pol.* 14.1-2 shares with Dan 3:39-40 a cluster of six terms:

LXX/Th Dan 3:39-40		*Mart. Pol.* 14.1-2	
3.39a	προσδεχθείημεν	14.2	προσδεχθείην
3.39b	ἐν ὁλοκαυτώμασι	14.1	ὁλοκαύτωμα
3.39b	κριῶν	14.1	κριός
3.39c	πιόνων	14.2	πίονι
3.40a	θυσία	14.2	ἐν θυσίᾳ
3.40a	ἐνώπιόν σου σήμερον	14.2	ἐνώπιόν σου σήμερον

A reference to Daniel 3 in connection to the *Martyrdom of Polycarp* 14–15 is not given by the *Biblia Patristica* and Bodenmann, *Naissance*. However, it is noted by W. Reuning, *Zur Erklärung des Polykarpmartyriums* (Darmstadt: C. F. Wintersche Buchdruckerei, 1917) 40; W. R. Schoedel, *Polycarp. Martyrdom of Polycarp. Fragments of Papias* (The Apostolic Fathers 5; London: Nelson, 1966) 69–71; T. Baumeister, *Die Anfänge der Theologie des Martyriums* (MBT 45; Münster: Aschendorff, 1980) 298.

[25] Cf. the *Martyrdom of Montanus and Lucius* 3.3-4, which also draws an

concern the Lord's invocation to rescue the Jewish people, as in the
Greek Daniel 3. In line with some other early Christian interpretations of Daniel 3 and 6, the deliverance is individual and posthumous. The analogy underlines Polycarp's post-mortem vindication, by
the resurrection of body and soul (14.2). It implies that Polycarp
deserved a vindication similar to that of the righteous Hananiah,
Mishael and Azariah, who were miraculously rescued because of their
perfect obedience to the Lord. The analogy is strengthened by details
and phrases in chapter 15, indicating that Polycarp's body could not
be burned, which are reminiscent of the three men's rescue in Dan
3:46-50LXX/Th.[26] *Mart. Pol.* 14.2 emphasizes Polycarp's wish to be
received by God "this day" (σήμερον), which probably means that
Polycarp's resurrection was thought to take place immediately after
his death and not at the end of time (cf. 19.2).[27]

4. EARLY CHRISTIAN READINGS OF DANIEL 6

4.1 Matt 27:62-66: The Sealing of the Grave

The brief pericope about the guard at Jesus' tomb after the request
of chief priests and Pharisees (Matt 27:62-66),[28] which only appears

---

analogy with the deliverance of Hananiah, Azariah and Mishael: the fire is
extinguished by the Lord's dew. The death by burning of Fructuosus and his
deacons Augurius and Eulogius is compared with the punishment of Daniel's
companions. The Father, the Son and the Holy Spirit are present with them in the
fire and Fructuosus starts a prayer as Azariah did in the Greek versions of Daniel
3, being certain of the resurrection and making the form of the Cross with his
arms as a sign of victory (*Mart. Fruct.* 4.2-3).

[26] Cf. the allusions to the wind (πνεῦμα, Dan 3:50LXX/Th) and furnace
(κάμινος) in *Martyrdom of Polycarp* 15. See Van Henten, "Zum Einfluß
jüdischer Martyrien auf die Literatur des frühen Christentums, II.Die Apos-
tolischen Väter," *ANRW* II.27 (1993) 1.700–23, esp. 719–23.

[27] H. W. Surkau, *Martyrien in jüdischer und frühchristlicher Zeit* (FRLANT
NF 36; Göttingen: Vandenhoeck & Ruprecht, 1938) 27 n.97; J. Holleman,
*Resurrection and Parousia: A Traditio-Historical Study of Paul's Eschatology in
1 Corinthians 15* (NovTSup 84; Leiden: Brill, 1996) 141–52.

[28] J. Kremer, *Die Osterbotschaft der vier Evangelien. Versuch einer
Auslegung über das leere Grab und die Erscheinungen des Auferstandenen*
(Stuttgart: Katholisches Bibelwerk, 1969); E. L. Bode, *The First Easter Morning.
The Gospel Accounts of the Women's Visit to the Tomb of Jesus* (AnBib 45;
Rome: Biblical Institute Press, 1970); I. Broer, *Die Urgemeinde und das Grab
Jesu. Eine Analyse der Grablegungsgeschichte im Neuen Testament* (SANT 31;

in Matthew, is probably an allusion to Daniel 6.[29] Matthew's description of the grave's protection does not match any practice attested by archaeological or epigraphical sources. There is, however, significant corresponding terminology in Matt 27:62-66 and Dan 6:18LXX/Th: compare "they ... made the tomb secure by sealing the stone" (Matt 27:66)[30] with "and they brought a stone and laid it on the mouth of the den, and the king sealed it with his own signet and with the signet of his great men, so that nothing might be changed concerning Daniel" (Dan 6:18Th).[31] The priests' and Pharisees' motivation for excluding every possible means of deceit (cf. ὁ πλάνος, Matt 27:63, and πλάνη, 27:64) corresponds to the concern of Daniel's colleagues in Daniel 6. The Septuagint version explicitly refers to the exclusion of deceit: "... so that Daniel could not be taken away from them [the lions] or the king could pull him out of the den."[32]

At first sight Matthew's interpretation has turned Daniel 6 upside down, since reading Daniel 6 in light of Matt 27:62-66 implies that the lion's den is interpreted as a grave, or as a place (for example the underworld) where the dead remain. As a consequence, Daniel's rescue becomes a *post mortem* deliverance. Such a reading can be found, among others, in the *Commentary on Daniel* by Hippolytus of Rome (died 235 CE), which links Matt 27:66 to Dan 6:[17]18 and, in this, is closest to the Septuagint version:

> Since they (the satraps) were anxious that the king should not secretly give orders to pull him up out of the den, they asked him to let the stone be sealed. In similar manner the chief priests and the Pharisees acted concerning our Savior "sealing the stone with the guard" (author's translation).[33]

At the end of the third book of his commentary, Hippolytus interprets

---

München: Kösel, 1972).

[29] W. Grundmann, *Evangelium nach Matthäus*, 566. E. Klostermann, *Das Matthäusevangelium* (4th ed., HNT 4; Tübingen: Mohr-Siebeck, 1971) 227; and W. D. Davies & D. C. Allison, *A Critical and Exegetical Commentary on the Gospel According to S. Matthew* (3 vols., ICC; Edinburgh: T & T. Clark, 1988-97) 3.655–66.

[30] Cf. *Gospel of Peter* 8:28-34.

[31] Matt 27:66, Dan 6:18LXX and 6:18Th share the combination of σφραγίζω and λίθος

[32] Dan 6:18LXX: ... ὅπως μὴ ἀπ᾽ αὐτῶν ἀρθῇ ὁ Δανιηλ ἢ ὁ βασιλεὺς αὐτὸν ἀνασπάσῃ ἐκ τοῦ λάκκου. See also *Bel et Draco* 1-22.

[33] Hippolytus, *Com. in Dan*, 3.27.4-5.

Daniel 6 symbolically as a resurrection story. The lions' den now symbolizes the underworld, and the lions act as angels of punishment (3.31.2-3). This interpretation is followed by a paranetic passage in which he emphasizes that Christians have to follow Daniel and should not fear satraps or human decrees

> in order that ... you will be brought up from the den alive, you will be found a companion in the resurrection, you will be lord over your enemies and will thank the ever living God.

This passage clearly shows that Daniel 6 was interpreted in the first part of the third century as a resurrection story. Matt 27:62-66 can, of course, already be understood along similar lines, but it has to be emphasized that the Matthean passage contains no explicit reference to resurrection. The early readers of Matt 27:62-66 may well have interpreted the allusion to Daniel 6 as a reference to the protection of the tomb only.

4.2 2 Tim 4:17: The Analogy of Fate and Deliverance

2 Tim 4:17 mentions Paul's deliverance from the lion's mouth in a trial scene that first seems to end happily (4:16-17) but, ultimately, might lead to his execution (4:18).[34] The author lets Paul describe his own fate as that of a persecuted righteous one (cf. also 4:6-8), deserted by all but, like other Christian martyrs, assisted by Christ (ὁ κύριός μοι παρέστη;[35] ἐνεδυνάμωσέν με, 4:17).[36] The context is that of a trial in which the accused answers the hostile government (cf. 2 Tim 4:16). The metaphor of being rescued from a lion's mouth is rather

---

[34] N. Brox, *Die Pastoralbriefe* (RNT 7.2; Regensburg: Pustet, 1969) 31; 275–77. M. Prior (*Paul the Letter-Writer and the Second Letter to Timothy* [JSNTSup 23; Sheffield: Sheffield Academic Press, 1989] 113–39) takes Paul as the author and offers an alternative interpretation.

[35] Παρίστημι can indicate the assistance by a lawyer; cf. C. Spicq, *Saint Paul. Les Épitres Pastorales* (4th ed., Ebib; Paris: Lecoffre, 1969) 2.819.

[36] In Christian martyr texts the motif of the martyr's support can be found in various ways. Christ may assist the martyr during trial, torture or execution, sometimes through a vision. In addition, the angel of the Lord may help (cf. Luke 21:43), or a heavenly voice may encourage the martyr after his arrest, as in *Polycarp's Martyrdom* (9.1; cf. Acts 23:11). See H. Delehaye, *Les passions des martyrs et les genres littéraires* (2nd ed., SH 13b; Brussels: Société des Bollandistes, 1966) 213–17. The motif also occurs in the *passio Pauli* in Acts (23:11; 27:23-4; cf. Phil 4:13; 1 Tim 1:12; 2 Tim 2:1). Acts 27:23-4 refers to the assistance of the angel of the Lord; cf. Luke 22:43).

common in the Hebrew Bible (cf. Ps 7:2-3; 22:22; 35:17; cf. Daniel 6).[37] Nevertheless, 2 Tim 4:17 may be a quotation of, or at least an allusion to, two passages: Ps 22:22, as several scholars have noted,[38] as well as Daniel 6. The vocabulary of 2 Tim 4:17 (καὶ ἐρρύσθην ἐκ στόματος λέοντος) closely corresponds to Ps 21(22):22LXX (σῶσόν με ἐκ στόματος λέοντος). Both 2 Tim 4:17 and Ps 21[22]:22LXX have the verbal form in the first person sing. and refer to just one lion, which can be interpreted as a metaphor for the emperor in 2 Timothy.[39] On another point, however, 2 Tim 4:17 differs from Ps 21[22]:22LXX,[40] and corresponds closely to Daniel 6.[41] Daniel's rescue takes place because the Lord closes the lions' mouth (6:32; cf. 6:21Th), and the verb ῥύεσθαι used in 2 Tim 4:17 also occurs in 6:28Th.

If we are allowed to consider 2 Tim 4:17 as an allusion to Daniel 6 as well, the correspondence may imply that the contexts of 2 Timothy 4 and Daniel 6 may be viewed similarly. This would invite the reader to compare Paul's situation with that of Daniel in the lions' den (see especially Dan 6:21, 23, 28). At the same time, this analogy presupposes a shift from metaphor to reality. The focal point of the analogy would be, of course, Paul's rescue. Ps 21[22]:22LXX only refers to a future rescue (σῶσον), while 2 Timothy 4—like Dan 6:21, 23, 28

---

[37] V. Hasler (*Die Briefe an Timotheus und Titus [Pastoralbriefe]* [Zürcher Bibelkommentare NT 12; Zürich: Theologischer Verlag, 1978] 81) notes that the metaphor originates in the language of prayer of persecuted righteous ones and refers to Pss 7:2-3; 21(22):22; 34(35):17; 90(91):13; *Pss. Sol.* 13:3.

[38] E.g. J. Torrance, "Ps. xxii – As used by Christ and St. Paul." *ExpTim* 44 (1932-33), 382; W. Lock, *A Critical and Exegetical Commentary on the Pastoral Epistles* (ICC, Edinburgh: T & T Clark, 1966) 119; Spicq, *Épitres Pastorales*, 821; A. T. Hanson, *The Pastoral Epistles. Based on the Revised Standard Version* (NCB; Grand Rapids: Eerdmans; London: Marshall, Morgan & Scott, 1982) 161.

[39] Est. 4:17-8LXX; Josephus, *Ant.* 18 §228; more references are given in Spicq, *Épitres Pastorales*, 821.

[40] The verb ῥύεσθαι is lacking in Ps 21(22):22LXX (but cf. 21:5, 9, 21).

[41] Cf. G. Holtz, *Die Pastoralbriefe* (THKNT 13, Berlin: Evangelische Verlag-anstalt, 1965) 198: "ἐκ στόματος λέοντος ist als Redewendung aus Dan 6,27 genommen. Der Löwe kann als Symbol des Teufels auftreten (Ps 91,13; I.Petr. 5,8) und wie in Ps 22,22 als Symbol des Todes. Beide Möglichkeiten sind für unsere Stelle gegeben." Baumeister (*Theologie*, 199) is not certain that the passage refers to Dan 6:21, 28. Brox (*Pastoralbriefe*, 276) refers to Ps 22:22, Dan 6:21, 28 and 1 Macc 2:60.

(6:27Th)—refers to a rescue in the past (ἐρρύσθην, 4:17), as well as to
a rescue by the Lord in the future (4:18, ῥύσεταί με ὁ κύριος ... καὶ
σώσει).[42] The assumption underlying this analogy between Paul and
Daniel may be that Paul was considered a righteous person who could
count on God's or Christ's intervention in case he should be in
danger.[43] Thus the Timothy passage may suggest that Paul is writing
in the 1st pers. sing. that, like Daniel, he has been saved from an
execution and hopes to be rescued in the future as well (as is prayed
for in Psalm 22). This rescue may concern also other oppressive acts
by the Roman government,[44] but may be seen as posthumous as well,
implying that Paul would partake in the heavenly kingdom[45] or even
share the fate of being resurrected as a martyr right after his death. A
similar reasoning underlies the analogy between Polycarp and
Daniel's three companions in the *Martyrdom of Polycarp* 14.[46] Thus
Daniel 6 may already be interpreted in 2 Timothy 4 as a story about
resurrection, as it certainly was in later Christian passages.[47]

5. THE RECEPTION OF DANIEL 3 AND 6 COMBINED
IN EARLY CHRISTIAN LITERATURE

5.1 Acts 12:11: An Analogous Deliverance

Acts 12:3-19 describes Peter's miraculous deliverance from prison
in Jerusalem, and belongs to the so-called *Passio Petri et Pauli*
passages in the Book of Acts. In 12:11 Luke presents Peter's own
retrospective of his deliverance with the following statement:

> Now I know that the Lord truly has sent his angel and rescued me from
> Herod's hands (ὅτι ἐξαπέστειλεν ὁ κύριος τὸν ἄγγελον αὐτοῦ καὶ

---

[42] The motif of the deliverance of righteous ones, whether individually or
collectively, is often indicated by phrases with the verb ῥύεσθαι, see LXX Est
4:8.17t, 17z; 10:3f; Dan 3:17, 88LXX; 88Th, 96Th; 6:28Th; 3 Macc 2:12; 5:8;
6:6., 10-1, 39. Cf. Wis 2:18; 1 Macc 12:15.

[43] Cf. 1 Macc 2:60: "Because of his sincerety (ἐν τῇ ἁπλότητι αὐτοῦ) Daniel
was delivered from the mouth of the lions," which is applied to Mattathias's sons
through an argument of analogy which can be summarized as: similar deeds will
bring a similar reward.

[44] Baumeister, *Theologie*, 199.

[45] Hanson, *Pastoral Epistles*, 161–62; O. Knoch, *1. und 2.Timotheusbrief.
Titusbrief* (Die Neue Echter Bibel; Würzburg: Echter-Verlag, 1988) 66.

[46] *Ibidem*. Cf. Holtz, *Pastoralbriefe*, 198–99.

[47] See esp. Hippolytus, *Com. in Dan*, 3.31.3; Cassin, "Daniel," 155–56.

ἐξείλατό με ἐκ χειρὸς Ἡρῴδου) and from all that the people of the Jews were expecting.

Part of this statement is reminiscent of the deliverance of Daniel and his friends.[48] The Greek vocabulary of Acts 12:11 partly corresponds to that of Dan 3:95Th (ἀπέστειλεν τὸν ἄγγελον αὐτοῦ καὶ ἐξείλατο [LXX: ἔσωσε] τοὺς παῖδας αὐτοῦ) as well as to that of Dan 6:23Th, which offers Daniel's explanation of his deliverance to the king (ὁ θεός μου ἀπέστειλεν τὸν ἄγγελον αὐτοῦ). Reading Acts 12:11 with both stories of deliverance in Daniel as background seems to imply that Peter's fate can be interpreted analogously to that of Hananiah, Azariah, Mishael and Daniel. Dan 6:23 is especially close to Acts 12:11, since both Daniel's and Peter's statements can be interpreted as the explanation of the deliverance by the victim himself.[49] The analogy makes the reader wonder whether the Jewish people mentioned in Acts 12:11 may be compared with the satraps of Daniel 6.[50] In that case, the passage may hint at a punishment for the Jewish people, since Daniel's accusers are thrown into the lions' den together with their wives and children at the command of king Darius (Dan 6:25).

5.2 Heb 11:32-38: Models of Faith and Endurance

Hebrews 11 offers an extensive catalogue of famous persons from Israel's history, culminating in Jesus Christ who has shown, in an exemplary way, how one should live in accordance with faith (πίστις, cf. the definition in 11:1).[51] In 11:33-38 a list of anonymous heroes

---

[48] Of course, the motif of deliverance by the Lord from the hands of a ruler is common in the Jewish Bible; see esp. Exod 18:8; 1 Sam 17:37; 2 Sam 22:1; Jer 38(31):11LXX; as well as Dan 3:88Th/LXX. Daniel 3 and 6 share with Acts 12:11 that this deliverance is brought about by the angel of the Lord.

[49] Cf. E. Jacquier, *Les Actes des Apôtres* (2 vols., Ebib; Paris: Lecoffre, 1926) 2.365; E. Haenchen, *Die Apostelgeschichte* (16th ed., Kritisch-exegetischer Kommentar über das NT 3; Göttingen: Vandenhoeck & Ruprecht, 1977) 369 n.10.

[50] Cf. Haenchen, *Apostelgeschichte*, 371. The execution of the guards (Acts 12:19) ordered by Herod Agrippa may be compared with the fact that the executioners are themselves killed according to Daniel 3 (vv. 22-23, 48LXX/Th).

[51] G. Schille, "Katechese und Taufliturgie. Erwägungen zu Hbr 11," *ZNW* 51 (1960) 112-31; M. R. Cosby, *The Rhetorical Composition and Function of Hebrews 11 in Light of Example Lists in Antiquity* (Macon, GA: Mercer, 1988); D. Hamm, "Faith in the Epistle to the Hebrews: the Jesus Factor," *CBQ* 52 (1990) 270-91; I. G. Wallis, *Where Opposites Meet. The Faith of Jesus Christ in Early Christian Traditions* (SNTSMS 84; Cambridge: Cambridge University Press,

follows upon the series of ancient heroes of faith mentioned by name
(11:2-31). This list is introduced by a well-known rhetorical phrase in
v. 32 ("And what more can I say? For time fails me to tell about
...").[52] After referring to six other names only, the passage proceeds
with references to anonymous prophets[53] who, however, could easily
be associated with biblical figures by readers familiar with Jewish
Scriptures through a series of catch phrases. As in the earlier series,
the key phrase is "faith."[54] Read in connection with Hebrew Bible
passages, the anonymous references seem to share a common context
of death, oppression and/or military violence. Several of these
references take up the motif of the persecution of Israel's prophets.[55]

The beginning of the anonymous series (11:33d-34a) probably
alludes to the deliverance of Daniel and his companions with brief
paraphrases from both Daniel 3 and 6. The first instance echoes
vocabulary of the Greek versions of Daniel 6, corresponding closely
to Dan 6:23 in the version of Theodotion (Heb 11:33d: ἔφραξαν
στόματα λεόντων, "they [the prophets] shut the mouth of lions"; cf.
Dan 6:23Th: ἐνέφραξεν τὰ στόματα τῶν λεόντων, "he [God through
his angel] blocked the mouth of the lions"). If Heb 11:33d is a
quotation of Dan 6:23Th, two adaptations seem to have been made:
(1) Daniel's rescue by the angel remains unmentioned (as with the
deliverance of his three companions; cf. Heb 11:34a with Dan

1995); P. M. Eisenbaum, *The Jewish Heroes of Christian History: Hebrews 11 in
Literary Context* (SBLDS 156; Atlanta: Scholars Press, 1997).

[52] Cf. Cicero, *De natura deorum* 3.81. Cicero uses a similar formula to
interrupt two series of examples and to prove a statement, namely that the gods do
not reward people in accordance to their deeds. See C. Spicq, *L'Épitre aux
Hébreux* (2 vols., Ebib; Paris: Lecoffre, 1952-53) 2.362.

[53] Heb 11:32 introduces the second series of models as a series of prophets,
which implies that if 11:33-38 refers to Daniel and his companions they were
considered prophets.

[54] Cf. the inclusion of διὰ (τῆς) πίστεως in 11:33, 39; and H. W. Attridge,
The Epistle to the Hebrews. A Commentary on the Epistle to the Hebrews
(Hermeneia; Minneapolis: Fortress, 1989) 347. On so-called *Beispielreihen*, see
K. Berger, "Hellenistische Gattungen im Neuen Testament," *ANRW* II 25 (1984)
2.1145–48, 1205; B. Fiore, *The Function of Personal Example in the Socratic and
Pastoral Epistles* (AnBib 105; Rome: Biblical Institute Press, 1986).

[55] Heb 11:34, 37, cf. 1 Kings 19; 11:36: cf. Jer 37:11-40:6 [44:11-47:6LXX];
11:37: cf. 2 Chron 24:20-2; *Life of Jeremiah* 1; *Ascension of Isaiah* 5:11-4; *Life of
Isaiah* 1; 11:38: cf. 1 Kings 18–19.

3:28MT; 3:25, 49-50, 92, 95LXX/Th); (2) because of the plural verbal form ἔφραξαν and the omission of the article before λεόντων, the reader gets the impression that several persons were saved from lion's dens. These changes can be understood as adaptations to the context of Hebrews 11. All examples are given in an unspecified plural form, which makes it easy to read the list as a continuous story of heroic perseverance during suffering. The correspondences between Heb 11:34a ("they quenched the fury of fire," ἔσβεσαν δύναμιν πυρός) and the Greek version of Daniel 3 are of a more general nature. Nevertheless, Heb 11:33d-34a probably alludes to Daniel 6 and 3,[56] since Daniel and his three companions were well-known as models in post-biblical Jewish as well as early Christian writings and often function together as models in lists of *exempla*.[57] Besides, there is the obvious connection with the overall motif of πίστις in Hebrews 11, since Daniel 3 and 6 already emphasize the faithfulness of the four heroes (Dan 3:28MT/95Th; 3:40LXX; 6:24MT/Th).[58]

Together with other *exempla*, the references to Daniel and his companions fulfill several functions in the rhetorical context of Hebrews 11. First, they illustrate and exemplify the definition of πίστις in Heb 11:1. Second, they have a paranetic function, since the readers are being incited by the many references to past witnesses, as well as by Jesus' death and vindication (12:2-3), to remain steadfast in their faith (cf. ὑπομονή, 10:36; 12:1; ὑπομένω 10:32; 12:2-3, 7).[59] That might result in violent death, but would also lead to participation in God's promise and to salvation in the end (cf. 10:36-9). Third, the two series of *exempla* lead anaphorically to Jesus, the founder and perfecter of faith (12:2; cf. 5:8-9). Fourth, Hebrews 11 as well as some other lists of exempla imply that staying faithful to God could lead to severe suffering or even violent death (11:4, 17, 25-27, 33-38). In this connection Hebrews 11 may be compared with 4 Maccabees' presentation of Abraham, Isaac, Daniel, Hananiah, Azariah and Mishael as models of faith and steadfastness for the seven Maccabean martyrs,

---

[56] With Attridge, *Hebrews*, 348.

[57] See, for example, 1 Macc 2:59-60; 3 Macc 6:6-7; 4 Macc 13:9; 16:3, 21; 18:12-13 and *1 Clem.* 45:6-7.

[58] Dan 6:24Th: "And Daniel was taken up out of the den, and no kind of harm was found on him, because he had trusted in his God" (ὅτι ἐπίστευσεν ἐν τῷ θεῷ αὐτοῦ). See also 1 Macc 2:59.

[59] Cf. 4 Macc 16:17, 19, 21.

who are urged by their mother to opt for a noble death (4 Macc 16:16-23).[60]

5.3 1 Clem. 45.6-7: Models of Perseverance and Trust

In his plea for unity in the Christian community of Corinth, Clement of Rome notes that the Holy Scriptures show that the righteous are being persecuted, imprisoned and stoned by wicked, godless and lawless persons. He mentions Daniel and his companions to make this point:

> Shall we say that Daniel was cast into the lions' den (ἐβλήθη εἰς λάκκον λεόντων) by men who really had the fear of God in their hearts? Shall we say that Ananias, Azarias and Mishael were shut up in the fiery furnace (κατείρχθησαν εἰς κάμινον πυρός) by men who were engaged in the honorable and illustrious service of the Most High? A thousand times no.[61]

These brief paraphrases have a dual function in this passage. They indicate what could be the shocking ultimate consequence of the vice of jealousy (ζῆλος), which was unfortunately so common among the Corinthian Christians in Clement's opinion (cf. 45.1, 4). Besides, the scriptural figures function as models of the right attitude, which would be suitably rewarded:

> ... because their [the villains'] victims, whose trusting endurance won them a heritage of honor and renown, are now exalted on high, and enrolled by God in his Tablets of remembrance for all future ages; Amen. It is the example of such men as these, my brothers, that we must make our own (45.8–46.1).

Thus, Daniel and his three companions are presented as examples (ὑποδείγματα) for the Corinthian Christians (46.1; cf. 55.1).[62] Their exemplary attitude is characterized by the catch phrases ὑπομονή

---

60   Van Henten, *Maccabean Martyrs*, 131–32 and 241–42.

61   Translation by M. Staniforth, *Early Christian Writings: The Apostolic Fathers* (Penguin Classics; Harmondsworth, UK: Penguin, 1975).

62   From chapter 55 it is apparent that Clement was familiar with Jewish and non-Jewish *exempla* of persons who were willing to sacrifice themselves for their people. See L. Sanders, *L'Hellénisme de Saint Clément de Rome et le Paulinisme* (Studia Hellenistica 2; Leuven: Universitas Catholica Lovaniensis, 1943) 41–56; Baumeister, *Theologie*, 229–48; van Henten, "The Martyrs as Heroes of the Christian People: Some Remarks on the Continuity between Jewish and Christian Martyrology, with Pagan Analogies," in M. Lambardigts and P. van Deun (eds.), *Martyrium in Multidisciplinary Perspective: Memorial Louis Reekmans* (BETL 117; Leuven: Peeters, 1995) 318–22.

("perseverance") and πεποιθήσις ("trust").[63] Such phrases, as well as the reference to ζῆλος as the cause of death (which is only true in a certain way for Daniel 6, of course), are strongly reminiscent of Clement's vocabulary used in connection with the *exempla* of Christian martyrs mentioned in chapters 5–6; thus the four heroes from Daniel seem to have been associated with Christian martyrs.[64] This connection is not elaborated, however, in Clement.

6. CONCLUSION

Various readings of Daniel 3 and 6 have been discussed in this essay. Matthew refers to the fiery furnace as an image of punishment at the end of time (13:42, 50) and constructs a parallel between the sealing of the lions's den and of Jesus' grave (27:62-66). Other readings focus upon analogies between the fate and deliverance of Daniel and his companions on the one hand, and early Christians on the other (Acts 12:11; Rev 13:7; 14-15; 2 Tim 4:17; *Mart. Pol.* 14–15). Finally, the four heroes from Daniel are presented as models of endurance and faith or faithfulness (Heb 11:33-38; *1 Clem.* 45–46). Some of the passages discussed link Daniel and his companions to Christian heroes of faith, who died a violent death (especially *1 Clement* and the *Martyrdom of Polycarp*; but cf. already 2 Timothy 4). These passages are part of a trajectory which ends with the depiction of the four righteous ones from Daniel as models for and forerunners of Christian martyrs.

Christian martyrologies and calendars of martyrs evidence the ritualization of this role attributed to Daniel and his companions. At the literary level, Origen's *Exhortatio ad martyrium* (235 CE)[65] shows the final stage of this trajectory. Together with the Maccabean martyrs, Daniel and his companions are referred to extensively (*Exh.*

---

[63] The *Martyrdom of Montanus* compares the martyrs' faithfulness to the Lord with that of Daniel's companions (13.9; 16.21; 18.12-3), of Isaac and Abraham (Genesis 22; *Mart. Mont.* 9.21; 13.12; 14.20; 15.28; 16.20; 17.6; 18.11, 20, 23), and of the mother of the seven Maccabean brothers (16.3-5).

[64] *1 Clem.* 5.1; 6.1: ὑπόδειγμα; and 5.5, 7: ὑπομονή. See also 5.6; 6.2: πίστις which is semantically closely related to πεποιθήσις; cf. *Bauer-Aland* 1296 s.v. 1.

[65] J. J. O'Meara, *Origen, Prayer, Exhortation to Martyrdom. Translated and Annoted* (Ancient Christian Writers 19; London: Newman Press-Longman, Green, 1954); P. Hartmann, "Origène et la théologie du martyre d'après le ΠΡΟΤΡΕΠΤΙΚΟΣ de 235," *ETL* 34 (1958) 773–824.

Mart. 22–27; 33),[66] and their exemplary behaviour should be imitated by Christian martyrs (23; 33).[67] The self-sacrifice of these Jewish heroes, however, is re-interpreted from a Christian perspective. Like the Christian martyrs, the Jewish heroes function as models (παρα-δείγματα) of belief and the love of God. Origen's summary of the significance of the Maccabean martyrs clearly shows this:

> So that we see how much power piety and the love of God have against the most toughest and heavy tortures ... (ἵν' ἴδωμεν, ὅσον δύναται κατὰ τῶν τραχυτάτων πόνων καὶ τῶν βαρυτάτων βασάνων εὐσέβεια καὶ τὸ πρὸς θεὸν φίλτρον, *Exh. Mart.* 27).

The Jewish identity of Daniel and his companions, and the political dimension of their behaviour, are thereby ignored and substituted for by Origen's Christian ideal of martyrdom. Thus part of the *Nachleben* of Daniel, Hananiah, Mishael and Azariah requires the amazing observation that they were integrated into a group of Christian heroes, to the point of functioning as paragons of a Christian identity.

7. SELECT BIBLIOGRAPHY

Beale, G. K. *The Use of Daniel in Jewish Apocalyptic Literature and in the Revelation of St. John* (Lanham, MD: University Press of America, 1984).

Bentzen, A. "Daniel 6. Ein Versuch zur Vorgeschichte der Märtyrerlegende," in W. Baumgartner, O. Eißfeldt a.o. (eds.), *Festschrift Alfred Bertholet zum 80.Geburtstag gewidmet* (Tübingen: Mohr-Siebeck, 1950) 58–64.

Bodenmann, R. *Naissance d'une exégèse: Daniel dans l'église ancienne des trois premiers siècles* (BGBE 28; Tübingen: Mohr-Siebeck, 1986).

Cassin, E. "Daniel dans la 'fosse' aux lions," *RHR* 139 (1951) 129–61.

Henten, J.-W. van. *The Maccabean Martyrs as Saviours of the Jewish People: A Study of 2 and 4 Maccabees* (JSJSup 57; Leiden: Brill, 1997).

Koch, K. *Deuterokanonische Zusätze zum Danielbuch. Entstehung und Textgeschichte* (AOAT 38; Neukirchen-Vluyn: Butzon & Bercker/Neukirchener Verlag, 1987).

Kuhl, C. *Die drei Männer im Feuer* (BZAW 55; Giessen: Töpelmann, 1930).

Levinger, J. "Daniel in the Lions' Den: A Model of National Literature of Struggle," *Beth Mikra* 70 (1977) 329–33*; 394–95* (Hebrew).

---

[66] Cf. Cyprian, *Ep*. 58.5-6, who gives the following list of martyrs: Abel, Abraham, Daniel and his three companions, the Maccabean martyrs, the prophets and the apostles.

[67] *Exh. Mart.* 33 alludes to Dan 3:50LXX/Th (δρόσος); cf. 27.

Müller, H. P. "Die weisheitliche Lehrerzählung im Alten Testament und seiner Umwelt," *WO* 9 (1977) 77–98.

Toorn, K. van der. "In the Lions' Den: The Babylonian Background of a Biblical Motif," *CBQ* 60 (1998) 626–40.

Wills, L. M. *The Jew in the Court of the Foreign King: Ancient Jewish Court Legends* (HDR 26; Minneapolis: Fortress, 1990).

Yarbro Collins, A. "The History of Interpretation: B. The Christian Interpretation," in J. J. Collins, *Daniel. A Commentary on the Book of Daniel* (Hermeneia; Minneapolis: Fortress, 1993) 90–117.

PART FOUR

SOCIAL SETTING

THE SOCIAL SETTING OF THE ARAMAIC AND HEBREW BOOK OF DANIEL

RAINER ALBERTZ

1. INTRODUCTION

In his lexicon article on "Apocalypticism" one German expert in this field, K. Müller, states: "daß es bis heute keine wirkliche Klarheit über die soziologische Basis der apokalyptischen Hinterlassenschaft im Judentum gibt."[1] Twelve years later this statement is still true. Even if we confine ourselves to the Book of Daniel, we have to concede that we remain far from any consensus among Old Testament scholars as to who its author or authors might have been, and how his or their social setting can be determined. Many scholars still follow the widely-held opinion that the author of Daniel can be identified with the Ḥasidim mentioned in the books of Maccabees,[2] but this theory has been disputed by others with sound arguments.

One such argument holds that—in contrast to the information which is given in 1 Macc 4:42—the Ḥasidim joined the Maccabees and reinforced their troops, whereas the book of Daniel does not espouse a militant ideology.[3] Somewhat confusingly perhaps, O. H.

---

[1] K. Müller, "Apokalyptik," in M. Görg and B. Lang (eds.), *Neues Bibel-Lexikon* (Zürich: Benzinger, 1988) 1.124–32, esp. 132.

[2] Very influential in this respect were the books of O. Plöger, *Theokratie und Eschatologie* (2nd ed., WMANT 2; Neukirchen-Vluyn: Neukirchener Verlag, 1962) 27, 33; and M. Hengel, *Judentum und Hellenismus. Studien zu ihrer Begegnung unter besonderer Berücksichtigung Palästinas bis zur Mitte des 2.Jhs. v.Chr.* (2nd ed., WUNT 10; Tübingen: Mohr-Siebeck, 1973) 320–21. See most recently E. Haag, "Die Hasidäer und das Danielbuch," *TTZ* 102 (1993) 51–63, esp. 62–63, although he suggests 1 Maccabees may reflect a later development of the group.

[3] See especially J. J. Collins, *The Apocalyptic Vision of the Book of Daniel* (HSM 16; Missoula, MT: Scholars Press, 1977) 201–05; idem, "Daniel and His Social World," *Interpretation* 39 (1985) 131–43, esp. 132–33; idem, *Daniel. A Commentary on the Book of Daniel* (Hermeneia; Minneapolis: Fortress, 1993) 66–70; G. W. E. Nickelsburg, "Social Aspects of Palestinian Jewish Apocalypticism," in D. Hellholm (ed.), *Proceedings of the International Colloquium on Apocalypticism: Uppsala, August 12-17, 1979* (Tübingen: Mohr-Siebeck, 1983) 641–54, esp. 647–48.

Steck[4] and R. G. Kratz[5] located the Daniel stories in particular, but also the whole book, among cultic and wisdom circles of Jerusalem, which represented a theocratic position like that of the authors of the Chronicler's History. This would mean that the social setting of Daniel was rooted precisely in those groups which in O. Plöger's and M. Hengel's view constituted the opposition to the eschatological circles, to which the Ḥasidim belonged.[6] J.-C. Lebram took a similar direction in regarding the author of the Hebrew visions (Daniel 8–12) as a priest[7] or a temple official.[8] In P. Lampe's view the Daniel apocalyptist is a learned scribe, trained in the exegesis of prophetic literature and belonging to the urban upper-class.[9] On the basis of

---

[4] O. H. Steck, "Weltgeschehen und Gottesvolk im Buche Daniel" (1980), in idem, *Wahrnehmungen Gottes im Alten Testament: Gesammelte Studien* (TB 70; München: Kaiser, 1982) 262–90, esp. 265–70. Steck reckoned on a transformation of the genuine theocratic position under prophetic influences in the traditio-history of the book (pp. 270ff.).

[5] R. G. Kratz, *Translatio imperii. Untersuchungen zu den aramäischen Daniel-erzählungen und ihrem theologiegeschichtlichen Umfeld* (WMANT 63; Neukirchen-Vluyn: Neukirchener Verlag, 1991) 279. In his opionion the separate stories came from a "Kreis priesterlich-weisheitlich geschulter Erzähler," probably of the eastern diaspora at the end of the 5th or the beginning of the 4th century BC (pp. 273–74). The story collection of Daniel 1-6* was shaped by "kultisch-weisheitliche Kreise" who identified themselves with the priestly restoration in Jerusalem, which can be seen behind the Chronicler's History. In his article "Reich Gottes und Gesetz im Danielbuch und im werdenden Judentum," in A. S. van der Woude (ed.), *The Book of Daniel in the Light of New Findings* (BETL 56; Leuven: Leuven University Press and Peeters, 1993) 435–79, Kratz wrote: "So entspricht die theologische Konzeption der Erzählsammlung Daniel 1–6* ... ziemlich genau dem eigentlich theokratischen Konzept, nach dem im chronistische Geschichtswerk die nachexilische Geschichte Judas neu geschrieben und aus dieser Optik die vorexilische Königszeit rekapituliert wird" (pg. 454). Going beyond the subject of his dissertation Kratz speaks about a "Kehre ins Eschatologische" (pg. 454), which should have taken place in the later history of the book.

[6] O. Plöger, *Theokratie*, 37ff., 57–68; M. Hengel, *Judentum*, 322.

[7] J.-C. Lebram, "Apokalyptik and Hellenismus im Buche Daniel," *VT* 20 (1970) 503–24, esp. 515, 523–24, regarding the cultic interest of the visions in Daniel 8; 9; and 11.

[8] J.-C. Lebram, "Daniel/Danielbuch und Zusätze," *TRE* 8 (1981) 325–49, esp. 339, pointing out that the term מַשְׂכִּיל in Dan 11:33, 35; 12:3-10 also appears in many Psalm headings.

[9] P. Lampe, "Die Apokalyptiker—ihre Situation und ihr Handeln," in U. Lutz (ed.), *Eschatologie und Friedenshandeln. Exegetische Beiträge zur Frage christ-*

the court-tales (Daniel 1–6) J. J. Collins thought of wise men, trained in mantic wisdom, who might have returned from the Babylonian diaspora to Jerusalem in the early second century BC.[10] Thus for him, too, they were "like Daniel, upper-class, well-educated Jews," but—in contrast to Steck and Kratz—"not closely affiliated with the Jerusalem establishment."[11] Referring to the Persian magicians, K. Koch asked whether we should reckon in late Israel "mit einem vergleichbaren Stand von Wanderpredigern mit apokalyptischer Schriftgelehrsamkeit und eigenen Revelationserfahrungen."[12]

In considering the wide range of scholary opinions, we have to admit that nearly all the possible social and cultural classifications enjoy some support: Did the Daniel apocalypticists stand in the prophetic, priestly or the wisdom tradition? Did they belong to "pious conventicles" next to the lower class, as the Ḥasidim were situated by O. Plöger and M. Hengel?[13] Or did they belong to the well-educated upper class? Moreover, were they a part of the Jerusalem establishment? Or did they represent a group of immigrants from the diaspora?

In my opinion three main obstacles prevent Old Testament scholarship from attaining a more generally accepted reconstruction. The first of these is the still disputed traditio-history of the book of Daniel. Obviously, scholars arrive at very different or even contradictory results depending on whether they focus on the stories (Daniel 1–6) or on the visions (Daniel 7–12) of the book. Taking this division for granted, scholars feel urged to recognize very different or even conflicting tendencies between both parts, especially in their attitude to gentile rulers. Thus, for example, are we to suppose different groups behind Daniel 1–6 and Daniel 7–12, or to assume a sudden swing of opinion that took place in one group?[14] However,

---

licher Friedensverantwortung (SBS 101; Stuttgart: Katholisches Bibelwerk, 1981) 59–114, esp. 85–88.

[10] J. J. Collins, "The Court-Tales in Daniel and the Development of Apocalyptic," *JBL* 94 (1975) 218–34, esp. 230–34; cf. his commentary *Daniel*, 69–70, where Collins admits that this reconstruction is "very hypothetical."

[11] Idem, "Daniel and His Social World," 136.

[12] K. Koch, *Das Buch Daniel* (EdF 144; Darmstadt: Wissenschaftliche Buchgesellschaft, 1980) 178.

[13] Plöger, *Theokratie*, 16–18, 27–33; Hengel, *Judentum*, 320–23.

[14] Cf. for the latter, Steck, "Weltgeschehen," 270ff.; Kratz, "Reich Gottes," 454; Collins, "Daniel and His Social World," 137.

the widely-accepted division into non-apocalyptic stories and apocalyptic visions may be simply incorrect, which would mean that the sharp contrast in tendency does not really exist.

The second obstacle is the model of Israelite society that is usually used for the reconstruction of the social setting. In the past, the model of O. Plöger—which was followed by M. Hengel—was very influential, whereby a long lasting dichotomy was constructed in post-exilic Israel between two theological currents labelled "theocracy" and "eschatology." Both offered the model of a fundamental opposition between the temple and the Jerusalem state establishment (priests, aristocrats), with "eschatological conventicles" being on the side of the ordinary people.[15] In this eschatological group were located not only the author of Daniel, but also the writers of late prophetic and other apocalyptic literature. However, this model is far too simple and rigid to facilitate a sufficient reconstruction of the complicated and vivid religious history of post-exilic Israel and early Judaism.[16] Accordingly, more and more scholars are looking for a solution apart from this model. Most promising are the attempts of J. J. Collins[17] and P. Lampe[18] at distinguishing between several apocalyptic groups who pursued partly different goals and came from different backgrounds. However, the older simplistic model is still influential among some scholars,[19] and as yet no consensus regarding a better one exists.

The third obstacle is the sociological classification of the Ḥasidim. There is a wide consensus that they constitute an established group of some sort, since 1 and 2 Maccabees use the Greek transcription

---

[15] Hengel, *Judentum*, 320ff.

[16] Cf. R. Albertz, *A History of Israelite Religion in the Old Testament Period* (2 vols., OTL; Louisville, KY: Westminster John Knox, 1994) 2.438–43; 564–66.

[17] Collins, *The Apocalyptic Vision*, 195–218.

[18] Lampe, "Die Apokalyptiker," 85–93.

[19] Cf. O. H. Steck, "Strömungen theologischer Tradition im Alten Israel," in idem, *Wahrnehmungen Gottes im Alten Testament. Gesammelte Studien* (TB 70; München: Kaiser, 1982) 311ff.; Kratz, "Reich Gottes," 438–39; 455ff., but with some modifications. Kratz is aware of the fact that his thesis concerning the book of Daniel is in contrast with Plöger's model: "Daß der von Plöger konstruierte Gegensatz von 'Theokratie und Eschatologie' in dieser einfachen Weise nicht stimmen kann, haben wir bereits aufgrund der Schichtung des Danielbuchs festgestellt" (pg. 477). He is forced to postulate an eschatological trend within the theocracy.

'Ασιδαῖοι of the Aramaic term חֲסִידַיָּא, "the pious (people)." But just how this group can be classified is widely disputed: Are they to be identified as "pious conventicles" next to the lower-class as proposed by O. Plöger and M. Hengel, or—as suggested by V. Tcherikover?[20] —were they the pious "scribal class" who had already risen to the rank of a religious elite during the conservative restoration under Simon the Just, and who were first to organize military resistance against the Hellenistic reform? Recently, J. Kampen has sustained the latter viewpoint, but with some modifications: downplaying the military aspect, he defines the Ḥasidim as learned scribes and "leading citizens devoted to the law ... who bore some weight in matters concerning the Jews of Judea."[21] Kampen himself sees no evidence for the assumption that the Ḥasidim had anything to do with apocalyptic literature.[22] However, it is only his and Tcherikover's approaches that admit any discussion of the positions of scholars who regard the authors of apocalyptic literature as well-educated scribes, temple officials, priests, or members of the upper-class in connection with the Ḥasidim-hypothesis.

2. THE TRADITIO-HISTORY OF THE BOOK OF DANIEL

Social-historical research is dependent on careful investigation of the main *Tendenz* of a given text. In the case of Daniel we are faced with the problem that a clear shift of *Tendenz* exists. In the entire Aramaic section of the book (Daniel 2–7) we can clearly identify a main goal, the realization of God's kingdom against the mighty foreign empires of the world, which links each chapter like a chain (Dan 2:44-45; 3:31-33; 4:31-32; [5:21]; 6:26-28; 7:13-14). However, in the Hebrew part of the book (Daniel 1; 8–12) this theme is completely absent. Its goals "are more elusive," as J. J. Collins correctly points out: "Chapters 8 and 9 look only for the demise of the king and the restoration of the cult .... Finally, chapter 12 speaks of the resurrection of the dead."[23]

---

[20] V. Tcherikover, *Hellenistic Civilization and the Jews* (3rd ed., New York: Atheneum, 1975), 125–26; 196–98.

[21] J. Kampen, *The Hasideans and the Origin of Pharisaism. A Study in 1 and 2 Maccabees* (SBLSCS 24, Atlanta: Scholars Press, 1988) 113–14, 150; cf. 120.

[22] *Ibidem*, 219.

[23] Collins, "Daniel and His Social World," 139; I do not discuss here the fact that Collins ascribes Daniel 7 to the second part of the book.

It is thus of crucial importance that this shift in *Tendenz* be properly explained by a reconstruction of the book's traditio-history.

In explaining the emergence of the book of Daniel, the so-called "Aufstockungshypothese," put forward by J. Meinhold in 1884, is very influential. This hypothesis distinguishes four main phases of growth: (1) Separate Daniel stories (end of the 4th century BC); (2) The collection of Daniel stories, including that of the three friends which is perhaps complemented by an introduction[24] (Daniel 1–6, the "Aramaic Daniel biography": 3rd century BC); (3) The extended Aramaic Daniel book (Dan 1:1-7:27*:[25] beginning of the 2nd century BC); and (4) The received Aramaic-Hebrew book of Daniel (Daniel 1–12: 167-164 BC).[26]

The main problem of this hypothesis is the widely accepted assumption that the Daniel stories in the first phase—chapters 2 to 6, more or less in their present form—constituted a non-apocalyptic collection, a kind of "Daniel biography." This assumption presents problems for determining the *Tendenz* of the book, since it forces scholars to presume a sharp contrast between an alleged friendly attitude to the foreign ruler in the stories and the annihilation of all empires in the visions (especially Daniel 7), while offering no clear reason why such a shift could take place. Fortunately, however, this assumption is unwarranted. It can be demonstrated that Daniel 2–7* constituted a literary unit, and that a collection of Daniel stories never existed in the shape that they are now found in the Aramaic text. The following five observations may be made:

(a) In their present form two of the Daniel stories reach their climax in the praise of the everlasting kingdom of God by the gentile king (Dan 4:31; 6:27); also to be mentioned is Daniel 5, where Belshazzar is accused of refusing to acknowledge the kingdom of God over the kingdom of men like his father (v. 21). Even the story of the three friends, which contains more general praise of God's saving might (3:28), is connected to the main theme by Dan 3:31, which links it up to chapter 4. On the one hand, these central verses

---

[24] I do not deal here with the problem of the Hebrew chapter 1, which—in my opinion—was added in phase 4. The verses Dan 2:1-4a were translated from Aramaic into Hebrew in connection with this addition.

[25] The asterisk here indicates that not all of the verses are indicated.

[26] For the history of this hypothesis, cf. Koch, *Daniel*, 61ff. Some scholars regard the prayer in Dan 9:4-19 as a later addition.

are not removable from the text, since many other passages refer to the theme (cf. Dan 4:14, 22, 23, 29; 5:18-22). On the other hand, these verses all have similar wording, quoting with slight variation the hymnic passage Ps 145:13. Thus the traditio-historical conclusion is clear: the verses belong to the redactional level, and link the stories to a composition; but they, too, have been fully reworked to fit the topic of the composition and can no longer be separated.[27]

(b) Daniel 3–6, however, does not constitute a unit of its own, but also includes Daniel 2 and 7. This can be proved in that an identical link is made with the climax in Daniel 7: after the judgement over the four cruel beasts representing the empires, God will establish his everlasting kingdom by handing it over to "sombody like a man" (Dan 7:13). Clearly the vision will reveal the goal of the entire composition: God will establish his kingdom, as opposed to the deteriorated worldly empires. But in revealing the final end of history, Daniel 7 does not stand alone. Daniel's interpretation of Nebuchadnezzar's dream in Dan 2:31-45 constitutes a parallel apocalyptic instruction, although it makes use of a different symbolism: the statue representing the system of decaying empires was totally destroyed by a rock representing the final establishment of God's everlasting kingdom (2:44). Moreover, the praise of the linking hymn is echoed (לָא תִתְחַבַּל, cf. 6:27; 7:14). The fact that the story of Daniel 2 comprises a clear apocalyptic instruction (cf. vv. 20-23, 28-30; cf. 8:19; 10:14) argues strongly against the assumption that a collection of non-apocalyptic Aramaic stories of Daniel ever existed. Furthermore, those scholars who argue for such a collection are forced to reduce the text of Daniel 2 by arbitrary literary-critical decisions,[28] or by weakening its apocalyptic character.[29]

---

[27] Thus it is methodologically invalid for Steck, "Weltgeschehen," 265–66, to use these hymnic passages for determining the intention of the separate stories. Kratz, *Translatio imperii*, 161ff., correctly assigned them to the story collection.

[28] See Kratz, *Translatio imperii*, 61–70, who selects Dan 2:1aα, 28aβγb; the words דִּי נֶחְשָׁא and תְּלִיתָיָא in v. 39; and 40-44. Kratz wishes us to believe that originally signified were only the three governments of the Babylonian empire that was destroyed by "the rock," i.e. the Persian empire. The only possible argument in favour is that in this form Daniel 2 would better accord with the other Daniel stories, but it should be rejected as a *petitio principii*. In any case, Kratz admits that in its present form Daniel 2 accords perfectly with the eschatological perspective of Daniel 7 (pg. 49). The only provable literary additions are Dan 2:41*, 42, 43.

[29] Cf. for example, Collins, "Court-Tales," 222–24; and his more reserved

(c) These results from traditio-criticism are sustained by the form-critical insight that Daniel 2–7 constitutes a well-structured composition, one that must be considered intentional.[30] The outer frame is formed by the two parallel apocalyptic instructions of Daniel 2 and 7; indeed, the vision is an intensification of the dream interpretation. The whole system of worldly empires will be destroyed, and God's kingship will be erected in their place. The inner frame constitutes the two martyr legends found in Daniel 3 and Daniel 6, the "three men in the fiery furnace," and "Daniel in the lions' den." In these cases pious Jews, who bravely withstood the self-divinizing claims of the empires, were rescued from death by God who thereby demonstrated his superior kingship. The inner core consists of the antitypical stories about Nebuchadnezzar and Belshazzar. Whereas the former was humbled by God and was restored to the kingship—after acknowledging the kingship of God—the latter, having learned nothing from his father, uttered blasphemies against the only true God and lost his kingship. This well thought-out structure makes it highly probable that Daniel 2–7* is a literary unit, composed and written by one author.

(d) The thesis suggesting that each chapter of Daniel 2–7* must be seen as a literary unit in its own right, easily explains the strange fact that the book of Daniel comprises texts in two languages. Similar to the Aramaic chapters of Ezra 4–6, the entire Aramaic section of Daniel 2–7 can be interpreted as an older source that was incorporated by a Hebrew-writing editor.

(e) In comparison to these arguments, observations as to why Daniel 7 was not an original part of Daniel 2–6 but a later addition, are rather weak. While there are only a few stylistic pecularities in Daniel 7 as compared with 2–6,[31] many identical or similar formulations are to be found.[32] The only serious argument against an original literary unity is the observation that the dating of Daniel 7 "in the

---

comments nearly twenty years later in *Daniel*, 174–75.

[30] Cf. A. Lenglet, "La structure littéraire de Daniel 2–7," *Bib* 53 (1972) 169–90; R. Albertz, *Gott*, 181–82.

[31] For example, the use of the particle וַאֲרוּ (Dan 7:2, 5, 6, 7, 13) instead of וַאֲלוּ (Dan 2:31; 4:7, 10).

[32] For detailed discussion, cf. P. Weimar, "Daniel 7. Eine Textanalyse," in R. Pesch and R. Schnackenburg (eds.), *Jesus und der Menschensohn* (Freiburg: Herder 1975) 13–29; Albertz, *Gott*, 172–74.

first year of Belshazzar" (v. 1) springs back behind the period that has already been reached in Daniel 6 and 5. However, there are good reasons for this apparent inconsistency, which induced the Septuagint editor to place chapters 7 and 8 between Daniel 4 and 5. First, the author did not want to destroy the strong links between Daniel 4 and 5, which were crucial for his presentation. Second, he wished to connect chapters 5 and 7 in parallel: during the reign of Belshazzar, whose kingship broke down so quickly, Daniel saw the vision that all empires will be destroyed. Third, because Daniel 7 also includes the destruction of the Babylonian empire as an event in the future, the vision had to be dated before its fall. Finally, as a revelation concerning the mystery of the future, Daniel 7 constitutes the climax of the Aramaic book and thus had to be placed at its end.[33]

To conclude this literary discussion, the assumption that the book of Daniel contains a collection of non-apocalyptic stories (Daniel 1–6) and three apocalyptic visions (Daniel 7–12) is unfounded. There are good reasons for distinguishing in the present form of Daniel between two apocalyptic books: the Aramaic Daniel apocalypse (Daniel 2–7*), and the Hebrew Daniel apocalypse (Daniel 1; 8–12),[34] which re-edited and interpreted the former during the Maccabean crisis. The Aramaic apocalypse arose at an earlier date. Thus, in order to locate the social setting of the book of Daniel we must investigate the *Tendenz*, date, and social background of the two apocalyptic books separately.[35]

3. *TENDENZ*, DATE, AND SOCIAL BACKGROUND OF THE DANIEL NARRATIVE COLLECTION IN THE OLD GREEK (DANIEL 4–6* LXX)

The *Tendenz* of the Aramaic Daniel apocalypse may be described most precisely by comparing Daniel 2–7 with the narrative collection

---

[33] The observation that the datings of Hebrew chapters reiterated the periods of the Aramaic section of the Daniel stories (Daniel 8: Babylonian, Daniel 9: Median, Daniel 10: Persian; cf. Daniel 2–5; 6; 6:29) does not mean that Daniel 7 did not originally belong with them. On the contrary, the dating in Dan 8:1 "In the third year of the reign of Belshazar" presupposes the dating of Daniel 7 and continues it.

[34] Thus an increasing number of scholars now oppose the majority, for example Weimar, "Daniel 7," 33–34; Lebram, *Das Buch Daniel*, 21; Albertz, *Gott*, 170ff.; idem, *History of Israelite Religion*, 584ff.

[35] It is interesting to note that J. J. Collins ("Daniel and His Social World," 139–40) recognizes some differences between Daniel 7 and 8–12, although he regards the visions as a literary unity.

in chapters 4–6 as transmitted by the Septuagint.[36] It can be proved
that these Old Greek stories, which differ markedly from their
Aramaic counterparts, are not late and inaccurate midrashim as is
often thought, but represent an independent shape of the Daniel
stories which in my view is even older than the Aramaic, perhaps not
in all their details, but in their basic narrative plot.[37] The most

---

[36] Only a few sentences are later additions by the Septuagint translator (4:18*,
37*, 37C; 5 praefatio; 6:1a). For additional details, see my exegesis in *Gott*, 13–
42, 77–84, 113–28.

The material has been artificially divided by the tradents of the Septuagint who
inserted Daniel 7 and 8 between Daniel 4 and 5 (so even in the oldest manuscript, P
967, from the 2nd or 3rd century AD). It is difficult to decide whether the division
of Daniel 4 and 5 LXX is a secondary adjustment, caused by the dating of Daniel 7,
or represents an older shape of the Book in the Old Greek Daniel tradition (Daniel
2–4; 7; 5–6, followed by Bel and the Dragon) as posited by J. Lust, "The
Septuagint Version of Daniel 4–5," in A. S. van der Woude (ed.), *The Book of
Daniel in the Light of New Findings* (BETL 56; Leuven: Leuven University Press
and Peeters, 1993) 39–53. In any event, Lust's assumption says nothing against
my thesis that Daniel 4–6* LXX belonged together, as he seems to suppose (pg.
39). The Greek narrative collection of Daniel 4–6* represents a stage of tradition
more ancient than the oldest edition of the Greek Daniel book. That Daniel 4 and 5
are not as tightly connected in the Greek version as in the Aramaic (Lust, pg. 39), I
have already shown (Albertz, *Gott*, 91–94). Daniel 4–6* LXX still has the features
of a collection, not a composition like the Aramaic apocalypse. In any event, the
Greek keyword links between Daniel 4, 5, and 6, which I pointed out previously
(*Gott*, 159–60), cannot be overlooked. For reasons why the Greek translator of the
Book of Daniel included an older Greek narrative collection in his edition, see R.
Albertz, "Bekehrung von oben als 'messianisches Programm.' Die Sonderüber-
lieferung der Septuaginta in Dan 4–6," in H. Graf Reventlow (ed.), *Theologische
Probleme der Septuaginta und der Hellenistischen Hermeneutik* (Veröffent-
lichungen der Wissenschaftlichen Gesellschaft für Theologie 11; München: Kaiser
& Gütersloher Verlagshaus, 1997) 46–62, esp. 56–61.

[37] Cf. my detailed investigations in *Gott*, 19ff; 77ff.; 113ff.; 155–56; 159ff.,
with a synopsis in German translation. There are still some reservations in the
scholary debate against my conclusions, mainly against the priority of the Old
Greek narratives; for example, Collins, *Daniel*, 262–63; E. Haag, "Hasidäer," 59
n.13. It is somewhat odd that certain scholars believe in their ability to reconstruct
one or more older "Vorlagen" of a given biblical text by literary-critical means, but
cannot entertain the existence of a biblical text outside the Hebrew Bible, which
could be a "Vorlage" of the Hebrew. While I cannot unfold my argument here, I
offer one oberservation that is most convincing in my view: nearly all compository
links found in the Aramaic Daniel apocalypse are still lacking in the Old Greek
narratives! Without knowledge of my book, L. M. Wills, *The Jew in the Court of*

interesting difference of Daniel 4–6* in the LXX is evident in that it almost completely lacks the main topic of the Aramaic apocalypse: the praise and establishment of God's kingdom.[38] The Old Greek presents instead the topic of conversion to the one true God, which the gentile ruler underwent, forced by God's might or impressed by pious Jews. Using Nebuchadnezzar as an example, the Greek author wished to demonstrate that God himself could turn the destroyer of the temple into an adherent and defender of Jewish religion if only he was guided by a wise Jewish interpreter of dreams (Daniel 4 LXX). Certainly there were constant setbacks, as is made clear by the example of Belshazzar, so that a world ruler lapsed from the true God and turned blasphemously to pagan idolatry, with the result that God also deprived him of his rule (Daniel 5 LXX). However, these were not irreversible setbacks, as the Greek author showed by the example of Darius: Despite the intrigues of malicious minions which brought pious and loyal Jewish officials into discredit, with God's help there arose time and again the opportunity to convert the ruler of the world and create a form of political rule in which pious Jews even occupied leading posts in government (Daniel 6 LXX).[39]

The perspective offered by the Greek narrator is principally an optimistic one. Even if in the Jewish diaspora living in the service of gentile rulers might became dangerous, generally this could be understood as a wonderful opportunity for converting heathens of high rank and for spreading monotheistic belief to all nations. Admittedly, there existed certain points of conflict such as the Hellenistic ruler cult (Dan 6:8-9 LXX), but through the brave witness of pious Jews in pagan service there was the opportunity to

---

Foreign King. Ancient Jewish Court Legends (HDR 26, Minneapolis: Fortress 1990) 144–52, reached a similar conclusion on the priority of the Old Greek narratives. However, Wills did not present a clear picture of their tendency, since he is more interested in details of "court legends." Furthermore, he does not conclude that the Aramaic chapters 2–7 constitute a literary unit.

[38] Dan 4:37c is clearly a doublet and in secondary alignment with the MT, propably added by the LXX-translator. Dan 4:31 in MS 88 and the Syrohexapla seems to allude to it, but the variant in P 967 clearly shows that this is a later accomodation; cf. Albertz, *Gott*, 20–21. In the LXX stories what is praised is not God's kingdom, but his might in nature and history, partly against the idols (4:17, 27, 31, 37; 5:4, 23; 6:27-28).

[39] For more details, see Albertz, *Gott*, 159–70; the summary is taken from my *History of Israelite Religion*, 577.

reform the empires from within. Of course, the hope of the ultimate conversion of all peoples to YHWH is also nourished by the eschatological promises of late prophets,[40] but in contrast[41] the Greek narrator expects this to be a harmonious inner-worldly development without any judgement and destruction. Consequently, all typical apocalyptic features are lacking in his account.

It is highly probable that this optimistic tendency derives from the upper-class of the Alexandrian diaspora.[42] The concept of a "mission from above," that the converted ruler of the world will enact protective laws in favour of the Jewish faith and accord it the status of a state religion (Dan 4:37a, b; 6:26-28 LXX), is a typical upper-class perspective. The Jewish audience for whom the narratives are written can be located in the group of cosmopolitan officials in pagan service and their environs. Their service is justified against any possible criticism from pious Jewish circles that dissociated themselves from the pagan world, by illuminating it beneath the eschatological horizon of world mission. The upper-class members are admo-nished to stay faithful to their Jewish beliefs and practices, even though this might provoke conflicts with their pagan environment, and are confirmed in their intention that belief in God is compatible with loyalty to gentile rulers.

Regardless of the probable Persian origin of the separate Daniel stories, the Greek narrative collection was composed in the Hellenistic Period. The redactional links were made on the level of Greek language, and there are some allusions to typical Hellenistic cultural features such as the ruler cult (Dan 6:8-9.). Because of its optimistic expectations this collection should be placed in the first part of the 3rd century BC, before the Syrian wars damaged the reputation of the Hellenistic empires in Jewish eyes. A very possible period of origin is the reign of Ptolemy II Philadelphos (285-246 BC), who—if the legendary Aristeas letter is not completely incorrect—encouraged the Egyptian Jews to translate their religious and legal writings. Another possibility is the reign of Ptolemy VI Philometer

---

[40] Cf. Isa 44:5; 45:18-25; 55:3; 56:3, 6; 66:18, 20; Zech 2:15; 8:20-22; and 14:16-21.

[41] Cf. Isa 66:5ff.; Zech 14:1ff.

[42] In spite of the Babylonian mileu of the strories, the Greek language and the prominent role that the narrative collection must have played in Alexandria point to an Egyptian origin of the collection.

(180-145 BC), when Jews in Egypt had good opportunities of rising to high state offices; but this date is probably too late. In that case it would be difficult to explain why the Greek stories became more popular in Alexandria than their Aramaic counterparts, when the latter already existed. But the later opportunity for Jews to engage in the Ptolemaic state can explain why the Alexandrian translator of Daniel, who worked about 130 BC, included the older Greek narrative collection, whose *Tendenz* differed widely from those of the Aramaic and Hebrew apocalypses.

4. *TENDENZ*, DATE, AND SOCIAL BACKGROUND OF THE ARAMAIC DANIEL APOCALYPSE

Awareness of what the Daniel stories look like that are clearly derived from the upper-class makes it impossible to relate the Aramaic book of Daniel to any establishment as is done by O. H. Steck, R. G. Kratz, and others.[43] The author of the Aramaic Daniel apocalypse, who probably knew a narrative collection very similar to that transmitted in Old Greek, could no longer share the optimistic estimation of foreign power and positive assessment of collaboration that were so popular with the Jewish upper-class in Egypt. For this reason he reworked the Daniel stories throughout. He prefaced the collection with the martyr legend of the "three men in the fiery den" (Daniel 3), which hitherto had circulated independently, using it to demonstrate the self-divinizing claim of the Hellenistic state power with which pious Jews necessarily came into conflict, and which they had to resist. He also transformed the story "Daniel in the lions' den" (Daniel 6), previously only a limited intrigue of minor officials, into a showpiece of totalitarian state power that could no longer tolerate the religious loyalty of pious Jews. In this author's view the Jewish upper-class hope of reforming the pagan state from within by collaboration was a dangerous illusion. All that was left was for pious Jews was to offer resistance against the violent pressure of the hellenistic state, even to the point of martyrdom.

Consequently our author almost completely removed all statements about the conversion of the world ruler[44] and replaced it with his new general theme of the unstoppable establishment of God's kingdom (Dan 3:31-33; 4:31-32; 6:26-28; cf. 5:21). For him the gentile

---

[43] See the Introduction above.

[44] A trace of this topic can be found only in Dan 3:28-29.

empires were no longer reformable, neither by Jews nor by others. In his view God would himself impose his rule, not with but against the political world powers. By humiliating the mad king Nebuchadnezzar to the level of a beast, God was compelling him to acknowledge the divine kingdom (4:31-32). Only in this way did he grant a limited existence to the Babylonian empire. In casting down Belshazzar the blasphemer, God demonstrated that he could establish his rule against a world empire. And by exploding the totalitarian claim of the Median empire via Daniel's rescue from the lions' den, he compelled Darius to be subject voluntarily to his eternal, universal rule. But these events are only examples demonstrating how God's kingdom had already been at work behind the history of past empires.

With two apocalyptic instructions the Aramaic author placed a framework around the narratives, and proved that the history of the world empires, which unrelentingly descended to brutality, hubris and instability, would necessarily come to an end in the near future. They will be destroyed by the kingdom of God, which like a big rock will cast down a fragile statue without any human activity (Dan 2:44-45). In his personal vision at the end of his work (chapter 7), Daniel raised a corner of the veil of mystery concerning the positive characteristics of God's kingdom in contrast to all previous empires. After the four terrible beasts that trampled and devoured everything have been judged and destroyed by God, Daniel suddenly sees appear in God's bright world "one like a man" (כְּבַר אֱנָשׁ), to whom the kingship of God is given (Dan 7:13-14). This figure is then identified with the "saints of the Most Hight" in the interpretation of v. 18.

What is meant by this mysterious figure is hotly debated. In my opinion "son of man" here is not yet a messianic title as is found in later texts.[45] Likewise, it is highly improbable that the "saints of the Most High" originally mean angels,[46] as some scholars assume, even though the author of the Hebrew edition might have interpreted them in this manner.[47] Since in v. 28 the "people (עַם) of the saints of the

---

[45] Cf. for example, Steck, "Weltgeschehen," 272; Collins, *Daniel*, 305–306, 318 (for discussion, 306–310; 312ff.); and H. S. Kvanvig, *Roots of Apocalyptic. The Mesopotamian Background of the Enoch Figure and the Son of Man* (WMANT 61, Neukirchen-Vluyn: Neukirchener Verlag, 1988) 345–53.

[46] Thus in *1 Enoch* 37-71, *4 Ezra* 13, and in the NT.

[47] Cf. his characterization of Gabriel and other angels: כְּמַרְאֵה־גָבֶר (Dan 8:15; likewise 10:16-18).

Most High" is mentioned, a kind of human group must be meant.[48] In the imagery of Daniel 7, the "one in human form" simply represents the human as opposed to the inhuman beasts. This means that the author of the Aramaic apocalypse wanted to indicate that God's kingdom will have profoundly human features, in contrast to the bestial and destructive rule of the previous world empires. In the view of the Aramaic author, this new kind of political rule, essentially shaped by humanity, would be executed by a human community deeply devoted to God. He most likely envisaged pious Jewish circles who had previously been the victims of totalitarian state power. Moreover, he presumably expected that they who had suffered so long had learned to see through the inhumane consequences of self-divinization of political power, to resist its seduction, and to treat all mankind humanely.

That this interpretation is in accordance with the author's intention is demonstrated by two observations. First, he provides a hidden hint of how the handing over of power in chapter 7 is to be understood. Already in Dan 4:14, he lets Daniel announce that by removing Nebuchadnezzar from power, God wants to teach all men that "he gives the kingdom to whom he will and he may set over it the humblest of mankind (שְׁפַל אֲנָשִׁים)." The "saints of the Most High" to whom God's kingdom is finally given are "the humblest of mankind." In the background is the well-known psalm motif that "God casts the highest down and raises the humblest up."[49] Second, in Psalm 145, where the author cites v. 13 repeatedly in mentioning God's kingdom, God's rule is characterized in the next verse as follows: "the Lord holds up those who stumble and straightens the backs which are bent" (v. 14). The kingdom of God, which is carried out by the humblest of mankind, will not suppress and exploit like the world empires, but will hold up the weak.

Thus the theologumenon of God's kingdom constituted for the author of the Aramaic apocalypse not only the basis for questioning

---

[48] The assumption that עַם is a later addition is very suspect, since in the later tradition of the book there is a clear tendency for strengthing the transcendence of salvation. However, both interpretations can be reconciled if we take into account the early Jewish concept that the eschatological community on earth has its heavenly counterpart; cf. for example CD 20:8; 1QM 3:5; 6:6; 10:10-11; 16:1.

[49] Cf. 1 Sam 2:8; Ps 107:40-41; 113:7-9; 145:14; 147:6; Job 5:11-16; and Lk 1:52-53.

the legitimacy and existence of world powers, but also allowed him
to outline an ideal form of political government that is rooted in
humanity and is immune to the self-divinization of power.

We may conclude that the Aramaic apocalypse is clearly a political
manifesto which tried to encourage pious Jews, who felt victimized
under Hellenistic empires, to resist their political, ecomomic, and
cultural pressure. This apocalypse does not call for military
resistance; the destruction of human empires, or the establishment of
God's kingdom, will be brought about by God himself without any
human participation (Dan 2:44-45; 7:11-12). But it calls for a clear
and public religious resistance against the totalitarian claim of the
state, including political consequences such as martyrdom. It announ-
ces the destruction of the Hellenistic empire in the near future and
draws up an ideal form of political government instead, in which the
pious audience of the apocalypse will participate.

From this plain concept a social setting of the author and his
audience may be determined. He is clearly an intellectual, not only
trained in the knowledge of Jewish traditions but also familiar with
Near Eastern and Hellenistic concepts.[50] He is especially devoted to
the psalmic tradition, however, and used Psalm 145 as the backbone
of his theological concept—not representing the official Jerusalem
temple cult as O. H. Steck[51] and R. G. Kratz[52] have assumed. As M.
Millard and E. Zenger have pointed out,[53] the book of Psalms cannot
generally be seen as the official prayer book of the Second Temple.
On the contrary, Psalm 145 constitutes the redactional climax of the
fifth psalm book (Psalms 107–145), which is strongly shaped by the
idea of an eschatological kingdom of God in relationship to pious
devotion.[54] The psalmic base of our author is to be seen as an

---

[50] Note the Persian-Hellenistic concept of three or four world empires
combined with the idea of four deteriorating world ages in Daniel 2, and the Ancient
Near Eastern background of the vision in Daniel 7; cf. Collins, *Daniel*, 166–70;
280–94.

[51] Steck, "Weltgeschehen," 266–67.

[52] Kratz, *Translatio imperii*, 163ff.

[53] Cf. M. Millard, *Die Komposition des Psalters* (FAT 9, Tübingen: Mohr-
Siebeck, 1994) 227ff.; E. Zenger, "Das Buch der Psalmen," in idem (ed.), *Ein-
leitung in das Alte Testament* (Kohlhammer Studienbücher 1.1; Stuttgart:
Kohlhammer, 1995) 309–26.

[54] Cf. E. Zenger, "Komposition und Theologie des 5.Psalmenbuchs 107–145,"
BN 82 (1996), 97–116, who argues: "Problematisch erscheint mir sowohl bei

alternative concept to the sacrifical temple theology, and composed by eschatologically-oriented pious groups.[55] Thus the author of the Aramaic apocalypse may come from a circle of learned psalmic poets who worked not only for the temple, but also for pious communities. He clearly stood in opposition to the aristocratic and priestly establishment which was prepared to collaborate with the Hellenistic empires. Not only did he lose all hope of the ability to reform the foreign world power, but also felt a deep sympathy for its victims, and by his work made the attempt to encourage their resistance against it.

The problem of dating the Aramaic apocalypse has to do with the interpretation of the "little horn" in Dan 7:8. There are many good reasons for the assumption that Antiochus IV Epiphanes is intended. However, in contrast to Dan 8:11-13 the profanation of the temple is not mentioned. Dan 7:25 can be interpreted to the effect that the king introduced a foreign calendar so that it was impossible to celebrate Sabbaths and feasts properly (cf. 1 Macc 1:45; 2 Macc 6:6). Accordingly, J. J. Collins has placed the addition of Daniel 7 in an early phase of the Maccabean crisis (late 167 BC).[56] Consequently, there would be only a few years between the Aramaic and the Hebrew apocalypses. Alternatively, J.-C. Lebram has identified the "little horn" with Antiochus III.[57] This actually offers a much better period for dating, but the interpretation cannot explain specific details of the vision, especially the three horns which are torn out (vv. 8, 24).[58]

Koch wie bei Kratz, daß die Theologie des 5.Buchs und insbesondere des Schlußhallels 146–150 viel zu nahe an die Theologie der Chronikbücher bzw. des chronistischen Geschichtswerkes herangerückt wird" (pg. 106).

[55] In contrast to the chronistic concept in Psalm 145, the kingdom of God (vv. 1, 11, 12, 13) is not related to Zion, the Davidic Monarchy, or even Israel, but to pious Jewish circles, and is directed universally to all the pious and needy people (see 1:10-12, 19-21). The same is true for the Aramaic book of Daniel. Apart from the close theological agreement between Psalm 145 and Aramaic Daniel, there are many similarities in wording (see Albertz, *Gott*, 187, n.363) which permit the conclusion that this psalm was important for the Aramaic author, or even that he composed it.

[56] Collins, *Daniel*, 323–24.

[57] Lebram, *Das Buch Daniel*, esp. 21, 84.

[58] Antiochus III was a younger son of Seleucus II Callinicus, and followed his elder brother Seleucus III Soter 223 BC to the throne, after the latter was murdered during a campaign against Attalus I of Pergamon; see H. H. Schmitt, *Unter-*

Thus I follow P. Weimar, R. G. Kratz and many others who assume for good reason that Daniel 7 was secondarily actualized during the Maccabean crisis by inserting Antiochus IV into the vision,[59] but in contrast to these authors I agree with J. J. Collins who dates this Aramaic addition in the early phase of the crisis, before the Hebrew visions were added in a later phase.

Nevertheless, the second part of J.-C. Lebram's thesis is highly probable, that the original Aramaic apocalypse should be dated during the reign of Antiochus III. Two observations support this position. First is the strange fact that the author of the Hebrew apocalypse, who felt obliged to re-edit the Aramaic work, paid so much attention to Antiochus III, more than to any other Hellenistic king besides Antiochus IV (Dan 11:10-20). In his vision all the military campaigns by which Antiochus III invaded Coelesyria and Palestine since 221 BC, finally bringing to an end the long rule of the Ptolemies in that area, are mentioned and commented on in great detail: his first successful attacks against Ptolemy IV (Dan 11:10), his suprising defeat at Raphia in 217 BC after an initial success (vv. 11-12), his new campaign down to Gaza in 202/1 BC against the young and weak Ptolemy V (v. 13), his victory in Paneas over the Ptolemaic commander Scopas in 200 BC (v. 15), and his final conquest of Palestine in 198 BC (v. 16). Obviously this earlier period is still of crucial importance for the Hebrew author, and by mentioning the hybris and fall of Antiochus III (vv. 12, 13) he intended to present him as the bad forerunner of Antiochus IV (vv. 36-41).

The second observation is that the Hebrew author mentioned in his vision—apart from his own time—only one inner-Jewish event, which took place during the reign of Antiochos III before his victory in Paneas:

> In those times many will rise against the king of the south, and some violent men among your own people will rise themselves to fulfill the vision, but they will stumble (Dan 11:14).

---

suchungen zur Geschichte Antiochos' des Großen und seiner Zeit (Historia 6, Wiesbaden: Steiner, 1964) 1–3. There is no evidence that Antiochus III was involved in this murder or that there were two other rivals.

[59] Cf. Weimar, "Daniel 7," 15–28; and, somewhat differently, Kratz, *Translatio imperii*, 21–31. In my opinion the secondary verses are 7bβ, 8, 11*, 12, 20f., 22b, 24f., and 26bβ. The assumption of a literary reworking of Daniel 7 is the only weak point of the thesis that Daniel 2–7 constitutes an older apocalypse. But in contrast to Daniel 2, the literary-critical separation in Daniel 7 is not unfounded!

This verse, often judged to be "obscure,"[60] testifies clearly to a violent uprising in Judah, possibly against the Ptolemies, which was induced by "a vision" (חָזוֹן), that—in the terminology of the Hebrew book of Daniel—clearly means an apocalyptic instruction.[61] It probably has to do with the recapture of Judah by Scopas during the winter of 201/200 BC, when Antiochus III had left Palestine after his successful conquest of Gaza, as is mentioned by Polybius (cf. Josephus, *Antiquities* 12 §135). In the insecure and disastrous political situation caused by several occupations and reoccupations, the inhabitants of Jerusalem and Judah were split into pro-Seleucid and pro-Ptolemaic factions. It is especially probable that the poorer people, who had to suffer the enormous pressure of the Ptolemaic tax system, hoped that Seleucid rule would lighten their hard lot. The surprising reoccupation by Scopas seemed to destroy all those hopes; and his persecutions of members of the pro-Seleucid party may well have provoked a violent rebellion against the Ptolemaic empire in Jerusalem and Judah.

For the Hebrew apocalyptist this event was doubtlessly of crucial importance, since it involved the same kind of apocalyptic instruction he felt obliged to give himself. However, he painted a negative picture of his forerunners by calling them "violent men" or "robbers" (בְּנֵי פָּרִיצִים),[62] denoting people who obviously tried to force the fullfillment of a given apocalyptic vision by recourse to violent means, such as upheaval, rebellion or military attempts. As we will see below, the Hebrew apocalyptist totally disagreed with any kind of violence in the apocalyptic movement; in his judgement such apocalyptic engagements were bound to fail.

It was probably Scopas who quickly put down the anti-Ptolemaic upheaval in Judea. To what extent this event was still straining Jewish-Egyptian relationships as many as 70 years later is evident by the fact that the Septuagint translator completely changed the text of

---

[60] Cf. Collins, *Daniel*, 379–80.

[61] Cf. Dan 1:17; 8:1–2, 13, 15, 17, 26; 9:21, 27; 10:14; also 7:1–2, 7, 13, 20.

[62] It is of interest that the term ληστής, the Greek equivalent of פָּרִיץ (cf. Jer 7:11), is later used by Josephus to name the Zealots; cf. A. van der Kooij, "A Case of Reinterpretation in the Old Greek of Daniel 11," in J. W. van Henten, H. J. de Jonge, P. T. van Rooden, and J. W. Wesselius (eds.), *Tradition and Interpretation in Jewish and Early Christian Literature. Essays in Honor of J.-C. Lebram* (Leiden: Brill, 1986) 72–80, esp. 75, n.12.

Dan 11:14 for his Alexandrian audience:

> And in those times thoughts shall stand up against the the king of Egypt,
> and he shall rebuild the ruins of your people, and he shall stand up in order
> to realize the prophecy, and they (that means the plots) shall stumble.[63]

From this perspective Ptolemy V, disregarding the failing plots
against him, wished to fulfill the prophetic promises by rebuilding
the devasted Judah (Amos 9:11). Here the Jewish origin of the
rebellion was concealed, and a little of its positive eschatological
horizon was transferred to Scopas' brutal mission.

Thus Dan 11:14, both in its Hebrew and its Greek versions,
testifies to the existence of an earlier apocalyptic movement in Judah
at the end of the 3rd century BC. This earlier movement is probably
also meant in *1 Enoch* 90:6-7, where the start of the apocalyptic
enlightenment and instruction is set clearly in a period before the
High Priest Onias III, who was removed from his office in 175 BC
(v. 8), and the start of the Maccabean revolt (v. 9). Since it is
unlikely that the period of conservative restoration under Simon the
Just could be meant (198-180 BC), we should look to the end of the
3rd century. In my opinion it is highly probable that the Aramaic
Daniel apocalypse can be connected in some way with this early
apocalyptic movement. Admittedly, the Daniel apocalypse does not
call for violent resistance and does not indicate a special anti-
Ptolemaic attitude; rather, it polemicizes fundamentally against the
Greek empire as a whole.[64] Thus we cannot say that the first Daniel
apocalypse emerged directly from the anti-Ptolemaic rebellion
during the winter of 201/200 BC. Instead, it was written some years
before the upheaval caused by the militant, economic and cultural
pressures (Dan 2:40; 7:7) exerted by the Hellenistic empires in
Palestine during the invasions of Antiochus III and Ptolemy IV/V
from 221 BC. Nevertheless, the promise of this apocalypse could
stand behind the rebellion because of its clear political content: by
offering hope that the destructive Hellenistic empires would come to

---

[63] Here I follow the translation and interpretation of van der Kooij, "Old
Greek," 77ff.

[64] It is only by the early Maccabean addition in Daniel 7 that the Daniel
apocalypse received an anti-Seleucid perspective. In the event that Daniel 7
originally polemicized against Antiochus III (as assumed by J.-C. Lebram, *Das
Buch Daniel*, 21, 84), the Aramaic book of Daniel would not fit in the conflict
testified by Dan 11:14.

an end, and that God would hand over the rule to the pious in the near future. This could in fact motivate pious circles among the poor classes to mount active political resistance.

Obviously, this first heated phase of the apocalyptic movement failed (Dan 11:14; *1 Enoch* 90:7). Scopas was defeated at Paneas by Antiochus III only half a year later, but the system of Hellenistic empires did not collapse. Nevertheless, under Seleucid rule (198-180 BC) the conservative party of the upper-class, including the learned scribes, gained the opportunity for a religious and political restoration which improved the situation of Judah, albeit only a little. It may be assumed that apocalyptic hope faded away and that its pious supporters were once more reintegrated into society.

5. *TENDENZ*, DATE, AND SOCIAL BACKGROUND OF THE HEBREW DANIEL APOCALYPSE

Inasmuch as the Aramaic Daniel apocalypse played an important, though somewhat dangerous, role in the social and political upheaval near the end of the 3rd century, it is understandable why the author of the Hebrew Daniel re-edited and commented upon it. Because of its previous popularity, he published the Daniel apocalypse in its original Aramaic language, presumably chosen to make it more readily understood by the ordinary people who spoke Aramaic in daily life. With its closing vision, Daniel 7 was probably made topical, still in Aramaic,[65] at the beginning of the Maccabean crisis. The Hebrew author wished to make full use of the older apocalypse during the ongoing rebellion against Antiochus IV Epiphanes (about 165 BC) by supplementing it with new apocalyptic instructions of topical interest (chapters 8, 9, and 10–12). Thus he provided the Aramaic Daniel apocalypse with a Hebrew frame (Daniel 1; 8–12) so as to give to it a more traditional outlook, and—as will be shown below—corrected its political character to prevent any military misuse.

The *Tendenz* of the Hebrew apocalypse differs from that of the Aramaic, which is clearly demonstrated by comparing their closing visions (Daniel 10–12 and Daniel 7). Both visions have in common, following the nadir of deterioration, the final collapse of the Hellenistic empire. In Dan 7:11-12 this is brought about by God's judgement, but in Dan 12:1 by the victory of the archangel Michael. From this point onwards the two visions differ completely: whereas

---

[65] See above, pp. 187–88.

the former expects the establishment of God's kingdom and its operation by the community of the pious, the latter envisages the resurrection of the dead, God's judgement on the pious and the wicked, one to eternal life the other to eternal shame, and finally the elevation of the pious teachers (מַשְׂכִּילִים) as ever-shining stars in God's heavenly world (Dan 12:2-3). Clearly, the political theme of a new form of human government is replaced with a purely individual eschatology; instead of an eschatological reality still operating on earth, the eschatological salvation described in Daniel 12 distinctly transcends this world and will operate in heaven hereafter.[66] No doubt the author of the Hebrew apocalypse intended to depoliticize the Aramaic imagery and reinterpret it on an individual and transcendent level of expectation.

The reasons for this noticeable shift in *Tendenz* may be explored by looking at the visionary description of the Maccabean crisis, which the author of the Hebrew apocalypse provides in Dan 11:21-35. Here it is already evident that the author emphasized the responsibility of Antiochus IV for the crisis; it is he who expelled the High Priest Onias III (Dan 11:22), who raged against Judah and Jerusalem after the failure of his campaigns against Egypt (vv. 28-30), and who violated the temple, stopped the daily temple cult, and introduced a pagan symbol (v. 31). By his attack against the "holy covenant" (vv. 28, 30) and the temple of Jerusalem (v. 31) he provoked YHWH blasphemously (Dan 8:10-11, 25). This is the main reason for and issue of the crisis from the perspective of the Hebrew author. On the other hand, the inner-Jewish political and religious conflict between Hellenizers and conservatives, which played a prominent role in the crisis (1 Macc 1:15; 2:15ff., 44; 2 Macc 4–5) is only hinted at (Dan 11:30, 32), and the economic and social clashes have completely faded. In contrast to the Aramaic apocalypse, which emphasizes pious circles mostly from the lower classes (cf. "saints of the Most High," Dan 7:18, 28), the Hebrew author stresses the unity

---

[66] J. J. Collins, who takes for granted the unity of the visions in Daniel 7–12, tries to interpret Daniel 7 and 11–12 along the same lines, but is aware of the incongruity: "We might expect from this that the eschatological kingdom would be ruled by the *maśkîlîm* (sic!) and exclude the violators of the covenant, but this is never asserted. Daniel 11–12 does not pick up the notion of the kingdom .... While the hope for an earthly kingdom remains part of Daniel's expectation, the primary goals of the *maśkîlîm* are not in the political realm." Also see idem, "Daniel and His Social World," 140.

of the people (vv. 32-33) who are threatened from without.

In any case, the author of the Hebrew apocalypse is interested in another conflict, which has been mostly ignored so far: the conflict between the מַשְׂכִּילִים, to whom he dedicates six verses (Dan 11:33–35; 12:3, 9-10)—more than what he has said about the attacks of Antiochus IV against Judah! Concerning the identity of the מַשְׂכִּילִים, we read that their task is "to impart knowledge to many" (Dan 11:33; cf. 12:10) and "to lead many to righteousness" (12:3). Thus it is clear that the term denotes the apocalyptic teachers, who were instructing the ordinary people in the mysteries of the present and future, so that they could resist all the temptations of the religious crisis and attain righteousness in the Last Judgement. As they are called also "teachers of the people" (מַשְׂכִּילֵי עָם, v. 33), they may be imagined as a group of learned elite who felt responsible for the whole society. Since Daniel is identified with this group (12:3-4, 9-10), it is highly probable that the author of the Hebrew apocalypse also regards himself as a member of it.[67]

However, in his visionary interpretation of the Maccabean crisis, the Hebrew author distinguishes between at least two different groups of apocalyptic teachers. "Some of the teachers will stumble" (Dan 11:35; cf. v. 33-34): since כשל is used in all instances, it cannot mean that some of the teachers will die or even suffer martyrdom as is often interpreted on the basis of v. 33b, where sword, flame, and captivity are mentioned.[68] כשל in the nipʿal usually denotes the failure of an action and/or the bad end of the wicked,[69] which is clearly the case in two other passages of Daniel 11: in v. 14 the failure of the previous apocalypticists is meant, in order to enforce the fulfillment of the vision, and v. 19 describes the failure and death of Antiochus III, when he tried to plunder the temple of Elymais.[70]

Thus we have to reconstruct the conflict between the apocalyptic teachers as follows. In carrying out their task of instructing the

---

[67] With Collins, *Apocalyptic Vision*, 212, and others.

[68] Against Collins, *Apocalyptic Vision*, 207, 211; *The Apocalyptic Imagination. An Introduction to the Jewish Matrix of Christianity* (New York: Crossroad, 1984) 89; and *Daniel*, 385–86, who regards the *maskîlîm* as "true heroes of the persecution" and think that "their deaths are said to refine and purify them until the appointed end" (*Apocalyptic Imagination*, 89).

[69] Cf. Lebram, "Piety," 182–83, who translates כשל as "to fall from truth, to go astray," a meaning that is attested at Qumran: 1QS 11:12; CD 2:16; 1QS 3:24.

[70] Only the third passage, Dan 11:41, is not very clear.

people in the crisis (v. 33a) the teachers, or most of them, were not successful for some time; they failed in convincing the people to resist the Hellenizers because the masses were frightened by the cruelty of civil war (v. 33b). Frustrated at the failure of their teaching, the intellectual leaders were ready to accept the "little help" (v. 34a), i.e. the offer from the Maccabees to form a coalition (cf. לוה *nip'al*), and to fight together against Antiochus and the Hellenizers.[71] However, through the acceptance of military resistance the teachers were thrown into theological conflicts; they had to struggle with groups that were not very interested in keeping the people from the apostasy of Hellenism, but acting rather in their own dubious or purely military interests (v. 34b). By forming a coalition with the Maccabean troops, the apocalyptic teachers themselves ran into the danger of apostasy, and some of the author's colleagues already had broken with the truth in his eyes (v. 35aα). Thus, the Maccabean crisis was seen by him as a judgement of purification, distinguishing between the true and false apocalyptic teachers before the last days arrived (v. 35aβb; cf. 12:10). They were not favoured above the ordinary people, who had to be purified from the danger of temptation (12:10).[72] Only those teachers who resisted the seduction of political activism and limited themselves to encouraging others to attain salvation would be raised up to splendour in God's heavenly world (12:3). All others failed, and would fail again. The apocalyptic teachers, so the author of the Hebrew book concludes, have only to teach (יָבִינוּ), nothing else. Even though the wicked Hellenizers did not accept their doctrine, they were not allowed to use other means in the political conflict (12:10).

The polemics of the apocalyptic teacher behind the Hebrew book of Daniel against a group closely associated with the Maccabees are better unterstood if we take into account the emergence at that time

---

[71] This old identification, already made by Porphyry, is still the best. It is disputed by Collins, *Apocalyptic Vision*, 207; *Daniel*, 386, but his own varied solutions are less convincing. Moreover, Collins concedes that the Maccabees could well be included in the group who joined the *maśkîlîm* insincerely (cf. Dan 11:34b).

[72] In the context of the verse, the verbs constructed in the *hithpa'el* are probably not to be understood in the reflexive sense of "self-purification." This purification, of course, should take place through the teaching of the מַשְׂכִּילִים. Thus the form is to be interpreted, like the Aramaic *itpa'el*, as passive. If this is true, Dan 11:35 likewise cannot be understood as self-purification of the מַשְׂכִּילִים by martyrdom or other means.

of another apocalyptic instruction. This is the "Animal Apocalypse" in *1 Enoch* 85–90, which recognized the Maccabean struggles as having crucial importance for the last days. Here the uprising of Judas Maccabeus is explicitly mentioned as a "great horn shooting up from a goat" (90:9), and the coalition with the Maccabees is judged a great help in spreading apocalyptic enlightment to many people (90:10). And here the Maccabean struggles are considered as holy wars—conducted with angelic help—leading directly to the great eschatological battle in which God and Israel, side by side, would put all their enemies to flight (90:18ff.). As J. J. Collins points out,[73] we need to distinguish between different apocalyptic options in the Maccabean crisis: the one voting for militant resistance and supporting the Maccabees, sentiments shared by the author of the Animal Apocalypse; the other opting for non-violent, purely religious resistance, a view defended by the author of the Hebrew book of Daniel. The position of the Hebrew author may be more sharply defined as quietistic.[74]

Moreover, we can identify the false apocalyptic teachers, from which the author of the Hebrew apocalypse dissociated himself, with the group behind the Animal Apocalypse. While still acknowledging them as members of the same intellectual group to which he belonged, in his view they had broken with the truth by teaching that the fulfillment of the promises could be forced by the Maccabean wars, a view similar to that of their forerunners in 201/200 BC. Although the Hebrew book is directed to all the people, not to any specific class—in contrast with the Aramaic book[75]—it engages in an inner-group dispute between different apocalyptic factions as to what kind of resistance should be advocated and what man's contribution might be in realizing God's last judgement and salvation .

It is not by chance that a member of the quietistic wing of apocalyptic teachers used just the Aramaic book of Daniel in his theological dispute. First, he found in this apocalyptic tradition the clear opinion that the last judgement and salvation would be brought about by God himself; the rock, which symbolizes God's kingdom,

---

[73] Cf. Collins, *Apocalyptic Vision*, 194–214; he also refers to the *Testament of Moses*, but the date of this work is disputed.

[74] Cf. my interpretation in greater detail: Albertz, *History of Israelite Religion*, 591–94.

[75] So correctly, Collins, *Apocalyptic Vision*, 213.

would destroy all empires and would be detached from the mountain
"not by hands," i.e. without human influence (Dan 2:45). For him,
this motif was so important that he took it over in his own vision
describing the destruction of the blasphemous Antiochus IV (Dan
8:25). Along these lines he clarified in his final vision that Antiochus
would not be defeated by the Maccabees (11:28), and described the
war of the last days as not being carried out by them but by the
archangel Michael (12:1).

Second, as has been shown, the Hebrew apocalyptist tried to
depoliticize the Aramaic book in order to protect it from misuse.
This attempt is more easily understood as we become aware of the
popularity of Daniel and his friends among the Maccabean fighters.
In idealizing retrospective, one of their descendants described in the
first book of Maccabees how the progenitor Mattathias admonished
his sons before his death, "to recompense fully the heathen" and "to
take heed of the commandments of the law" (1 Macc 2:68), by
reminding them of the heroes of the past. After Abraham, Joseph,
Pinehas, Joshua, Caleb, David and Elijah, both Daniel and his friends
are mentioned:

> Hananiah, Azariah, and Mishael had faith, and they were saved from the
> blazing furnace (1 Macc 2:59)
>
> Daniel was a man of integrity (ἁπλότης), and he was rescued from the
> lions' jaws (1 Macc 2:60).

By these examples the sons were taught to draw their courage and
strength from the law in order to win great glory (v. 64). As far as
can be seen in 1 Maccabees, the Maccabean rebels themselves were
not eschatologically-oriented, but were inspired by the tradition of
"Holy War" that provided a picture of Israel's ideal past. Thus it is
not clear whether their appreciation of the Daniel figures includes
any interest in the Aramaic Daniel apocalypse.[76] However, it is

---

[76] From the terminology used in 1 Macc 2:60 it is unclear whether the author
has in mind the story of "Daniel in the lions' den" in the Old Greek or the Aramaic
version (cf. the expression στόματα τῶν λεόντων in Dan 6:19 LXX and 6:19, 21,
23 θ'). In the case of the "three men in the fiery furnace" it is more problable that the
author had in mind the version transmitted in Daniel 3 LXX, and still retained the
shape of a separate narrative. First, all the keywords in 1 Macc 2:59 also occur in
Daniel 3 LXX (πιστεύειν, v. 40; σώζειν, vv. 88, 95; φλόξ, vv. 23, 47, 49, 88).
Second, I. Kottsieper has shown that the "Prayer of Azariah" inserted in this
version is of Maccabean origin, written in the beginning of the rebellion: "Zusätze
zu Ester und Daniel," in O. H. Steck, R. G. Kratz, and I. Kottsieper, *Das Buch*

beyond doubt that the resistance shown by these martyr legends is interpreted as a religious-political one with clear military consequences. Moreover, that the Maccabean author stresses the "sincerity" or "integrity" (ἁπλότης) of Daniel may be understood as a defence against the suspicion of other conservative groups that they would carry out their fights insincerely, as was expressed by the Hebrew apocalypticist (Dan 11:34) and others.[77] Taking into account that the Daniel figure was exploited by the Maccabees for their military resistance and political self-defence, it becomes clear why the author of the Hebrew Book had to protect the apocalyptic Daniel tradition firmly from any political misuse, unless he was willing to surrender his goal of strengthening his quietistic position in the ungoing civil war.[78]

6. THE APOCALYPTICISTS IN THE MACCABEAN CRISIS AND THE ḤASIDIM

On the basis of Daniel 11–12 and *1 Enoch* 90, it can be shown that a group of educated teaching apocalypticists (מַשְׂכִּילִים) probably existed at the beginning of the Maccabean crisis (172 BC), which was then split during the start of military resistance (167 BC) into at least two different fractions: a militant one that legitimized military resistance as ushering in eschatological salvation, and a quietistic one that deligitimized any violent actions and restricted itself to teaching

---

Baruch—Der Brief des Jeremia—Zu Ester und Daniel (ATD Apokryphen 5, Göttingen: Vandenhoeck & Ruprecht, 1998) 223; 229ff.

[77] The request of the probable Maccabean "Prayer of Azariah" (Dan 3:44 LXX) is directed against a similar suspicion: "Let all who spoke ill of thy servants be humbled; may they be put to shame and stripped of all their power, and may their strength be crushed." This request testifies that the criticism came from very influental groups of society; these were not only the Hellenizers, as I. Kottsieper, *Daniel*, 236, believes. That the young leadership of the Maccabees praised their own ἁπλότης against the established leadership, which is regarded as corrupt, is seen in the original independent frame of the Susanna story (vv. 5-6* and 63 LXX); for a literary reconstruction and interpretation, see Kottsieper, *Daniel*, 286ff.

[78] That the author of 1 Maccabees could use even the Hebrew book of Daniel as a source for his historical review (cf. especially chapter 1) is a much later development from a time when it had had nearly achieved canonical status. In any event, there are points of interest shared the Maccabees and the Hebrew apocalypsist: both agreed that the crisis was mainly induced by foreign enemies and both stressed the desecration of the temple.

pious steadfastness to the people by stressing the hope of individual salvation to come. A point of dispute over which the two factions differed was the willingness of one section of apocalyptic teachers to accept a coalition with the Maccabees (Dan 11:34; cf. לוה *nip'al*, "to be joined") for mutal support.

It is most significant that a very similar coalition with the Maccabees is mentioned in 1 Macc 2:42, and is judged to be the starting-point of a successful military resistance:

> It was then that they were joined (συνάγομαι) by a group of Ḥasidim, leading citizens (ἰσχυροὶ δυνάμαι) of Israel, every one of them devoted to the law.

Admittedly, there are some differences. First, the Maccabean source maintains that the Maccabees were joined by a pious group, while the Hebrew Daniel author claims that the apocalyptic teachers were joined by many people including the Maccabees (the "little help"). Second, 1 Macc 2:42 uses the term 'Ασιδαῖοι, while Dan 11:33-35 takes מַשְׂכִּילִים. Third, 1 Macc 2:42, 44 stresses the military activity of the group and makes no mention of any apocalyptic engagement, while Daniel 11 stresses the apocalyptic task and gives only indirect hints of a—disputed—military engagement (vv. 14, 34-35).

Nevertheless, all these differences can be explained. First, the coalition is viewed from different perspectives: for the book of Maccabees, the leadership of Israel consists of the Maccabees, and for the book of Daniel, the apocalyptic teachers. Second, the Hebrew word מַשְׂכִּיל is not a usual term for a profession. In the period before the book of Daniel it is only attested as a technical term for a specific kind of psalm;[79] and not until the Qumran period is it used to denote a profession, a kind of leader of the community.[80] Using the *hip'il* participle in a technical sense, the author of the Hebrew apocalypse wished to reveal a little of the apocalypticists's self-understanding as "wise, teaching, and finally successful experts," but at the same time tried to hide the identity of the group in accordance with his visionary style. However, the original Aramaic word חֲסִידַיָּא ("the Pious") may be interpreted as the specialized use of a term for a common group, probably a significant group of outstanding religious people called from without. Thus it is not strange for this term to be

---

[79] Cf. Psalms 32; 42; 44–45; 52-55; 74; 78; 88–89; 142; and Ps 47:8.

[80] Cf. 1QS 3:13; 9:12, 21; CD 12:21; 13:21; 4Q401 frg. 1.1; 4Q403 frgs. 1.30; 2.18; etc.

used in the Book of Maccabees, but not to be used in the book of
Daniel. Third, the emphasis on the Ḥasidim's military functions in
the First Book of Maccabees can easily be explained by the military
interest of its author. That he had no interest in mentioning this
group's eschatological horizon is not strange, if we remember that
the Maccabeean fighters were not noticeably eschatologically-
oriented, and that the author wrote retroperspectively from a standpoint of the established Hasmonean kingdom, after the eschatological
hopes had already failed. However, the military aspect concerning
the Ḥasidim should not be exaggerated; the Hebrew equivalent of
ἰσχυροὶ δυνάμει, גִּבּוֹרֵי חַיִל, must not be rendered here by the usual
"mighty warriors." The term is not restricted to a military meaning,
but can denote other people of social importance;[81] in 1 Macc 2:42 it
should be translated by "leading citizens," as J. Kampen has argued.[82]
Thus the Ḥasidim should not necessarily be considered as warriors; it
is more likely that they supported the fighting ideologically by their
apocalyptic propaganda.

Nevertheless, even the pro-Maccabean author concedes the
Ḥasidim as possessing an outstanding religious quality; when he calls
it "devoted to the law," he denotes the common basis with the
Maccabees—but this does not deny that the Ḥasidim were also
engaged in the apocalyptic field. The Animal Apocalypse (1 Enoch
85–90) attests to the existance of apocalyptists who supported the
wars of the Maccabees with their apocalyptic instructions while Judas
Maccabaeus lived (up to 162 or 160 BC). Thus there is no reason
why the coalitions mentioned in Dan 11:34 and 1 Macc 2:42 cannot
be identified. From a different perspective and ideological background, both texts deal with the same event, which was of crucial
importance for the development of both the military resistance and
the apocalyptic movement during the Maccabean crisis.

The other two passages that mention the Ḥasidim fit perfectly into
this scenario. The statement of Alcimus before king Demetrius in 2
Macc 14:6 that Judas Maccabeus is seen as the leader of the Ḥasidim

---

[81] Such as the general free land owner, who was also responsible for military
support; cf. 1 Kings 15:20. In Chronicles the term denotes influential family leaders
with several functions; cf. 1 Chr 5:24; 7:2, 5, 7, 9, 11, 40; 9:13; 26:6, 31; 2 Chr
26:12; Neh 11:14.

[82] J. Kampen, Hasidaeans, 106–107; cf. his understanding of πρῶτοι (1 Macc
7:13) not as an adverb, but as a predicative nomen in the following note.

and that they are responsible for the ongoing upheavals and wars, may be interpreted as the exaggerated claim of a disappointed Hellenizer emphasizing the close coalition of both groups, which he previously opposed.

The report of 1 Macc 7:12-13 that Alcimus was received by a group of scribes mainly consisting of the Ḥasidim[83] testifies that the Ḥasidim were learned scribes. This information fits very well with the picture drawn from the apocalyptic sources: not only the term מַשְׂכִּילִים, but also the sophisticated shape of the Hebrew Daniel apocalypse. Moreover, Daniel 9 and most parts of *1 Enoch* 85–90 display certain features of learned exegesis. Thus the assumption that the author of the Hebrew apocalypse belonged to the circle of learned scribes is highly probable.

Moreover, another item in 1 Macc 7:12-13—that a considerable number of Ḥasidim made their peace with the new High Priest Alcimus and thus revoked the coalition with the Maccabees early on—becomes perfectly clear when we consider how much this coalition was debated between the different factions of the religious elite. After the temple had once more been purified and the despised Antiochus IV had been murdered, this group of Ḥasidim saw their goal reached and thus refused to support military resistance any longer, even though the political situation remained dangerous.[84] One might say that the polemic of the quietistic apocalyptic teachers against their militant colleagues, as is evident in Dan 11:33-35, was not without success.

Thus, with respect to the social setting of the Hebrew book of Daniel, we may conclude that the old hypothesis that the author of the present book of Daniel was one of the Ḥasidim remains true. Nevertheless, three qualifications are to be made. First, this conclusion is valid for only the final stage of traditio-history: the Hebrew book, which included the Aramaic. There is no evidence that

---

[83] Note the convincing interpretation of J. Kampen, *Hasidaeans*, 115ff. There are not only striking parallels between both groups (cf. συναγωγὴ γραμματέων in 1 Macc 7:12 with συναγωγὴ Ἀσιδαίων in 2:42, and ἐκζήτησαι δίκαια in 7:12 with ἐπεζήτουν ... εἰρήνην in 7:13). 1 Macc 7:13 has to be rendered as follows: "But the Ḥasidim were the first (πρῶτοι, i.e the leaders) among the Israelites, and they sought peace with them."

[84] Whether 60 persons really suffered martyrdom, as 1 Macc 7:16-17 claims, is uncertain. The scenario looks more like Maccabean propaganda.

the group of Ḥasidim already existed when the Aramaic Daniel book was written.[85]

Second, the Ḥasidim have nothing to do with "pious conventicles" next to the lower class as O. Plöger and M. Hengel assumed, but are rather identified as learned scribes, outstanding in their piety and widely acknowledged as the religious elite during that period.[86] During the dramatic Maccabean crisis some of these scribes engaged in apocalyptic speculations, previously restricted to smaller pious groups, which now became widespread in the anti-Hellenistic movement. Although the Ḥasidim stood in opposition to the radical Hellenizers and their Seleucid allies, they saw themselves as teachers of the whole people. Their interest in playing down conflicts from within society may be viewed as a typical characteristic of the middle-class. Thus the Ḥasidim should be located sociologically somewhere between the aristocratic/priestly establishment and the lower-classes.[87]

Third, the Ḥasidim did not form an unchangeable unity, but were split at least into two factions on the question of whether a coalition with the Maccabees was theologically justified or not. The author of the Hebrew Daniel belonged to the quietistic wing of the Ḥasidim who fought against the militant one, emphatically denying the theological legitimacy of military resistance. Nevertheless, since the Ḥasidim were not only seen from without as a unity ("the pious"), but also revealed a clear in-group awareness (acknowledging each other as "teachers"), "Ḥasidim" should not be defined as an "umbrella-term" covering a wide range of different pious groups.[88] There was a common social and religious root, as well as a common responsibility for the whole people, which united all the Ḥasidim

---

[85] The assumption of V. Tcherikover, *Hellenistic Civilization*, 125–26, that the group was founded in the restoration period under Simon the Just, is still plausible.

[86] Cf. the similar conclusion of E. Haag, "Hasidäer," 62, although his view that the author of the Book of Daniel had a relatively positive attitude towards the Maccabees (pg. 55) does not fit with the scenario given here and is exegetically questionable. Haag supposes that the "little help" (Dan 11:34a) is to be regarded in comparison with the "great help" of God, but fails to take into account that the coalition with the Maccabees is sharply criticized in vv. 34b, 35.

[87] The similar social setting of Jesus Sirach might be an example; cf. Sir 33:16-17; 34:9ff.; 38:24-39:11; 51:13-29.

[88] Thus Collins, "Daniel and His Social World," 134, in his rejection of the Ḥasidim hypothesis.

even where they disagreed in political options. Amidst ongoing fierce debates they maintained contact, with the result that some members of one wing felt convinced by the other wing and changed their opinion. It is thus possible to situate the author of the present book of Daniel amidst a lively political and theological debate in 2nd century BC Jewish society.

7. SELECT BIBLIOGRAPHY

Albertz, R. *A History of Israelite Religion in the Old Testament Period* (2 vols., OTL; Louisville, KY: Westminster John Knox, 1994).

—. "Bekehrung von oben als 'messianisches Programm.' Die Sonderüberlieferung der Septuaginta in Daniel 4–6," in H. Graf Reventlow (ed.), *Theologische Probleme der Septuaginta und der Hellenistischen Hermeneutik* (Veröffent-lichungen der Wissenschaftlichen Gesellschaft für Theologie 11; München: Kaiser & Gütersloher Verlagshaus, 1997) 46–62.

—. *Der Gott des Daniel. Untersuchungen zu Daniel 4–6 in der Septuagintafassung sowie zu Komposition und Theologie des aramäischen Danielbuches* (SBS 131; Stuttgart: Katholisches Bibelwerk, 1988).

Collins, J. J. *Daniel. A Commentary on the Book of Daniel* (Hermeneia; Minne-apolis: Fortress, 1993).

—. "Daniel and His Social World," *Interpretation* 39 (1985) 131–43.

—. *The Apocalyptic Imagination. An Introduction to the Jewish Matrix of Christianity* (New York: Crossroad, 1984).

—. *The Apocalyptic Vision of the Book of Daniel* (HSM 16; Missoula, MT: Scholars Press, 1977).

—. "The Court-Tales in Daniel and the Development of Apocalyptic," *JBL* 94 (1975) 218–34.

Haag, E. "Die Hasidäer und das Danielbuch," *TTZ* 102 (1993) 51–63.

Hellholm, D. (ed.). *Proceedings of the International Colloquium on Apocalyp-ticism: Uppsala, August 12-17, 1979* (Tübingen: Mohr-Siebeck, 1983).

Hengel, M. *Judentum und Hellenismus. Studien zu ihrer Begegnung unter beson-derer Berücksichtigung Palästinas bis zur Mitte des 2.Jhs. v.Chr.* (2nd ed., WUNT 10; Tübingen: Mohr-Siebeck, 1973).

Kampen, J. *The Hasideans and the Origin of Pharisaism. A Study in 1 and 2 Maccabees* (SBLSCS 24; Atlanta: Scholars Press, 1988).

Koch, K. *Das Buch Daniel* (EdF 144; Darmstadt: Wissenschaftliche Buchgesell-schaft, 1980).

Kooij, A. van der. "A Case of Reinterpretation in the Old Greek of Daniel 11," in J. W. van Henten, H. J. de Jonge, P. T. van Rooden, and J. W. Wesselius (eds.), *Tradition and Interpretation in Jewish and Early Christian Literature.*

Essays in Honor of J.-C. Lebram (Leiden: Brill, 1986) 72–80.

Kottsieper, I. "Zusätze zu Ester und Daniel," in O. H. Steck, R. G. Kratz, and I. Kottsieper (eds.), *Das Buch Baruch—Der Brief des Jeremia—Zu Ester und Daniel* (ATD Apokryphen 5; Göttingen: Vandenhoeck & Ruprecht, 1998) 206–328.

Kratz, R. G. "Reich Gottes und Gesetz im Danielbuch und im werdenden Judentum," in van der Woude (ed.), *The Book of Daniel in the Light of New Findings*, 435–79 [see under van der Woude].

—. *Translatio imperii. Untersuchungen zu den aramäischen Danielerzählungen und ihrem theologiegeschichtlichen Umfeld* (WMANT 63; Neukirchen-Vluyn: Neukirchener Verlag, 1991).

Lampe, P. "Die Apokalyptiker—ihre Situation und ihr Handeln," in U. Lutz (ed.), *Eschatologie und Friedenshandeln. Exegetische Beiträge zur Frage christlicher Friedensverantwortung* (SBS 101; Stuttgart: Katholisches Bibelwerk, 1981) 59–114.

Lebram, J.-C. "Apokalyptik and Hellenismus im Buche Daniel," *VT* 20 (1970) 503–24.

—. "Daniel/Danielbuch und Zusätze," *TRE* 8 (1981) 325–49.

—. *Das Buch Daniel* (ZBK.AT 23, Zürich: Theologischer Verlag, 1984).

—. "The Piety of the Jewish Apocalyptists," in Hellholm (ed.), *Apocalypticism in the Mediterranean World and the Near East*, 171–210 [see under Hellholm].

Lenglet, A. "La structure littéraire de Daniel 2–7," *Bib* 53 (1972) 169–90.

Lust, J. "The Septuagint Version of Daniel 4–5," in van der Woude (ed.), *The Book of Daniel in the Light of New Findings*, 39–53 [see under van der Woude].

Müller, K. "Apokalyptik," in M. Görg and B. Lang (eds.), *Neues Bibel-Lexikon* (Zürich: Benzinger, 1988) 1.124–32.

Nickelsburg, G. W. E. "Social Aspects of Palestinian Jewish Apocalypticism," in Hellholm (ed.), *Apocalypticism in the Mediterranean World and the Near East*, 641–54 [see under Hellholm].

Plöger, O. *Theokratie und Eschatologie* (2nd ed., WMANT 2; Neukirchen-Vluyn: Neukirchener Verlag, 1962).

Steck, O. H. "Strömungen theologischer Tradition im Alten Israel" (1978), in idem, *Wahrnehmungen Gottes im Alten Testament: Gesammelte Studien* (TB 70; München: Kaiser, 1982) 291–317.

—. "Weltgeschehen und Gottesvolk im Buche Daniel" (1980) in idem, *Wahrnehmungen Gottes im Alten Testament*, 262–90 [see the previous entry].

Tcherikover, V. *Hellenistic Civilization and the Jews* (3rd ed., New York: Atheneum, 1975).

Weimar, P. "Daniel 7. Eine Textanalyse," in R. Pesch and R. Schnackenburg (eds.), *Jesus und der Menschensohn* (Freiburg: Herder, 1975) 11–36.

Wills, L. M. *The Jew in the Court of Foreign King. Ancient Jewish Court Legends* (HDR 26; Minneapolis: Fortress, 1990).

Woude, A. S. van der (ed.). *The Book of Daniel in the Light of New Findings* (BETL 56; Leuven: Leuven University Press and Peeters, 1993).

THE BOOK OF DANIEL AND ITS SOCIAL SETTING

STEFAN BEYERLE

1. A QUESTION OF METHOD

In his recent book the late Norman Cohn, to my knowledge one of the few scholars who wrote an all-embracing history of apocalyptic ideas and their relation to sectarian groups,[1] writes negatively:

> The authors of the Book of Daniel and of the Enochic writings certainly thought of themselves as men set apart by God, endowed with a wisdom not available to ordinary mortals, the only ones to understand the past and to foresee the future .... Yet there is no convincing evidence that they were sectarians in the sense of belonging to an identifiable group.[2]

But with regard to an appropriate interpretation, the historical method requires identifiable groups pertaining to themes, motifs and notions found in apocalyptic writings. And it is indeed a "question of method" how to relate those motifs to data about conventicles and parties of the Second Temple Period. Despite the no less negative assumptions by Lester Grabbe,[3] who has underscored that there "is no necessary connection between apocalypses and apocalyptic communities" and that "much work on the sociological level has heretofore been circular,"[4] no modern scholar who asks historical questions can ignore the social environment of apocalyptic

---

[1] N. Cohn, *The Pursuit of the Millennium: Revolutionary Messianism in Medieval and Reformation Europe* (2nd ed., New York: Harper, 1961).

[2] N. *Cohn, Cosmos, Chaos and the World to Come. The Ancient Roots of Apocalyptic Faith* (New Haven: Yale University Press, 1993) 187–88. This approach suffers from an overestimation of Zoroastrian influences on Jewish apocalypticism; see also idem, "How Time Acquired a Consummation," in M. Bull (ed.), *Apocalypse Theory and the Ends of the World* (Wolfson College Lectures; Oxford and Cambridge, MA: Blackwell, 1995) 21–37.

[3] L. Grabbe, "The Social Setting of Early Jewish Apocalypticism," *JSP* 4 (1989) 27–47, who seeks to show that it is too simplistic to approach the phenomenon of apocalypticism from the "apocalypses" alone.

[4] Grabbe, "The Social Setting," 29, 39. See also the response to Grabbe by D. C. Sim, "The Social Setting of Ancient Apocalyticism: A Question of Method," *JSP* 13 (1995) 6–7, 9–11.

literature.[5] Precisely the more we know the social world of biblical writings—including apocalyptic ones—the more we can determine the historical circumstances of these ancient books. Notwithstanding solemn declarations to the contrary, the sociological approach is a major tool for the historical-critical investigation of apocalyptic texts.

Despite their obvious mythological language and otherworldly placements and eschatological orientation towards a transcendent sphere, the apocalyptic writings of the Second Temple Period provoke questions of social setting. In my view this is for two reasons: first, the recent debate of how to define "apocalypses" in terms of genre still incorporates the insights of classical Form Criticism.[6] Accordingly, each genre arises in and is appropriate for its use in a particular situation. Second, the scholarly distinction between "apocalypse" (as a literary genre), "apocalypticism" (as a religio-social movement), and "apocalyptic eschatology" (as a religious perspective),[7] frequently used to distinguish literary evidence from a broader movement, calls for further knowledge about the circles that composed and/or transmitted apocalyptic ideas and ideologies. Some of these "apocalyptic communities" died in late antiquity—for example, the Qumran community. Others survived

---

[5] See, for example J. J. Collins, "Inspiration or Illusion: Biblical Theology and the Book of Daniel," *Ex Auditu* 6 (1990) 29–38, esp. 31, who emphasises that the "Books of Enoch and Daniel appear to have originated in circles which held these traditional, legendary, figures in high respect." For a further description of these circles see idem, "Daniel and His Social World," *Int* 39 (1985) 131–43; and S. L. Cook, *Prophecy and Apocalypticism: The Postexilic Social Setting* (Minneapolis: Fortress, 1995) 2–17.

[6] See the morphology of the genre "apocalypse" by J. J. Collins, "Introduction: Towards the Morphology of a Genre," *Semeia* 14 (1979) 1–20. The inter-relationship between genre and social movement is explained in Collins, "Genre, Ideology and Social Movements in Jewish Apocalypticism," in his *Seers, Sibyls and Sages in Hellenistic-Roman Judaism* (JSJSup 54; Leiden: Brill, 1997) 25–38.

[7] For this differentiation see P. D. Hanson, "Apocalypticism," *IDBSup* 29–31; idem, "Apocalypse and Apocalypticism," *ABD* 1.280–81. For a critique of Hanson's approach see P. R. Davies, "The Social World of Apocalyptic Writings," in R. E. Clements (ed.), *The World of Ancient Israel. Sociological, Anthropological and Political Perspectives* (2nd. ed., Cambridge: Cambridge University Press, 1991) 252–53, 257–58; and more recently D. C. Sim, *Apocalyptic Eschatology in the Gospel of Matthew* (SNTSMS 88; Cambridge: University Press, 1996) 23–31.

until the Middle Ages—for example, Enochic apocalypticism in later Hekhalot literature, *3 Enoch*, or in the Kabbalah. But none has survived until the present time. The loss of every "living witness" calls for rigid scrutiny of the ancient primary sources. Furthermore, since contemporary sociological models are only of limited help, the starting-point should be the text itself, not a theory or a hypothetical movement that may be related to the sources.[8]

The Qumran community may function as a helpful example. There is no doubt that the Qumranites can be described, with some limitations, as an "apocalyptic community."[9] At the same time, the caves brought to light several manuscripts that relate to the book of Daniel:[10] biblical manuscripts in Cave 1, 4 and 6;[11] texts that have a genetic relationship to the biblical book (*Pseudo-Daniel*);[12] manuscripts with quotations from biblical Daniel (as in 4QFlor or

---

[8] On the problematic relationship between apocalyptic communities and apocalyptic writings see Sim, "Social Setting of Ancient Apocalypticism," 12–14. In the history of scholarship, G. Behrmann was the first interpreter of the book of Daniel who sought to identify groups and a "social framework" from within the Danielic text and who identified the "Proto-Essenes" (*Das Buch Daniel* [HKAT 3/2.2; Göttingen: Vandenhoeck & Ruprecht, 1894], xxv–xxvi; cf. also K. Koch [with T. Niewisch and J. Tubach], *Das Buch Daniel* [ErFor 144; Darmstadt: Wissenschaftliche Buchgesellschaft, 1980] 164–68).

[9] See esp. F. García Martínez, *Qumran and Apocalyptic. Studies on the Aramaic Texts from Qumran* (STDJ 9; Leiden: Brill, 1992). For an alternative view see J. J. Collins, *Apocalypticism in the Dead Sea Scrolls* (Literature of the Dead Sea Scrolls; London and New York: Routledge, 1997).

[10] See the relevant overviews by P. W. Flint, "The Daniel Tradition at Qumran," in C. A. Evans and P. W. Flint (eds.), *Eschatology, Messianism, and the Dead Sea Scrolls* (SDSRL; Grand Rapids: Eerdmans, 1997) 41–60; and J. J. Collins, "New Light on the Book of Daniel from the Dead Sea Scrolls," in F. García Martínez and E. Noort (eds.), *Perspectives in the Study of the Old Testament and Early Judaism. A Symposium in Honour of Adam S. van der Woude on the Occasion of His 70th Birthday* (VTSup 73; Leiden: Brill, 1998) 180–96.

[11] E. Ulrich, "Daniel Manuscripts from Qumran. Part 1: A Preliminary Edition of 4QDan^a," *BASOR* 268 (1987) 17–37; idem, "Daniel Manuscripts from Qumran. Part 2: Preliminary Editions of 4QDan^b and 4QDan^c," *BASOR* 274 (1989) 3–26; K. Koch and M. Rösel, *Polyglottensynopse zum Buch Daniel* (Neukirchen-Vluyn: Neukirchener Verlag, 2000).

[12] J. J. Collins and P. W. Flint, "243-245. 4Qpseudo-Daniel^a–c ar," in J. VanderKam (consulting ed.), *Qumran Cave IV.XVII: Parabiblical Texts, Part 3* (DJD 22; Oxford: Clarendon Press, 1996) 95–164 + pls. VII–X.

4QHistorical Text)[13] and references from the Additions (possibly in 4Q551?); and two more manuscripts with contents closely related to Daniel.[14] On the other hand, these texts were only transmitted, not written, by the Qumranites, because no "Daniel-Text" from Qumran contains specifically "sectarian" features (as found, in contrast, in CD, 1QS, and 1QM).[15] Thus the Danielic literature, as attested in the Dead Sea Scrolls, says more about the social setting of the book of Daniel than about the Qumran community itself.[16] Several examples could be added, especially from Qumran and early Christian literature; in fact, it is striking to see how neither of the two "classical" apocalyptic movements, Qumran and early Christianity, were characterized by the production of apocalypses.[17]

What nevertheless becomes apparent from the above example is that any sociological analysis of ancient societies must start with the sources, whether literary (Hebrew Bible, Inscriptions) or non-

---

[13] See M. Broshi and E. Eshel, "The Greek King is Antiochus IV (4QHistorical Text = 4Q248)," *JJS* 47 (1997) 120–29; and the contribution of E. Eshel in this volume.

[14] The *Prayer of Nabonidus* (4Q242) and the *Son of God Text* (4Q246). For the *Prayer of Nabonidus* see J. J. Collins, "242. 4QPrayer of Nabonidus ar," DJD 22.83–93. For the *Son of God Text* see É. Puech, "246. 4QApocryphe de Daniel ar," DJD 22.165–84; and J. Zimmermann, *Messianische Texte aus Qumran. Königliche, priesterliche und prophetische Messiasvorstellungen in den Schriftfunden von Qumran* (WUNT 2/104; Tübingen: Mohr-Siebeck, 1998) 128–70.

[15] For a "sketch of Qumran thought and practice" see J. C. VanderKam, *The Dead Sea Scrolls Today* (Grand Rapids: Eerdmans, 1994) 108–19.

[16] If G. Boccaccini is correct, the purpose of *Pseudo-Daniel* (4Q243–45) was to read biblical Daniel in light of *1 Enoch* 83–90. The aim may well have been to mediate between Enochic apocalypticism and Danielic eschatology. In Boccaccini's view, the collectors of the Dead Sea Scrolls were "ideologically closer" to the apocalypticism of *1 Enoch* 83–90 than to the apocalypticism of the Book of Daniel (*Beyond the Essene Hypothesis: The Parting of the Ways between Qumran and Enochic Judaism* [Grand Rapids and Cambridge: Eerdmans, 1998] 81–86).

[17] See Davies, "The Social World of Apocalyptic Writings," 253; and J. J. Collins, *The Apocalyptic Imagination: An Introduction to Jewish Apocalyptic Literature* (2nd ed., Grand Rapids: Eerdmans, 1998) 13. The question of whether or how many apocalypses were written by the Qumranites is highly disputed; cf. H. Stegemann, "Die Bedeutung der Qumranfunde für die Erforschung der Apokalyptik," in D. Hellholm (ed.), *Apocalypticism in the Mediterranean World and the Near East. Proceedings of the International Colloquium on Apocalypticism Uppsala, August 12-17, 1979* (2nd ed., Tübingen: Mohr-Siebeck, 1989) 511–29.

literary (archaeological or ecological data)—and not with models from modern sociologists, since sociology lays emphasis upon and begins with modern-day social realities. Accordingly, the interpreter should bear in mind this major methodological difference between the approaches adopted by historians and sociologists.[18] As George W. E. Nickelsburg states:

> These theories [i.e. those developed by modern sociologists and anthropologists, S. B.] may serve as useful models that help us to understand ancient texts, but primary attention must be given to the documents themselves and to their peculiar contours.[19]

Of late, the identities of "apocalyptic communities" have been closely linked to the theological understanding of scriptures which these communities composed and sometimes preserved. For example, Sheldon R. Isenberg has emphasized the necessity of a mainly phenomenological comparison between patterns of religious belief, behaviour and structures.[20] While the main questions he raises are applicable in the present context, Isenberg's approach primarily examines groups such as the Pharisees, Sadducees and Essenes, not the sources. Isenberg has apparently identified the doctrines of the Pharisees and the Sadducees with the Jewish "belief-system" in order to confront their religion with millenarian groups. Besides such problematic assumptions he also poses the following questions:

---

[18] A very influental sociological method is the "Sociology of Knowledge." See P. L. Berger and T. Luckmann, *The Social Construction of Reality. A Treatise in the Sociology of Knowledge* (Garden City, NY: Doubleday, 1966).

[19] G. W. E. Nickelsburg, "Social Aspects of Palestinian Jewish Apocalypticism," in Hellholm (ed.), *Apocalypticism in the Mediterranean World and the Near East*, 648. See also D. C. Sim, "Social Setting of Ancient Apocalypticism," 14–15. For an application of sociological methods to apocalyptic texts (other than the book of Daniel) see J. R. Mueller, "A Prolegomenon to the Study of the Social Function of 4 Ezra," in K. H. Richards (ed.), *SBLSP 1981* (SBLSP 20; Chico, CA: Scholars Press, 1981) 259–68; S. B. Reid, "*1 Enoch*. The Rising Elite of the Apocalyptic Movement," in K. H. Richards (ed.), *SBLSP 1983* (SBLSP 22; Chico, CA: Scholars Press, 1983) 147–56; idem, *Enoch and Daniel. A Form Critical and Sociological Study of the Historical Apocalypses* (BIBAL.MS 2; Berkeley: BIBAL, 1989) 38–52, 59–67; and G. W. E. Nickelsburg, "The Apocalyptic Construction of Reality in *1 Enoch*, in J. J. Collins and J. H. Charlesworth (eds.), *Mysteries and Revelations. Apocalyptic Studies since the Uppsala Colloquium* (JSPSup 9; Sheffield: Sheffield Academic Press, 1991) 51–64.

[20] S. R. Isenberg, "Millenarism in Greco-Roman Palestine," *Religion* 4 (1974) 26–46, esp. 28–30, 41 nn.6–7.

... how did the Jews in this period [i.e. the Greco-Roman period, S. B.]
experience the universe? what were their hopes and fears? what were their
values? Then, how did these ultimate interests express themselves?[21]

The purpose of what follows is to investigate the relationship
between the "belief-system" and the "social-system" of the book of
Daniel in two steps. Firstly, an investigation of a certain group, the
maśkîlîm, in this book seeks to analyze the social setting of the
apocalypse. The *maśkîlîm* represent a group within the Danielic
visions, and have long been suspected of contributing to the milieu in
which Daniel was composed.[22] The aim of a textual approach to the
visions of Daniel is to reconstruct the "belief-system" via
examination of the traditio-historical background of Dan 11:33-35
and 12:1-3 and the genre of Daniel 7-12. Secondly, the reciprocal
links between a "belief-system" and a "social-system" will be
discussed.

2. SOCIOLOGICAL AND THEOLOGICAL DIFFERENTIATIONS WITHIN THE BOOK OF DANIEL

2.1 The Social Setting of the Daniel-Apocalypse

The need for social differentiation within the book of Daniel stems
from the textual evidence of this Hebrew-Aramaic apocalypse—more
specifically, from the manner in which this biblical book combines
forms and genres.[23] As Philip R. Davies correctly emphasizes:
"[Daniel] chapters 1–6 are widely accepted as not only earlier, but
reflecting a different social setting from the visions of 7–12."[24]

---

[21] *Ibidem,* 30.

[22] See esp. Collins, "Daniel and His Social World," 137–43; and the more
critical evaluation of Reid, *Enoch and Daniel,* 107–8, 119.

[23] By means of historical criticism, one becomes aware that the delimitation of
the canonical shape of biblical books, especially Daniel, is no mere scholarly
argument. This is because, from a historian's point of view, the emergence of a
canonical book is the result of an ongoing canonical process that lies far behind the
historical situation that is reflected in that book. On the other hand, the major
theological themes in Daniel can only be examined by rigid scrutiny of all relevant
traditions. For instance, the central theological theme of "punishment and
atonement," as attested in Daniel 4, requires a discussion of non-canonical texts
such as 4QPrNab and *Lives of the Prophets* 4:4, 13 (cf. A. M. Schwemer, *Studien
zu den frühjüdischen Prophetenlegenden Vitae prophetarum* [TSAJ 49; Tübingen:
Mohr-Siebeck, 1995] 1.318–29).

[24] Davies, "The Social World of Apocalyptic Writings," 256, against H. H.

In this case, the focus on biblical Daniel tries to take into account the social grouping reflected in an apocalyptic source, i.e. the visions in Daniel 7–12. Comment on social grouping can only be offered with qualifications about the court-tales in Daniel 1–6 and the Danielic writings preserved in the Septuagint (e.g. Susanna or Bel and the Dragon).[25] Furthermore, if the text is taken as a starting-point, the court-tales and visions—representing two different genres—go back to different social settings (Sitze im Leben): the court-tales reflecting the fate of Jews in the diaspora, and the visions offering examples of persecuted, pious Jews in Jerusalem.

After reaching several misleading conclusions about the social milieu of Daniel (such identifying the Danielic apocalyptists with the *hasîdîm* [חסידים], cf. 1 Macc 2:42; 7:12-13; 2 Macc 14:6: συναγωγὴ Ασιδαίων/ʼΑσιδαῖοι),[26] several scholars have focused on groups (or a group) within the book of Daniel itself (e.g. the *maśkîlîm* [משכילים], cf. Dan 11:33-35; 12:3, 10)[27] in order to describe the

---

Rowley, *The Relevance of Apocalyptic* (London: Athlone, 1994; repr. Greenwood, SC: Attic, 1980); and recently, P. L. Redditt, "Daniel 11 and the Sociohistorical Setting of the Book of Daniel," *CBQ* 60 (1998) 463–74, esp. 469.

[25] For the social setting of the Danielic court-tales, see the theses of R. Albertz, *Der Gott des Daniel. Untersuchungen zu Daniel 4–6 in der Septuagintafassung sowie zu Komposition und Theologie des aramäischen Danielbuches* (SBS 131; Stuttgart: Verlag Katholisches Bibelwerk, 1988). For the Greek additions to the book of Daniel, see C. A. Moore, "Daniel, Additions to," *ABD* 2.18–28; M. D. Mendels, "Susanna, Book of," *ABD* 6.246–47; and S. Lasine, "Solomon, Daniel, and the Detective Story: The Social Functions of a Literary Genre," *HAR* 11 (1987) 257–62. The differences between the social milieus in the court-tales and the visions have been shown by R. R. Wilson, "From Prophecy to Apocalyptic: Reflections on the Shape of Israelite Religion," *Semeia* 21 (1981-82) 79–95, esp. 91–93.

[26] L. F. Hartman and A. A. DiLella, *The Book of Daniel* (AB 23; New York: Doubleday, 1978) 43–45; and A. Lacocque, "The Socio-Spiritual Formative Milieu of the Daniel Apocalypse," in A. S. van der Woude (ed.), *The Book of Daniel in the Light of New Findings* (BETL 106; Leuven: University Press, 1993) 315–343. For a recent critique see Redditt, "Daniel 11 and the Sociohistorical Setting," 465–66. Whether apocalypses such as the Apocalypse of Weeks, the Animal Apocalypse or the book of *Jubilees* can be traced back to the "apocalyptic movement" of the *hasîdîm* remains very tentative; see P. A. Tiller, *A Commentary on the Animal Apocalypse of 1 Enoch* (SBLEJL 4; Atlanta: Scholars Press, 1993) 109–15; Collins, *The Apocalyptic Imagination*, 77–79.

[27] Davies, "The Social World of Apocalyptic Writings," 265–67 and the

social setting. One crucial passage characterizes the *maśkîlîm* as "wise men" in a typical apocalyptic setting (Dan 11:33-35): "the wise (מַשְׂכִּילִים) of the people will cause many to understand" when there is oppression by evil power. Moreover, recent scholarship often denies the identification of this group with an "apocalyptic movement" or a "community." The *maśkîlîm*, as observers of the Torah and recorders of the new revelation, fit better with the contemporary Jewish "upper class," in terms of a highly educated intellectual elite, rather than being representatives of an oppressed and under-privileged community. The social position of these scribes becomes apparent not only through their role and function within the book of Daniel (see below), but also through the Danielic reception and re-interpretation of several motifs and forms that originate mostly from earlier prophetic literature. Examples include the "seventy years" and "seventy weeks" from Jer 25:11-12; 29:10 and 2 Chr 36:20-22 in Daniel 9 (esp. vv. 2, 24-27), or the "Vision of the Ram and the He-goat" in Daniel 8 compared with earlier prophetic visions (especially Amos 7:1-3).[28] The shift from "oral prophecy" to "written apoca-lypticism" and the productive manner in which the author of Daniel took over traditional motifs and forms, not only from Israelite traditions, but also makes an intellectual and "upper-class" milieu more propable. As David Syme Russell points out:

> "The wise," then, were in all probability a rather small elite, a spiritual aristocracy as it were, who believed they had been given special insight into the hidden mysteries of God and his universe.[29]

Moreover, a few motifs and forms in early Jewish and Christian lite-rature may be traced back to the Danielic visions. Some examples are the "Son of Man" figure from Dan 7:13-14 in *4 Ezra* 13:1-13a and Mark 13:26-27; the "Four Beasts" (Dan 7:2b-7) in the eagle vision (*4 Ezra* 10:60–12:51); and the "Dragon from the Sea" (Rev 13:1-4).[30]

---

completely different approach by Collins in "Daniel and His Social World," 133–40, and *Daniel. A Commentary on the Book of Daniel* (Hermeneia; Minneapolis: Fortress, 1993) 61–67; and by Wilson, "From Prophecy to Apocalyptic," 81–82.

[28]   For a comparison of Daniel 8 and Amos 7, see K. Koch, "Vom profetischen zum apokalyptischen Visionsbericht," in Hellholm (ed.), *Apocalypticism in the Mediterranean World and the Near East*, 423–25.

[29]   D. S. Russell, *Divine Disclosure. An Introduction to Jewish Apocalyptic* (Minneapolis: Fortress, 1992) 31.

[30]   On the hermeneutics of Jewish apocalypticism in an early Christian context

The above observations permit a first concluding remark: that the manner in which Daniel arranged ancient motifs—from both Israelite and from Near Eastern sources—and used forms and literary tools to create a new genre underlines the literary character of the composition. Nevertheless, it represents neither the first ancient Jewish literary source nor the first known apocalypse.[31] Yet its position between earlier prophetic traditions of the Old Testament and the very productive ancient apocalyptists from the Second Temple Period explains the crucial significance of Daniel. Moreover, the social milieu of this apocalypse is distinguished from other Jewish groups in terms of well-educated, "upper class" people,[32] not oppressed and deprived outsiders. This observation is attested by a characterization of Daniel in Josephus' *Antiquities* (10 §266):[33]

> [...] and during his [i.e. Daniel's, S. B.] lifetime he received honour and esteem from kings and people [τιμή τε καὶ δόξα ἡ παρὰ τῶν βασιλέων καὶ τοῦ πλήθους], and, since his death, his memory lives on eternally.

The observation that the book of Daniel, like apocalyptic literature in

---

see C. Rowland, "Upon Whom the Ends of the Ages have Come: Apocalyptic and the Interpretation of the New Testament," in Bull (ed.), *Apocalypse Theory and the Ends of the World*, 40–51.

[31] The Qumran remains of *1 Enoch* and related texts (e.g. the "Book of Giants") predate the only apocalypse in the Old Testament (see recently G. W. Nickelsburg, "The Books of Enoch at Qumran. What We Know and What We Need to Think about," in B. Kollmann, W. Reinbold and A. Steudel [eds.], *Antikes Judentum and Frühes Christentum: Festschrift für Hartmut Stegemann zum 65.Geburtstag* [BZNW 97; Berlin: de Gruyter, 1999] 99–113).

[32] As the *maśkîlîm*; see S. Freyne, "The Disciples in Mark and the Maskilim in Daniel. A Comparison," *JSNT* 16 (1982) 8–10.

[33] Text and translation: R. Marcus, *Josephus VI* (LCL 326; Cambridge, MA: Harvard University Press; London: Heinemann, 1978) 304–305. A. I. Baumgarten sees Josephus as a source for finding in the book of Daniel a "victorious sort of millenarianism" (*The Flourishing of Jewish Sects in the Maccabean Era: An Interpretation* [JSJSup 55; Leiden: Brill, 1997] 169–70). On the general criticism against the assumption "that apocalyptic was the prerogative of the marginalized alone" see Cook, *Prophecy and Apocalypticism*, 35–52; J. M. Knight, "Apocalyptic and Prophetic Literature," in S. E. Porter (ed.), *Handbook of Classical Rhetoric in the Hellenistic Period: 330 B.C.-A.D. 400* (Leiden: Brill, 1997) 469, 471, 487. The works of Baumgarten, Cook and Knight criticise especially the "conventicle approach" of O. Plöger (*Theocracy and Eschatology* [Richmond, VA: John Knox, 1968] and P. D. Hanson (*The Dawn of Apocalyptic* [2nd. ed., Philadelphia: Fortress, 1979]).

general, answers to a certain crisis does not call into question the suggested social environment. Even if this response from the Danielic apocalypticists were originally caused by a political or social struggle, in their eyes it was interpreted as referring to a theological, i.e. inner-Jewish, crisis (see below). As Albert I. Baumgarten has recently shown, it is simply misleading to equate millenarian or apocalyptic with oppressed or deprived groups:

> To summarize, I have no quarrel with the conclusion that millenarianism is often a phenomenon of the deprived or the "down and outs" of various sorts. I maintain, however, that we should not overlook another type ... the triumphant version which emerges as a result of events which produce the conviction that we humans and God are now marching together towards the most glorious of all possible new worlds.[34]

In sum, the present investigation of the social milieu from within the apocalyptic book of Daniel takes place on a twofold level: hermeneutical and theological. The first takes into account the manner of literary production in which the book of Daniel was composed (see above). The second level, properly described as theological, takes cognizance of the positive hope of apocalyptists (for which Dan 12:1-3 may function as a point of focus).

2.2 The Maśkîlîm and the "Belief-System" of the Daniel-Apocalypse

In order to proceed further, it is necessary to explain the term מַשְׂכִּיל,[35] which is the masculine *hip‘il* participle of שׂכל, and is often used as a noun: literally, "causing to know" or "one who makes (another) understand or become wise." Together with its several synonyms בִּין (בִּינה), חכם (חכמה) or ידע (דעת)—all found in Dan 1:4 (וּמַשְׂכִּילים בְּכל חכמה וידעי דעת ומביני מדע), "and versed in every branch of wisdom, endowed with knowledge and insight" [cf. Dan 1:17])[36]—

---

[34] A. I. Baumgarten, "The Pursuit of the Millennium in Early Judaism," in G. N. Stanton and G. G. Stroumsa (eds.), *Tolerance and Intolerance in Early Judaism and Christianity* (Cambridge: Cambridge University Press, 1998) 47, cf. 40–44.

[35] See the relevant overviews from H. Kosmala, "Maśkîl," *JNES* 5 (T. H. Gaster issue, 1973) 235–41; C. A. Newsom, "The Sage in the Literature of Qumran: The Functions of the Maśkîl," in J. G. Gammie and L. G. Perdue (eds.), *The Sage in Israel and the Ancient Near East* (Winona Lake, IN: Eisenbrauns, 1990) 373–82; A. Lange, "Exkurs: Der maśkîl," in his *Weisheit und Prädestination. Weisheitliche Urordnung und Prädestination in den Textfunden von Qumran* (STDJ 18; Leiden: Brill, 1995) 144–48.

[36] K. Koch makes the important suggestion that מַשְׂכִּיל in Dan 1:4 is used of

מַשְׂכִּיל forms is a central term in early Jewish wisdom literature. For references contemporaneous with the book of Daniel, see Sir [Heb.] 7:21; 10:23; 13:21, 47:12, and wisdom texts from Qumran such as the cryptic 4Q298, the *Songs of a Sage* (cf. 4Q510 frg. 1.4; 4Q511 frg. 2 i.1), the passage on the "Two Spirits" within the *Community Rule* (1QS 3:13–4:26; cf. also 9:21 and 9:26–10:5), or some of the *Hodayot* (1QHª 20:11-13 [4-36]).[37]

In scholarly debate on the "wise" in the book of Daniel, quotations from the Wisdom of Solomon are highly significant.[38] In contrast to the מַשְׂכִּילִים who know (בִּין, Dan 12:10; 1:4), the "godless men" (Wis 1:16–2:24)[39]

> were ignorant of God's mysteries (οὐκ ἔγνωσαν μυστήρια θεοῦ); they entertained no hope that holiness would have its reward, and passed up the prize of unblemished souls (γέρας ψυχῶν ἀμώμων) [Wis 2:22].

And of the "souls of the just in the hand of God" (δικαίων δὲ ψυχαὶ ἐν χειρὶ θεοῦ, Wis 3:1), it is said:

> For even if in the sight of men they shall have been punished, their hope is full of immortality (ἡ ἐλπὶς αὐτῶν ἀθανασίας πλήρης) ... they will blaze forth, and like sparks in the stubble will fly in all directions (Wis 3:4, 7).

Wis 3:7 in particular alludes to the "wise [that] shall shine like the brightness of the sky ... like the stars" in Dan 12:3. This comparison of the *maśkîlîm's* brightness with the כּוֹכָבִים of heaven places those "wise instructors" among the heavenly host. Echoing the Fourth Servant Song in Isa 52:13–53:12 (cf. 52:13; 53:11),[40] an early

---

someone who is wise, while in Dan 11:33-35 he makes the audience wise (*Daniel* [BKAT 22.1; Neukirchen-Vluyn: Neukirchener Verlag, 1986] 18, 20, 44).

[37] Newsom, "The Sage in the Literature of Qumran," 373–82; D. J. Harrington, *Wisdom Texts from Qumran* (Literature of the Dead Sea Scrolls; London and New York: Routledge, 1996) 65–66, 76–78.

[38] J. J. Collins, *The Apocalyptic Vision of the Book of Daniel* (HSM 16; Missoula, MT: Scholars Press, 1977) 210–11.

[39] Translations are from D. Winston, *The Wisdom of Solomon: A New Translation with Introduction and Commentary* (AB 43; Garden City, NY: Doubleday, 1979) 111–13, 124–25. Translations from the Bible are from the *NRSV*.

[40] It is generally accepted that the מַשְׂכִּילִים allude to the suffering servant in Second Isaiah: compare the role of the "wise servant" (הִנֵּה יַשְׂכִּיל עַבְדִּי) in Isa 52:13 (setting the multitude right [צָדַק, *hipʿil*]: 53:11) with the function of the "wise" in Dan 12:3 (leaders of the multitude towards righteousness [צָדַק, *hipʿil*]); compare also the exaltation motif in Isa 52:13 (the servant "shall be exalted [רוּם] and lifted up, and shall be very high") with "those who are wise shall shine like the

parallel interpretation of this song, or motifs from it, in both apocalyptic literature (Dan 11:33-35; 12:1-3) and wisdom literature (Wis
1:1–6:21) seems very likely.[41]

Nevertheless, there remains a striking difference between the
eschatological constructions in the Wisdom of Solomon and those in
Daniel. Whereas Dan 12:2 (cf. קיץ, see also Isa 26:19) certainly
attests to a resurrection, Wis 2:23; 3:4; 5:15 clearly alludes to the
"immortality of the soul." This is a concept based on the "ambiguity
of death"—i.e. Pseudo-Solomon's negative attitude towards the death
of the "wicked" and his contrasting attitude, guaranteed by the
distinction between physical and spiritual mortality towards the death
of the "just."[42] This notion is closely related to Hellenistic-Jewish
interpretations of Gen 1:1–3:24 and 4:1-16 (for example, Philo,
Opif. §134; *L. A.* 1 §§105-107; see also *Sib. Or.* 3.767–71 and
Pseudo-Phocylides 97-115) in the light of Platonic and Stoic ideas.[43]
In addition to this result, we must acknowledge several apocalyptic
writings that simply combine the concepts of (astral) immortality
(*Jub.* 23:31; Pseudo-Philo's *Bib. Ant.* 33:5; *2 Bar.* 51:9-10),[44] deifi-

---

brightness (יזהרו כזהר) of the sky" in Dan 12:3. See the recent commentaries of J.
E. Goldingay, *Daniel* (WBC 30; Dallas: Word, 1989) 284, 303, 317; and Collins,
Daniel, 385, 393.

[41] J. J. Collins, *Jewish Wisdom in the Hellenistic Age* (OTL; Louisville, KY:
Westminster John Knox, 1997) 183–85; and the very thorough analysis of L.
Ruppert, "Gerechte und Frevler (Gottlose) in Sap 1,1–6,21. Zum Neuverständnis
und zur Aktualisierung alttestamentlicher Tradition in der Sapientia Salomonis," *in*
H. Hübner (ed.), *Die Weisheit Salomos im Horizont Biblischer Theologie*
(Biblisch-Theologische Studien 22; Neukirchen-Vluyn: Neukirchener, 1993) 22–
35, 49.

[42] See Collins, *Jewish Wisdom*, 188: "The cessation of physical life has
different meanings for the righteous and the unrighteous, and herein lies its
ambiguity."

[43] M. Kolarcik, *The Ambiguity of Death in the Book of Wisdom 1–6. A Study
of Literary Structure and Interpretation* (AnBib 127; Rome: Pontifical Biblical
Institute, 1991) 159–90; Collins, *Jewish Wisdom in the Hellenistic Age*, 185–87;
and K. M. Hogan, "The Exegetical Background of the 'Ambiguity of Death' in *The
Wisdom of Solomon*," *JSJ* 30 (1999) 1–24. For Pseudo-Phocylides and its mixture
of several different understandings of death and the afterlife, see Collins, *Jewish
Wisdom in the Hellenistic Age*, 165–66.

[44] On ancient Jewish quotations pertaining to astral immortality, see already P.
Volz, *Die Eschatologie der jüdischen Gemeinde im neutestamentlichen Zeitalter:
Nach den Quellen der rabbinischen, apokalyptischen und apokryphen Literatur*

cation (Ezekiel the Tragedian [*Exag.*] 68-82; at Qumran, e.g. 4Q374 frg. 2 ii.6; 4Q491 frg. 11 i.12-15; also the *Ascension of Isaiah* 9:27-28),[45] and resurrection as may be seen in several passages from the (Ethiopic) Epistle of Enoch (*1 Enoch* 102:4-8; 103:2-4 [= 7Q4 frg. 1 + 7Q12 + 7Q14]; 104:2-6; see also *4 Ezra* 7:96-97, 125; and the *Assumption of Moses* 10:9).[46]

Up to a point, it is probable that the משכילים represent not only a particular social class, but also a certain theological system or "belief-system." As such, the system reflects a theological tradition found within later prophetic writings (e.g. Isa 52:13; 53:11; see also Isa 42:1 LXX and Isa 42:4LXX: ἀναλάμψει).[47] From there the Danielic משכילים adopted two theological aspects of their role: teaching and exaltation. The second of these appears explicitly in both texts, Isaiah's song of the Suffering Servant and Daniel, but in a paradoxical fashion. First, the servant's exaltation is embedded within a theological concept of humility and atonement (Isa 53:10):

> Yet it was the will (חפץ) of the Lord to crush him with pain. When you make his life an offering for sin (אשם), he shall see his offspring, and shall prolong his days; through him the will (חפץ) of the Lord shall prosper.

Secondly, the servant's function of teaching and instruction is closely connected to his change of outer appearence as well as to his

---

(Tübingen: Mohr-Siebeck, 1934; repr. Hildesheim: Olms, 1966) 396–401.

[45] For further references, see J. M. Knight, *The Ascension of Isaiah* (Sheffield: Sheffield Academic Press, 1995) 79–81; C. Fletcher-Louis, "4Q374: A Discourse on the Sinai Tradition: The Deification of Moses and Early Christology," *DSD* 3 (1996) 240–41.

[46] *1 Enoch* 104:2-6 is of particular interest; cf. E. Isaac, "1 (Ethiopic Apocalypse of) Enoch," in *OTP* 1.85: "But now you shall shine like the lights of heaven.... Be hopeful, and do not abandon your hope, because there shall be a fire for you; you are about to be making a great rejoicing like the angels of heaven." On *1 Enoch* 102–104 see G. W. E. Nickelsburg, *Resurrection, Immortality, and Eternal Life in Intertestamental Judaism* (HTS 26; London: Oxford University Press; Cambridge, MA: Harvard University Press, 1972) 114–29; and on *4 Ezra* 7:96-97 see M. E. Stone, *Fourth Ezra. A Commentary on the Book of Fourth Ezra* (Hermeneia; Minneapolis: Fortress, 1990) 244–45.

[47] H. L. Ginsberg, "The Oldest Interpretation of the Suffering Servant," *VT* 3 (1953) 400–404; Ruppert, "Gerechte und Frevler (Gottlose) in Sap 1,1–6,21," 40–41, 49; Hartman and DiLella, *The Book of Daniel*, 300; and also S. B. Reid's critical remarks (*Enoch and Daniel*, 107–8). For additional influence of the Suffering Servant motif in the Similitudes of Enoch (*1 Enoch* 37–71), see Collins, *The Apocalyptic Imagination*, 186–87.

perception by the nations (גוים, Isa 52:14-15):

> Just as there were many who were astonished at him—so marred was his appearance, beyond human semblance, and his form beyond that of mortals—so he shall startle many nations; kings shall shut their mouths because of him; for that which had not been told (ספר) them they shall see (ראה), and that which they had not heard (שמע) they shall contemplate (בין, hithpolel).

Nevertheless, the tradition of the Suffering Servant from Isa 52:13 and 53:11 was combined with neither the motif of resurrection, as in the book of Daniel, nor with that of the immortality of soul, as in the Wisdom of Solomon.[48] Yet precisely these are decisive features of "apocalyptic eschatology" (Wis 1:1–6:21) or an "apocalypse" (Dan 7:1–12:13). The fourth Servant Song and its earliest interpretations in the Wisdom of Solomon and the Book of Daniel reveal the development of an eschatology in three different stages. At the starting-point in Isa 52:13–53:12 "teaching" and "exaltation" are connected to the transformation of the Servant's status or personality. As a further step, the Wisdom of Solomon expresses the hope of the righteous for immortality and everlasting life (cf. Wis 5:15: δίκαιοι δὲ εἰς τὸν αἰῶνα ζῶσιν), but no resurrection is attested. The Book of Daniel, representing the ultimate stage of the development, explains the teaching and exaltation of the "wise" by referring to a transcendent reality: "Those who are wise shall shine *like* the brightness of the sky ... *like* the stars for ever and ever" (Dan 12:3).

This passage may function as an explanation for "awakening to everlasting life" in Dan 12:2abα. In any case, vv. 2-3 refer to an otherworldly, heavenly reality, i.e. a "spatial eschatology" that represents a central feature of the genre "Apocalypse."[49] This "spatial eschatology" is not necessarily implied by the Hebrew terminology. The *hipꜤil* of קיץ ("to awake," Dan 12:2a), here related to awakening from death, is attested in Jer 51:39, 57 and Isa 26:19 (cf. Job 14:12; 1QpHab 8:14). Comparison with the Isaiah-Apocalypse demonstrates that a resurrection indicated by this verb is probable but not self-

---

[48] In the light of Dan 12:3 the Suffering Servant becomes a new character (Isa 52:13); see K. Baltzer, *Deutero-Jesaja* (KAT X.2; Gütersloh: Gütersloher Verlag, 1999) 497, 537.

[49] See the definiton of an apocalypse as a literary genre by Collins, *Daniel*, 54; also Cook, *Prophecy and Apocalypticism*, 22–25.

evident. At any rate, the question of whether Isa 26:19 is to be understood literally as denoting resurrection or metaphorically as describing national restoration (cf. Hos 13:14; Ezek 37:1-14) is highly disputed.[50] Even if an "awakening from the dust or (death-) sleep" is used for bodily resurrection in later traditions,[51] the two contemporary references in *1 Enoch* 91:10 and 92:3 are just as ambiguous as Isa 26:19.[52]

The notion of resurrection in Daniel 12:1-3 is clear nonetheless because of the visionary context of the pericope as a whole. Most notably, Dan 12:3 takes us back to the first vision in chapter 7, especially vv. 21-23: the horn wages war against the holy ones (קדישין) until the "Ancient of Days" arrives for judgement and the holy ones take possession of the kingdom. Eventually the victory of the holy ones over the horn—i.e. the apocalyptic depiction of Antiochus Epiphanes' persecutions and his defeat (cf. Dan 11:36)—will be completed, when the *maśkîlîm* "shall shine like the stars" (12:3) and shall join the angelic hosts (cf. *1 Enoch* 104:2-6).[53] Thus the composition and structure of Daniel highlights the eschatology of the *maśkîlîm* as hope for an otherworldly reality. The decipherment

---

[50] J. Day has recently argued against the resurrection-motif in Isa 26:19 ("The Dependence of Isaiah 26:13–27:11 on Hosea 13:4–14:10 and Its Relevance to Some Other Theories of the Redaction of the 'Isaiah Apocalypse'," in C. C. Broyles and C. A Evans [eds.], *Writing and Reading the Scroll of Isaiah. Studies of an Interpretive Tradition* [FIOTL 1 and VTSup 70; Leiden: Brill, 1997] 358–61).

[51] J. F. A. Sawyer, "Hebrew Words for the Resurrection of the Dead," *VT* 23 (1973) 223–24; and Collins, *Daniel*, 392.

[52] See the Aramaic text from Milik's reconstruction (4QEn^g ar 1 ii, lines 13-14): ...ה[וקשיטי]א [יתעירון מן שנתהון] (?) חכמתא תהוא קאמ[ה והלכ]ה... ("[And the right-eou]s [shall awake from their sleep [?] ... wisdom shall aris]e and go ..."), text and translation from J. T. Milik, with M. Black, *The Books of Enoch. Aramaic Fragments of Qumran Cave 4* [Oxford: Clarendon Press, 1976] 260). The "arising of wisdom" alludes to the idea of hidden wisdom (cf. *1 Enoch* 42:1-3; 84:3; *2 Enoch* 30:8[7]) that will be revealed at the end of the days as a mystery (cf. *Odes of Solomon* 33:5-8). Yet revelation, not resurrection, is the focus of such passages (see *4QInstruction*, which may also be related to the משכילים; cf. T. Elgvin, "The Mystery to Come: Early Essene Theology of Revelation," in F. H. Cryer and T. L. Thompson [eds.], *Qumran between the Old and New Testaments* [JSOTSup 290; Sheffield: Sheffield Academic Press, 1998] 115, 146–47).

[53] J. J. Collins, "Apocalyptic Eschatology and the Transcendence of Death," in his *Seers, Sibyls and Sages in Hellenistic-Roman Judaism*, 87–88, 95–96; and the critique of Hartman and DiLella, *The Book of Daniel*, 310.

of world-history as truth (אמת, Dan 11:2), extending from Cyrus to Antiochus Epiphanes (Dan 11:2-45), reaches its goal in that hope (see section 3 below).

Further evidence of the hope for an otherworldly reality as the center of the *maśkîlîm*'s "belief-system" stems from the Jewish reaction to the "Hellenization" of the Temple in Jerusalem. Since Elias Bickerman it is accepted that the Maccabean revolt, together with its precursory conflicts, primarily reflects a struggle within the Jewish community.[54] For the book of Daniel in particular, compare the "violent ones (NRSV: 'lawless') of your own people" (Dan 11:14, בני פריצי עמך) who will "stumble." These are probably a Jewish, pro-Seleucid party related to earlier pro-Syrian activity by Jews at the battle of Paneas (200 or 198 BCE).[55] In the eyes of the pre-Jews of the Maccabean era, including the *ḥasîdîm*, those who had chosen to obey the Torah died at that time. "Thus piety caused death, and disobedience led to life."[56] The same may be said about the *maśkîlîm* and the terminology in Dan 12:2: those who "awake to everlasting life" (לחיי עולם) are to be identified with the Jews who died because of their obedience of the Torah, while those who "awake to reproach and everlasting abhorrance" (לחרפות לדראון עולם) are to be identified with Hellenizing Jews (cf. 1 Macc 1:52-53, 55; cf. 2 Macc 6:1-11).[57]

---

[54] E. Bickerman, *The God of the Maccabees. Studies on the Meaning and Origin of the Maccabean Revolt* (SJLA 32; Leiden: Brill, 1979). For an alternative view see V. Tcherikover, *Hellenistic Civilization and the Jews* (Jerusalem: Magnes and Philadephia: JPS, 1959; repr. Peabody, MA: Hendrickson, 1999) 183–203; and F. Millar, "The Background to the Maccabean Revolution: Reflections on Martin Hengel's *Judaism and Hellenism*," *JJS* 29 (1978) 1–21. For a recent approach, especially a critique of terms like "Hellenizer" and "Hellenizing Jews," see E. S. Gruen, *Heritage and Hellenism. The Reinvention of Jewish Tradition* (Hellenistic Culture and Society 30; Berkeley: University of California Press, 1998) 1–40.

[55] Hartman and DiLella, *The Book of Daniel*, 291–92; Collins, *Daniel*, 379–80. Goldingay (*Daniel*, 297) identifies the "wild men" with the Tobiads.

[56] Nickelsburg, *Resurrection, Immortality, and Eternal Life*, 19. From the standpoint of pious Jews the wisdom doctrine of retribution was obviously no longer of any help.

[57] The criterion of obedience of the Torah becomes evident via a comparison of Dan 12:2 with 1QS 4:6-14, where the same terminology is used: the "Sons of Truth" will find "endless joy in everlasting life" (ושמחת עולמים בחיי נצח, 1QS 4:7). But the "Spirit of Deceit" will lead to "everlasting terror and endless shame" (לזעות נצח וחרפת עד, 1QS 4:12-13. Whereas 4:9 mentioned the "Spirit of Deceit"

In contrast to the prayer in col. 10^{58} of 1QH^a, the *maśkîlîm* saw no chance of redress for their affliction in this world.

Nevertheless, the *maśkîlîm* of Daniel did not emphasize the law in terms of studying and teaching the Torah, as may be seen, for example, in *Jubilees* and in the attitude of the *ḥasîdîm* (cf. 1 Macc 2:42; 7:12-13). They were indebted to the Torah inasmuch as they lived in accordance with the law from the God of Israel who had become a universal God. His privileged revelations made the "wise" examples of distinguished knowledge and protagonists of eschatological hope (Dan 12:9-10; cf. *4 Ezra* 14:42-48). As John Collins observes: "The teaching they impart is not primarily the Torah, which they surely assume, but the apocalyptic world view of the Book of Daniel itself."[59]

In sum, the transcendent character of Dan 12:1-3 only comes to light in the context of a vision-like reality that discloses a heavenly salvation. We must also take into account the historical reality of the *maśkîlîm* as a group of persecuted, pious Jews who were oppressed by Hellenizing Jews. Their hope of salvation is eschatological, i.e. a future expectation and transcendent hope, but is already concrete as they receive privileged knowledge through revelations (cf. Dan 12:10).

3. THE SOCIAL CONSTRUCTION OF REALITY IN THE BOOK OF DANIEL

Examination of the belief-system in Daniel leads to a twofold reality that constitutes the faith and hope of the "wise." The first component is a vision-like reality which relates to the formal aspect,

---

(רוח עולה), col. 9 refers to the "men of deceit" (אנשי העול, line 17). In their midst the "counsel of the Torah" (עצת התורה) "might be concealed." But the members of the יחד are "guided with knowledge and instructed (שכל) in the mysteries (רז) of wonder" (line 18). For the text and translation of 1QS, see E. Qimron and J. H. Charlesworth, "Rule of the Community," in J. H. Charlesworth (ed.) *The Dead Sea Scrolls: Hebrew, Aramaic, and Greek Texts with English Translations*. Vol. 1: *Rule of the Community and Related Documents* (PTSDSSP 1; Tübingen: Mohr-Siebeck; Louisville, KY: Westminster John Knox, 1994) 16–19, 40–41, 78–79.

[58] The speaker of the prayer is set "as a reproach and a mockery of traitors, a foundation of truth and of knowledge for those on the straight path" (1QH^a 10:9-10: ותשימני חרפה וקלס לבוגדים סוד אמת ובינה לישרי דרך). For text and translation see F. García Martínez and E. J. C. Tigchelaar, *The Dead Sea Scrolls Study Edition* (Leiden: Brill, 1997) 1.160–61.

[59] Collins, "Daniel and His Social World," 140.

while the second is the historic reality which emphasizes the
background of the *maśkîlîm*'s faith. Accordingly, any future hope
could only be received and articulated by means of a "mantic
genre."[60] At the same time, the eschatology of the "wise" became
concrete through revelation of secrets, since the *maśkîlîm* found
themselves in an historical situation of intense persecution.
Nevertheless, they continued to assume the doctrines of the forefathers (cf. the function of the Torah); they "shall give understanding
to many" (Dan 11:33). The latter component, i.e. the historic reality,
contradicts the sociological assumption that an "individual's
'knowledge' of the world is socially derived and must be socially
sustained."[61] This is because the main peculiarity of the *maśkîlîm*'s
knowledge is that it is enshrouded in mystery and in no way
originates in this world—what is more, this knowledge should be
termed "anti-social." From this viewpoint, it is plausible that—in
contrast to the Qumran community and more or less comparable to
Enochic apocalypticism—the group of the Danielic *maśkîlîm* became
isolated and eventually disappeared.[62] At the same time, their
reliance on contemporaneous political expectations and on the
witness of the prophets (cf. Dan 11:2-39, 40-45 with Isaiah's
prediction of the fall of Assyria in Isa 10:12-14, 24-27, 33-34;
14:24-27) illuminates the historical and traditio-historical background of this group.[63]

But how did this isolated group of *maśkîlîm* find its "legitimation"?[64] In a creation of worldly realities, other than those of

---

[60] On "mantic" wisdom in apocalyptic writings, see H.–P. Müller, "Mantische
Weisheit und Apokalyptik," in G. W. Anderson and the Board of VT (eds.),
Congress Volume, Uppsala, 1971 (VTSup 22; Leiden: Brill, 1972) 268–93.

[61] P. L. Berger and T. Luckmann, "Sociology of Religion and Sociology of
Knowledge," in N. Birnbaum and G. Lenzer (eds.), *Sociology and Religion. A
Book of Readings* (Englewood Cliffs, NJ: Prentice-Hall, 1969) 414.

[62] Berger and Luckmann, *The Social Construct of Reality*, 61–62; and A. D.
H. Mayes, *The Old Testament in Sociological Perspective* (London: Marshall
Pickering, 1989) 131–33.

[63] A. S. van der Woude, "Prophetic Prediction, Political Prognostication, and
Firm Belief. Reflections on Daniel 11:40–12:3," in C. A. Evans and S. Talmon
(eds.), *The Quest for Context and Meaning. Studies in Biblical Intertextuality in
Honor of James A. Sanders* (BIS 28; Leiden: Brill, 1997) 66–68.

[64] Berger and Luckmann, "Sociology of Religion and Sociology of
Knowledge," 416–18; eidem, *The Social Construction of Reality*, 85–118. See also

everyday life, a society's "symbolic universe" comprises a certain level of legitimation. Furthermore, in a theory where the society is more or less a symbolic system, social change is symbolic change.[65] Eventually, legitimation by means of a symbolic universe draws closer to the world of apocalyptic writings when we consider the almost overwhelming multitude of symbols in the book of Daniel (cf. Daniel 7; also *1 Enoch* 14)[66] and the important role of legitimation within apocalypticism in general—consider, for example, the importance of "scripture" in Dan 7:10; 10:21; 12:1, 4, 9; *Jub.* 23:32; *1 Enoch* 81:1-2, 6; 82:1; 93:1-2; 103:3; 104:12-13; *4 Ezra* 14:42-48; and Rev 13:8.

But if we return to the sociological theory of Berger and Luckmann, it soon becomes apparent that a certain function is peculiar to the symbolic universe. Berger and Luckmann later explain the "nomic function of the symbolic universe" that "puts everything in its right place:"

> ... whenever one strays from the consciousness of this order (that is, when one finds oneself in the marginal situations of experience [i.e. the world of dreams and visions: S. B.]), the symbolic universe allows one "to return to reality"—namely, to the reality of everyday life.[67]

It is obvious that Berger and Luckmann identify the function and meaning of symbols. Their content is identical with "interrelation" between an object and its meaning, between different kinds of "knowledge," and between different subjects. As Émile Durkheim

---

Mayes, *The Old Testament in Sociological Perspective*, 136–37; and J. G. Gager, *Kingdom and Community. The Social World of Early Christianity* (Prentice-Hall Studies in Religion Series; Englewood Cliffs, NJ: Prentice-Hall, 1975) 66–92.

[65] J. Z. Smith, "The Influence of Symbols upon Social Change. A Place on Which to Stand," in his *Map is Not Territory. Studies in the History of Religions* (SJLA 23; Leiden: Brill, 1978) 143–46. For a definition of "symbol" see Berger and Luckmann, *The Social Construction of Reality*, 88: "... symbolic processes are processes of signification that refer to realities other than those of everyday experience."

[66] Furthermore, for the use of symbols in the Animal Apocalypse (*1 Enoch* 85–90) as elements of an "allegory" see Tiller, *A Commentary on the Animal Apocalypse*, 21–60. For the importance of symbols to the social setting of the Book of Revelation, see A. Yarbro Collins, "The Book of Revelation," in John J. Collins (ed.), *The Encyclopedia of Apocalypticism*. Vol. 1: *The Origins of Apocalypticism in Judaism and Christianity* (New York: Continuum, 1998) 394–403.

[67] Berger and Luckmann, *The Social Construction of Reality*, 91.

has shown, symbols have an effect on the society that uses them.[68]
Yet the unspecific definition of a symbol by Berger and Luckmann
remains especially unstatisfactory in religio-historical discourse.
Even a phenomenological approach, as represented in the work of
Mircea Eliade, distinguishes six criteria of application: (1) revealing
a condition of the world that lies besides immediate experience;
(2) multivalence and versatility of symbols; (3) fitting diverse
realities together in a system; (4) expressing paradoxical situations;
(5) existential value; and (6) sometimes religion and symbol are
identified (in "primitive religions").[69]

It is beyond doubt that ancient Jewish apocalypses use symbols as a
means of indicating a "symbolic transformation of the world."[70] For
example, the symbolic world of the beasts in Dan 7:3-8, 11-12 and
the war of the "horn" (Antiochus IV) against the "holy ones" (vv 20-
21)—including the defeat of the "horn" (vv. 26-27)—mirror the
two realities of a corrupt and lost world on the one hand, and an
everlasting world of salvation on the other (cf. Dan 7:22, 27: מלכותה
מלכות עלם). While the persecutions of Antiochus IV were taking
place, there was already a world of heavenly hosts that was closely
related to a future hope which include the identification of the
persecuted with these heavenly beings (cf. Dan 12:1-3; *1 Enoch*
104:2-6). Thus the symbolic world of the book of Daniel has both
temporal and spatial dimensions, and the symbols become concrete
through the association of the risen *maśkîlîm* (Dan 12:3) with the
angels.[71]

As regards the symbolic world of Daniel, it is not only the goal of
the resurrected shining like stars, but also the means of reaching that
goal (cf. Daniel 10)—i.e. the elimination of earthly distress towards

---

[68] J. W. Heisig, "Symbolism," *Encyclopedia of Religions* 14.201–2, 204–6.
For a functional definition of "Religion," see T. Luckmann, *The Invisible Religion*
(New York: MacMillan, 1967).

[69] M. Eliade, *The Two and the One* (New York: Harper & Row, 1969) 201–
208; see also T. Fawcett, *The Symbolic Language of Religion. An Introductory
Study* (London: SCM, 1970) 26–38.

[70] D. L. Barr, "The Apocalypse as a Symbolic Transformation of the World: A
Literary Analysis," *Int* 38 (1984) 39–50.

[71] See Collins, "Daniel and His Social World," 140–142; idem, *Daniel*, 393–
94. Against this, see the unconvincing comments of P. R. Davies, "Reading Daniel
Sociologically," in van der Woude (ed.), *The Book of Daniel in the Light of New
Findings*, 345–61, esp. 355.

heavenly salvation through an angelic host—that makes the Danielic symbols so different from any "symbol" that affords a fallback to the reality of everyday life.[72] Thus the major sociological function of symbols fails with respect to the Daniel apocalypse and apocalypses in general. Even if these apocalyptic symbols were derived from older well-known traditions, their rearrangement in a visionary setting leaves them disconnected from the symbolic universe of everyday experience. It is not ultimately the change of symbols, but a new understanding of rearranged traditional symbols, that constitutes the distinctive reality of the Daniel apocalypse. This conclusion is based not only on references to mythical symbols (for example, the beasts or the "Ancient of Days" in Daniel 7, alluding to a Canaanite or Mesopotamian context),[73] but it also rests on a reinterpretation of ancient Israelite traditions (as is the case with the *maśkîlîm*; see section 2 above).[74]

4. CONCLUSION

To sum up, the sociological approach directs the reader's attention to the inherent belief-system of the apocalypse.[75] Furthermore, the book of Daniel envisages a radical replacement of social organization and should thus be called "utopian" (Karl Mannheim).[76] This

---

[72] This assumption is also true of the three symbols examined by P. R. Davies: "book," "the court," and "secret" ("Reading Daniel Sociologically," 352–57). All three function as heavenly symbols within Daniel 7–12.

[73] H. S. Kvanvig, *Roots of Apocayalptic. The Mesopotamian Background of the Enoch Figure and the Son of Man* (WMANT 61; Neukirchen-Vluyn: Neukirchener Verlag, 1988) 459–535; J. J. Collins, "Stirring up the Great Sea. The Religio-Historical Background of Daniel 7," in his *Seers, Sibyls and Sages in Hellenistic-Roman Judaism*, 139–155.

[74] For further references in Daniel 9–11, mainly from prophetic books, see M. Fishbane, *Biblical Interpretation in Ancient Israel* (Oxford: Clarendon Press, 1985) 482–99; and M. A. Knibb, "'You are Indeed Wiser than Daniel.' Reflections on the Character of the Book of Daniel," in van der Woude (ed.), *The Book of Daniel in the Light of New Findings*, 399–411.

[75] Lacocque, "The Socio-Spiritual Formative Milieu of the Daniel Apocalypse," 317, 330–31, 335–37; and section 2 above.

[76] Lacocque (*ibidem*, 321) distinguishes between revolutionist (e.g. the Animal Apocalypse), introversionist (e.g. Qumran), manipulationist (e.g. the Hellenists), and utopian sects (e.g. Daniel). On Utopianism, see K. Mannheim, *Ideology and Utopia: An Introduction to the Sociology of Knowledge* (London: Routledge, repr.

replacement includes the hope for salvation within a transcendent reality that only comes to light through the visionary context of Daniel. In addition, the belief-system incorporates symbols which had been embedded in (mainly prophetic) traditions of ancient Israelite writings, but which were then rearranged in the Danielic predictions.[77] As regards the social setting of the Daniel apocalypse, the most probable solution is to identify the apocalypticists with the *maśkîlîm*. This conventicle lived in an historical situation of intense persecution, but should nevertheless be characterized as a highly-educated elite. The *maśkîlîm* were observers of the Torah and recorders of the new revelation.

To conclude these explanations with some speculation, the *maśkîlîm* were never aware of two or more realities. Their only reality was the vision of salvation, which was concrete in their hope for resurrection and legitimated through the traditions of their forefathers.[78]

5. SELECT BIBLIOGRAPHY

Albertz, R. *Der Gott des Daniel. Untersuchungen zu Daniel 4–6 in der Septuagintafassung sowie zu Komposition und Theologie des aramäischen Danielbuches* (SBS 131; Stuttgart: Verlag Katholisches Bibelwerk, 1988).

Barr, D. L. "The Apocalypse as a Symbolic Transformation of the World: A Literary Analysis," *Int* 38 (1984) 39–50.

Baumgarten, A. I. *The Flourishing of Jewish Sects in the Maccabean Era: An Interpretation* (JSJSup 55; Leiden: Brill, 1997).

Berger, P. L. and T. Luckmann. *The Social Construction of Reality. A Treatise in the Sociology of Knowledge* (Garden City, NY: Doubleday, 1966).

—. "Sociology of Religion and Sociology of Knowledge," in N. Birnbaum and G. Lenzer (eds.), *Sociology and Religion. A Book of Readings* (Englewood Cliffs, NJ: Prentice-Hall, 1969) 410–18.

Broshi, M. and E. Eshel. "The Greek King is Antiochus IV (4QHistorical Text = 4Q248)," *JJS* 47 (1997) 120–29.

Cohn, N. *The Pursuit of the Millennium: Revolutionary Messianism in Medieval*

1991) 173; and Knight, *The Ascension of Isaiah*, 86–87.

[77] Fishbane, *Biblical Interpretation in Ancient Israel*, 491–93; and van der Woude, "Prophetic Prediction, Political Prognostication, and Firm Belief," 68.

[78] In contemporary terms, the *maśkîlîm* may be characterized as "realists" who had only one (utopian) reality in mind; see the theoretical discussion by J. R. Searle, *The Construction of Social Reality* (London: Penguin, 1995).

and Reformation Europe (2nd ed., New York: Harper, 1961).

—. *Cosmos, Chaos and the World to Come. The Ancient Roots of Apocalyptic Faith* (New Haven, CT: Yale University Press, 1993).

Collins, J. J. "Introduction: Towards the Morphology of a Genre," *Semeia* 14 (1979) 1–20.

—. "Daniel and His Social World," *Int* 39 (1985) 131–43.

—. "Genre, Ideology and Social Movements in Jewish Apocalypticism," in idem, *Seers, Sibyls and Sages in Hellenistic-Roman Judaism* (JSJSup 54; Leiden: Brill, 1997) 25–38.

Cook, S. L. *Prophecy and Apocalypticism: The Postexilic Social Setting* (Minneapolis: Fortress, 1995).

Davies, P. R. "Reading Daniel Sociologically," in A. S. van der Woude (ed.), *The Book of Daniel in the Light of New Findings* (BETL 106; Leuven: University Press, 1993) 345–61.

—. "The Social World of Apocalyptic Writings," in R. E. Clements (ed.), *The World of Ancient Israel. Sociological, Anthropological and Political Perspectives* (2nd. ed., Cambridge: Cambridge University Press, 1991) 251–71.

García Martínez, F. *Qumran and Apocalyptic. Studies on the Aramaic Texts from Qumran* (STDJ 9; Leiden: Brill, 1992).

Grabbe, L. "The Social Setting of Early Jewish Apocalypticism," *JSP* 4 (1989) 27–47.

Isenberg, S. R. "Millenarism in Greco-Roman Palestine," *Religion* 4 (1974) 26–46.

Hanson, P. D. "Apocalypse and Apocalypticism: The Genre and Introductory Overview," *ABD* 1.279–82.

Lacocque, A. "The Socio-Spiritual Formative Milieu of the Daniel Apocalypse," in van der Woude (ed.), *The Book of Daniel in the Light of New Findings*, 315–43. [see under Davies]

Mayes, A. D. H. *The Old Testament in Sociological Perspective* (London: Marshall Pickering, 1989).

Nickelsburg, G. W. E. "Social Aspects of Palestinian Jewish Apocalypticism," in D. Hellholm (ed.), *Apocalypticism in the Mediterranean World and the Near East. Proceedings of the International Colloquium on Apocalypticism Uppsala, August 12-17, 1979* (2nd. ed., Tübingen: Mohr-Siebeck, 1989) 641–54.

Redditt, P. L. "Daniel 11 and the Sociohistorical Setting of the Book of Daniel," *CBQ* 60 (1998) 463–74.

Reid, S. B. *Enoch and Daniel. A Form Critical and Sociological Study of the Historical Apocalypses* (BIBAL.MS 2; Berkeley: BIBAL, 1989).

—. "1 Enoch: The Rising Elite of the Apocalyptic Movement," in K. H. Richards (ed.), *SBLSP 1983* (SBLSP 22; Chico, CA: Scholars Press, 1983) 147–56.

Searle, J. R. *The Construction of Social Reality* (London: Penguin, 1995).

Sim, D. C. "The Social Setting of Ancient Apocalyticism: A Question of Method," *JSP* 13 (1995) 5–16.

Wilson, R. R. "From Prophecy to Apocalyptic: Reflections on the Shape of Israelite Religion," *Semeia* 21 (1981-82) 79–95.

Yabro Collins, A. "The Book of Revelation," in John J. Collins (ed.), *The Encyclopedia of Apocalypticism*. Vol. 1: *The Origins of Apocalypticism in Judaism and Christianity* (New York: Continuum, 1998) 384–414.

A DAN(IEL) FOR ALL SEASONS:
FOR WHOM WAS DANIEL IMPORTANT?

LESTER L. GRABBE

Many Jews and Christians through the centuries have been intrigued by Daniel. In many ways it has been "all things to all men," not least to those curious about what the future might hold. The purpose of this essay is primarily to look at how the book has functioned in Second Temple Judaism. Since our Second Temple sources are somewhat limited, and in order to gain some perspective on the book, certain early Christian literature will also be considered. To achieve its ends the study is divided into four main parts: (1) which circles might have given rise to the book (i.e. determining those to whom it was originally important); (2) the "author" of Daniel; (3) interpretations of this book in the couple of centuries or so from its final compilation to the end of the Second Temple period; (4) Daniel's social location.

1. ORIGINS OF THE BOOK OF DANIEL

There are no magical keys to Daniel. With such a small corpus, we are continually driven back to the text to re-examine what we know. It will be useful here to summarize certain conclusions about Daniel that can be gleaned from the book itself, since it is from these that we must determine authorship. Many of them will be uncontroversial—perhaps even represent a consensus—and only the new ones will be argued at greater length. [1]

(a) Daniel was completed sometime during the period of the Maccabean revolt, i.e. between the halting of the daily *tamid* sacrifice and its resumption (168-165 BCE). [2] The book is quite aware of the

---

[1] Like so many students of Daniel, I am indebted to J. J. Collins' *The Apocalyptic Vision of the Book of Daniel* (HSM 16; Missoula, MT: Scholars Press, 1977) for many insights. See also P. R. Davies, *Daniel* (Old Testament Guides; Sheffield: Sheffield Academic Press, 1985) for an overview. A number of the points listed here will agree to a greater or lesser extent with Collins' and Davies' views, but others may differ; however, I have not felt it useful to catalogue the differences and agreements.

[2] On these dates, see Grabbe, "Maccabean Chronology: 167-164 or 168-165 BCE?" *JBL* 110 (1991) 59–74.

coming of Antiochus IV Epiphanes (Dan 7:19-27), but shows no knowledge of Judas' retaking of the temple. The ending of the "abomination of desolation" seems to be predicted (Dan 8:13-14; 11:31-45; 12:11), but this is as a genuine prediction, not a *vaticinium ex eventu*.[3]

(b) Daniel 1–6 are pre-Maccabean and were apparently taken up by the Maccabean author/compiler who wrote Daniel 7–12 and attached them to the earlier cycle of tales.[4] Nebuchadnezzar's vision of the statue (Daniel 2) indicates knowledge of Alexander's conquest and the Greek empires but shows no awareness of Antiochus' reign or anything specifically from the second century BCE, which indicates that Daniel 1–6 belong to the period earlier than the Maccabean crisis.

(c) The book was the product of "wisdom" circles. There is a strong emphasis on wisdom (for example, Daniel 1) and the use of wisdom vocabulary.[5] But this is essentially mantic wisdom. Although the book makes a point of wisdom acquired by learning, it is clear that the main source of wisdom is seen to be the Deity who imparts it by direct revelation (Dan 2:19-20; 9:20-23).

(d) The persona of Daniel seems to be based on a figure in the Neo-Babylonian and/or Persian period, evidently a Jewish visionary and dream interpreter. That the memory of some actual historical figure gave rise to the stories in the present book is plausible for the simple reason that the pseudepigraphic writer is unlikely to have invented a previously unknown character as the vehicle for his tales. As is well known, the name Daniel may have been derived from an ancient sage noted for wisdom (cf. Ezek 14:20; 28:3; *Jub.* 4:20),[6] but this is

---

[3] The explanation that the different figures represent different calculations, including recalculations when the prediction failed to materialize is a reasonable one. See Collins, *A Commentary on the Book of Daniel* (Hermeneia; Minneapolis: Fortress, 1994) 400–401, who notes that the first to propose this was H. Gunkel, *Schöpfung und Chaos in Urzeit und Endzeit: Eine religionsgeschichtliche Untersuchung über Gen 1 und Ap Joh 12* (Göttingen: Vandenhoeck & Ruprecht, 1895) 269.

[4] For a literary analysis of the book's structure which looks convincing to me, see Collins, *Apocalyptic Vision of the Book of Daniel*, 1–25.

[5] 1:4, 17, 19-20; 2:29-30. The root שׂכל (esp. in the form מַשְׂכִּל) is used several times (1:4, 17; 11:33, 35; 12:3).

[6] An attempt to disconnect the Ezekiel references from the Daniel of Ugaritic legend by H. H. P. Dressler ("The Identification of the Ugaritic *Dnil* with the Daniel of Ezekiel," *VT* 19 [1979] 152–61) cannot be considered convincing. See

probably not the origin of the legends here. The story is too embedded in the Babylonian and Persian courts to be derived from legends of an ancient Northwest Semitic hero. The name of an ancient figure could have been attached to the legends of a Persian-period hero, but this is not a necessary development.

(e) The writer was very concerned about being able to divine the future. Many of the visions are of course *ex eventu* prophecies rather than genuine predictions. Nevertheless, the writer gives genuine predictions, especially at the end of Daniel 11 but also probably in the statements about how long the "abomination of desolation" would last (8:13-14; cf. 12:11).

(f) The writer of Daniel 7–12 (who was also probably the editor and compiler of the whole) was an educated person, knowledgable in Greek learning, and likely of high standing in the Jewish community.

2. THE "AUTHOR" OF DANIEL[7]

The diverse origins of the material in the book complicates any attempt to characterize the compiler. Since the material in Daniel 1–6 arose earlier (probably in Ptolemaic times), it may have interests not so important to the final author. The use of earlier material suggests that the final writer found it generally sympathetic to his concerns (for example, God's sovereignty, refusal to disobey the law even in the face of death, and vindication of the obedient Jews). He also did not find anything in it particularly objectionable, though it would be a mistake to see any point in Daniel 1–6 alone as a special concern of the final compiler. A number of the themes in 1–6 carry through to 7–12, however, and are clearly of interest to the final editor, especially

---

Grabbe, "'Canaanite': Some Methodological Observations in Relation to Biblical Study," in G. J. Brooke, et al. (eds.), *Ugarit and the Bible: Proceedings of the International Symposium on Ugarit and the Bible, Manchester, September 1992* (Ugaritisch-Biblische Literatur 11; Münster: Ugarit-Verlag, 1994) 113–22, esp. 119–20; also J. Day, "The Daniel of Ugarit and Ezekiel and the Hero of the Book of Daniel," *VT* 30 (1980) 174–84; and B. Margulit, "Interpreting the Story of Aqht: a Reply to H. H. P. Dressler," *VT* 29 (1979) 152–61, *VT* 30 (1980) 361–65. Dressler replied to Day and Margulit in "Reading and Interpreting the Aqhat Text," *VT* 34 (1984) 78–82; I have seen no response to my own critique.

[7] This article was virtually complete when I came across P. L. Redditt, "Daniel 11 and the Sociohistorical Setting of the Book of Daniel," *CBQ* 60 (1998) 463–74. I have not changed my argument, which is parallel to Redditt's in certain aspects but also different, though I have added some references to his article.

the concern with dream interpretation and mantic wisdom in general.

This final editor was very likely a single individual who may also have done the editing of the stories in 1–6 and arranged the material to form a single coherent structure. He then wrote 7–12 to accompany it.[8] In that sense, we can speak of an "author" of the final version of the book in Hebrew and Aramaic. Thus, we find that the compiler was someone concerned with apocalyptic speculation and prediction of the future, a respecter of the wisdom tradition in certain forms, a person steeped in the Jewish historical traditions but also having access to Greek sources. He was also a biblical exegete, trying to make sense of earlier Scripture as he knew it, such as Jeremiah's 70-years prophecy which he reinterpreted as 70 weeks of years.

Who could this author have been? It has been conventional to ascribe the book to conventicle circles; the "Ḥasidim" have been popular as proposed authors. There are serious problems with this interpretation, especially with regard to the Ḥasidim.[9] No apocalypticist hiding in the desert or conventiclist writing out of Jewish oral and even written tradition would have had access to such information about external history. Such a person might have made certain vague references to some major events or figures, particularly recent ones, but would not have evinced an extensive knowledge of Hellenistic history over a century or more as we find in Daniel 11.

The writer does show a fair knowledge of the Neo-Babylonian and Persian periods. Although drawing on legendary material, he exhibits

---

[8] In postulating a single author for Daniel 7–12, I do not deny that he used pre-existing material in some cases, such as the four-empires schema (known from various sources as fairly widely extant in the Ancient Near East), the elements from mythology such as the "Son of Man" and "Ancient of Days," a source for Daniel 11 (see below), and an earlier oracle as the basis of Dan 9:24-27 (On this last, see Grabbe, "'The End of the Desolations of Jerusalem': From Jeremiah's 70 Years to Daniel's 70 Weeks of Years," in C. A. Evans [ed.], *Early Jewish and Christian Exegesis: Studies in Memory of William Hugh Brownlee* [Hommage Series 10; Atlanta: Scholars Press, 1987] 67–72).

[9] See esp. Collins (*Apocalyptic Vision of the Book of Daniel*, 201; idem, *Commentary on the Book of Daniel*, 67–69. The "Ḥasidim" of much scholarship is an invention more or less of whole cloth; see the classic study of P. R. Davies, "*Hasidim* in the Maccabean Period," *JJS* 28 (1977) 127–40. For a summary of scholarship on the Ḥasidim, see Grabbe, *Judaism from Cyrus to Hadrian*. Vol. I: *Persian and Greek Periods*. Vol. II: *Roman Period* (Minneapolis: Fortress, 1992; British edition in one volume, London: SCM, 1994) 465–67 (pagination continuous).

a surprising number of genuine historical remembrances. One of the most interesting is the description of Belshazzar who has otherwise dropped out of classical and ancient Near Eastern memory. Some knowledge of Nabonidus also seems to be preserved, though this is ascribed to Nebuchadnezzar.[10] Finally, Darius "the Mede" may well have elements of genuine historical memory behind him.[11] We should not exaggerate this knowledge since it shows a good deal of error or reworking, but it evidences someone with access to perhaps the best Jewish memory of the Persian period, which is otherwise fairly obscure in Jewish sources. The writer also had an interest in court matters and apparently also a genuine interest in historical events.[12] This is in contrast with the additions to Daniel found in the Septuagint where the tales are cruder (for example, Bel and the Dragon) and there seems little interest in the court as such.

Does the writer's knowledge of Neo-Babylonian and Persian matters prove a learned author? Perhaps, but not necessarily. Most of this could have been passed down in folk memory (even though there is a danger that we read our modern perspective of what is crude and legendary into the judgment of an ancient writer). Despite its intriguing remembrances, it is still often far removed from the actual history of the Babylonian and Persian courts as known today. The writer is probably not drawing on archival material or written historical sources; Jewish legendary and religious tradition (whether oral or written) can still explain most of what we see in this part of Daniel. The same applies to much of the knowledge relating to the Greeks. The references to Alexander and the Greek empires does not generally

---

[10] As far as I am aware this was first recognized by W. von Soden, "Eine babylonische Volksüberlieferung von Nabonid in den Danielerzählungen," ZAW 53 (1935) 81–89. His instincts have been supported more recently by the finding of 4QPrayer of Nabonidus which looks like the sort of intermediate stage in the development of the tradition that von Soden's theory had envisaged. See Grabbe, "Fundamentalism and Scholarship: The Case of Daniel," in B. P. Thompson (ed.), Scripture: Method and Meaning: Essays Presented to Anthony Tyrrell Hanson for His Seventieth Birthday (Hull: University Press, 1987) 133–52, esp. 142–45.

[11] Cf. Grabbe, "Another Look at the Gestalt of 'Darius the Mede'," CBQ 50 (1988) 198–213; Brian E. Colless, "Cyrus the Persian as Darius the Mede in the Book of Daniel," JSOT 56 (1992) 113–26.

[12] One cannot help smiling at those who have labeled apocalypticism as a-historical; on the contrary, some of the apocalyptists like Daniel are obsessed with historical concerns.

rise above folk memory (Dan 7:7-8, 23-24; 8:5-8, 21-22),[13] while Antiochus' doings (7:8, 24-27; 8:9-12, 23-26) would have been known to many Jews of Palestine at the time.

But when we come to Daniel 11, we are in completely different territory. Here is a detailed account of the interactions between the Ptolemaic and Seleucid courts over more than a century. Much of the chapter is usable as a historical source in its own right, so accurate is it (even if hidden under thinly disguised prophetic symbol). It is unthinkable that this is based on anything but a sophisticated historical document (or documents) of some sort. Such a document is unlikely to have been written by the Jews but is almost certainly a Greek writing (or writings) which has been used by the writer.[14] It need not have been translated or used verbatim or even in close paraphrase; rather, the historical information has been extracted and fitted into the needs of the apocalyptic "vision" contained in the chapter. This is clear from 11:21-39 where the Maccabean revolt is specifically taken up, and then from 11:40 to the end of the chapter where a genuine prophecy is made.

Who could this compiler have been? One person of the time known to possess a number of the characteristics associated with the proposed author is Eupolemus, son of John (1 Macc 8:17; 2 Macc 4:11). He was of the priestly family Hakkoz (Hebrew הקוץ; 1 Chr 24:10; Ezra 2:61; Neh 3:4, 21; 7:63), and probably the author of the fragments of a work of history preserved by Eusebius and others.[15]

---

[13] The statement that Alexander's empire was divided four ways does not of course correspond to historical reality, where the final division was between the Seleucids, the Ptolemies, and the Antigonids. The treaty of 301 after the battle of Ipsus provided for a four-fold division, but this was soon overtaken by events.

[14] Redditt's argument that this was written by Jewish scribes in the employ-ment of the Seleucids ("Daniel 11," 472–73) is not necessarily antithetical to my position, since we both postulate authors knowledgable in Greek. However, I have trouble with his assumption that these were "lower-level workers in the Seleucid governmental structure." It seems to me that such individuals were less likely to have access to a document like the one required by Daniel 11 than a prominent figure in Jerusalem, especially one close to the high priest.

[15] A convenient collection and study of the fragments of Eupolemus are found in C. R. Holladay, *Fragments from Hellenistic Jewish Authors*. Volume I: *Historians* (SBLTT 20; Pseudepigrapha Series 10; Atlanta: Scholars Press, 1983) 93–156. See also F. Fallon, "Eupolemus," in J. H. Charlesworth (ed.), *Old Testament Pseudepigrapha* (2 vols., Garden City, NY: Doubleday, 1983-85) 2.861–72.

Earlier commentators—and no doubt many present ones—would find this a rather strange suggestion because of assumptions about the origins and place of apocalypticism. Yet there is no reason to deny the possibility to a person like Eupolemus.

I do not suggest that it was certainly Eupolemus who wrote the book, but it was most likely someone very much like him in background, education, and status. We know it was someone who expected the eschaton in his own time, who favored a passive approach to persecution,[16] and who saw the military resistance as only "a little help" (Dan 11:34). What we do *not* know is what happened to the author after the success of the armed revolt and the restoration of the temple.

Eupolemus was most likely a part of Jason's "Hellenistic reform" in which Jerusalem was turned into a Greek polis. This episode in Jewish history is routinely misrepresented because of ancient and modern bias, but the reform was in fact widely welcomed, especially among the Jerusalem aristocracy including the leading priests.[17] Yet it is also clear that many of these same people opposed the actions of Menelaus and joined the side of the Maccabees when Judaism was suppressed (cf. 2 Macc 4:39-44). Eupolemus was apparently one of those Jason supporters who joined the Maccabees. But was he an apocalypticist?

Again, there is no reason why priests could not write apocalypses; indeed, there is good circumstantial evidence to suggest that they were the authors of some of the known Jewish apocalypses.[18] While there is nothing in the book to require priestly authorship, there is also nothing to oppose it. The cessation of the daily *tamid* offering would have been traumatic in the extreme (cf. Daniel 8), not least to priests of the temple. For a priest to have dreams and visions of the endtime in which God himself would intervene to restore the temple and true worship would have been perfectly understandable. On the other hand,

---

[16] Cf. Collins, *Apocalyptic Vision of the Book of Daniel*, 198–201, 206–10.

[17] For a discussion, see Grabbe, *Judaism from Cyrus to Hadrian*, 276–81; idem, "The Hellenistic City of Jerusalem," in J. Bartlett (ed.), *Jews in the Hellenistic and Roman Cities* (Royal Irish Academy; London: Routledge, in press).

[18] This is discussed in Grabbe, "The Social Setting of Early Jewish Apocalypticism," *JSP* 4 (1989) 27–47. A recent study coming to the same conclusion is S. L. Cook, *Prophecy and Apocalypticism: The Postexilic Social Setting* (Minneapolis: Fortress, 1995). The connection between the priesthood and apocalyticism was already noted by M. E. Stone, *Scriptures, Sects and Vision: A Profile of Judaism from Ezra to the Jewish Revolts* (Oxford: Blackwell, 1980) 44.

when the temple had been re-taken and proper worship restored, the passing of danger may have brought the author back to practical participation in the new Maccabean government. The author may not have been Eupolemus, but nothing presently known rules him out.

3. INTERPRETATIONS OF THE BOOK OF DANIEL

A thorough survey of how Daniel was used by later Jewish and Christian interpreters is beyond the scope of this paper.[19] Here I simply offer a quick overview as it relates to the possible social context of later usage of the book and its contents.

3.1 Jewish Interpretations

The earliest interpretation was the Greek translation of the book.[20] Some of the differences between the Hebrew and Aramaic text of the MT and the earliest Greek version can be explained by textual development.[21] While the extent of interpretation in the LXX version needs further exploration,[22] a number of recent studies have emphasized the interpretative aspects of the so-called "Theodotion" version.[23]

---

[19] For such a survey see Collins (with A. Yarbro Collins), *Commentary on the Book of Daniel*, 72–123, though some of the passages I shall be discussing are not mentioned there. For the 70 weeks prophecy of Dan 9:24-27, see Grabbe, "The 70-Weeks Prophecy (Daniel 9:24-27) in Early Jewish Interpretation," in C. A. Evans and S. Talmon (eds.), *The Quest for Context and Meaning: Studies in Biblical Intertextuality in Honor of James A. Sanders* (BIS 28; Leiden: Brill, 1997) 595–611. A useful survey of Christian interpretations is also found in J. G. Gammie, "A Journey Through Danielic Spaces: The Book of Daniel in the Theology and Piety of the Christian Community," *Int* 39 (1985) 144–56.

[20] This is the so-called OG or LXX version, found in only a few manuscripts. For the text, see J. Ziegler (ed.), *Susanna, Daniel, Bel et Draco* (2nd ed., edited by R. Smend; Septuaginta: Vetus Testamentum Graecum 16/2; Göttingen: Vandenhoeck & Ruprecht, 1999).

[21] Cf. Grabbe, "The 70-Weeks Prophecy," 596–99. In the case of Dan 9:24-27 most of the differences are explained by textual development. Apart from slightly different readings (for example, involving metathesis), one section of the LXX text seems to be a case of dittography and rearrangement. In this particular case, the MT seems overall to be more original.

[22] One such recent study is S. P. Jeansonne, *The Old Greek Translation of Daniel 7–12* (CBQMS 19; Washington, DC: Catholic Biblical Association, 1988); see also T. McLay, *The OG and Th Versions of Daniel* (SBLSCS 43; Atlanta: Scholars Press, 1996).

[23] In addition to Jeansonne and McLay (previous note) see T. J. Meadowcroft,

Daniel was well known by the community that produced the Qumran scrolls, with eight manuscripts of the book found in three caves (1QDan[a–b]; 4QDan[a–e]; pap6QDan). Daniel is referred to as a "prophet"[24] in at least one scroll, and several passages are quoted or made the basis of exegetical development. Unfortunately, despite considerable study the exact relationship of the fragments known as Pseudo-Daniel, now formally published,[25] to the book of Daniel is still unclear. Although one explanation is that they represent an interpretation of Daniel, this is not at all certain; they could instead show an independent tradition of some sort. One intriguing question concerns how the 70-weeks prophecy of Dan 9:24-27 was interpreted at Qumran. This is a difficult question: there are some passages that suggest that the passage was used to calculate the future, but these are not straightforward.[26]

A recent study has seen the judgment scene of Dan 7:9-14, with the Ancient of Days and the Son of Man, as the basis for the judgment scene in *Testament of Abraham* 11:1–13:8.[27] There are a number of parallels, and this is certainly a possibility. But, if so, it has developed considerably from the picture of Daniel 7, with rather different details.

Josephus is an important writer who saw Daniel as prophesying about Rome and his own times or perhaps even the future.[28] With

---

Aramaic Daniel and Greek Daniel: A Literary Comparision (JSOTSup 198; Sheffield: Sheffield Academic Press, 1995). Meadowcroft generally agrees with S. P. Jeansonne that most differences between the LXX and the MT are due to a different *Vorlage* for the LXX or to translation difficulties. However, contrary to Jeansonne, he finds many examples which can only be explained by "a particular mind set" or theological *Tendenz* on the part of the translator(s) (pp. 262–63). See further my review of Meadowcroft in *CBQ* 59 (1997) 128–29.

[24] 4QFlor frg. 1 ii.3, 24 and frg. 5.3 state: "[a]s is written in the book of Daniel, the prophet [הנביא]."

[25] 4Q243-45 (*4Qpseudo-Daniel[a–c] ar*); see J. J. Collins and P. Flint in J. VanderKam (consulting ed.), *Qumran Cave 4. XVII: Parabiblical Texts, Part 3* (DJD 22; Oxford: Clarendon Press, 1996) 95–164 + pls. VII–X, including earlier studies.

[26] For further discussion, see Grabbe, "The 70-Weeks Prophecy," 601–604.

[27] P. B. Munoa III, *Four Powers in Heaven: The Interpretation of Daniel 7 in the Testament of Abraham* (JSPSup 28; Sheffield Academic Press, 1998).

[28] See especially L. Grabbe, "Eschatology in Philo and Josephus," in A. Avery-Peck and J. Neusner (eds.), *Judaism in Late Antiquity*, Part 4. *Death, Life-After-Death, Resurrection & the World-to-Come in the Judaisms of Antiquity* (Handbuch der Orientalistik: Erste Abteilung, Der Nahe und Mittlere Osten 17;

regard to Daniel 2 (*Ant.* 10.10.3–4 §§195–210), the empire of the king
from the West (who can only be Alexander) is eventually brought
down by a power like iron which, though not explicitly identified,
must be Rome. The last is destroyed by a "stone made without hands,"
about which Josephus states (*Ant.* 10.10.4 §210):

> And Daniel also revealed to the king the meaning of the stone, but I have
> not thought it proper to relate this, since I am expected to write of what is
> past and done and not of what is to be; if, however, there is anyone who
> has so keen a desire for exact information that he will not stop short of
> inquiring more closely but wishes to learn about the hidden things that are
> to come, let him take the trouble to read the Book of Daniel, which he will
> find among the sacred writings.

He almost certainly applied this prophecy to Rome and expected its
destruction by supernatural means, though whether he expected that
destruction to be imminent is rather less certain. Josephus does not
write as one who anticipated Rome's imminent fall, but gives unmistakable hints that his interpretations of prophecy were strongly eschatological.

Even after the fall of the temple in 70 CE, we have evidence that
eschatological expectations were still strong in some circles. Especially important are *4 Ezra* and *2 Baruch*, both of which see the events
of their own times as heralding the eschaton. *4 Ezra* 11:10-34 applies
the fourth beast of Daniel 8 to Rome. The heavenly figure (messiah?)
called the "man from the sea" in *4 Ezra* 13 seems to be based on the
"son of man" figure in Dan 7:13-14. Although *2 Baruch* shows no
special dependence on Daniel, the vision of the light and dark waters
leads to the revelation of the messiah (chapters 53–74, cf. 29) and
illustrates the continuing eschatological outlook in this particular
writer.

The Bar-Kokhba Revolt seems to have brought overt eschatalogical
expectations to an end. Daniel is not referred to in the Mishnah, while
in the Tosefta the activities in Daniel 8 are related to various rabbis (*T.
Miqvaot* 7:11). The messianic and eschatological interpretation does
not appear to fit the world-view of those who produced the Mishnah
and related documents.[29] Later rabbinic literature, including the two
Talmuds, re-introduce a messiah into their world-view, though the

---

Leiden: Brill, 2000) 163–85.

[29] See especially J. Neusner, *Messiah in Context: Israel's History and Destiny in Formative Judaism* (Philadelphia: Fortress, 1984).

concept has been "rabbinized." Daniel is sometimes still seen to be prophetic, but as either fulfilled or perhaps for a more distant future. One especially interesting interpretation of Dan 9:24-27 is found in the *Seder Olam Rabbah* which reckons 490 years from the destruction of the First Temple to that of the Second Temple (chapters 28 and 30). This requires the artificial shortening of the Persian period to 34 years, but a similar reckoning occurs in *b. ʿAboda Zara* 9a. The passage has lost its eschatological meaning and has become just another fulfilled prophecy.

3.2 Christian Interpretations

Although explicit quotation of Daniel in the NT is rare, there appear to be many allusions. These are primarily in eschatological contexts. First is the Gospel Apocalypse (Mark 13//Matthew 24//Luke 21), where Daniel 7:13 is quoted (Mark 13:26//Matt 24:30//Luke 21:27) and the expression "abomination of desolation" (Dan 11:31; 12:11) appears (Mark 13:14//Matt 24:15); many other allusions have also been identified.[30] Secondly, Daniel 11:36 lies at the core of 2 Thess 2:1-12 (cf. also Dan 7:25; 8:25). Finally, the book of Revelation is filled with borrowings from and allusions to Daniel.[31] The *Epistle of Barnabas* similarly holds expectations of the imminent eschaton and draws on Daniel in support (4:3-5, quoting Dan 7:7 24; 16:15 16, quoting Dan 9:24-25). It is also argued that the expression "son of man" frequently used in the Gospels is based on the figure in Daniel, but this is controversial at the moment.[32]

After this period, the strong feeling of living in the eschaton disappears from the extant sources, at least for much of Christianity, and many aspects of eschatology became reinterpreted as relating to the history of the church. Nevertheless, belief in a literal return of Christ was retained, even if it tended to be put off to a distant future. Much of Daniel could still be applied to the first or second coming of

---

[30] See especially L. Hartman, *Prophecy Interpreted: The Formation of Some Jewish Apocalyptic Texts and of the Eschatological Discourse of Mark 13 par.* (ConBNT 1; Lund: Gleerup, 1966), even if he presents a rather maximalist case.

[31] See the list in R. H. Charles, *A Critical and Exegetical Commentary on the Revelation of St. John* (2 vols., ICC; Edinburgh: T & T Clark, 1920) 1.lxviii–lxxxii.

[32] See the convenient summary and discussion of the debate by Collins and Yarbro Collins in Collins, *Commentary on the Book of Daniel*, 79–82, 90–105.

Christ, though aspects were also applied to the activities of the church. A long section of Daniel 7 (vv. 9-28) is quoted by Justin Martyr (*Dialogue with Trypho* 31) with reference to the second coming of Jesus Christ. Irenaeus cites Daniel a number of times as a prophecy of the activities of Jesus, including his second coming (3.21.7; 4.20.11; 4.23.10; 4.33.1; 5.26.2; 5.28.2-4; 5.34.2). Hippolytus' *Commentary on Daniel* is apparently the first Christian commentary known as such.[33] He naturally makes the fourth kingdom of Daniel 7 identical with Rome (2.12; 4.5). Dan 9:24-27 ends with the birth of Christ, except that the final week is reserved to the endtime activities of the Antichrist. The "little horn" of Dan 7:20 is the Antichrist (4.5), but the one of Dan 8:9 was Antiochus Ephiphanes (4.26). Tertullian cites Daniel a number of times in his book *Contra Marcionem* (3.7; 3.25; 4.10; 4.21; 4.40), applying the Son of Man figure to Jesus. Perhaps his most interesting comments make up a long section on Dan 9:24-27 in his *Adversus Judaeos* 8 in which he proves by (often erroneous) historical data how the 70 weeks ended with the birth of Jesus and the fall of Jerusalem.[34] Clement of Alexandria also relates Dan 9:24-27 to the birth of Jesus and to the destruction of Jerusalem in 70 CE (*Stromata* 1.21).

Origen refers to the prophecies of Daniel several times. In his *Contra Celsum*, he says that Daniel 7 covers the future from his own times to the end of the world (6.46), and ascribes several passages (Dan 7:23-26; 8:23-25; 9:27; 11:36) to the Antichrist (2.50; 6.44, 46). As one would expect, Dan 12:1-3 is applied to the resurrection of the righteous (4.30; 5.10). Origen used Dan 9:27 to calculate the time

---

[33] Much of the Greek text has been lost, but the whole has been preserved in Old Slavonic. The remains of the Greek text and a German translation of the Old Slavonic are given in G. N. Bonwetsch and H. Achelis (eds.), *Hippolytus Werke. Erster Band: Exegetische und homiletische Schriften: Erste Hälfte Die Kommentare zu Daniel und zum Hohenliede;* Zweite Hälfte: *Kleinere exegetische und homiletische Schriften* (GCE; Leipzig: Hinrichs, 1897) i–xx, 1–340. Depending on Bonwetsch, but giving the Greek text (including a few additional readings from a newly discovered manuscript) and a French translation, is G. Bardy and M. Lefèvre (eds.), *Hippolyte, Commentaire sur Daniel* (SC 14; Paris: Cerf, 1947).

[34] The text of Daniel quoted by him refers to 62 and a half heptads plus seven and a half. The 62.5 heptads culminate in the birth of Jesus, while the remaining seven and a half fill out the time to the fall of Jerusalem. However, the dates for the Persian and Greek kings and the Roman emperors often bear little relation to modern knowledge, and the emperor Claudius is completely omitted.

between the crucifixion and the destruction of Jerusalem by the Romans (*Comm. in Matt.* 40 [on Matt 24:15]; *De Principiis* 4.5). Eusebius of Caesarea sees the prophecies as already fulfilled; for example, in the *Demonstratio Evangelica* he gives a number of ways of calculating the 70 weeks of Daniel 9:24-27, one of which begins with Cyrus and ends with the death of Alexander Janneus.[35] Jerome's *Commentary on Daniel* is best known for its quotations from the lost work of Porphyry which anticipated modern critical conclusions about the growth of the book. He takes Daniel as a prophet, but most of his prophecies have already been fulfilled except for those applying to a rather remote endtime.

These all fit with the general tendency of patristic writers to downplay the eschatological element in the biblical text.[36] This does not mean that there were no periods of intense apocalyptic speculation, such as the time of the Montanist controversy around 200 CE, but these tend to be shortlived. One of the few to use Daniel to predict the future was Apollinaris of Laodicea.[37] Most patristic figures accept the idea of a distant eschatological event and return of Christ, but it is not imminent. Some of the early Christian writers thought that Jesus' birth was in 5,500 *anno mundi*, leaving another 500 years to the end.[38] This is very much paralleled in literature being produced at this

---

[35] This is a period said to be 482 years. However, Eusebius goes on to say that "the first seven weeks must be reckoned from Cyrus to Darius, and the remaining sixty-two from Darius to Pompey the Roman general" (*Dem. Ev.* 8.2 §394b-d), translated by W. J. Ferrar, *The Proof of the Gospel, Being the Demonstratio Evangelica of Eusebius of Caesarea* (TCL Series I: Greek Texts; London: SPCK; New York: Macmillan, 1920) 2.129. There is some confusion here, since Eusebius himself recognizes that it was several years after Janneus' death that Pompey took Jerusalem. This is also quoted by Jerome (*Com. in Dan.* [PL 25.544–47 = CCL 75A.869–77]).

[36] This trend is well exemplified in the original version of Victorinus of Pettau's *Commentary on Revelation*, with explicit millenarian views, and Jerome's reworking of it which deleted them.

[37] Apollinaris applied the 70-weeks prophecy in this way. According to Jerome (*Comm. in Dan.* [PL 25.548–49]), he thought the 70 weeks began with the birth of Jesus. After 69 weeks of years, the temple would be rebuilt, after which for a time it would be taken over by the Antichrist who would deceive the Jews. This would usher in the return of Christ, placing the culmination of the prophecy in the late 5th century CE.

[38] Cf. L. L. Grabbe, "The End of the World in Early Jewish and Christian Calculations," *RevQ* 11/41 (1982) 107–108. Those who mention this dating

time within Judaism. Neither Jewish nor Christian literature is particularly eschatologically-minded during this period, as far as we can tell.

3.3 Conclusions from the Interpretations

Only a brief survey of the book's interpretative history could be given, but it leads to several inferences. In one sense Daniel is like any other biblical text which was taken over and used in a variety of contexts, with certain words, phrases, or sections reused in a way not envisaged in their original setting. There are plenty of examples to illustrate this point. However, in the early period of both Jewish and Christian interpretation Daniel was seen fundamentally as holding the key to the future. Those who read the book seem to have read it as describing monumental events affecting their own lives or events shortly to take place. Although written centuries before (as they saw it), it described their own times in terrifying detail but also gave hope, for their present oppression and subjugation was about to be relieved through divine intervention. The Jews expected Rome to be destroyed by the coming of the messiah or a similar event. The Christians expected Jesus to return imminently, not as a suffering figure as at his first coming, but as a heavenly warrior who would bring the Roman empire to its knees, vindicating those presently being persecuted and executing judgment on the persecutors.

As time went on and two intense Jewish revolts were put down with great bloodshed, the expectation of an impending eschaton faded. From the known Jewish documents (primarily the Mishnah and Tosefta) Daniel ceased to form the basis of speculation, and a different world-view began to prevail. These later Jewish and Christian interpretations often still treated Daniel as foretelling the future—only the future foretold by him was now a part of their past. Daniel was a true prophet, but his prophecies had now been fulfilled. Christians still found Daniel useful because they could interpret the book as foretelling Jesus' first coming, demonstrating that God was behind his prophecies but also as giving insight into the second coming, an event sufficiently distant in the future that it need not trouble them at the moment. Jerome, for example, was very happy to write a commentary

include Julius Africanus (apud Syncellus, *Chronographia*, pp. 31 and 614 [Dindorf edition]), and Hippolytus, *Comm. in Dan.* 4.23–24. Theophilus of Antioch also seems to calculate the birth of Jesus as about 5500 AM (*Ad Autolycum* 3.24-28), even though he does not state this explicitly.

on Daniel even though the eschaton was not within his immediate horizon. However, in both Judaism and Christianity there were periodic enthusiasms which interpreted their own day as the endtime—and Daniel often played a role in these.

4. DANIEL'S SOCIAL LOCATION: A SUMMARY

The book of Daniel has its roots in the Greek period. It was most likely under Ptolemaic rule of Palestine that a number of legends about a Jewish dream interpreter at the Neo-Babylonian and/or Persian court circulated and were collected and written down. These legends were community literature and probably not the product of a single author; the stories were most likely based on an actual historical figure, though the memory of his real historical context was often hazy and inaccurate. Whether this figure was named Daniel is uncertain. It is indeed possible that he was, but the legends as we now have them might have drawn on the name of an ancient (Canaanite?) sage who was still remembered in the Greek period. In either case, these tales were available to the final compiler during the Maccabean crisis.

The final book in Hebrew and Aramaic was the product of a single author who wrote Daniel 7–12 sometime between the suppression of the daily sacrifice in December 168 BCE and its restoration in 165 BCE. He saw the tales of Daniel as representing a kindred spirit, a fellow visionary and wisdom figure. Many aspects of the tales probably appealed to him, including the wisdom elements, the steadfastness and obedience to the Jewish law regardless of personal risk, God's sovereignty over the world, and his solicitude for his people. But it was especially the divinely-inspired visions revealing the future that attracted his interest at a time when the Judaic religion was under threat of extinction. Whether the tales were already a block of material used with little change, or whether the author put together a set of separate tales, is uncertain. What is clear is that the tales were not rewritten to take account of the Maccabean crisis since there are no certain allusions to the Maccabean period in them.

Far from being an obscure apocalyptist hiding in a cave in the desert, the author of the book was an educated individual who knew Greek and had access to Hellenistic books of history and learning. He was likely to have been a member of the aristocracy, perhaps a priest, and probably a prominent member of the community in Jerusalem. Eupolemus the son of John is a possible candidate for the role, but if not he, someone like him.

Once the book had been written, it seems to have established itself rather quickly. It is already being alluded to in the books of Maccabees, which may have been no more than half a century after the book of Daniel was completed (cf. 1 Macc 16:23-24; 2 Macc 1:10).[39] Clear references to the book after this do not really come until the first century of the Common Era, but those who quote or allude to it see Daniel as prophesying the imminent time of the end. This applies to both Jewish interpretations and Christian ones. The book had evidently become a collection of prophecies for contemporary times which were also seen as the endtime. Daniel was by no means the only book to be viewed in this way, but there is no doubt that it lent itself to being used by those trying to find clues to what was shortly about to happen.

The interpretation of the book of Daniel has a long history in Judaism and Christianity. Much of the time it was seen as a source of knowledge about the future; in that function it seems to have been "all things to all men," serving up the future in potted form. It was easy to fit your favorite historical scenario into its visions and calculations. For those who saw history as a long-term affair, ending in the far-distant future, Daniel was still a sign that God had predicted certain things in the past and then brought them to pass on schedule. In the same way, his word about Israel/the church was sure and future vindication according to God's own timetable was certain. Yet at varying intervals Daniel was seized upon as proof that God's plan was about to be fulfilled in the very lifetime of the interpreters, in much the same way that early Jewish and Christian commentators had done.

Scholars of our own times see the book of Daniel as an apocalypse, but for centuries Daniel was the prophet *par excellence*. It was he who provided the key to "the times and the seasons"—as many still believe to this very day.

5. SELECT BIBLIOGRAPHY

Bardy, G. and M. Lefèvre (eds.). *Hippolyte, Commentaire sur Daniel* (SC 14; Paris: Cerf, 1947).

Bonwetsch, G. N. and H. Achelis (eds.). *Hippolytus Werke. Erster Band: Exegetische und homiletische Schriten: Erste Hälfte Die Kommentare zu Daniel und*

---

[39] This assumes that the expression "abomination of desolation" is taken from Daniel. If this phraseology originated independently and was simply drawn on by the author of Daniel, then the earliest reference to Daniel becomes more uncertain.

zum Hohenliede; Zweite Hälfte Kleinere exegetische und homiletische Schriften (GCE; Leipzig: Hinrichs, 1897).

Charlesworth, J. H. (ed.). *Old Testament Pseudepigrapha* (2 vols., Garden City, NY: Doubleday, 1983-85).

Colless, B. E. "Cyrus the Persian as Darius the Mede in the Book of Daniel," *JSOT* 56 (1992) 113–26.

Collins, J. J. *The Apocalyptic Vision of the Book of Daniel* (HSM 16; Missoula, MT: Scholars Press, 1977).

—. *A Commentary on the Book of Daniel* (Hermeneia; Minneapolis: Fortress, 1994).

Collins, J. J. and P. W. Flint. "Pseudo-Daniel," in J. C. VanderKam (consulting ed.), *Qumran Cave 4. XVII: Parabiblical Texts, Part 3* (DJD 22, Oxford. Clarendon Press, 1996) 95–164 + pls. VII–X.

Cook, S. L. *Prophecy and Apocalypticism. The Postexilic Social Setting* (Minneapolis: Fortress, 1995).

Davies, P. R. "*Hasidim* in the Maccabean Period," *JJS* 28 (1977) 127–40.

—. *Daniel* (Old Testament Guides; Sheffield: Sheffield Academic Press, 1985).

Dressler, H. H. P. "The Identification of the Ugaritic Dnil with the Daniel of Ezekiel," *VT* 19 (1979) 152–61.

Gammie, J. G. "A Journey Through Danielic Spaces: The Book of Daniel in the Theology and Piety of the Christian Community," *Int* 39 (1985) 144–56.

Grabbe, L. L. "The End of the World in Early Jewish and Christian Calculations," *RevQ* 11/41 (1982) 107–108.

—. "Fundamentalism and Scholarship: The Case of Daniel," in B. P. Thompson (ed.), *Scripture: Method and Meaning: Essays Presented to Anthony Tyrrell Hanson for His Seventieth Birthday* (Hull: University Press, 1987) 133–52.

—. "'The End of the Desolations of Jerusalem': From Jeremiah's 70 Years to Daniel's 70 Weeks of Years," in C. A. Evans (ed.), *Early Jewish and Christian Exegesis: Studies in Memory of William Hugh Brownlee* (Hommage Series 10; Atlanta: Scholars Press, 1987) 67–72.

—. "Another Look at the *Gestalt* of 'Darius the Mede'," *CBQ* 50 (1988) 198–213.

—. "The Social Setting of Early Jewish Apocalypticism," *JSP* 4 (1989) 27–47.

—. "Maccabean Chronology: 167-164 or 168-165 BCE?" *JBL* 110 (1991) 59–74.

—. *Judaism from Cyrus to Hadrian.* Vol. I: *Persian and Greek Periods.* Vol. II: *Roman Period* (Minneapolis: Fortress, 1992; British edition in one volume, London: SCM, 1994).

—. "'Canaanite': Some Methodological Observations in Relation to Biblical Study," in G. J. Brooke, et al. (eds.), *Ugarit and the Bible: Proceedings of the International Symposium on Ugarit and the Bible, Manchester, September 1992* (Ugaritisch-Biblische Literatur 11; Münster: Ugarit-Verlag, 1994) 113–22.

—. "The 70-Weeks Prophecy (Daniel 9:24-27) in Early Jewish Interpretation," in C. A. Evans and S. Talmon (eds.), *The Quest for Context and Meaning: Studies in Biblical Intertextuality in Honor of James A. Sanders* (BIS 28; Leiden: Brill, 1997) 595–611.

—. Review of T. J. Meadowcroft, *Aramaic Daniel and Greek Daniel, CBQ* 59 (1997) 128–29.

—. "Eschatology in Philo and Josephus," in A. Avery-Peck and J. Neusner (eds.), *Judaism in Late Antiquity*, Part 4. *Death, Life-After-Death, Resurrection & the World-to-Come in the Judaisms of Antiquity* (Handbuch der Orientalistik: Erste Abteilung, Der Nahe und Mittlere Osten 17; Leiden: Brill, 2000) 163–85.

—. "The Hellenistic City of Jerusalem," in J. Bartlett (ed.), *Jews in the Hellenistic and Roman Cities* (Royal Irish Academy; London: Routledge, forthcoming).

Gunkel, H. *Schöpfung und Chaos in Urzeit und Endzeit: Eine religionsgeschichtliche Untersuchung über Gen 1 und Ap Joh 12* (Göttingen: Vandenhoeck & Ruprecht, 1895).

Hartman, L. *Prophecy Interpreted: The Formation of Some Jewish Apocalyptic Texts and of the Eschatological Discourse of Mark 13 par.* (ConBNT 1; Lund: Gleerup, 1966).

Holladay, C. R. *Fragments from Hellenistic Jewish Authors.* Volume I: *Historians* (SBLTT 20, Pseudepigrapha Series 10; Atlanta: Scholars Press, 1983).

Jeansonne, S. P. *The Old Greek Translation of Daniel 7–12* (CBQMS 19; Washington, DC: Catholic Biblical Association, 1988).

McLay, T. *The OG and Th Versions of Daniel* (SBLSCS 43; Atlanta: Scholars Press, 1996).

Margulit, B. "Interpreting the Story of Aqht: a Reply to H. H. P. Dressler," *VT* 29 (1979) 152–61, *VT* 30 (1980) 361–65.

Meadowcroft, T. J. *Aramaic Daniel and Greek Daniel: A Literary Comparision* (JSOTSup 198; Sheffield: Sheffield Academic Press, 1995).

Munoa, P. B. III. *Four Powers in Heaven: The Interpretation of Daniel 7 in the Testament of Abraham* (JSPSup 28; Sheffield Academic Press, 1998).

Neusner, J. *Messiah in Context: Israel's History and Destiny in Formative Judaism* (Philadelphia: Fortress, 1984).

Redditt, P. L. "Daniel 11 and the Sociohistorical Setting of the Book of Daniel," *CBQ* 60 (1998) 463–74.

Soden, W. von. "Eine babylonische Volksüberlieferung von Nabonid in den Danielerzählungen," *ZAW* 53 (1935) 81–89.

Stone, M. E. *Scriptures, Sects and Vision: A Profile of Judaism from Ezra to the Jewish Revolts* (Oxford: Blackwell, 1980).

Ziegler, J. (ed.). *Susanna, Daniel, Bel et Draco* (2nd ed., edited by R. Smend; Septuaginta: Vetus Testamentum Graecum 16/2; Göttingen: Vandenhoeck & Ruprecht, 1999).

THE SCRIBAL SCHOOL OF DANIEL

PHILIP R. DAVIES

1. DANIEL AND THE SOCIAL-SCIENCE AGENDA

The integration of social-science methods into biblical scholarship is a fairly recent phenomenon, and hence the agenda of this essay does not carry a long history. Interest in the identity of the author of a biblical book *as an individual* is of course extremely ancient (to the point of pseudepigraphical attribution, be it of the Gospels or Epistles), but until the last two decades scholarship has tended to draw such a profile from a surface reading of the text, while the motivation for authorship itself has been addressed in theological terms: "what was the 'message' to be conveyed?" More recently, the problems of relating texts to real rather than implied authors, and a recognition of the many levels of "meaning" (and ambiguity) accessible from a text have made "authorship" a more recalcitrant issue. We have learnt, moreover, to distrust what authors tell us, until we know why they are writing and whom they wish to persuade of what. Applying this "hermeneutics of suspicion" to scriptural texts understandably meets with little interest in some quarters. But recent work has demonstrated the value of this approach for uncovering the underlying, as well as the overt, ideology of texts.

The various reasons for the advent of social-science perspectives on biblical literature deserve a lengthy review elsewhere. The outcome, however, is that the *social* dimension of authorship is now more fully in view. This is both in terms of the social construction of an author's world-view—the cultural formation, the class interest, the group ideology—and the function of writing, whether generally or in particular, as manifestations of economic and ideological impulses rather than personal inclination or impulse, or even theological reflection. One consequence for Hebrew Bible studies is that its writings are no longer simply treated either as the product of "ancient Israel," as a whole, expressing the beliefs of an entire society, nor as the fruit of an individual and autonomous mind. Nor is such writing explained simply in terms of the communication of a message, but in terms of various other functions also, such as

entertainment, ideological construction, group identity reinforce-
ment (and several other motivations). In short, the origins of the
literature of the Jewish scriptural canon are increasingly approached
from social-scientific presuppositions about the nature of human
behaviour, of which writing is but one category. Fundamentally, the
shift from a humanistic to a sociological approach is also a move
from the idealistic to the materialistic. This is, indeed, a major transition within the discipline of biblical studies, the wider contours of
which should not be obscured.

The history of research into the authorship of Daniel reflects a
trend from personal and historical, via theological and literary and
back, to socio-historical emphases. A century ago, the question of the
book's authorship and historicity were intertwined, and the notion
that Daniel himself was not the author—and that the author was
historically inaccurate—was once raised as a question of "fraud."
This battle was still being fought by H. H. Rowley, who very sharply
insisted on a single second-century setting for the entire contents and
elaborated greatly on its historical inaccuracies.[1] Rowley himself
accordingly played a major role in promoting the question of the
"origin" of "apocalyptic" as a product of persecution, and contributing to the revival of this genre in theological discussion, including
its dependence on either "prophecy" or "wisdom." More recently
still, "apocalypse" has been identified as a literary genre, or set of
genres; and the question of historical background has correspondingly re-emerged in various searches for an "apocalyptic
movement"[2] or "apocalyptic communities."[3] While these terms are a

---

[1] H. H. Rowley, *Darius the Mede and the Four World Empires of Daniel*
(Cardiff: University of Wales Press, 1935 [repr. 1959]); idem, "The Unity of the
Book of Daniel," in *The Servant of the Lord and Other Essays on the Old
Testament* (2nd ed., Oxford: Blackwell, 1965) 249–80.

[2] Although this term has now generally been abandoned, it continues in the so-
called "Groningen hypothesis" of the the Dead Sea Scrolls, where this "apocalyptic
movement" is the forerunner of the Essenes. See F. García Martínez, "Qumran
Origins and Early History: A Groningen Hypothesis," *Folia Orientalia* 25 (1988)
113–36.

[3] E.g. J. J. Collins, "Was the Dead Sea Sect an Apocalyptic Movement?" in L.
H. Schiffman (ed.), *Archaeology and History in the Dead Sea Scrolls* (JSPSup 8;
Sheffield: JSOT Press, 1990) 25–51; idem, *Apocalypticism in the Dead Sea Scrolls*
(London: Routledge, 1997). The idea originated with F. M. Cross, Jr., *The
Ancient Library of Qumran* (3rd ed., Sheffield: Sheffield Academic Press, 1995).

clear case of category confusion, the social-science agenda has again become quite clear, and "Daniel" has turned into a historically formed and ideologically motivated social group.

Attempts have been made since the mid-1960s at some kind of identification of this group for whom the book of Daniel speaks. O. Plöger recreated a post-exilic Judean society bifurcated between those wedded to the Temple establishment and those who, constituting small and closed communities ("conventicles"), preserved and developed the "prophetic eschatology."[4] The connection between apocalyptic and small visionary groups was developed by P. Vielhauer[5] and endorsed in a fashion by P. Hanson.[6] The theory entailed a view (derived almost exclusively by deduction from biblical literature) that "post-exilic" Judean society consisted of a pragmatic priestly establishment with a broadly theocratic ideology, and incipiently sectarian visionary groups with an "eschatological" ideology. The former was complacent, the latter pessimistic, about the quality of its contemporary society and history. The latter groups produced "apocalyptic" as an extension of "prophecy"—or at least of that bit of prophecy that could be seen as visionary.

The weaknesses of this (rather naïve) position have subsequently become evident. First, "prophetic eschatology" is itself a dubious construct, with "prophecy" itself an unexamined social category. Informed sociological studies of prophecy (such as those by B. Lang, R. Wilson and D. Petersen)[7] have exposed the wide range of "prophetic" activity and of world-view—though even some of these studies still confuse the social phenomenon of intermediation with the literary phenomenon of a corpus of texts.

Second, a useful corrective to several assumptions about the social setting of Second Temple Jewish apocalyptic literature has been

---

[4]   O. Plöger, *Theocracy and Eschatology* (Oxford: Blackwell, 1968).

[5]   P. Vielhauer, "Apocalypses and Related Subjects," in E. Hennecke and W. Schneemelcher (eds.), *The New Testament Apocrypha* (2 vols., London: SCM Press; Philadelphia: Westminster, 1963-65) 2.581–607.

[6]   P. D. Hanson, *The Dawn of Apocalyptic* (Philadelphia: Fortress, 1975).

[7]   B. Lang, "Prophetie, prophestische Zeichenhandlung und Politik in Israel," *Theologische Quartalschrift* 161 (1981) 273–80; R. R. Wilson, *Prophecy and Society in Ancient Israel* (Philadelphia: Fortress, 1980); D. L. Petersen, *The Roles of Israel's Prophets* (JSOTSup 17; Sheffield: JSOT Press, 1981). See also R. C. Culley and T. W. Overhol, *Anthropological Perspectives on Old Testament Prophecy* (*Semeia* 21, 1982).

issued by Stephen Cook, who points to the "central-priestly" nature of much "proto-apocalyptic" material; he also advocates the abandonment of the "deprivation-theory" of apocalyptic, whereby it was ascribed to conditions of persecution or exclusion; and, finally, suggests that apocalyptic writings should not be assigned to any one stream of tradition.[8]

Third, it is increasingly recognized that the values of the book of Daniel are clearly those of a scribal elite; and further, as H.-P. Müller observed (following a cue from G. von Rad),[9] its intellectual ethos is that of "mantic wisdom": a divinatory culture permeating Mesopotamian (Sumerian, Semitic and Persian) religious practice.

Despite these considerations, the danger remains of trying to match a reconstructed "apocalyptic world-view" simplistically with a certain kind of social phenomenon, or even a "movement."[10] But not only are apocalyptic texts plentiful and diverse among Jewish writings of the Greco-Roman period, they were produced outside Jewish societies as well. To seek a purely Jewish explanation for "apocalyptic" is absurdly myopic.[11] Moreover, much of what has been described as typical of apocalyptic (such as a "vertical" view of reality, a belief in a transcendental world about to break into the world of human affairs) is simply a staple of much ancient Near Eastern and Mediterranean thought. Rather, one has to see apocalyptic literature as a genre of writing that can be used to express metaphysical or ethical beliefs, for one purpose or another. It is characteristically used when the sense of current events appears challenged by common understandings, or as a fashionable means of communicating religious dogma. But the genre itself does not hold any key to a social description of its producers.

The identity and social location of the writers of Daniel requires investigation from the book itself (which, in any case, partakes of at

---

[8] S. L. Cook, *Prophecy and Apocalypticism: The Postexilic Social Setting* (Minneapolis: Fortress, 1995).

[9] G. von Rad, *Old Testament Theology* (2 vols., Edinburgh: Oliver and Boyd, 1965 [repr. London: SCM, 1975]) 2.I "Daniel and Apocalyptic"; H.-P. Müller, *Mantische Weisheit und Apokalyptik* (VTSup 22; Leiden: Brill, 1971) 268–93.

[10] See n. 3 above.

[11] An honourable exception to this is E. P. Sanders, "The Genre of Palestinian Jewish Apocalytic," in D. Hellholm (ed.) *Apocalypticism in the Mediterranean World and the Near East* (Tübingen: Mohr-Siebeck, 1983) 447–60.

least two different genres). With an appropriately nuanced reading, such a task turns out to be surprisingly fruitful. We can begin with the implied authorship of the book.

2. *MASKILIM* IN DANIEL

It is unusual for a biblical book to name the group for whom it claims to speak. The book of Daniel is, by general consent, an exception, with the recognition[12] that the noun *maskilim* designates a specific group, class, or circle, at least as it is used in 11:33-35 and 12:3, 10:

> The wise among the people (מַשְׂכִּילֵי עַם) shall give understanding to many; for some days, however, they shall fall by sword and flame, and suffer captivity and plunder. When they fall victim, they shall receive a little help, and many shall join them insincerely. Some of the wise (מִן־הַמַּשְׂכִּילִים) shall fall, so that they may be refined, purified and cleansed, until the time of the end: for there is still an interval until the time appointed.

> Those who are wise (הַמַּשְׂכִּילִים) shall shine like the brightness of the sky, and those who lead many to righteousness, like the stars forever and ever.

> Many shall be purified, cleansed and refined, but the wicked shall continue to act wickedly. None of the wicked shall understand, but those who are wise (הַמַּשְׂכִּלִים) shall understand.[13]

Three main features of these references may be noted: (1) Allusions to Isa 52:13 (הִנֵּה מַשְׂכִּיל עַבְדִּי) and 53:11 (מִצְדִּיקֵי הָרַבִּים) have long been detected[14] in Dan 11:33 and 12:3. The exact significance of such allusions depends, of course, on how the "servant" of Isaiah was understood by the writers and readers of Daniel ("messianic" is most certainly both too loose and too loaded a term to use here). However, the claim to a divinely-appointed role, foretold in a text of ancient prophecy, is significant enough, and it is clear that such a role combines both enlightening others and also suffering. The portrait of Isaiah's "servant" thus fits very well that of the *characters* of Daniel in the narratives of chapters 1–6, where these roles

---

[12]   J. J. Collins is fairly typical of this consensus: "There can be little doubt that the author of Daniel belonged to this circle" (*Daniel: A Commentary on the Book of Daniel* [Hermeneia; Minneapolis: Fortress, 1993] 385).

[13]   All biblical quotations in English are those of the NRSV unless otherwise stated.

[14]   See especially H. L. Ginsberg, "The Oldest Interpretation of the Suffering Servant," *VT* 3 (1953) 400–404.

alternate (enlightening in chapters 2, 4, 5 and being persecuted in chapters 3 and 6). There exists, therefore, a fundamental unity between the real authors (the *maskilim*) and the implied author (Daniel—at least for chapters 7–12). Moreover, the editors ("real authors") of the book of Daniel have, it seems, applied or adapted existing stories of the wise courtier Daniel (or Belteshazzar, as in chapter 2,[15] or an unnamed Jew, as perhaps in chapter 4)[16] to fit a profile of themselves—just as Daniel's exile is intended to mirror, or perhaps more accurately to initiate (see Daniel 9) the "exilic" predicament of the group of second century *maskilim*.

The identification of the figure of Daniel with the self-designation of the authorship of the book is apparent in the way Daniel and his friends are introduced in 1:4, a chapter that belongs to the editorial stratum of the book rather than to a source-narrative:[17]

> ... young men without physical defect and handsome, versed in every branch of wisdom (משׂכילים בכל־הכמה), endowed with knowledge and insight, and competent to serve in the king's palace; they were to be taught the literature and language of the Chaldeans.

The young men, then, are introduced into the royal scribal school, where they become familiar with, among other things, the mantic arts (since mantic texts constitute a large proportion of the "Chaldean" literature). Dan 2:13 (again, an editorial gloss)[18] assumes Daniel and his friends to be numbered among the wise men and thus to be sought for execution. We should note, however, that the root used for the Chaldean wise is √חכם and not √שׂכל, for the latter term is restricted to divinely-acquired Jewish wisdom. The contrast between non-Jewish and Jewish wisdom (a major theme of Daniel 2) is thus linguistically as well as ideologically articulated.

(2) The implied relationship between the authors of Daniel and other sectors of Judaism is also instructive as an element in the social world-view of the *maskilim*. Where did they see themselves within "Israel"? Elements of a dualistic outlook can certainly be identified—at least in the final chapters of the book. Such a dualism is

---

[15] See P. R. Davies, "Daniel Chapter Two," *JTS* 27 (1976) 392–401.

[16] As in the text 4QPrNab, which features (very probably) a version of the story featuring Nabonidus and an unknown Jew.

[17] Compare P. R. Davies, *Daniel* (OT Guides; Sheffield: JSOT Press, 1985) 42–43.

[18] See Davies, *Daniel*; 45–46; and idem, "Daniel Chapter Two."

explicitly evoked through the contrast between the verbs צדק and
רשע in Dan 12:10, where the issue is one of "understanding" (בין√);
but it is also implied in 11:22-23, where a group called מרשיעי ברית
is mentioned before the משכילי עם, and in 12:2 where those to be
raised from the dead are divided into two, each awaiting an opposite
fate.

There is a hint of a temporal aspect of such dualism in Daniel 9,
where the past, on which Daniel reflects in his prayer, is characterized by sin and wickedness (see especially v. 5), while the
period of "seventy times seven" years is decreed "to bring in
everlasting righteousness" and to end transgression (פשע), sins
(חטאות) and iniquity (עון).

It is important to realise, however, that while the *maskilim* see
themselves as the elite among the righteous, they do not represent
themselves as exclusively one side of a dualistic divide, for alongside
the "wicked" and the "righteous" are a third group, the "many"
(רבים), those still to be "made righteous" by the *maskilim*. Nor is the
world universalized into two camps, as is the case in certain Qumran
texts, through lexical pairs (for example, light/darkness, truth/
falsehood). We are, perhaps, closer to that way of speaking that is
characteristic of the instructional wisdom literature of the Hebrew
Bible that divides people into (potentially) wise/foolish, and the
possibilities of human existences into life/death. The *maskilim*
responsible for the book of Daniel identify themselves with good-
ness, of course, and also categorize certain others with the opposite.
But they see their own role as extending צדק to others (the *rabbim*),
and, as noted, they foresee a post-mortem allocation of reward and
punishment to these groups, though with a specially glorious status
for themselves. It is important, then, to recognize that in Daniel
dualism is modified by a elitism that recognizes a privileged group
among the "righteous." Yet it is a privilege that has no place for
separatism, but belongs and operates within a wider community.
Here is a clear contrast with the Damascus and *Yaḥad* sects of the
Qumran scrolls

Again, in Daniel we generally find no clear delineation among the
"wicked," nor can we identify as the counterparts of the *maskilim*
any other clearly-defined group. We know from some of the
Qumran scrolls (for example, the *pesharim* or the *Damascus
Document*) that it is possible for one group to single out another
group as its target ("builders of the wall," "seekers of smooth

things"). In such cases an apparently universalistic dualism may mask an essentially inter-group rivalry. In Daniel, we find one possible case of a Qumran-like sobriquet: the מרשיעי ברית. However, these are not directly opposed to the *maskilim*, but to the עם ידעי אלהיו. If we look at the narratives, too, we find no consistent counterpart to Daniel and his friends among the villains. Mostly the antagonist is the imperial king; but in each case this king is finally won over to Daniel's cause—Belshazzar being a significant exception. In chapter 6 the enemies of Daniel are other courtiers, the "presidents and satraps" (6:4). Rival courtiers are a staple of the ancient Near Eastern wisdom tale, and their plottings are often the immediate cause of the hero's temporary misfortune (as the case of Haman illustrates).[19] It remains possible, but no more, that the privilege of the *maskilim* is most directly challenged by another scribal group or groups. But such a group is certainly not featured in the book. From a surface reading of chapters 7–12 it would appear that the group sees its ideological target as the Hellenistic monarchy, which now appears as much less amenable to demonstrations of divine wisdom and power and incapable of repentance; but this focus is clouded both by the narratives of chapters 2–6 and the final chapter, which is set after the death of the king.

These observations and deductions are reasonably consistent with what we know of the political, social and religious crises that led to the Hasmonean uprising, the political context in which the stories and the visions came together to form a book of Daniel. Reports of that period suggest a number of conflicting parties within Judean society,[20] for, despite the *Tendenz* of contemporary or near-contemporary Jewish sources[21] and the glosses of some more recent writers, it is impossible to present this episode simply as a conflict between two parties or groups representing "reform" and "tradition." We can

[19] For a study of this genre, see L. M. Wills, *The Jew in the Court of the Foreign King* (Minneapolis: Fortress, 1990).

[20] See J. Sievers, *The Hasmoneans and Their Supporters: From Mattathias to the Death of John Hyrcanus I* (SFSHJ 6; Atlanta: Scholars Press, 1990).

[21] A similar simplification of the issues into two sides can also be seen in 1 Maccabees, for whose author the "righteous" are clearly the Hasmonean dynasty and its supporters, and their opponents (no doubt of many colours) presented vaguely as "lawless" or "covenant violaters" (the latter term borrowed from Daniel's מרשיעי ברית).

rather reconstruct a growing tension—and presumably a growing polarization—within Judean society between those supporting some degree of accommodation with aspects of Hellenistic culture, and those wishing to defend the traditional customs from such inroads, as well as degrees of compromise. It is clear that among those who broadly opposed the Seleucid regime's policies there were differences of opinion, which emerged more clearly under the rule of the Hasmonean dynasty. In this rather messy situation of mixed allegiances and ambitions, the *maskilim* do not exclusively constitute one side of a dualism; they are within a cluster of groups opposed to Antiochus IV, a distinct interest group with ambivalent attitudes towards living under a non-Jewish regime.

(3) The values of the *maskilim* are clearly those of an educated elite. Daniel is trained in the wisdom of the Chaldeans, and it is assumed that he can both read (chapter 5) and write (chapter 12). The natural social context of the hero and his friends is the royal court. A corresponding theology is also apparent: while religion is certainly a matter of devout behaviour (prayer, especially), religious insight is essentially an intellectual matter. For the contrast of chapter 12 is between the *wise* and *wicked*. Piety is identified with *understanding*. Such an observation hardly needs developing or explaining: it is a fundamental premise of manticism that the secrets of the universe can be discovered because the gods give signs, and that the interpretation of these signs can be learned. While Daniel opposes the learning of the Chaldeans to the inspiration of the Jewish wise man, the distinction is not entirely fundamental, only the mechanism for decipherment. Daniel is instructed by God or by one of his intermediaries, and the *maskilim* accordingly instruct others in that wisdom. The *maskilim* of Daniel are, therefore, undoubtedly to be understood as a scribal community, and indeed concerned with one of the basic issues of scribal values: the definition of what constitutes correct behaviour, based on observation of (or enlightenment about) the way the world works. The question remains only: what sort of scribal community was provoked to produce the book of Daniel, and why?

3. IDENTIFICATION OF THE *MASKILIM*

What can be inferred from the text of Daniel, then, is its authorship by a group who see themselves as endowed with special understanding, as divinely appointed to teach their "righteousness" to the Judeans, and as undergoing suffering in the process. Attempts have, inevitably, been made to identify the authorship of Daniel with specific known (or partially-known) groups. P. Redditt[22] has recently reviewed a number of these proposals. The most influential has been Plöger's identification with the *Ḥasidim* of 1 and 2 Maccabees, a suggestion which has since been accepted in many quarters, but has also been comprehensively dismantled. When the relevant passages in 1 Maccabees are exegeted in detail, they simply do not provide a suitable profile, while the portrait in 2 Maccabees is quite different.[23] It remains unclear whether the term actually refers to a distinct group at all. Another candidate mentioned by Redditt, the group referred to in 1 Macc 2:29 as "seeking righteousness and justice," who attempted to escape from Jerusalem and were slaughtered on a sabbath, is not depicted as "scribal" and their reaction was to flee persecution rather than suffer it.

Redditt's third candidate is a party of "scribes associated with Jesus ben Sira." He refers to R. Albertz's suggestion[24] (following an earlier proposal of V. Tcherikover[25]) that a number of temple scribes banded together to form the *Ḥasidim*, and observes that other scribes may have "flourished beside them."[26] But that seems a forlorn identification, and most commentators have pointed out the contrasts between the mantic wisdom of Daniel and that of our conventional, Jerusalem scribe. Redditt is thus probably correct to dismiss all proposed identifications in favour of an otherwise unknown scribal group,[27] of which we may imagine there were plenty in the Jerusalem of the Second Temple period. We do not, it appears, have any credible allusion in other literature of the period to the authors of Daniel—with one possible exception, which Redditt curiously does not mention: the Qumran literature. But we shall consider this later.

---

[22] P. L. Redditt, "Daniel 11 and the Sociohistoical Setting of the Book of Daniel," *CBQ* 60 (1998) 463–74. See also his *Daniel* (NCB; Sheffield: Sheffield Academic Press, 1999).

[23] P. R. Davies, "Hasidim in the Maccabean Period," *JJS* 28 (1977) 127–40.

[24] R. Albertz, *A History of Israelite Religion in the Old Testament Period*. Vol. 2: *From the Exile to the Maccabees* (OTL; London: SCM Press, 1994) 539.

[25] V. Tcherikover, *Hellenistic Civilization and the Jews* (2nd ed., Philadelphia: Jewish Publication Society, 1961) 125–26, 196–67.

[26] Redditt, "Daniel 11," 467.

[27] Following P. R. Davies, *Daniel*; 124.

4. BEHIND THE *MASKILIM*

But if one cannot name a group, one may still describe it. The book of Daniel itself turns out to be a reasonably fulsome witness to the self-understanding of its authors. Does it also permit us to infer anything of their history?

The use of court-narratives and their diaspora setting seem to suggest that, as also with the authors and tradents of *1 Enoch*, the group behind Daniel has inherited non-Palestinian traditions. While the stories of Daniel 2–6 are clearly intended to be read, in the context of the book as a whole, somewhat allegorically, it is probable (perhaps not certain) that stories about rule under foreign kings flourished among Jews outside rather than within Palestine, where presumably a native scribal class administered the local affairs.

Nevertheless, the book of Daniel as a whole, and thus its authors, is fundamentally concerned with the fate of the Jerusalem temple and its cult. It is the use of Temple vessels in chapter 5 and their blasphemous use that precipitates the inscription of Belshazzar's fate, while in chapters 8–11 the cessation of the daily sacrifice is the crucial trigger for the movement of history towards its preordained end.[28] Concern for the temple itself, of course, does not point to a Judean origin, but it is the political circumstances of Judah that the visions reflect. If the *maskilim* originated outside Judah, at some point they immigrated to the city of the Jewish temple.

Can we suggest either when or why this move happened, or indeed, whether the move had any direct connection with the production of the book of Daniel? R. Wilson has suggested that the *maskilim* were a group who aspired to service in foreign courts, and I have also suggested that court service underlies the visions as well as the narratives and constitutes an important part of the social world of the authors. In other words, the *maskilim* belonged to the class of professional scribes employed in the administration of political affairs. This might explain their interest in problems of the interpretation of historical affairs, as well as a detailed knowledge (exhibited in chapter 11) of Seleucid and Ptolemaic relations. This particular chapter, according to U. Rappaport,[29] may indeed reflect

---

[28] The likelihood that the morning and evening sacrifices were also key times for diaspora Jews, as occasions for prayer (Dan 9:21), must also not be overlooked.

[29] See U. Rappaport, "Apocalyptic Vision and Preservation of Historical

a non-Palestinian source, or possible perspective, on these matters. Redditt[30] has taken the suggestion further, identifying within chapter 11 a Greek source that was editorially modified (for example, by phrases such as "king of the north" and "king of the south" which very probably point to a Palestinian locus). Citing S. Reid's characterization of the authors of Daniel as a "fallen elite,"[31] Redditt concludes that the *maskilim* may have been erstwhile officials of the Seleucid court, ousted or estranged by Antiochus IV. At any rate, they "harbored hopes of serving in the Seleucid court, or at least found the thought attractive."[32] This profile coheres with my own analysis of the scribal-diplomatic ideology of Daniel's authors.[33] But should such administrative service be assigned to Jerusalem, or elsewhere? Did the *maskilim*, if indeed they did move to Judah, serve in the Seleucid court before or after that move? Or both?

The reasons for such a move, if it occurred, can be no more than guessed at; the same is true of the point of departure. As in the case of Abraham, we have the choice of Ur or Harran, or rather Mesopotamia or Syria—both originally within the Seleucid kingdom.[34] Specific instances of, or occasions for, migration hardly need to be sought, since the movement of Jews from Babylonia was probably continuous throughout the Persian and Seleucid periods (and possibly not discouraged during the Ptolemaic era). Indeed, considerable migration in the other direction too created and enlarged the considerable Jewish diaspora in Egypt, Syria and Asia Minor.

5. DANIEL AND THE EVIDENCE OF THE QUMRAN MANUSCRIPTS

Inferences from the book of Daniel itself about the prehistory of its *maskilim* can probably take us no further. But concerning the

---

Memory," *JSJ* 23 (1992) 222–24.

[30] Redditt, "Daniel 11," 470–73.

[31] S. B. Reid, *Enoch and Daniel: A Form Critical and Sociological Study of Historical Apocalypses* (Berkeley, CA: Bibal, 1989) 134–35.

[32] Redditt, "Daniel 11," 467.

[33] P. R. Davies, "Reading Daniel Sociologically," in A. S. van der Woude (ed.), *The Book of Daniel in the Light of New Findings* (BETL 106; Leuven: Peeters, 1993) 345–61.

[34] I am not taking into account here the fascinating but ultimately improbable thesis of J. Lebram (*Das Buch Daniel* [Zurich: Theologische Verlag, 1984]) that Daniel is to be connected with Egypt.

later history of this group, we have a range of possible clues from the Qumran scrolls.

It is first of all interesting to observe that the *Hasidim* of 1 and 2 Maccabees have also long been suggested as the ancestors of the Essenes. This was for several decades the dominant theory of Qumran origins, and it surely implied that the "Qumran sect" stood in direct descent from the writers of the book of Daniel. Another connection between Daniel and Qumran stems from the suggestion of J. Murphy-O'Connor that the Essenes migrated to Palestine from Babylonia where they gradually formed into a separate group, and finally into a sect.[35] Finally, and, perhaps most tellingly, the *Community Rule* illustrates use of *maskil* and *rabbim* as technical designations within the *yahad*. The invitation to connect Daniel's *maskilim* with the authors and/or keepers of some or all of the Qumran archive is accordingly impossible to evade—and has indeed attracted a great deal of scholarly attention, though no systematic sociological analysis has yet emerged. ˙

The most ambitious of recent attempts to incorporate both Daniel and the Scrolls into a coherent picture of Second Temple Judaism is that of G. Boccaccini.[36] Though not a social historian but a historian of ideas, if he is correct there are immediate implications for our understanding of Judean society in the Second Temple period. Boccaccini traces from *1 Enoch*, through Daniel, *Jubilees* and the *Temple Scroll*, a merging of two different forms of Judaism: Enochic and Mosaic.[37] The former he identifies with the "apocalyptic" stream which, like his mentor P. Sacchi, is synonymous with "Enochic"; the Zadokite traditions, on the other hand, flow from Ezekiel and through Daniel. Thus, interestingly, Boccaccini divorces his "apocalyptic" tradition from Daniel. In the

---

[35] J. Murphy-O'Connor, "An Essene Missionary Document? CD II,14–VI,1," *RB* 77 (1970) 201–29; and idem, "The Essenes and Their History," *RB* 81 (1984) 215–44.

[36] G. Boccaccini, *Beyond the Essene Hypothesis. The Parting of the Ways Between Qumran and Enochic Judaism* (Grand Rapids: Eerdmans, 1998) 76–77.

[37] Here Boccaccini follows P. Sacchi (*Jewish Apocalyptic and Its History* [JSPSup 20; Sheffield: Sheffield Academic Press, 1987]) in suggesting a split between these two in the fourth century. This is not a topic to be pursued here, but I wonder how far the notion of an originally unified "Judaism" in the early Second Temple period is necessary or justified. Might it be better to assume an original independence of the two religious cultures?

Qumran scrolls he finds a combination of the two Judaisms, and especially in the Halakhic Letter 4QMMT finds a manifesto of the Enochic priesthood against a now disenfranchised Zadokite priesthood. The *Damascus Document*, in his view, represents an attempt by followers of the Teacher of Righteousness to control the Enochic movement which was accommodating its views to those of the Zadokites. The Teacher's failure led to the founding of a community at Qumran which broke with the main Enochic movement, producing a dualistic and strongly predestinarian ideology.

The attempt to link Daniel to a Zadokite theology is not unattractive: Daniel's adherence to the Temple and to the legitimacy of the Zadokite high priest supports that view. Moreover, Cook, as noted earlier, identified Zadokites as authors of early "apocalyptic" texts. The difficulty, it seems to me, is that Daniel's *maskilim* do not seem to be priestly. Daniel is not identified (as he easily might have been) as a priest, and nothing is said of priestly activities in connections with the *maskilim*. It is, of course, possible to argue that the term "Zadokites" applies also to those who supported the Zadokite priests and shared their ideology. But from a sociological point of view, one ought to respect the difference between a priestly and a lay group and not employ a terms that might confuse that distinction. Daniel represents a non-priestly group, even though ideologically and perhaps at one time professionally associated with the Temple. More recently, T. Elgvin has also underlined the notable fact that the Qumran literature

> represents a merger between two different streams: a lay community that fostered the apocalyptic and dualistic traditions of *1 Enoch* and *4QInstructions*, and a priestly group that brought with it Zadokite temple traditions.[38]

Boccaccini's stimulating thesis may clarify in some respects the ideological connections between Daniel and Qumranic literature. Yet the most concrete of connections between the two concern the terms *maskil* and *rabbim*, both used in the *Community Rule*.[39] The *maskil*

---

[38] T. Elgvin, "The Mystery to Come: Early Essene Theology of Revelation," in F. H. Cryer and T. L. Thompson (eds.), *Qumran Between the Old and New Testaments* (JSOTSup 290; Sheffield: Sheffield Academic Press, 1998) 113–50, esp. 150.

[39] One probably should not speak any longer of "The Community Rule" as a stable document, but rather about various manuscripts of an evolving work.

is the person for whom the various recensions of the *Rule* are apparently composed, and by whom they are to be used. 4QS^d opens with the heading מדרש למשכיל; in 1QS 3:13 we find למשכיל להבין וללמד אתכול בני אור; and in 1QS 9:12.21 a heading indicates rules for a/the *maskil*. On the same manuscript as 1QS is the text 1QSb, which opens with דברי ברש[ה]ן לשכיל (cf. 3:22).

It is widely deduced, therefore, that in the *yaḥad* the title *maskil* was the name given to a superior. Those whom he is responsible to instruct and for whom he also leads the liturgy are referred to, at least in one section (other terms are also used) as the *rabbim* (1QS 6:7ff.; 7:10ff.). In 4Q298 those instructed by the *maskil* are called the בני שחר. In *4QSapiential Work A* (4Q415–18, 4Q423) we have another term: the individual being instructed is known as a *mebin* (מבין). In this and other Qumran texts we get a picture of personal instruction (but within a defined group) into the "mystery of life."[40] It seems to me, in fact, that *maskil* is not, as the majority of scholars tend to suppose, a single individual (G. Vermes, for example, translates "The Master"),[41] but one of a number of persons accorded a recognized status. He is a senior member of the group, who has attained full knowledge and (in theory) practises full virtue. If this is the case, the plural usage in Daniel and the singular at Qumran are not incompatible. The teaching of the *rabbim* by the *maskilim* has, however, been institutionalized, at least as the manuscripts of the *Community Rule* represent the matter, within a sect. But within the Qumran wisdom texts we are offered an insight into a relationship between an individual teacher and his disciple.

In these two cases, in the *Community Rule* and the wisdom texts, can we draw any direct lines to the *maskilim* of Daniel? Can we conclude that the use of *maskil* and *rabbim* in the *Community Rule* is an instance of literary inspiration from Daniel or that it constitutes a *historical* connection between the writers of Daniel and one

---

[40] On the sapiential texts in general, see J. Fitzmyer (consulting ed.), *Qumran Cave 4.XV: Sapiential Texts, Part 1* (DJD 20; Oxford: Clarendon Press, 1997). On Sapiential Work A, see T. Elgvin, "The Reconstruction of Sapiential Work A," *RevQ* 16 (1995) 559–80; and now J. Strugnell, D. J. Harrington and T. Elgvin, *Qumran Cave 4.XXIV: Sapiential Texts, Part 2* (DJD 34; Oxford: Clarendon Press, 1999). The phrase "mystery of life" renders the rather enigmatic Hebrew expression רז נהיה.

[41] G. Vermes, *The Complete Dead Sea Scrolls in English* (New York: Allen Lane and Penguin, 1997).

community represented in the Qumran scrolls? In the case of the
wisdom texts, the question is whether we are dealing with long-
standing and widely-used terminology from the world of the scribal
school.

These questions can be answered, at least provisionally, by
considering an important and fundamental connection between
Daniel and both the wisdom texts and a large number of the Qumran
texts: the notion of eschatological salvation for some, earned by a
righteousness (צדק) that is based on divine revelation but also taught.
While obedience to the Mosaic law and traditional practices are not
abandoned, they are insufficient. An esoteric *knowledge* is required;
the God of its religion is one who *knows*. This divine characteristic
is basic to a great deal of the book of Daniel—the stories in which
the future can be revealed by the "God in heaven who reveals
mysteries" (Dan 2:28) and by the visions. The "righteousness" that
the *maskilim* teach the *rabbim* can hardly consist of anything but
understanding.

In the *Community Rule*, it is also clear that the members of the
yaḥad receive instruction from the *maskil* in the mysteries of the
"God of Knowledge." And in the distinctive wisdom texts from
Cave 4 (such as *4QSapiential Work B* [4Q420–21]) "righteousness"
is explicitly stated as the goal and practice of wisdom. Whether or
not the *content* of the knowledge that the *maskilim* imparted was
identical to that claimed within the *yaḥad*, there is an important
development in the understanding of "wisdom." Now the instructional tradition (still reflected in ben Sira), which taught the benefits
of a life well led, has been married to elements of manticism,
whereby the mysteries of the heavens can be discerned by a learned
knowledge of their signs; and the two are married to a belief in post-
mortem reward.

There is enough evidence to suggest that the *maskilim* of Daniel
and the writings from Qumran, which belong mostly to the century
and a half that follow the writing of Daniel, are connected by more
than literary dependence. There are significant similarities in what
we can legitimately call a "gnostic" form of Jewish religion, in
which possession of esoteric knowledge is the key to eschatological
salvation. That in the *Community Rule*, as well as in Daniel, this
knowledge is imparted through a *maskil* may point to something
socially more concrete.

It is inviting to draw further some possible lines of historical connection between the *maskilim* of Daniel and the *yaḥad*. But there are serious complications to be confronted, for instance in the *Damascus Document*, with which Daniel might be held to have important connections. One such link is the hint of a diaspora origin; another is the strong exilic/diaspora ideology, expressed in terms of a calendar of exile culminating in an eschatological moment.[42] Yet another is a concern, even an obsession, with temple purity. In the *Damascus Document*, however, the word *maskil* hardly appears.[43] On the contrary, leadership in the *Damascus Document* is assigned to the *mebaqqer*, who has priority even over the priests.

Another complication is the *Community Rule* itself. While the interpretation of the evidence remains disputed, there is widespread agreement that a "Zadokite" and a "lay" stage can be distinguished in the evolution of the materials. Despite the palaeographical evidence (which would place 1QS, with its references to "sons of Zadok" as authority, within the *yaḥad*), it seems intrinsically more likely that the introduction of Zadokites is a secondary development.[44] But because of the difficulties in extracting from the Qumran texts themselves a clear and agreed history of sectarian evolution, any relationship between Qumranic literature and the book of Daniel must be expressed rather cautiously.

Yet a third complication is the fact that Enochic literature has exercised a considerable influence on much of Qumranic literature (which, of course, also contains copies of Enochic books). The

---

[42] In the case of the *Damascus Document* this caledar is implied in CD 43:18–4:6, where a genealogy (perhaps similar to those of Ezra and Nehemiah?) seems to have stood; and also in references to the "epoch of wickedness" (e.g. 6:10). Adherence to a Jubilean word-calendar is probably implied in the reference to the *Book of Jubilees* in CD 16:3-4.

[43] The word *maskil* appears once in CD (13:22; and its parallel in 4Q266 frg. 9 iii 15); the context is unfortunately missing in each case. It would be extremely helpful if we could establish that *maskil* was also in use to indicate a status or office within the "Damascus" community; however, we must conclude that this was not the title accorded to any leadership figure in that community.

[44] See Philip R. Davies, "Sons of Zadok," in his *Behind the Essenes* (BJS 94; Atlanta: Scholars Press, 1987) 51–72. That analysis, which was undertaken before the publication of the Cave 4 manuscripts of the *Community Rule*, seems to be supported by the recensional history that these fragments indicate. See S. Metso, *The Textual Development of the Qumran Community Rule* (STSJ 21; Leiden: Brill, 1997).

theory of Boccaccini, referred to earlier, would set the Qumran texts at a point of convergence between Zadokite and Enochic forms of Judaism; this is a welcome exercise in the kind of bold thinking that is needed to accommodate the quite distinct strands of the Qumran corpus. The question of whether or not the *maskilim* of Daniel belong to the prehistory of the Scrolls is probably obsolete. The proper (and more difficult) question is: where, among the several prehistories implied in the Scrolls, are the Danielic *maskilim* most plausibly to be situated?

6. CONCLUSION

As far as the social identity and immediate history of the *maskilim* of Daniel are concerned, we can perhaps claim to have come fairly close to the limits of intelligent inference. But a suitably sophisticated analysis of the relationships between the book of Daniel and the Qumran writings, taking into account both ideological and social factors, may enable a larger theory to be constructed of the history of the Danielic *maskilim* after the advent of the Hasmonean dynasty. That these *maskilim* betray some diaspora roots, and see themselves as a disenfranchised, erstwhile elite makes them plausible candidates for membership of sectarian movements opposed to the Hasmoneans, and potential allies of the Zadokite priests. Daniel 12 may imply that these *maskilim* developed a system of esoteric wisdom designed to teach "righteousness" to those willing to accept it. There also seem to be no reasons for them to have abandoned either their belief in an "exilic calendar" or in an eschatological vindication of the righteous. These features alone make it entirely plausible, if not probable, that among the texts from Qumran are those written by the successors of the Danielic *maskilim*.

But in order for such plausilibities, even probabilities, to be developed into hypotheses, further progress needs to be made on the origins of the Qumran writings and the histories to which they obliquely refer. At the present moment this prospect is distant; however, a growing recognition of the complexity of the problem, and a correspondingly more sophisticated reconstruction of the social realities of Palestinian Jewish society in the late second and first centuries BCE, may lead eventually to a fuller history of the *maskilim* of the book of Daniel.

7. SELECT BIBLIOGRAPHY

Boccaccini, G. *Beyond the Essene Hypothesis. The Parting of the Ways between Qumran and Enochic Judaism* (Grand Rapids: Eerdmans, 1998).

Collins, J. J. *Daniel: A Commentary on the Book of Daniel* (Hermeneia; Minneapolis: Fortress, 1993).

Cook, S. L. *Prophecy and Apocalypticism: The Postexilic Social Setting* (Minneapolis: Fortress, 1995).

Davies, P. R. *Daniel* (OT Guides; Sheffield: Sheffield Academic Press, 1985).

—. "The Social World of the Apocalyptic Writings," in R. E. Clements (ed.), *The World of Ancient Israel* (Cambridge: Cambridge University Press, 1989) 251–71.

Redditt, P. L. "Daniel 11 and the Sociohistoical Setting of the Book of Daniel," *CBQ* 60 (1998) 463–74.

—. *Daniel* (NCB; Sheffield: Sheffield Academic Press, 1999).

Wilson, R. R. "From Prophecy to Apocalyptic: Reflections on the Shape of Israelite Religion," *Semeia* 21 (1981) 79–95.

PRAYERS AND DREAMS: POWER AND DIASPORA IDENTITIES IN THE SOCIAL SETTING OF THE DANIEL TALES

DANIEL L. SMITH-CHRISTOPHER

1. NEGOTIATING IDENTITY AS AN ASPECT OF THE SOCIAL SETTING OF THE BOOK OF DANIEL: PRELIMINARY CONSIDERATIONS

At their core, the Daniel tales represent Jews who are "re-negotiating" their cultural and religious identities in circumstances of cross-cultural contact that also presumes a significant perception of threat and unequal distribution of power and authority. Any analysis of the "social setting" of the Daniel tales (a category in which I include not only chapters 1–6, but also the LXX additions, and most likely also the Qumran fragment entitled *The Prayer of Nabonidus*) must therefore attend to the implications of this forced inter-cultural contact that is a part of the social realities of living under Imperial dominion throughout the Second Temple period. These dynamics are important irrespective of whether we locate the tales' origins in the Persian period (my own view of the oral and functional origins of the earliest tales) or as late as the 2nd Century, under Seleucid Hellenistic rule (still the majority view). This fact of forced inter-cultural contact alone justifies the recent interest of Biblical scholars in issues of ancient "ethnicity,"[1] but also suggests prospects of applying aspects of the contemporary debates surrounding such issues as the *fluidity* of cultural identity.

Furthermore, it seems clear that this cross-cultural encounter was both fascinating and threatening. The "exotic" and the dangerous are

---

[1] See, for example, M. Brett, (ed.), *Ethnicity and the Bible* (BIS 19; Leiden: Brill, 1996); D. L. Smith-Christopher, (ed.), *Text and Experience: Toward a Cultural Exegesis of the Bible* (Sheffield: Sheffield Academic Press, 1995); R. S. Sugirtharajah, *Voices from the Margin* (2nd ed., New York: Orbis, 1997). It is interesting to note that the determination of "ethnicity" is also emerging as a central issue in contemporary archaeological debates. See William Dever, "Archaeology and the Emergence of Early Israel," in J. R. Bartlett, (ed.), *Archaeology and Biblical Interpretation* (New York: Routledge, 1994) 20–50; idem, "Archaeology, Ideology, and the Quest for an 'Ancient' or 'Biblical' Israel," *NEA* 61 (1998) 39–52.

not entirely separate, of course.[2] For example, the setting for the Daniel tales (as also Esther, Neh 1:1–2:10, 1 Esdras 3–4, Tobit 1, perhaps also the Joseph tales in their present form, etc.) is clearly in the most sumptuous and exotic circumstances imaginable for Jews in late Persian and/or Ptolemaic or Seleucid Hellenistic cultures—the very court of the Babylonian or Persian Emperors. In all six stories, the exotic enticements include political influence and wealth. But the encounter is also dangerous. There are no less than four threats of death in these stories—threats often spectacular in their calculated frightfulness, e.g. dismemberment, burning in over-heated furnaces, or mauling by starved wild animals. Thus we find the ambiguities of minority existence illustrated in the folklore of Daniel.

2. READING DANIEL THROUGH CULTURAL STUDIES: METHODOLOGICAL CONSIDERATIONS

In order to read ancient stories involving cross-cultural contact, we must not only assess the themes of the stories themselves in the light of this contact, but recognize that our assessment of these themes is inextricably bound to our own appreciation of such themes as late 20th century readers and exegetes. At the end of the 20th century we are involved in an unprecedented discussion of ethnic identity, cultural traditions, and the persistence of such questions under circumstances of tremendous population shifts. As Pnina Werbner has stated in her analysis of the concept of "hybrid" cultural identities:

> ...what has evidently rendered holistic models of culture and society unviable is the reality of postwar population movements, transnational capitalism, global telecommunications and the explosion of consumption. What now seems pressing is to theorize the problems of cultural translation and reflexivity, inter-ethnic communication and cross-cultural mobilisation, hybridity and creolisation.[3]

---

[2] A. Memmi, in my view, is especially aware of this aspect of the colonial situation; see his *Colonizer and the Colonized* (Boston: Beacon, 1965), and *Dependence: A Sketch for a Portrait of the Dependent* (Boston: Beacon, 1984). See also F. Fanon, in *The Wretched of the Earth* (New York: Grove, 1963): "The settler's world is a hostile world, which spurns the native, but at the same time, it is a world of which he is envious" (pg. 52).

[3] P. Werbner, "Introduction: The Dialectics of Cultural Hybridity," in P. Werbner and T. Modood (eds.), *Debating Cultural Hybridity, Multi-Cultural Identities and the Politics of Anti-Racism* (London: Zed Books, 1997) 1–28, esp. 6.

The book of Daniel obviously also demands attention to issues raised by population movements (ours *and* theirs!) and the issues of identity formation that are raised by that movement and interaction ("... mobilization, hybridity, and creolization ...") as well as the setting of unequal distribution of power and/or resources. A helpful set of questions that focus on this can be cited from "Postcolonial Criticism." Summarized recently by Bart Moore-Gilbert, Post-Colonial Criticism is: ".... preoccupied principally with analysis of cultural forms which mediate, challenge or reflect upon the relation of domination and subordination—economic, cultural and political—between (and often within) nations, races or cultures ...."[4]

Of course, when we attempt to understand ancient texts, we are speaking of different circumstances than the colonialist legacy of the last centuries—but it is now widely recognized that these questions are suggestive for the study of ancient as well as modern societies. A reading of Daniel can benefit from thinking about questions such as those raised, for example, by post-colonial theorist Homi Bhabha:

> The social articulation of difference, from the minority perspective, is a complex, on-going negotiation that seeks to authorize cultural hybridities that emerge in moments of historical transformation ... [it] does not depend on the persistence of tradition; it is resourced by the power of tradition to be reinscribed through the conditions of contingency and contradictoriness that attend upon the lives of those who are "in the minority."[5]

Similarly, Werbner notes the potential creativity of minorities who live, effectively, on the margins of a dominant society. As a result of such a "liminal state" (Turner), or by occupying "trickster places" (Levi-Strauss), there is potential for cultural criticism from a place outside the mainstream.[6] Yet Werbner is particularly intrigued with *the intentionality of a conscious choice to remain different*, which, in turn, encourages the development of a critical perspective: "What is felt to be most threatening [to majority cultures] ... is the deliberate, provocative aesthetic challenge to an implicit social order and identity ...."[7] What might be called intentional nonconformity can thus be oppositional in character—a form of cultural or spiritual resistance.

---

[4] B. Moore-Gilbert, *Postcolonial Theory: Contexts, Practices, Politics* (New York: Verso, 1997) 12.

[5] H. Bhabha, *The Location of Culture* (London: Routledge, 1994) 2.

[6] Werbner, "Introduction," 2–4.

[7] *Ibidem*, 4.

Issues of re-negotiating identity are, finally, also related to issues of re-location and therefore one takes note of the rise of sociological and anthropological interest in studies of actual "borderlands" where identities mix, and traditions, languages, music, and even histories, converge.[8] Akhil Gupta and James Ferguson helpfully summarize the complexity of the factors involved in such rescribing identity in conditions of exile:

> In a world of diaspora, transnational culture flows, and mass movements of populations, old-fashioned attempts to map the globe as a set of culture regions or homelands are bewildered by a dazzling array of postcolonial simulcra, doublings and redoublings, as India and Pakistan seem to reappear in postcolonial simulation in London, prerevolution Teheran rises from the ashes in Los Angeles, and a thousand similar cultural dramas are played out in urban and rural settings all across the globe. In this culture-play of diaspora, colony and metropole, "here" and "there," center and periphery, become blurred.[9]

To leave a familiar location (for whatever reason) forces the person and group to try to "make sense" of the world in the absence of reliable information that is available in familiar terms. This is *particularly* critical in circumstances of unequal power distribution where it is difficult to secure information that is not tainted by imperial biases or otherwise from suspicious and/or untrusted sources. John D. Peters, for example, argues that the construction of "grand pictures" may be a creative source of resistance among modern minority cultures:

> Part of what it means to live in a modern society is to depend on representations of that society. Modern men and women see proximate fragments with their own eyes and global totalities through the diverse media of social description. Our vision of the social world is bifocal. Institutions of the global constitute totalities that we could otherwise experience only in pieces, such as populations, the weather, employment, inflation, the gross national product, or public opinion. The irony is that the general becomes clear through representation, whereas the immediate is subject to the fragmenting effects of our limited experience.[10]

---

[8] A. Gupta and J. Ferguson, "Introduction," in eidem (eds.), *Culture, Power, and Place: Explorations in Critical Anthropology* (London: Duke University Press, 1997) 3.

[9] Gupta and Ferguson, "Beyond 'Culture': Space, Identity and the Politics of Difference," in *Culture, Power and Place*, 33–51, esp. 38.

[10] J. D. Peters, "Seeing Bifocally: Media, Place, Culture," in Gupta and Fer-

Peters goes on to make the following point:

> The representation of a social totality that transcends the circumference of an
> individual's possible experience is always potentially a political act, an act
> of constitution or revelation: for many social critics in the nineteenth cen-
> tury, to document society was already to protest it (Engels, Dickens, Zola,
> Riis, Tarbell, and so forth).[11]

One way that contemporary analysis has approached a study of these
attempts to construct alternative "grand pictures" is to note the place
of popular rumour as a kind of street theatre, or "people's news" (cf.
Ezekiel's frequent references to sayings and proverbs among the
exiled communities, in chapters 12, 16, and 18). Rosemary Coombe,
for example, looked at the role of popular urban myths and rumours
of industrial conspiracies in various African-American communities
and concluded that:

> Rumour campaigns such as those directed at Proctor & Gamble, Church's,
> Reebok, Philip Morris, and Troop Sport must be understood in the context
> of a consumption society in which corporate power maintains silence and
> invisibility behind a play of media signifiers without referents, a circulation
> of signs without meaning. In a world in which the presence of power lies
> increasingly in the realm of the imaginary, such rumors may be understood
> as cultural guerilla tactics—"political" in their significance—if not in their
> self-consciousness.[12]

In such a context, we are reminded of the recent trends toward
reading Ancient Near Eastern texts (building inscriptions, annals,
etc.) as rhetorically stereotyped propaganda.[13] What has yet to be
determined, however, is whether the ancient Hebrews were any more
gullible than we are in accepting such Imperial claims! Inasmuch as
Isa 44:9-20, Ezek 20:32; Jer 10:8 attest to a refusal to be cowed by
religious propaganda, we may also read the stories in Daniel as a
"counter-history" to the ubiquitous Babylonian, Persian, Ptolemaic,
or Seleucid monumental claims to be "King of Kings," "King of the

---

guson (eds.), *Culture, Power, and Place*, 75–92, esp. 79.

[11] Peters, "Seeing Bifocally," 82.

[12] R. Coombe "The Demonic Place of the 'Not There': Trademark Rumors in
the Postindustrial Imaginary," in Gupta and Ferguson (eds.), *Culture, Power, and
Place*, 249–74, esp. 270.

[13] A. Laato, "Assyrian Propaganda and the Falsification of History in the
Royal Inscriptions of Sennacherib," *VT* 45 (1995) 198–226; L. Rowlett, *Joshua
and the Rhetoric of Violence: A New Historicist Analysis* (JSOTSup 226; Sheffield:
Sheffield Academic Press, 1996).

Four Corners of the Earth," and so forth.

To summarize, the circumstances of cross-cultural contact give rise to the need to re-negotiate the meaning of identity for a conscious social group in new circumstances. Furthermore, when these contacts are in circumstances of uneven distribution of power, we need to be alive to the various ways in which communities engage in forms of resistance on a popular level—such as the use of a popular mythology or "folklore" in order to make sense of what is otherwise a faceless and overwhelming social reality. What might it mean, therefore, to read the Daniel tales as "counter-history"? Are the Daniel tales more helpfully seen as a folklore of resistance that particularly involves the need to re-negotiate Jewish identity?

3. PRESUMING THE SOCIAL SETTING FOR THE DANIEL TALES

In what is to date the most important commentary on Daniel, published as a volume of the Hermeneia series,[14] John J. Collins acknowledges the influence of an essay published in 1973 by W. Lee Humphreys entitled: "A Life-Style for Diaspora: A Study of the Tales of Esther and Daniel."[15] Humphreys' article, based on a dissertation at Union Theological Seminary (1970) inaugurated what may be described as a paradigm for viewing the *social* significance of the Daniel stories in Chapters 1–6, and one might also argue, the additional Greek stories as well. Although the social setting was notably not a central part of Humphrey's argument (which was mainly concerned with literary forms), his assumptions about the social setting are clearly stated when he surmises that the stories presume that: "... in certain circles at least the possibility of a cre-

---

[14] J. J. Collins, *Daniel: A Commentary on the Book of Daniel* (Hermeneia; Minneapolis: Fortress, 1993) 45.

[15] W. L. Humphreys, "A Lifestyle for Diaspora: A Study of the Tales of Esther and Daniel," *JBL* 92 (1973) 211–23. We can note that James Montgomery's commentary (*Daniel* [Edinburgh: T&T Clark, 1927]) contained relatively few comments suggesting his assumptions about a "social setting" behind his analysis of chapters 1–6. One can presume, however, that he had an eye to contemporary events when he wrote, for example, that:

> ... we see the Jews of the Golah, no longer hanging their harps on the willows, but bravely taking their place in the world and proving themselves the equals and superiors of their Pagan associates, not by reason of their race or human excellences, but through their constancy of character founded on faith and trust in God (pg. 19).

ative and rewarding interaction with the foreign environment was present and could work for the good of the Jew."[16] He concluded this influential study along similar lines, suggesting that: "One could, as a Jew, overcome adversity and find a life both rewarding and creative within the pagan setting and as a part of this foreign world"[17]

It is not difficult to trace the persistence of this view of the "attitude" of the stories of Daniel. Let a few examples suffice from the literature in English. L. Hartman and A. DiLella's Anchor Bible commentary suggests: "The fact that Daniel and his companions are said in chapters 1–5 to have achieved high position in the Babylonian court may perhaps suggest that life for the Israelites in exile was not all hardship and distress."[18]

N. Porteous, noting that previous scholars often suggested that the positive attitude to foreigners in chapters 1–6 is different from the more negative portrayal in chapters 7–12, cautions that there is a "double attitude,"[19] that is, both positive and negative, throughout the book as a whole. A. Lacocque, however, repeats the standard view that the "atmosphere" of chapters 7–12 and chapters 1–6 are quite different, and that chapters 7–12 are more negative precisely because: "... it is no longer a question of the apparently tranquil existence of the Jews in the midst of pagans, but of religious persecution and martyrdom."[20] Collins himself largely concurs:

> At a time when the Jews were subject to foreign powers, whether in their own land or in the diaspora, they could take vicarious pride in the figure of an exile who rose to the highest position in the kingdom. At the same time, these tales express a basically optimistic view of the world.... Wise courtiers will succeed, even at the court of an alien king.[21]

Finally, we can cite a recent important study by Lawrence Wills, when he concludes his impressive study about the genre of Hebrew court tales by concluding that:

> ... it is a popular genre, but it probably does not extend to the lower classes. It reflects the orientation of the administrative and entrepreneurial class. The

---

[16] Humphreys, "Lifestyle," 213.

[17] *Ibidem*, 223.

[18] L. Hartman and A. DiLella, *The Book of Daniel* (AB 23, Garden City, NY: Doubleday, 1978) 34.

[19] N. Porteous, *Daniel* (OTL, Westminster: Philadelphia, 1965) 19.

[20] A. Lacocque, *The Book of Daniel* (Atlanta: John Knox, 1979) 9.

[21] Collins, *Daniel*, 44.

scribal ideals inherent in the stories might restrict this circle somewhat to the extended court circles.[22]

There is a clear line of assumptions here about the social conditions of the community behind the Daniel tales—a diaspora setting certainly, but one that can be comfortable and even encourage aspirations to high office.[23]

---

[22] L. M. Wills, *The Jew in the Court of the Foreign King* (Harvard Dissertations in Religion, Minneapolis: Fortress, 1990) 197.

[23] Along these lines, it is important to mention the work of H. Barstad, *The Myth of the Empty Land* (Symbolae Osloenses Fasc. Sup 28; Oslo: Scandinavian University Press, 1996). Barstad's work is, in many ways, an extension of an important monograph published in 1956 by E. Janssen, *Juda in der Exilzeit* (Göttingen: Vandenhoeck & Reprecht, 1956). Janssen quite fairly warned that one cannot underestimate the vitality of religious practice and social life back in Palestine after the Babylonian Exile, but this is a view more widely held than Barstad seems willing to admit. Ephraim Stern, in what is still probably the most authoritative archaeological survey in print, stated that "... we can conclude that in the Babylonian period, despite the destruction of the temple, the culture of the Israelite period continued. Some 70-80% of every pottery group from this time consists of vessels which are usually attributed to the latest phase of the Israelite period ...," *Material Culture of the Land of the Bible in the Persian Period 538–332 BC* (Jerusalem: Israel Exploration Society, 1982) 229. See also recent work such as that of J. Zorn, "Mizpah: Newly Discovered Stratum Reveals Judah's Other Capital," *BAR* 23/5 (1997) 28–38, 66.

Barstad, incidentally, is certainly part of a trend toward downgrading the importance of the exile, when he designates the Babylonian exilic community itself with terms such as "wealthy landowners" who exercise authority and influence. This leads Barstad to a radical revision of the impact of the exile on the diaspora community itself:

"When reading the commentators on the biblical texts relating to these events, one sometimes get the Sunday school feeling that they regard the Babylonians as an evil people who came to destroy the true believers in Judah out of sheer wickedness, and that the bringing of Judeans into exile was a mean punishment or base revenge following the uprising of the Judean king. It is high time that we start thinking about the whole matter from a rather different perspective. The Neo-Babylonian empire represented a highly developed civilization, with an advanced political and economic structure.... Having no natural resources of its own, the whole existence of the empire depended entirely upon the import of materials like metals, stone, and timber, and all sorts of food and luxury items" (*Myth of the Empty Land*, 63–64).

The assumptions about the conditions of the exile here are very weighty indeed, and suggest that we must radically dismiss all the biblical and archaeological evidence that we have with regard to the enormity of the disaster, the depth of the

4. SOCIAL REALITIES OF POST-EXILIC JEWISH EXISTENCE: THE
SETTING OF IMPERIAL POWER IN THE SECOND TEMPLE PERIOD

The "rise" of small states on the Mediterranean coast—such as
Monarchical Israel, not to mention the Syro-Phoenecian and Trans-
Jordanian entities—were possible only because of a vacuum of power
among the larger warring states after the decline of Egyptian
hegemony over Palestine, and the eventual rise of Neo-Assyrian
power followed quickly by Neo-Babylonian usurpation after the rise
of the aggressive Chaldean tribes to power.[24] From the time of Neo-
Assyrian hegemony in the West, we can speak of "Imperial realities"
of military adventurism and control, extortion of tribute, and mass
movement of conquered populations. Summarizing recent work on
Assyrian deportations, Thomas Thompson suggests that among the
goals of deportation were: (1) punishment for resistance or rebellion; (2) the elimination of rivals to power; (3) the creation of a
population that was dependent in unknown settings on the central
administration; (4) the development of economic monopolies; and
(5) to restore empty or under-utilized lands.[25]

The historical circumstances of the rise of the Neo-Babylonian
regime, and the Babylonian Exile, are well known, and in this
context we need only remind ourselves of those salient points
relevant for the argument presented in this study—perhaps most

---

spiritual and social crises that resulted, and the continued conditions of subordination in Persian and Hellenistic societies. All this, it seems, on the basis of some
easily noted exaggerations in the Chronicler's literature about "total depopulation,"
combined with what seems to be a strange sympathy for the Neo-Babylonian
empire as a "highly developed civilization" that we must "understand." Is Barstad,
perhaps, exchanging biblical "propaganda" only to "believe" too much of the
Imperial propaganda of, for example, a Rab-Shakeh who promises every prisoner
"... their own vine and fig tree" (2 Kgs 18:32)?

[24] B. Otzen, "Israel under the Assyrians," *Mesopotamia* 7 (1979) 251–61; cf.
M. T. Larsen, "The Tradition of Empire in Mesopotamia," *Mesopotamia* 7 (1979)
pp. 75–103, esp. 86. The best source on the Assyrian deportation practices is B.
Oded, *Mass Deportations and Deportees in the Neo-Assyrian Empire* (Wiesbaden:
Reichert, 1979). Oded notes that Assyrian sources clearly identify families accom-
panying exiles. There is little reason to doubt that Babylonian policies were the
same—irrespective of the historical reliability one places in Jeremiah's advice to
"marry your sons and daughters" in exile (Jer 29:6).

[25] T. Thompson, *The Early History of the Israelite People from the Written
and Archaeological Records* (Leiden: Brill, 1994) 342.

notably their continued policies of conquest and military deportation. Barstad's recent call to modern scholars of the exilic period to "understand" the need of the "highly developed and advanced" Babylonian Empire to "import resources" (the latter an interesting euphemism for extorting tribute payments) might lead one to overlook the archaeological evidence strongly suggesting that Jerusalem was treated severely when it was destroyed by the Neo-Babylonian Empire. Nearby towns such as Lachish and Beth-Shemesh show total cessation of occupation, and D. J. Wiseman noted ash layers at Gezer and Tell el Hesi[26] indicating Babylonian battles. In a recent summary of digs at Ashkelon, Lawrence Stager writes:

> Archaeology cannot be so precise as to date the destruction of Ashkelon to 604 BCE, but the Babylonian Chronicle leaves little doubt that the late seventh-century destruction we found all over the site, followed by a 75-80 year gap in occupation until the Persian Period, was the work of Nebuchadnezzar in 604 BCE.[27]

Suggesting that the Neo-Babylonians had little interest in the populations along the route to his actual goal, Egypt, Stager states that Nebuchadnezzar was particularly severe in Palestine, and Ashkelon shows signs of intentional destruction and burning deep into the heart of the city itself: "... Throughout Philistia, and later throughout Judah, his scorched earth policy created a veritable wasteland west of the Jordan River."[28] With regard to Jerusalem, Saul Weinberg writes:

> ... excavations by Kathleen Kenyon yield a picture of ruin and desolation that confronted the first returnees of 539/8. While some people had no doubt continued to live in Jerusalem, the archaeological picture is one of their squatting among the rubble, which increased as the terrace walls ... collapsed through lack of care and the debris accumulated in impassable piles on the lower slopes. No great change in the condition of the city occurred until the time of Nehemiah's arrival in 445.[29]

Weinberg further considers it unlikely that in these circumstances

---

[26] D. J. Wiseman, *Nebuchadnezzar and Babylon* (London: British Museum, 1983) 28.

[27] L. Stager, "The Fury of Babylon: Ashkelon and the Archaeology of Destruction," *BAR* 22/1 (1996) 56–69, 76–77.

[28] *Ibidem*, 69.

[29] S. Weinberg, "Post-Exilic Palestine: An Archaeological Report," *Proceedings of the Israel Academy of Sciences and Humanities* 4 (1971) 78–97, esp. 80.

any viable material culture could have been maintained: "We must think more in terms first of squatters and then of people able to maintain only a mere subsistence level."[30]

More recent assessments concur. G. Ahlstrom states that the destruction of Jerusalem "... was thorough. The walls were broken down and the city was plundered.... Arrowheads of northern origin and destroyed buildings that have been unearthed in excavations from this period bear witness to the disaster of the city."[31]

But, even if a serious disaster is conceded for early in the Neo-Babylonian era, surely the Daniel tales come from so late in the Persian period, and perhaps entirely in the Hellenistic period, that such comments on early events are irrelevant? This would be true *only if we accept the notion that the devastation of Jerusalem and Judah was not really so bad.* But the literature is clear—the continued occupation of Palestine in the Second Temple period was frequently perceived by the Jewish community as simply a continued state of exile. The very ubiquity of "Babylon" imagery in tales like Daniel, and in later writings like Baruch and the Letter of Jeremiah (not to mention the recalculations of Jeremiah's "70 years")[32] long into the Hellenistic period (and arguably into the Christian period as well, noting 1 Peter and Revelation), all suggest that the *traditions about the Babylonian disaster were a source of effective and dramatic raw materials from which to construct stories about existence under late Persian, Ptolemaic, and Seleucid realities.* While this may suggest the presence of stereotypical language and established folklore patterns, it seems hardly acceptable that such "exilic" formulae were intended to communicate a comfortable existence.

When the Persian period is considered, negative assessments of exilic existence as the "social setting" for the Daniel tales have been

---

[30] *Ibidem*, 81.

[31] G. Ahlstrom, *The History of Ancient Palestine* (Minneapolis: Fortress, 1993) 798. P. King writes with reference to Y. Shiloh's excavations, "Shiloh found evidence of the Babylonian destruction everywhere: thick layers of dark ash, scattered iron and bronze arrowheads, and collapsed structures ...," ("Jerusalem," *ABD* 3.747–66, esp. 757). Finally, E. Stern ("Israel at the Close of the Period of the Monarchy: An Archaeological Survey," *BA* 38/2 [1975] 26–54) regards the severe destruction to be limited to Judah more than Benjamin—noting that evidence suggests that Bethel, Gibeon, and Tell en-Nasbeh continued to flourish.

[32] See the important article by Michael Knibb, "The Exile in the Literature of the Intertestamental Period," *Heythrop Journal* 17 (1976) 253–72.

resisted based on a reading of (for example) Ezra 1–6, which is perceived as indicating that the Persians were relatively generous in their return of exiles to their homelands, including the Jews. I have elsewhere suggested, however, that the constant need to seek permission at every turn in Ezra–Nehemiah creates a rather different picture of relations to the Persian administration. Other recent work on the Persian period reveals that their reputed "generosity"—this supposed "enlightened rule"—has been greatly exaggerated.[33] K. Hoglund, particularly, has invited modern scholars to a deeper appreciation of the missions of Ezra and Nehemiah as elements of Persian Imperial policy and increased military presence in the West, confronting the Greek enemies particularly after the Egyptian revolt in 460 BCE (the "Inarus Revolt"), which was eventually crushed by Artaxerxes I in 454 BCE.[34]

It is also frequently pointed out that many Jewish names appear in the Murašu Archive from Nippur, texts that were found in 1893, and were already being analyzed in print by 1898.[35] As these are business documents that appear to show Jews involved in commerce, the conclusion is quickly determined that life in exile was obviously not so bad.[36] But what do the Murašu Archive, from the reigns of Artaxerxes I and Darius II (464-404 BCE), actually reveal about socio-

---

[33] See my "Resistance in a 'Culture of Permission,'" in H. Macy and P. Anderson (eds.), *Truth's Bright Embrace: Essays and Poems in Honor of Arthur O. Roberts* (Newberg, IN: George Fox University Press, 1996) 15–38; also A. Kuhrt, "The Cyrus Cylinder and Achaemenid Imperial Policy," *JSOT* 25 (1983) 83–97; and two summaries of papers—R. J. van der Spek, "Did Cyrus the Great introduce a new policy towards subdued nations? Cyrus in Assyrian perspective," in *Persica* 10 (1982) 278–83; and K. D. Jenner, "The Old Testament and its appreciation of Cyrus," *Persica* 10 (1982) 283–84.

[34] K. Hoglund, *Achaeminid Imperial Administration in Syria-Palestine and the Missions of Ezra and Nehemiah* (SBLDS 125, Atlanta: Scholars Press, 1992). An alternative perspective is that of J. Berquist in *Judaism in Persia's Shadow: A Social and Historical Approach* (Minneapolis: Fortress Press, 1995), which is more along the lines of Ruben Richard's challenging dissertation, "The Role of the Imperial Decrees in Ezra-Nehemiah" (University of Cape Town, 1995), of which the publication will be very welcome. I am grateful to Mr. Richards for making his dissertation available to me.

[35] H. V. Hilprecht and A. T. Clay (eds.), *Business Documents of the Murashu Sons of Nippur* (Philadelphia: University of Pennsylvania Press, 1898).

[36] Lawrence Stager's article on Ashkelon even referred to the Murašu company as a "Jewish business."

economic activity and social standing? M. Coogan summarized that Jews appear as agriculturalists, fisherman, sheep-herders, and co-creditors in contracts.[37] Ran Zadok, however, challenges any assumptions that are made about an image of comfortable Jewish communities in exile:

> The highest positions in the Achaemenian administration of Babylonia were held by Persians and to some extent by Medes. The lower positions were manned mainly by Babylonians who constituted the majority.... Judging from their names, few officials were Arameans, Arabians and Phoenicians; nonetheless, collectively, these officials still largely outnumbered the Jews. Much like their Jewish colleagues ... these officials were mostly minor functionaries. Nehemiah, who held a senior position, was an exception among the Jews.[38]

Matthew Stolper's recent analysis is also suggestive:

> In both these matters, tenure and commercial practice, Achaemenid administration put new faces on old patterns. The Murašu texts point to some results of this policy: a tendency toward concentration of wealth, and a tendency toward relative impoverishment at the lowest ranks of the state-controlled agricultural sector, despite indications of overall prosperity in the province.[39]

Clearly there are questionable assumptions about whether the Murašu Archive is somehow representative of "economic opportunities" in the Persian Empire. The Persian "economy" (if it can be called that) was essentially a system for the hoarding of precious metals. Alexander, so it appears, was stunned with the amounts of bullion he found stashed at Susa, Ecbatana, and Persepolis,[40] but it can hardly be said that the Persian, or the Hellenistic rulers, were interested in "encouraging business" or spreading wealth among the populace.

The rare comment from standard histories of the Persian Empire on matters of economics are interesting. Richard Frye states that:

---

[37] M. D. Coogan, "Life in the Diaspora: Jews at Nippur in the Fifth Century BC," *BA* 37/6 (1974) 6–12, esp. 10.

[38] R. Zadok, *The Jews in Babylonia During the Chaldean and Achaemenian Periods According to the Babylonian Sources* (Haifa: University of Haifa Press, 1979) 87.

[39] M. Stolper, *Entrepreneurs and Empire: The Murašu Archive, the Murashu Firm, and Persian Rule in Babylonia* (Istanbul: Nederlands Historisch-Archaeologisch Instituut, 1985) 154.

[40] P. Green, *Alexander to Actium: The Historical Evolution of the Hellenistic Age* (Los Angeles: University of California Press, 1990) 157, quoting A. T. Olmstead.

Taxes, as usual, abounded in the Achaemenid empire. It seems there were harbour fees, market taxes, tolls on gates and roads and frontiers of various kinds, a tax on domestic animals, perhaps ten per cent, and other taxes as well. Gifts were received by the king on New Year's day, and when he travelled extra hardships were placed on the population. Most of these gifts and sundry taxes were mainly paid in kind rather than specie. Corveé labor, for roads, public buildings and the like, was employed extensively by satraps as well as the king. So life for the common person must have been at times oppressive. The local public works were probably financed by local taxes, while gold and silver streamed into the king's coffers.[41]

For his part, J. M. Cook comments:

> ... labour and production in Persis were organized on a huge scale by the central administration in a way that would seem to leave relatively little scope for what we should call modest private enterprise ... [even] ... sheep raising was also organized on a large scale. The Persians' criticism of Darius that he made a business of everything is not belied by the evidence from the one province of the empire that in theory was not subject.[42]

The same is true of the Hellenistic period. As P. Green summarizes: "... one central fact conditioned the conduct, outlook, and administration of both the Ptolemaic and Seleucid dynasties for the entire course of their existence: they treated the territories they controlled, however they might assign them, as royal estates."[43] The point was to facilitate the gathering of enormous amounts of precious metals in the treasuries of the rulers who would provide the occasional public displays, but who usually maintained large armies of mercenaries to ensure the constant flow of goods.[44] Green continues:

> To take your own superiority for granted does not necessarily, or even commonly, imply that you are altruistically eager to give others the benefit of it, especially when you are busy conquering their territory, exploiting their natural resources and manpower, taxing their citizens, imposing your government on them, and unloading their accumulated gold reserves into the international market in the form of military loot. The main, indeed the overwhelming, motivation that confronts us in these Greek or Macedonian torchbearers of Western culture, throughout the Hellenistic era, is the irresistible twin lure of power and wealth, with sex trailing along as a poor third and cultural enlightenment virtually nowhere.[45]

---

[41] *The Heritage of Persia* (London: Weidenfeld & Nicolson, 1962) 114–15.

[42] J. M. Cook, *The Persian Empire* (Shocken: New York, 1983) 89–90.

[43] P. Green, *Alexander to Actium*, 187.

[44] *Ibidem*, 386.

[45] *Ibidem*, 325.

The "social setting" of Daniel should not be presumed to be a land of of great opportunity for prosperity!

Is it so bold to suggest that Nebuchadnezzar's dreams in the Daniel tales—even though arguably reminiscent of Nabonidus' famed dream life[46]—could well be read to refer (also?) to Seleucus I Nicator, who was inspired by his dreams to consolidate Mesopotamian territories in his battles with Antigonus?[47] Or can Nebuchadnezzar's statue of Daniel 3 not only satirize communal memories of the building of Babylonian monuments, but equally serve to call to Jewish minds the 105 ft. statue that was erected at Rhodes to honor Ptolemy I Soter for his support during the siege of Demetrius?[48] Could Belshazzar's Feast even serve to pillory the extravagances of Antiochus IV? Green describes Antiochan tastes for excess as follows:

> ... the same kind of ostentation as Ptolemy II had affected was clearly a crowd-pleaser in Antioch, too. We find the same thousands of extras with gold shields and crowns, the same horses and elephants and ivory tusks, the gold jars of saffron ointment, the twelve-pound silver dishes, the thousand-table banquets, gigantism and vulgarity triumphant.[49]

Memories and traditions regarding the hubris of Babylonian rulers that formed the "raw materials" for the Daniel tales would not need extensive "revision" to be flexible enough to apply with equal cynicism to the pretensions of rulers throughout the Persian and Hellenistic eras. The point is simply this: irrespective of the very real differences between the political and ideological regimes from 587 to 164 BCE, it is also true that the Daniel tales reflect an awareness of the consistent social realities of Ancient Near Eastern Empire building. Furthermore, our analysis of the setting for the book of Daniel must always attend to the stubborn similarities of ancient imperial designs toward power and control over wealth, territory, and human resources.

Finally, then, I would like to suggest how *this* aspect of the social

---

[46] This supposition is made more likely by the specific identification of Nabonidus in the Qumran text known as the "Prayer of Nabonidus" which sounds very much like a "Daniel tale," although he is not named in the partial text that we have. See my commentary in the Introduction to "Daniel and the Additions to Daniel," in *The New Interpreters Bible* (Nashville, TN: Abingdon, 1996) 7.19–194.

[47] P. Green, *Alexander to Actium*, 26–27.

[48] *Ibidem*, 33.

[49] *Ibidem*, 164.

setting of the Daniel tales raises questions about some of the details in the tales—in this case the theme of dream interpretation.

5. DREAMING IN DIASPORA: "INTERPRETATION" AS RESISTANCE

Robert Gnuse[50] has identified the literary styles and themes of ancient "Dream Reports" in Biblical, Ancient Near Eastern and Classical literature on dreaming. In his outline of different types of dreams, Gnuse noted that:

> A dream in which a divine message was delivered demanded action in accord with the divine will, and usually kings, priests, and professional dreamers were the recipients. One suspects that ... [this] ... category of dream reports served political agendas more than anything else.[51]

Gnuse also points out that Daniel and Joseph occupy a special place in Biblical discussions of dreams:

> Israel differs somewhat from other cultures in the understanding of dreams. Dreams are not seen to come from the realm of the dead, magical practices for incubation are lacking, and the art of interpretation is connected only with Joseph and Daniel where special effort goes into attributing the power of interpretation to God, so that Joseph and Daniel appear as prophets not oneirocritics. *Dreams are clear messages freely given by God* ... [my emphasis].[52]

Although Gnuse is aware of the social and political dimension in many accounts of Jewish dream interpretation, it is understandably not a central concern in his more comprehensive literary approach.[53]

---

[50] See R. Gnuse, *The Dream Theophany of Samuel: Its Structure in Relation to Ancient Near Eastern Dreams and Its Theological Significance* (Lanham, MD: University Press of America, 1984); and idem, *Dreams and Dream Reports in the Writings of Josephus: A Traditio-Historical Analysis* (Leiden: Brill, 1996).

[51] Gnuse, *Dreams and Dream Reports*, 36.

[52] *Ibidem*, 73.

[53] For example, Gnuse (*Dreams and Dream Reports*, 131, 194) makes interesting comments on the dream of Archelaus in Josephus, *J. W.* 2 §§112–13, where a certain Simon, the Essene, intervenes to interpret the powerful leader's dream. Gnuse comments: "In *Ant.* 17 §346 it is noted that Simon 'asked for a guarantee.' In *J.W.* 2 §§112–13 no such reference is made. Josephus appears to be stereotyping the experience to make Simon appear more like Joseph and Daniel, outsiders to the court who come and interpret the dream when the established authorities in the court have failed" (pg.194). What we are more interested in, however, is the inherent social and political ramifications of such "outsiders" interpreting the dreams of potentially hostile, or certainly more powerful, monarchs.

But the very fact that Daniel interprets the dreams of the conqueror of Jerusalem, and that dreams are seen as *messages from God*, suggest that in the context of the Daniel tales, dreams represent a politically significant *power that is greater than the worldly power of the conquerors*. To assert the power of God over Nebuchadnezzar is an inherently political act and it is furthermore to identify the Jews with the power that even Nebuchadnezzar cannot resist. In short, in the context of the political subordination of the Jews under Babylon, Persia, and the Hellenistic inheritors of Alexander's conquests, the interpretation of dreams is an act of spiritual warfare.

There is an interesting comparative case which can assist us in highlighting the political significance of dreams as a literary form of "spiritual" warfare—Atossa's dream in Aeschylus' famed play, *The Persians*.

6. READING DANIEL AND AESCHYLUS: DREAMS AS WEAPONS

The Athenian Theatre is thought to have roots in Dionysian religious ritual, but the art form quickly became a forum as much for political and historical themes as for religious ones.[54] For students of post-exilic biblical literature, it is instructive to consider some of the interesting aspects of a reading of one of the Greek theatre's earliest masters, Aeschylus (525-456 BCE). In the spring of 472, Aeschylus produced *The Persians*, which was not, we know, the first of the plays dealing with Greek conflicts with Persia. Four years earlier, the Persian Wars had been a theme in Phrynichus' *Phoinissai* ("The Phoenician Women").

Notably, however, it was also Phrynichus' play, *The Capture of Miletus* —which dealt with a particularly brutal aspect of the Greek-Persian Wars—that reveals the potential political impact of Hellenistic drama. According to the historian Herodotus, when this play was performed

---

[54] For translations and studies of *The Persians*, see especially Aeschylus, *Persians*, translated by J. Lembke and C. J. Herington (Oxford: Oxford University Press, 1981); M. J. Smethurst, *The Artistry of Aeschylus and Zeami* (Princeton: Princeton University Press, 1989); D. J. Conacher, *Aeschylus. The Earlier Plays and Related Studies* (Toronto: University of Toronto Press, 1996); *The Persians by Aeschylus*, translated with Commentary by A. J. Podlecki (Englewood Cliffs, NJ: Prentice-Hall, 1970); L. Spatz, *Aeschylus* (Boston: Twayne, 1982); and H. D. Broadhead, *The Persae of Aeschylus* (Cambridge: Cambridge University Press, 1960).

... the whole audience at the theatre burst into tears and fined Phrynichus a thousand drachmas for reminding them of a calamity that was their very own; they also forbade any future production of the play.[55]

Aeschylus sets *The Persians* in the court of Susa, where dreams and visions occur. The play, dealing with the successful repulsion of Xerxes' attacks on the Greek heartlands not even a decade earlier (480-479 BCE), attributes much of the defeat to the intervention of gods—a Greek notion, generally held, of the gods' "ferocious punishment on anything that is unduly great, whether physical or mental."[56] Reminiscent of aspects of "Divine Warfare" in Ancient Near Eastern thought,[57] this intervention was seen as more important than the brilliance of the numerically smaller Greek resistance (although the latter theme is not entirely absent).[58]

As for the setting in the court, C. J. Herington notes it is highly unlikely that we are dealing with an attempt to provide historically convincing information:

> For affairs and personalities in the Persian capital at Susa, where his scene is set, and for the narrative of Xerxes' retreat through northern Greece, there was no way for a poet composing at Athens within eight years of the event to arrive at the objective historical particulars, even if it had occurred to him for one moment that such research was any part of a poet's trade.[59]

---

[55] Herodotus 6.21, in *The History*, translated by D. Grene (Chicago: University of Chicago Press, 1987) 416-417.

[56] Lembke and Herington (tr.), *Persians*, 9; also compare Spatz, *Aeschylus*, 20: "Aeschylus also builds a contrast between Persia and Athens which justifies the Athenian victory. The constant references to the immensity and extravagance of Persia, symbolized by the abundant gold, create a picture of an entire society which possesses more than its alloted portion (*moira*)." In addition, see W. G. Thalman, "Xerxes' Rags: Some Problems in Aeschylus' *Persians*," *AJP* 101 (1980) 260–82.

[57] The literature is growing. One of the classic statements is G. von Rad, *Holy War in Ancient Israel*, (translation of *Der Heilige Krieg im alten Israel*, 1958), with introduction by B. Ollenburger, (Grand Rapids: Eerdmans, 1991); see also Sa Moon Kang, *Divine War in the Old Testament and in the Ancient Near East* (BZAW 177; Berlin: de Gruyter, 1989).

[58] In his important commentary (*The Persae of Aeschylus*), H. D. Broadhead notes that at key points, when Aeschylus could have engaged in nationalist bravado, he does not do so (pg. xviii). A. E. Wardman, however, believes that the theme of superior armaments is not insignificant; see his "Tactics and Tradition of the Persian Wars," *Historia* 8/1 (1959) 49–60.

[59] Lembke and Herington (tr.), *Persians*, 5.

The choices for setting, then, were *dramatic* choices. Notable in the descriptions of the setting of the court in Aeschylus are the pomp and circumstance of the Persian court: "... the Messenger's first speech gathers up all the aspects of the Persian Empire which have emerged ambiguously so far in the play—wealth, majesty, command over all Asia, towering pride...."[60] L. Spatz notes the use of Persian loan-words, names, and even the titles of the Kings with their Persian eloquence.[61]

In lines 175–215, there are two interesting dreams or visions described by Atossa, mother of Xerxes. In the first, Xerxes tries to rein two women (to drive a chariot?)—one dressed like a Persian, the other like a Greek (in "Doric dress"). Scholars differ as to whether these women represent Europe and Asia, and therefore show the hubris of Xerxes in his attempt to shackle both lands, or Persia's ambition to rule over all Greeks, both Attic and Asia Minor (thus two related peoples). In any case, the attempt is a failure, and Atossa is deeply disturbed by what she sees. The second part seems to be a related vision, but perhaps implied as an actual omen, where an eagle is torn up by a smaller hawk as it approaches Apollo's altar, where Atossa has gone to offer sacrifices to ward off the evil of her previous "nightmare."

In each case, the dream or vision serves to inform Atossa of Xerxes' folly in trying to conquer the Greeks. The impact of such visions on the Athenian audiences can readily be imagined—the judgements of the gods will fall on the enemy. The nationalist fervor of the play can be measured in the celebratory lines toward the end of the play, with regard to the failure of Persian designs on Greece (lines 580–588):[62]

---

[60] *Ibidem*, 24.

[61] Spatz, *Aeschylus*, 28; cf. Podlecki (tr.), *The Persians by Aeschylus*, 4, 24 n.6. Broadhead further comments that some scholars believe that Aeschylus intended to hold Xerxes up to ridicule by making him appear on the stage in rags or to arouse the spectators' contempt by the spectacle of the dejected and humiliated monarch. "Such a view makes the *Persae* not a tragedy, but a farce" (*The Persae of Aeschylus*, xxiii). On the contrary, however, Spatz points out that the use of clothing is an effective device: "... when Xerxes returns in defeat, his finery is probably ragged and tattered. Aeschylus calls attention to the king's rags in his mother's dream, the messengers' advice to reclothe him, and Atossa's desire to obtain a fresh garment suitable to his position ..." (*Aeschylus*, 25).

[62] Podlecki (tr.), *The Persians by Aeschylus*, 76. Furthermore, Conacher

Those throughout Asia's land are ruled
No longer by Persian laws.
They carry their tribute no longer
By a master's necessity fixed,
Nor prostrate themselves to the ground and adore;
for the royal Strength is destroyed.

The point is this—given the political realities of Greek-Persian animosity, the use of the dream as political message is strikingly obvious. That this has appeared less obvious in analysis of the book of Daniel can be partially attributed to overemphasis of the significance of the presence in the court of a Jew who is the interpreter of the dream. The effect is to distract our attention (but probably not that of the original hearers) from the social realities of diaspora existence, cross-cultural contact, and social and political subordination that is presumed in these tales, whether they be in the late Persian or Hellenistic periods. Thus, when compared in this more generalized manner—keeping in mind that we have two quite different literary genres from different cultural settings—we note some parallels between Aeschylus and Daniel: (1) a literary portrayal of Persian culture; (2) pomp and circumstances, the presumed regalia of the central court (bowing, formal address to the kings, "Live Forever!", etc.); (3) assumption of the court's central importance (therefore the natural setting for a tale of power); (4) the military power of Persia—and a realistic sense of threat; (5) divine involvement against the enemy powers; and (6) symbolic dreams and portents as indications of divine involvement.

The use of all these elements clearly assisted Aeschylus in composing a patriotic theme which appeals to Greek impressions. That they also clearly appeal to Jewish sensibilities, fears, and impressions helps us to see elements in Daniel that are often undervalued, such as the setting of subservience to power, and the sense of threat. Although the presumed audience is *national* in Aeschylus, and necessarily *communal* in Daniel, both storytellers know that a dramatically effective location is the royal court, and so the *setting* ought not seriously to propose the notion of a pious *historical* Jew in the *actual* Persian court. Since the work of Humphreys, I would argue, we have misread the court setting as indica-

---

notes that the imagery of "yokes" is a central theme of *The Persians*, used in various combinations again and again (*Aeschylus. The Earlier Plays*, 120).

tive of a positive evaluation of the conditions of exile, and thus of a hopeful message for a diaspora Jew. But if these tales are read as oppositional literature, how might that impact our understanding of a theme such as the use of dreams and visions?

7. PRAYERS AND DREAMS IN DANIEL CHAPTER 2

Although I will focus on chapter 2, the dreams in both chapters 2 and 4 signal that the regime of the Babylonians is about to be terminated. Some interesting insights into the irony of these politicized dreams can be gleaned from following the vocabulary in the Aramaic sections of Daniel.

In chapter 2:20-23, a prayer is offered by Daniel and his friends when they are given the opportunity (after the other interpreters are threatened with mass execution) to interpret the elusive dream of Nebuchadnezzar. The terms used in this prayer contain a number of important concepts that connect the Danielic tales to Wisdom motifs which only heighten the significant political implications:

> 20 Daniel said:
>   Blessed be the name of God from age to age,
>   for *wisdom and power* are his.
> 21 He changes times and seasons,
>   *deposes kings and sets up kings*, …
> 22 He reveals deep and hidden things;
>   he knows what is in the darkness,
>   and *light* dwells with him.
> 23 To you, O God of my ancestors,
>   I give thanks and praise.
>   for you have given me *wisdom and power*, …

The "inclusio" formed by the phrase "wisdom and power" has been widely noted, but this also has strong political overtones. This inclusio suggests that God, the greatest power, "deputizes" Daniel and his companions. Thus the *identity* of the Jews (as followers of this God) also *empowers* them in relation to non-Jews. In this context, the use of (1) light, (2) power, and (3) "deposing" and "setting up" kings is suggestive.

The Aramaic term used in Dan 2:22 for "light," נְהִיר (read נְהוֹר), is used to contrast with חֲשׁוֹךְ, "darkness." This Aramaism occurs also in another post-exilic text: Isaiah 60 (elsewhere only in the poetry of Ps 34:6 and Job 3:4). In Isaiah 60, the theme of light is also used to speak of the power of God—a power that is celebrated *over the nations,* nations who will come to honor God: "Nations shall come to your light, and kings to the brightness of your dawn" (v. 3). Compare the light imagery in Isa 2:5 (this section is a post-exilic addition, as is the related passage in 9:2), which also completes the famous poem of the pilgrimage of the nations to learn peace with the phrase, "Come let us walk in the light of the Lord (בְּאוֹר יהוה)!" (Compare Ps 43:3—the light of God that leads to Zion, the "holy hill"; note also that light serves as a central theme of God's victory in Isa 30:26).

More generally, however, Wisdom literature, as is well known, terms the commandments of God "light" (Prov 6:23); and Job 24:13 calls disobedience and social injustice a rejection of God's "light" (cf. 30:26, where "good" and "evil" are parallel to "light" and "dark"). Eccl 2:13 proclaims that "... wisdom exceeds folly as light exceeds darkness ...," and in Ps 119:105 the word of God is "light to my path" (cf. v. 130). In Wis 5:6, truth is called "light of righteousness," and the writer furthermore engages in interesting speculation about the "light of the law" functioning during the plague of darkness before the Exodus (18:1-5; cf. Bar 3:14, 4:2 where wisdom is compared with light).

But in the context of a tale of conflicting loyalties and contrasting estimations of worldly power as in Daniel, it is clear that "light," and especially *wisdom as light,* develops even further toward the notion of light *as an expression of God's power over earthly powers (e.g. darkness).* The Qumran tradition is ample evidence for another aspect of this development, beginning with the *War Scroll* which famously calls the armies of God the "children of light" against the "children of darkness." At 1QM 10:10, the learning of Wisdom is associated with being among the children of Light: "... a people of holy ones of the covenant, learned in the law, wise in knowledge ...."[63] Compare the Qumran text identified as "Songs of the Sage" (*4QSongs of the Sage* [4Q510]), frg. 1.4-5, which makes the connection with wisdom, light, and judgement as spiritual warfare against malevolent powers:

> And I, the Sage,
> declare the grandeur of his radiance in order to frighten and terrify
> all the spirits of the ravaging angels and the bastard spirits,
> demons, Liliths, owls and [jackals ...]

---

[63] Florentino García Martínez, *The Dead Sea Scrolls Translated* (Leiden: Brill; Grand Rapids: Eerdmans, 1996) 102.

There is also a suggestive connection here with the final vision of Daniel, where the "Maskilim" will be made to "shine" (זהר) like the "splendor of the firmament" (vv. 12:2-3), and are then compared to stars in v. 3, *as a result of their engagement in the instruction of the people.*[64] The point is this—Daniel's prayer for wisdom explicitly uses politicized language of opposition or "spiritual warfare," since "wisdom" and "light" are among the armaments of the faithful in their struggle. And these are most certainly aspects of the Jews' unique identity over against "the nations."

What is also important, however, is that the "power" attributed to Nebuchadnezzar is not the same as that given to Daniel (2:37). When Daniel interprets the dream, Daniel says that the "God of heaven" has given Nebuchadnezzar the Kingdom, "power" (חִסְנָא), might, and glory—but none of these terms are גְּבוּרָה, that is, the power of God that is also given to Daniel! When Daniel interprets Nebuchadnezzar's dream in chapter 4 (a blunt warning of God's threat to "cut the tree" that is Nebuchadnezzar himself, vv. 19-24), Nebuchadnezzar nevertheless gloats of his "sovereign might" (4:27 Aramaic) which is, again, חִסְנִי.

The term for Daniel's power, on the other hand, is one that, when used in its Hebrew form גְּבוּרָה, is virtually always a military power (Ps 66:7; Jer 10:6; cf. the interesting notion of God "teaching" of his "power" to the nations in Jer 16:21), as opposed to what might be called the "majestic strength/power" (עז) of God.

Finally, the politicization of Daniel's prayer is made clearer by his proclamation that God has the power to "remove" kings, and "establish" kings. The term for remove, עדה (מְהַעְדֵּה in 2:21) turns up again in 4:28, when a "voice from heaven" makes good on the threat implied by Daniel when he claimed that God can depose kings—in chapter 4, the kingdom *is* taken (עֲדָת) from the emperor! At 5:20, too, Belshazzar is "removed" (cf. 7:12). Ironically, the laws of the Persians are said to "not pass away" (6:9, 13, using the same expression), yet the vision of chapter 7 has the enthronement of the "one like a son of man" (i.e. Michael, spiritual protector of the Heb-

---

[64] Collins (*Daniel*, 393–94) has noted this association, comparing texts such as *T. Mos.* 10:9; *2 Enoch* 1:5; 66:7; and *4 Ezra* 7:97, 125. Collins further notes the connection with stars and becoming angels; this association is clear and strengthens my point all the more, given that angels become warriors in apocalyptic literature.

rew people) given authority that will "not pass away." What is absolute in God is relativized in relation to the emperors of the world.

Similar comments are offered on קוּם (hap'el הֲקִים) used of
"establishing" or "setting up" kings, a term which has an equally
interesting career in the book of Daniel. The root is used in various
forms referring to the ubiquity of "declarations," "pronouncements,"
"establishments" that appear to be imperial prerogative. But the
"God of heaven" will "establish" a kingdom superior to the four predecessors (2:44) in Nebuchadnezzar's dream in chapter 2, although
the term is ironically used over and over with regard to his great
statue (3:1, 2, 3, 5, 7,12; 4:14; 5:11; 6:2).

To summarize—Daniel has "power" in his connection with God,
and therefore his power is lodged in his knowledge, or the light of
his wisdom. In the context of this language of comparative strength,
power, and wisdom, the interpretation of dreams has become
politicized. The emperor's dreams become an arena for the exercise
of God's power over the Babylonian monarch, and thus the dream
world is contrasted to the "real" world of Nebuchadnezzar. It is in
this dream world that God's sovereignty is first announced and em-
powered before it becomes, in the hopeful horizon of the tales, a
reality. It is thus in the dream world that the reader of the Daniel
tales comes to know his/her power, and just as important, their spiritual identity as the "mediators" of God's superior power. The world
of the minority is a world of emphasizing contrasts and differences—light and dark, "us" and "them," true gods and false gods.

In the context of exile—that is, with attention to the social setting
of empire—the survival of Jews as a diaspora people partially
involves the conviction of superior knowledge in the face of superior
strength (cf. Prov 16:32; 20:18; 21:22). It is precisely by teaching—
that is, instructing the hearer of the Daniel tales about their calling
and their relation to God—that these tales "re-negotiate" identity in
the context of diaspora existence. That wisdom is greater than
strength or money is the subversive strategy of minority cultural
survival, so relevant to Jewish existence throughout the periods from
587 BCE through 163 BCE. The Daniel tales teach that knowledge of
Jewish identity as the people of Yahweh's light and wisdom is the key
not only to survival, but also to the eventual defeat of the Imperial
rule of "the nations" on earth.

8. SELECT BIBLIOGRAPHY

Aeschylus, *Persians*, translated by J. Lembke and C. J. Herington (Oxford: Oxford University Press, 1981).

Collins, J. J. *Daniel: A Commentary on the Book of Daniel* (Hermeneia; Minneapolis: Fortress, 1993).

Conacher, D. J. *Aeschylus. The Earlier Plays and Related Studies* (Toronto: University of Toronto Press, 1996).

Fanon, F. *The Wretched of the Earth* (New York: Grove, 1963).

Green, P. *Alexander to Actium: The Historical Evolution of the Hellenistic Age* (Los Angeles: University of California Press, 1990).

Humphreys, W. L. "A Lifestyle for Diaspora: A Study of the Tales of Esther and Daniel," *JBL* 92 (1973) 211–23.

Laato, A. "Assyrian Propaganda and the Falsification of History in the Royal Inscriptions of Sennacherib," *VT* 45 (1995) 198–226.

Memmi, A. *Colonizer and the Colonized* (Boston: Beacon, 1965).

Moore-Gilbert, B. *Postcolonial Theory: Contexts, Practices, Politics* (New York: Verso, 1997).

Podlecki, A. J. (trans. and commentary). *The Persians by Aeschylus* (Englewood Cliffs, NJ: Prentice-Hall, 1970).

Rowlett, L. *Joshua and the Rhetoric of Violence: A New Historicist Analysis* (JSOTSup 226; Sheffield: Sheffield Academic Press, 1996).

—. *Dependence: A Sketch for a Portrait of the Dependent* (Boston: Beacon, 1984).

Smethurst, M. J. *The Artistry of Aeschylus and Zeami* (Princeton: Princeton University Press, 1989).

Smith-Christopher, D. L. "Resistance in a 'Culture of Permission,'" in H. Macy and P. Anderson (eds.), *Truth's Bright Embrace: Essays and Poems in Honor of Arthur O. Roberts* (Newberg, IN: George Fox University Press, 1996) 15–38.

—. "Daniel and the Additions to Daniel," in *The New Interpreters Bible* (Nashville, TN: Abingdon, 1996) 7.19–194.

Spatz, L. *Aeschylus* (Boston: Twayne, 1982). Broadhead, H. D. *The Persae of Aeschylus* (Cambridge: Cambridge University Press, 1960).

Stager, L. "The Fury of Babylon: Ashkelon and the Archaeology of Destruction," *BAR* 22/1 (1996) 56–69, 76–77.

Wills, L. M. *The Jew in the Court of the Foreign King* (Harvard Dissertations in Religion, Minneapolis: Fortress, 1990).

SUPPLEMENTS TO VETUS TESTAMENTUM

39. PARDEE, D. *Ugaritic and Hebrew poetic parallelism.* A trial cut. 1988.
    ISBN 90 04 08368 5
40. EMERTON, J.A. (ed.). *Congress Volume,* Jerusalem 1986. 1988. ISBN 90 04 08499 1
41. EMERTON, J.A. (ed.). *Studies in the Pentateuch.* 1990. ISBN 90 04 09195 5
42. MCKENZIE, S.L. *The trouble with Kings.* The composition of the Book of Kings in
    the Deuteronomistic History. 1991. ISBN 90 04 09402 4
43. EMERTON, J.A. (ed.). *Congress Volume,* Leuven 1989. 1991. ISBN 90 04 09398 2
44. HAAK, R.D. *Habakkuk.* 1992. ISBN 90 04 09506 3
45. BEYERLIN, W. *Im Licht der Traditionen.* Psalm LXVII und CXV. Ein Entwicklungs-
    zusammenhang. 1992. ISBN 90 04 09635 3
46. MEIER, S.A. *Speaking of Speaking.* Marking direct discourse in the Hebrew Bible.
    1992. ISBN 90 04 09602 7
47. KESSLER, R. *Staat und Gesellschaft im vorexilischen Juda.* Vom 8. Jahrhundert bis zum
    Exil. 1992. ISBN 90 04 09646 9
48. AUFFRET, P. *Voyez de vos yeux.* Étude structurelle de vingt psaumes, dont le
    psaume 119. 1993. ISBN 90 04 09707 4
49. GARCÍA MARTÍNEZ, F., A. HILHORST and C.J. LABUSCHAGNE (eds.). *The Scriptures
    and the Scrolls.* Studies in honour of A.S. van der Woude on the occasion of his
    65th birthday. 1992. ISBN 90 04 09746 5
50. LEMAIRE, A. and B. OTZEN (eds.). *History and Traditions of Early Israel.* Studies pres-
    ented to Eduard Nielsen, May 8th, 1993. 1993. ISBN 90 04 09851 8
51. GORDON, R.P. *Studies in the Targum to the Twelve Prophets.* From Nahum to
    Malachi. 1994. ISBN 90 04 09987 5
52. HUGENBERGER, G.P. *Marriage as a Covenant.* A Study of Biblical Law and Ethics
    Governing Marriage Developed from the Perspective of Malachi. 1994.
    ISBN 90 04 09977 8
53. GARCÍA MARTÍNEZ, F., A. HILHORST, J.T.A.G.M. VAN RUITEN, A.S. VAN DER
    WOUDE. *Studies in Deuteronomy.* In Honour of C.J. Labuschagne on the Occasion
    of His 65th Birthday. 1994. ISBN 90 04 10052 0
54. FERNÁNDEZ MARCOS, N. *Septuagint and Old Latin in the Book of Kings.* 1994.
    ISBN 90 04 10043 1
55. SMITH, M.S. *The Ugaritic Baal Cycle. Volume 1.* Introduction with text, translation
    and commentary of KTU 1.1-1.2. 1994. ISBN 90 04 09995 6
56. DUGUID, I.M. *Ezekiel and the Leaders of Israel.* 1994. ISBN 90 04 10074 1
57. MARX, A. *Les offrandes végétales dans l'Ancien Testament.* Du tribut d'hommage au
    repas eschatologique. 1994. ISBN 90 04 10136 5
58. SCHÄFER-LICHTENBERGER, C. *Josua und Salomo.* Eine Studie zu Autorität und Legi-
    timität des Nachfolgers im Alten Testament. 1995. ISBN 90 04 10064 4
59. LASSERRE, G. *Synopse des lois du Pentateuque.* 1994. ISBN 90 04 10202 7
60. DOGNIEZ, C. *Bibliography of the Septuagint – Bibliographie de la Septante (1970-1993).*
    Avec une préface de PIERRE-MAURICE BOGAERT. 1995. ISBN 90 04 10192 6
61. EMERTON, J.A. (ed.). *Congress Volume,* Paris 1992. 1995. ISBN 90 04 10259 0

62. SMITH, P.A. *Rhetoric and Redaction in Trito-Isaiah.* The Structure, Growth and
    Authorship of Isaiah 56-66. 1995. ISBN 90 04 10306 6
63. O'CONNELL, R.H. *The Rhetoric of the Book of Judges.* 1996. ISBN 90 04 10104 7
64. HARLAND, P.J. *The Value of Human Life.* A Study of the Story of the Flood (Gen-
    esis 6-9). 1996. ISBN 90 04 10534 4

65. ROLAND PAGE JR., H. *The Myth of Cosmic Rebellion*. A Study of its Reflexes in Ugaritic and Biblical Literature. 1996. ISBN 90 04 10563 8
66. EMERTON, J.A. (ed.). *Congress Volume*. Cambridge 1995. 1997.
    ISBN 90 04 106871
67. JOOSTEN, J. *People and Land in the Holiness Code*. An Exegetical Study of the Ideational Framework of the Law in Leviticus 17–26. 1996.
    ISBN 90 04 10557 3
68. BEENTJES, P.C. *The Book of Ben Sira in Hebrew*. A Text Edition of all Extant Hebrew Manuscripts and a Synopsis of all Parallel Hebrew Ben Sira Texts. 1997. ISBN 90 04 10767 3
69. COOK, J. *The Septuagint of Proverbs – Jewish and/or Hellenistic Proverbs?* Concerning the Hellenistic Colouring of LXX Proverbs. 1997. ISBN 90 04 10879 3
70,1 BROYLES, G. and C. EVANS (eds.). *Writing and Reading the Scroll of Isaiah*. Studies of an Interpretive Tradition, I. 1997. ISBN 90 04 10936 6 (*Vol.* I);
    ISBN 90 04 11027 5 (*Set*)
70,2 BROYLES, G. and C. EVANS (eds.). *Writing and Reading the Scroll of Isaiah*. Studies of an Interpretive Tradition, II. 1997. ISBN 90 04 11026 7 (*Vol.* II);
    ISBN 90 04 11027 5 (*Set*)
71. KOOIJ, A. VAN DER. *The Oracle of Tyre*. The Septuagint of Isaiah 23 as Version and Vision. 1998. ISBN 90 04 11152 2
72. TOV, E. *The Greek and Hebrew Bible*. Collected Essays on the Septuagint. 1999.
    ISBN 90 04 11309 6
73. GARCÍA MARTÍNEZ, F. and NOORT, E. (eds.). *Perspectives in the Study of the Old Testament and Early Judaism*. A Symposium in honour of Adam S. van der Woude on the occasion of his 70th birthday. 1998. ISBN 90 04 11322 3
74. KASSIS, R.A. *The Book of Proverbs and Arabic Proverbial Works*. 1999.
    ISBN 90 04 11305 3
75. RÖSEL, H.N. *Von Josua bis Jojachin*. Untersuchungen zu den deuteronomistischen Geschichtsbüchern des Alten Testaments. 1999. ISBN 90 04 11355 5
76. RENZ, Th. *The Rhetorical Function of the Book of Ezekiel*. 1999.
    ISBN 90 04 11362 2
77. HARLAND, P.J. and HAYWARD, C.T.R. (eds.). *New Heaven and New Earth Prophecy and the Millenium*. Essays in Honour of Anthony Gelston. 1999.
    ISBN 90 04 10841 6
78. KRAŠOVEC, J. *Reward, Punishment, and Forgiveness*. The Thinking and Beliefs of Ancient Israel in the Light of Greek and Modern Views. 1999.
    ISBN 90 04 11443 2.
79. KOSSMANN, R. *Die Esthernovelle – Vom Erzählten zur Erzählung*. Studien zur Traditions- und Redaktionsgeschichte des Estherbuches. 2000. ISBN 90 04 11556 0.
80. LEMAIRE, A. and M. SÆBØ (eds.). *Congress Volume*. Oslo 1998. 2000.
    ISBN 90 04 11598 6.
81. GALIL, G. and M. WEINFELD (eds.). *Studies in Historical Geography and Biblical Historiography*. Presented to Zecharia Kallai. 2000. ISBN 90 04 11608 7
82. COLLINS, N.L. *The library in Alexandria and the Bible in Greek*. 2001.
    ISBN 90 04 11866 7
83,1 COLLINS, J.J. and P.W. FLINT (eds.). *The Book of Daniel*. Composition and Reception, I. 2001. ISBN 90 04 11675 3 (*Vol.* I);
    ISBN 90 04 12202 8 (*Set*)
83,2 COLLINS, J.J. and P.W. FLINT (eds.). *The Book of Daniel*. Composition and Reception, II. 2001. ISBN 90 04 12200 1 (*Vol.* II); ISBN 90 04 12202 8 (*Set*).
    (In preparation).

11·22·65